The Prevention of Anxiety and Depression

The Prevention of Anxiety and Depression

Theory, Research, and Practice

Edited by

David J. A. Dozois and Keith S. Dobson

AMERICAN PSYCHOLOGICAL ASSOCIATION • WASHINGTON, DC

Published by
American Psychological Association
750 First Street, NE
Washington, DC 20002
www.apa.org

To order
APA Order Department
P.O. Box 92984
Washington, DC 20090-2984
Tel: (800) 374-2721; Direct: (202) 336-5510
Fax: (202) 336-5502; TDD/TTY: (202) 336-6123
On-line: www.apa.org/books/
E-mail: order@apa.org

In the U.K., Europe, Africa, and the Middle East, copies may be ordered from
American Psychological Association
3 Henrietta Street
Covent Garden, London
WC2E 8LU England

Typeset in Goudy by Page Grafx, Inc., St. Simons Island, GA

Printer: United Book Press, Inc., Baltimore, MD
Cover Designer: Naylor Design, Washington, DC
Technical/Production Editor: Casey Ann Reever

The opinions and statements published are the responsibility of the authors, and such opinions and statements do not necessarily represent the policies of the American Psychological Association.

Library of Congress Cataloging-in-Publication Data
The prevention of anxiety and depression : theory, research, and practice / David J.A. Dozois & Keith S. Dobson, editors. — 1st ed.
    p. cm.
   Includes bibliographical references and index.
   ISBN 1-59147-079-X (hardcover : alk. paper)
    1. Anxiety—Prevention. 2. Depression, Mental—Prevention. I. Dozois, David J. A.
  II. Dobson, Keith S. III. Title.

RC531.P736 2004
616.85'22305—dc21

                                      2003012671

British Library Cataloguing-in-Publication Data
A CIP record is available from the British Library.

Printed in the United States of America
First Edition

To the improvement of the lives of people who experience
mental health problems—in particular, anxiety and depression.

*Melius et utilius sit in tempore occurrere, quam post causam
vulnaratam remedium quaerere.*
(It is better and more useful to meet a problem in time
than to seek a remedy after the damage is done.)

—Bracton (Henry of Bratton), 1240,
De Legibus et Consuetudinibus Angliae

CONTENTS

CONTRIBUTORS

Martin M. Antony, PhD, Psychiatry and Behavioural Neurosciences, McMaster University and Anxiety Treatment and Research Centre, St. Joseph's Healthcare, Hamilton, Ontario, Canada

Peter J. Bieling, PhD, Psychiatry and Behavioural Neurosciences, McMaster University and Department of Psychology, St. Joseph's Healthcare, Hamilton, Ontario, Canada

Pascale Brillon, PhD, Sacred Heart Hospital of Montréal, Québec, Canada

David A. Clark, PhD, Department of Psychology, University of New Brunswick, Fredericton, New Brunswick, Canada

Michelle G. Craske, PhD, Department of Psychology, University of California, Los Angeles

Keith S. Dobson, PhD, Department of Psychology, University of Calgary, Calgary, Alberta, Canada

David J. A. Dozois, PhD, Department of Psychology, University of Western Ontario, London, Ontario, Canada

Michel J. Dugas, PhD, Centre for Research in Human Development, Department of Psychology, Concordia University, Montréal, Québec, Canada

Cecilia A. Essau, PhD, Westfälische Wilhelms-Universität Münster, Psychologisches Institut I, Münster, Germany

Ellen Flannery-Schroeder, PhD, Department of Social Sciences, University of the Sciences in Philadelphia, Pennsylvania

Jennifer L. Hudson, PhD, Department of Psychology, Macquarie University, Sydney, Australia

Rick E. Ingram, PhD, Department of Psychology, Southern Methodist University, Dallas, Texas

Philip C. Kendall, PhD, Department of Psychology, Temple University, Philadelphia, Pennsylvania

Randi E. McCabe, PhD, Psychiatry and Behavioural Neurosciences, McMaster University and Anxiety Treatment and Research Centre, St. Joseph's Healthcare, Hamilton, Ontario, Canada

Tish Mitchusson, BA, Department of Psychology, Southern Methodist University, Dallas, Texas

Mica Odom, BA, Department of Psychology, Southern Methodist University, Dallas, Texas

Nicole D. Ottenbreit, MSc, Department of Psychology, University of Calgary, Alberta, Canada

Adam S. Radomsky, PhD, Department of Psychology, Concordia University, Montréal, Québec, Canada

Tyler J. Story, MA, Department of Psychology, University of California, Los Angeles

Henny A. Westra, PhD, Anxiety & Affective Disorders Service, London Health Sciences Centre, London, Ontario, Canada

Bonnie G. Zucker, MA, Department of Psychology, University of California, Los Angeles

PREFACE

We are pleased to be able to offer this anthology on the issue of prevention to the field. From the genesis of the idea for the book, through to its final production here, the process has been fairly straightforward. We were pleased to find that the American Psychological Association (APA) and external reviewers were receptive to the way we conceptualized and developed the proposal for the book. Susan Reynolds, who was very helpful in the original thinking and planning for the book, and Linda McCarter at the APA, have been instrumental in bringing this book to its final production, and we would like to thank them, as well as the production staff at APA (notably Casey Reever), for the fine work that they have contributed to the publication of this volume. We were also fortunate to obtain the active support and involvement of leaders in the field to contribute to the book. These authors have risen to the challenge of addressing the salient issues in the prevention of anxiety and depression. From our perspective, they have made a conscientious effort to provide timely and important recommendations for future theory development, research, and practice.

Of course, we are grateful for the assistance that we have received from our funding agencies. Such assistance includes grants from the Ontario Mental Health Foundation, the Alberta Heritage Foundation for Medical Research, and the National Institute of Mental Health while we were working on this volume, as well as our regular support from our host universities. More personally, we want to express our thanks to our wives and families for enduring the vicissitudes of living with an academic person.

We are pleased to be able to provide this volume to the field. Having been involved in the project over the past two years, we have had the opportunity to read and think more in the area of models and strategies for preventing anxiety and depression. Given the widespread prevalence and often chronic nature of these disorders, their high degree of comorbidity, and the emergence of explanatory models and treatment methods, we believe that the time is ripe for the further development of targeted prevention efforts. It is our fervent hope that this volume captures some of the excitement we feel for this area and that it will encourage others to engage in further research and clinical development and application.

The Prevention
of Anxiety and
Depression

1

THE PREVENTION OF ANXIETY AND DEPRESSION: INTRODUCTION

DAVID J. A. DOZOIS AND KEITH S. DOBSON

Anxiety and depression are frequently referred to as the common colds of mental disorders. Although this statement is accurate in terms of the prevalence of these debilitating conditions, it tends to minimize their personal and social consequences. Among such consequences are the psychological, social, and emotional suffering of the individual as well as the interpersonal and economic costs to society (Barlow, 2002; Gotlib & Hammen, 2002). Given these serious and widespread implications of anxiety and depression, the development of models for their understanding and treatment is of paramount importance.

The empirical knowledge base has increased dramatically in recent years. Psychologists and psychiatrists now have well-developed and validated models of anxiety disorders and depression from a range of theoretical perspectives. These models have significantly enhanced the development of effective treatments. For example, biological models, new-generation anxiolytics, and selective serotonin reuptake inhibitors and related antidepressants have generated unprecedented excitement for the psychobiological approach to these mental illnesses. At the same time, from a psychological

1

perspective, the development of the cognitive–behavioral therapies in particular has generated a wide range of highly effective treatment methods tied to specific anxiety disorders and depression (Chambless & Ollendick, 2001; DeRubeis & Crits-Christoph, 1998).

As both participants in, and observers of, the strides made in treating the anxiety disorders and depression, we have been struck by the fact that whereas treatment for the acute phase of anxiety and depression has advanced significantly, our understanding of risk and vulnerability factors is relatively less developed. Consequently, the amount of empirical attention and research that has been devoted to preventing these disorders has been commensurately less. Our belief, which is echoed throughout this book, is that the time is right to adopt existing treatment models, our knowledge of risk and protective factors, and evolving conceptualizations of vulnerability and apply them to preventative efforts. This book evolved from discussions we have had over the years about anxiety and depression and was specifically crystallized at a conference we attended in Granada, Spain, that was devoted to cognitive–behavioral therapies. At that conference, we pondered the current state of the treatment literature and noted in particular the need for more sustained efforts at developing prevention models and testing them with current scientific methods. Although this is not a novel idea, it was and remains our conviction that the literature has developed to the point that prevention efforts are likely to be more fruitful than they have previously been.

On the basis of our discussions of the need for a book that would distill the work that has been accomplished to date, and also to provide directions for the future, we began to read and think more in the area of prevention. It quickly became clear that alternative ways of viewing prevention itself exist in the literature. The earliest well-accepted framework—perhaps what can now be called a classic model—entails a distinction between three levels of prevention (Commission on Chronic Illness, 1957): *primary prevention*, or intervention efforts at the broadest population level (Klein & Goldston, 1977); *secondary prevention*, or prevention focused on identifying groups at risk or those showing early symptoms of specific disorders; and *tertiary prevention*, or the use of maintenance strategies and the prevention of relapse to treat individuals with a disorder, shorten the length of a given episode, and minimize its long-term consequences (National Institute of Mental Health, 1993).

More recently, the Institute of Medicine (IOM, 1994) has recommended a spectrum of intervention efforts focused on prevention, treatment, and maintenance (see Table 1.1). Subsumed under prevention efforts are strategies that have been labeled *universal* (aimed at the general public without any predetermination of risk or vulnerability status), *selected* (intended for groups with a higher risk of developing a disorder than the population at large has), and *indicated* (targeted toward individuals who are developing

TABLE 1.1
Alternative Models and Stages of Prevention

Classic model (Commission on Chronic Illness, 1957)	Institute of Medicine (1994)	
	Intervention spectrum	Type of intervention
Primary	Prevention	Universal
Secondary	Prevention	Selective
Secondary	Prevention	Indicated
Case identification	Treatment	Case identification
Treatment	Treatment	Standard treatment
Tertiary	Maintenance	Compliance with long-term treatment
Tertiary	Maintenance	Aftercare

early signs and symptoms of a disorder). Prevention of relapse is categorized within the maintenance component of this paradigm.

These alternative models of prevention have their relative strengths and weaknesses. The classic model, for example, does not make the increasingly important distinction, captured in the IOM model, between selective and indicated prevention. It was, however, the chronic nature of anxiety and depression that ultimately most influenced the model adopted for this book. In our discussions of anxiety and depression as well as in our initial reviews of the literature, it became clear that because these disorders are often characterized by a chronic course and are known to have high rates of relapse and recurrence, neither of the existing models optimally captures the required focus on the prevention of relapse. In fact, to the extent that we considered the IOM framework, we discussed the idea that not only were certain indicated methods necessary, but "reindicated" strategies aimed at preventing the relapse and recurrence of anxiety and depression were also equally, if not more, important. Unfortunately, this type of prevention effort was not identified within the IOM framework, whose definition of prevention includes only the prevention of the first episode of a given condition. As a consequence of the aforementioned deliberations, the primary–secondary–tertiary framework, which explicitly identifies the need for maintenance strategies and the prevention of relapse in the tertiary level of prevention, became a more compelling framework around which to organize the book.

Given our decision to use the primary–secondary–tertiary distinction in this volume, we also had to decide the level of specificity with which to address the constructs of anxiety and depression. We were well aware of the ongoing debate about whether it is more appropriate to discuss anxiety and depression as continuous or dichotomous phenomena. We were also cognizant that notions of prevention can be applied equally well at either the symptom or the syndrome level. Because of the broad applicability of the concept of prevention, we decided not to constrain our contributors to look only at one or the other of these levels, or to be too prescriptive in terms of which specific anxiety disorder or subtype of depression was being discussed. That said, we encouraged those chapter authors writing in the area of secondary prevention to differentiate, as much as the literature permitted, prevention models organized around risk factors (more consistent with selective prevention) from those based on early signs or symptoms of disorder (more consistent with indicated prevention).

A third consideration related to the theoretical models to be addressed in the book. Our instructions to chapter authors encouraged them to broadly consider alternative theoretical models of anxiety and depression and to integrate these models into their contributions to the volume, to the extent that doing so was supported by the empirical literature.

The resulting volume comprises three distinct parts. The first consists of three chapters that highlight the nature of anxiety and depression and focus on the myriad conceptual and methodological issues related to the study and practice of prevention. Dozois and Westra (chap. 2) present information about the variety of disorders that exist within the broad domain of anxiety and depression, their epidemiology, and their comorbidity. They also examine the implications of these phenomena for models of risk and prevention. In chapter 3, Bieling, McCabe, and Antony focus on measurement issues in anxiety and depression. These contributors discuss the conceptual distinction between qualitative and quantitative (including dimensional) measures related to the diagnosis of anxiety and depression. Specific measures are described, and the reader is pointed toward other sources for obtaining them. Chapter 4 (Clark) focuses on conceptual and methodological issues—in particular, research methods that have a longitudinal emphasis, as prevention studies must.

Part II of the book (chaps. 5–11) was designed to address the complete matrix of primary, secondary, and tertiary prevention strategies for each of the constructs of anxiety and depression. In six chapters, the risk and vulnerability factors, as well as the prevention efforts that have been evaluated to date, are reviewed. These chapters also provide directions for the evolution of models and techniques for dealing with anxiety and depression. As the reader will observe, the amount of information available and research performed varies dramatically among these chapters. For example, while there is some limited information about primary prevention of anxiety (and what is available focuses mainly on prevention in children), there is a veritable dearth of controlled research in depression. In the domain of secondary prevention, by contrast, the available database regarding depression is stronger than that having to do with anxiety. In part, this phenomenon may be due to the fact that primary prevention of anxiety seems to focus more around general themes of anxiety sensitivity, whereas secondary (and tertiary) prevention of anxiety is organized around the range of specific anxiety disorders that have been identified. Thus, while the chapter authors have been able to elaborate risk factors for these different disorders, specific tests of the prevention strategies that follow from them are less in evidence. The last chapter in this section focuses on the co-occurrence of anxiety and depression and discusses the implications of this comorbidity for prevention theory, research, and practice.

Finally, in chapter 12, we summarized the 21 identifiable themes that emerged in the previous chapters. These themes are clustered in four broad areas: (a) theoretical issues, (b) population issues, (c) measurement issues, and (d) treatment issues. The final chapter also offers general recommendations for furthering the prevention of anxiety and depression. As the reader will note, the field is left with many unanswered questions and challenges, which can be the source of a major body of theory and research.

Our conviction is that, while efforts to understand and ameliorate the acute phase of anxiety and depression continue to be critical (cf. Antony & Swinson, 2000; Beutler, Clarkin, & Bongar, 2000; Weissman, 2001), a considerable increase is needed in our preventative intervention efforts to enhance our ability to help individuals who suffer from these devastating conditions. It is our hope that this book not only will provide readers with the most up-to-date review of prevention in anxiety and depression but also will encourage further research, theorization, and practical techniques. The focus on prevention is relatively new, especially in the mental health arena. Accordingly, this volume also represents a call for research. We are optimistic that a subsequent edition of the book will represent a response to this call and that the future will yield significant advances in our understanding of how to best prevent the onset, relapse, and recurrence of anxiety and depression.

REFERENCES

Antony, M. M., & Swinson, R. P. (2000). *Phobic disorder and panic in adults: A guide to assessment and treatment.* Washington, DC: American Psychological Association.

Barlow, D. H. (2002). *Anxiety and its disorders: The nature and treatment of anxiety and panic* (2nd ed.). New York: Guilford.

Beutler, L. E., Clarkin, J. F., & Bongar, B. (2000). *Guidelines for the systematic treatment of the depressed patient.* New York: Oxford University Press.

Chambless, D. L., & Ollendick, T. H. (2001). Empirically supported psychological interventions: Controversies and evidence. *Annual Review of Psychology, 52,* 685–716.

Commission on Chronic Illness. (1957). *Chronic illness in the United States. Volume 1.* Cambridge, MA: Harvard University Press.

DeRubeis, R. J., & Crits-Christoph, P. (1998). Empirically supported individual and group psychological treatments for adult mental disorders. *Journal of Consulting and Clinical Psychology, 66,* 37–52.

Gotlib, I. H., & Hammen, C. L. (Eds.). (2002). *Handbook of depression.* New York: Guilford.

Institute of Medicine. (1994). *Reducing risks for mental disorders: Frontiers for preventive intervention research.* Washington, DC: National Academy Press.

Klein, D. C., & Goldston, S. (1977). *Primary prevention: An idea whose time has come.* Washington, DC: Government Printing Office.

National Institute of Mental Health. (1993). *The prevention of mental disorders: A national research agenda.* Bethesda, MD: Author.

Weissman, M. M. (Ed.) (2001). *Treatment of depression: Bridging the 21st century.* Washington, DC: American Psychiatric Press.

I

CONCEPTUAL AND METHODOLOGICAL ISSUES

2

THE NATURE OF ANXIETY AND DEPRESSION: IMPLICATIONS FOR PREVENTION

DAVID J. A. DOZOIS AND HENNY A. WESTRA

In this chapter, we describe the nature of anxiety and depression. Beginning with the anxiety disorders, we review their descriptive features, summarize epidemiological findings, and consider the personal and economic cost of these disorders. We then address the phenomenology and symptomatology of depression, review its prevalence and course, and discuss the deleterious effects of this disorder to the individual and to society. Following this review, we concentrate on the covariation and comorbidity of anxiety and depression. We conclude by identifying some implications of our findings for the prevention of anxiety and depression.

ANXIETY DISORDERS

Descriptive Features of Anxiety

Anxiety disorders share a corresponding set of processes in which three major factors—somatic arousal, avoidance, and the (real or imagined) perception of a threat, or threat cognition—influence each other reciprocally. A state of heightened *somatic arousal* is a hallmark of all anxiety disorders and may consist of panic attacks, periods of intense and rapidly accelerating somatic arousal, or less intense, but generally heightened, anxiety. Arousal may be triggered by either external or internal (e.g., images) stimuli. *Avoidance*, or behavior initiated to control or reduce arousal, is another core feature of all anxiety disorders. Avoidance typically involves overt behavior and is directed at feared situations, but affected individuals also engage in more subtle avoidance strategies. For instance, a person may remain in a feared situation but initiate a behavioral (e.g., using alcohol to dampen anxiety) or cognitive (e.g., distraction) strategy to mitigate his or her anxiety. The particular form of avoidance or protective action varies, depending on the content of the underlying fear structure.

A third common component of anxiety, albeit with differential foci across the spectrum of anxiety disorders, is *threat cognition*, which includes (a) catastrophic beliefs (e.g., in panic disorder, the racing of one's heart may be interpreted as evidence of a heart attack); (b) the subjective experience of having limited personal control over feared events (e.g., in generalized anxiety disorder, the belief that one cannot predict or control the safety of one's children); (c) hypervigilance to, or chronic anticipation of, feared stimuli (e.g., in posttraumatic stress disorder [PTSD], vigilance toward cues reminiscent of an impending recurrent traumatic event); and (d) self-focused attention, or the tendency to narrow one's concentration on a perceived threat (e.g., in social phobia, rejection-related cues are often selectively attended to). These three primary aspects of anxiety are related to one another but do not invariably coincide (see, e.g., Rachman, 1990). For example, an individual may eliminate panic attacks but remain fearful and avoidant of body sensations associated with panic. In sum, although the features of anxiety disorders overlap, they differ primarily in the content of the fear.

The features of the major anxiety disorders listed in the *Diagnostic and Statistical Manual of Mental Disorders* (4th ed.; DSM–IV; DSM–IV–TR; American Psychiatric Association, 1994, 2000) are presented in Table 2.1. Beyond the disorders listed in the table, the *DSM–IV* includes panic disorder without agoraphobia, agoraphobia without a history of panic disorder, acute stress disorder, anxiety disorder due to a general medical condition, substance-induced anxiety disorder, and anxiety disorder not otherwise specified. These diagnostic categories apply to both children and adults, although some criteria are adjusted when evaluating youngsters to be more developmentally appropriate and sensitive. To meet the criteria for social phobia, for example, a child must show marked anxiety in the presence of peers, not just when interacting with adults. Separation anxiety disorder is the only anxiety-related diagnostic category that is reserved exclusively for children and adolescents.

TABLE 2.1
Key Features of Major Anxiety Disorders

Major anxiety disorders	Key features
Specific phobia	Fear or avoidance of circumscribed objects or situations (e.g., heights, flying, injections)
Social phobia	Fear or avoidance of social or public situations, due to the possibility of embarrassment or humiliation
Obsessive–compulsive disorder	Recurrent and intrusive thoughts, images, or impulses (e.g., fear of contamination, thoughts of harm toward others)
	Person recognizes thoughts as unreasonable or inappropriate
	Repetitive acts (behavioral or cognitive) aimed at reducing anxiety or neutralizing an obsessive thought (e.g., repeatedly checking under one's bed for the presence of some feared object)
	Excessive behavior, or behavior that is not logically related to the thought it is intended to neutralize
Panic disorder	Recurrent, unexpected panic attacks, fear of additional attacks, or fear of the implications of such attacks
	Change in behavior secondary to panic attacks
	Peaking of symptoms within 10 minutes of their onset
Panic disorder with agoraphobia	All of the features of panic disorder
	Fear of being unable to escape one's surroundings or of being alone in the event of a panic attack; avoidance of the suspect surroundings
Posttraumatic stress disorder	Persistent reexperiencing of a traumatic event (e.g., via nightmares, flashbacks, or acting as if the event were recurring)
	Distress or anxiety associated with exposure to cues related to the event
	Avoidance of reminders of the event (e.g., blocking thoughts of the event, avoiding stimuli associated with the event)
	Numbing or emotional detachment (e.g., no longer having strong feelings or feeling numb toward others)
Generalized anxiety disorder	Excessive, uncontrollable worry about a number of events (e.g., work performance, health and safety of self or others, finances, etc.)
	Worry associated with somatic symptoms or mood changes (e.g., worry producing irritability, sleep disruption, tension, or fatigue)
Separation anxiety disorder of childhood	Inappropriate and excessive anxiety regarding separation or anticipated separation from home or attachment figures

The commonalities across various forms of anxiety raise issues about the discriminant validity and use of contemporary classification systems for anxiety disorders. For instance, concern has been expressed that a focus on differentiating various disorders and identifying unique variance among them, has resulted in less consideration of the shared or overlapping features of emotional disorders, despite the fact that these features are potentially significant for prevention, treatment, and the conceptualization of the etiology of these disorders (Andrews, 1996; Brown & Barlow, 2002). The threshold criteria of classification systems, such as those listed in the *DSM–IV* (American Psychiatric Association, 1994), may also compromise the identification and treatment of subclinical or prodromal syndromes (Eisen & Kearney, 1995).

Several investigations have demonstrated that these subthreshold syndromes not only are highly prevalent but also result in substantial impairment. Ezpeleta, Keeler, Erkanli, Costello, and Angold (2001), for example, reported that 27% of children in a community sample experienced significant disability (with their peers, schools, or families) secondary to psychological problems, yet only 30% of these children met the full diagnostic criteria for a psychiatric disorder. In a similar fashion, Breton, Bergeron, Valla, Berthiaume, and Gaudet (1999) noted that the prevalence rates of anxiety disorders in children and adolescents approached 70% when the criterion that the disorder had to result in clinically significant impairment was eliminated. Such findings suggest that early and potentially serious problems may go undetected if one relies on a categorical diagnostic classification scheme.

Prevalence of Anxiety

The one-year and lifetime prevalence rates of various anxiety disorders are displayed in Table 2.2. These data are based largely on the National Comorbidity Survey (NCS), an epidemiological study of over 8,000 randomly sampled community residents in the United States (Kessler et al., 1994). According to the study, which established diagnoses by means of a structured diagnostic interview based on *DSM–III–R* criteria, anxiety disorders represent the most common of all mental disorders (Kessler et al., 1994).

TABLE 2.2
One-Year and Lifetime Prevalence Rates for Major Anxiety Disorders

Disorder	One-year prevalence (%)	Lifetime prevalence (%)
Specific phobia	8.8	11.3
Social phobia	7.9	13.3
Obsessive–compulsive disorder	1.8	2.5
Panic disorder	2.3	3.5
Agoraphobia without panic disorder	2.8	5.3
Posttraumatic stress disorder	3.6	7.8
Generalized anxiety disorder	3.1	5.1
Separation anxiety disorder	4.8	—

Note. Adapted from Kessler et al. (1994). Copyright © 1994 by the American Medical Association. Adapted by permission. The prevalence figures for obsessive–compulsive disorder and separation anxiety disorder are taken from Weissman et al. (1994) and Muris, Merckelbach, Mayer, and Prins (2000), respectively.

The cumulative one-year prevalence for anxiety disorders was 17%, compared with 11% for mood disorders and 11% for substance abuse disorders.

Kessler et al. (1994) also found that many of the major anxiety disorders occur more frequently in women than in men, with phobic disorders representing the most common mental health disorder in women and the second most widespread mental health problem in men. Reasons hypothesized to account for this gender discrepancy include greater cognitive vulnerability among females (i.e., a heightened sense of uncontrollability and a pessimistic attributional style), encountering a greater number of negative life events during childhood and adolescence (e.g., childhood sexual abuse), biological predispositions, and a learning history that fails to foster self-efficacy (Barlow, 2002). Some empirical support has accumulated for these hypotheses (Barlow, Chorpita, & Turovsky, 1996), but the precise mechanisms and risk factors placing females at greater risk of anxiety are largely unknown.

Determining accurate prevalence rates of anxiety disorders in children is difficult because the estimates vary widely, depending on the source of report. In specific phobia, for example, parental report of prevalence is significantly higher than is self-report in young children (ages 6–11). This trend reverses, however, in adolescents (Breton et al., 1999). Consistent with the adult literature, however, anxiety disorders are clearly the most prevalent psychiatric problems in childhood, and they are the most typical reason for referral to mental health services (Beidel, 1991). The overall prevalence rate of anxiety disorders in children and adolescents is approximately 10% (Breton et al., 1999; McGee et al., 1990), with specific phobia, generalized anxiety disorder, and separation anxiety disorder being the most common forms. Obsessive–compulsive disorder and panic disorder are relatively less well represented in youth, and there is limited information on the prevalence and manifestation of PTSD in this young population.

Just as women suffer from anxiety disorders more frequently than men, anxiety disorders are significantly more common in girls than in boys (Breton et al., 1999; Costello, 1989; Kashani & Orvaschel, 1990), with the exception of obsessive–compulsive disorder, which tends to be represented equally across the two genders (Kashani, Orvaschel, Rosenberg, & Reid, 1989). The specific type of anxiety presentation, however, varies with age. Younger children present with higher rates of separation anxiety disorder and specific phobia, adolescents show higher rates of generalized anxiety (Breton et al., 1999; Kashani et al., 1989), and social phobia and panic disorder materialize mainly among adolescents (Whitaker et al., 1990).

Course of Anxiety Disorders

Studies investigating the longitudinal course of untreated anxiety disorders in adulthood uniformly reveal an illness trajectory marked by chronicity and relapse over many years (Moreno & Delgado, 2000). For example, in a prospective study of selected anxiety disorders, 17% of individuals with panic disorder with agoraphobia and 39% of individuals with panic disorder alone were in remission one year later (Keller et al., 1994). Moreover, the cumulative probability of remission was only 21% for generalized anxiety disorder and 16% for social phobia after two years (Hirschfeld, 1996). These findings converge with those of other investigations of the naturalistic course of anxiety disorders. Noyes, Clancy, Hoenk, and Slymen (1980), for example, reported that 88% of their sample of patients with anxiety disorders continued to be symptomatic over nine years of follow-up. Similar results were reported by Agras, Chapin, and Oliveau (1972), who found that 53% of phobic individuals did not improve over the five-year study period.

Few studies have directly investigated the course of anxiety in children. Longitudinal studies, in which researchers use diagnostic interviews at multiple assessment points, imply that the rates of remission are high. A review of five prospective studies, with assessment intervals ranging from two to five years, revealed that only 20% to 30% of children with a subsequent anxiety disorder had an earlier anxiety disorder (Costello & Agnold, 1995), suggesting only a moderate degree of continuity. This finding concurs with that of Last, Perrin, Hersen, & Kazdin (1996), who reported a recovery rate of 92% for separation anxiety disorder four years after the initial diagnosis and a recovery rate of 80% for "overanxious disorder" (i.e., generalized anxiety disorder). However, 30% of the children in Last et al.'s study developed a new anxiety disorder, suggesting that improvement may be stable for specific anxiety disorders, but less so for anxiety in general. Consistent with this result are those of several other investigations which indicate that children with separation anxiety disorder have a higher probability of developing subsequent depression, social phobia, and panic disorder (Biederman et al., 1993; Black & Robbins, 1990; Moreau & Follett, 1993) and that children with social anxiety present an increased risk for the development of depression (Stein et al., 2001).

Retrospective studies of adults with anxiety disorders indicate greater stability of anxiety over the life span. Some anxiety disorders (e.g., panic disorder and PTSD) tend to have their onset in early adulthood, whereas others emerge in childhood or adolescence. For example, the age of onset for panic disorder is typically between 23 and 29 years of age (Craske, Miller, Rotunda, & Barlow, 1990). However, anxiety disorders tend to emerge more typically in childhood and adolescence. The onset of social phobia, for instance, is estimated to occur between 11 and 15 years of age (Juster, Brown, & Heimberg, 1996), and individuals with generalized anxiety disorder usually have difficulty identifying a clear age of onset but describe symptoms dating back to childhood (Sanderson & Barlow, 1990).

Given the paucity of longitudinal studies that follow anxious children into adulthood, coupled with the limitations of relying on retrospective self-reports in adult anxiety disorders, it is not possible to draw firm conclusions about the developmental trajectory of anxiety from childhood to adulthood. Some evidence suggests continuity for anxiety in general, even though a specific anxiety disorder may exhibit only moderate stability over time, and adult studies place the age of onset for many anxiety disorders in childhood and adolescence. Some research also posits that anxiety problems in children are precursors to later problems, such as depression (cf. Cole, Peeke, Martin, Truglio, & Seroczynski, 1998).

Even when treated, many individuals with anxiety disorders remain symptomatic. Katschnig and Amering (1994) reported that only 31% of panic patients recovered following a course of pharmacotherapy and that the majority of their sample continued to have symptoms over the six-year follow-up period. This recovery rate is consistent with other findings from studies of anxiolytic medications that demonstrate poor maintenance of treatment gains at follow-up assessments with benzodiazepines (see Westra & Stewart, 1998) and with suggestions that the efficacy of newer antidepressant agents are seen only as long as the medication is continued (Figgitt & McClellan, 2000; Sharp et al., 1996).

Notwithstanding the fact that cognitive–behavioral therapy is the empirically supported treatment most frequently recommended for anxiety disorder management (Chambless & Ollendick, 2001; DeRubeis & Crits-Christoph, 1998), response rates also vary widely in empirical evaluations of this approach. In their review of 11 data sets evaluating treatment for agoraphobia by exposure, Jacobson, Wilson, and Tupper (1988) found that only 27% of participants could be classified as "recovered" after treatment, and 34% at follow-up, when stringent criteria were used to define recovery. Similar findings have been reported for cognitive–behavioral therapy in generalized anxiety disorder. Fisher and Durham (1999) reanalyzed data from the State–Trait Anxiety Inventory—Trait Version, applying rigorous criteria for recovery in six controlled outcome trials. They noted an aggregate recovery rate of 40%, with over half of the trials obtaining recovery rates of 30% or less (see also Westen & Morrison, 2001). Similarly, up to 40% of individuals participating in cognitive–behavioral therapy for PTSD can be classified as nonresponders to treatment (Foa, 2000), and merely 50% of individuals receiving such therapy for social anxiety achieve clinically significant improvements (Clark, 1997). Comparable response rates have been obtained in treatment outcome studies with children, with 30% to 40% continuing to meet the criteria for a clinically significant anxiety disorder following treatment (Barrett, Dadds, Rapee, & Ryan, 1996; Kendall, 1994).

It is important to point out, though, that outcomes vary markedly, depending on how conservative the criteria for success are (Nathan, 2001). Brown and Barlow (1995), for instance, found that 75% of panic patients treated with exposure achieved high end-state functioning after 2 years. Only 21% of the sample, however, met the criteria when a "high end state" was defined as the absence of panic during the previous year.

Burden Associated With Anxiety

Anxiety disorders bear a substantial personal, societal, and health burden. In a large-scale review of epidemiological studies that investigated quality of life in the anxiety disorders, Mendlowicz and Stein (2000) noted that the studies portrayed an almost uniform picture of anxiety disorders causing marked impairment across multiple domains of functioning. The reduced quality of life reported in individuals with anxiety disorders is comparable to, and in some instances worse than, other major medical illnesses, such as diabetes (Candilis et al., 1999; Rubin et al., 2000). Leon, Portera, and Weissman (1995), for instance, reported that up to 29% of their sample of panic patients were chronically unemployed for five years or more, and up to 68% were unemployed at the time of the evaluation. Individuals with social anxiety exhibit significant restrictions in their relationships with their partners, in their educational and career development, and in family interactions (Schneier, Heckelman, & Garfinkel, 1994), and they also have a higher likelihood of being single and unemployed (Katzelnick & Greist, 2001), compared with control participants. In children, the presence of an anxiety disorder is associated with poorer academic performance, including repeating grades in school (Dweck, 1999), and family stress stemming from parental concern about the child (Costello, 1989; Ezpeleta et al., 2001).

The burden also extends to the families of people with anxiety disorders. Family members of patients with obsessive–compulsive disorder or generalized anxiety disorder, for instance, report substantial disruptions in the family's routine, leisure activities, and interpersonal interactions as well as increased financial difficulties (Chakrabarti, Kulhara, & Verma, 1993). Cooper (1996) found that a majority of family members of individuals with obsessive–compulsive disorder experienced significant interference in family activities, leading to loss of friendships, marital discord, financial problems, and hardship on siblings. Families living with clinically anxious individuals also show impaired problem-solving ability, dysfunctional behavior control, and a lowered capacity to regulate their emotions (Livingston-VanNoppen, Rasmussen, Eisen, & McCartney, 1990), and they have higher divorce rates than individuals without psychiatric disorders (Kessler, Walters, & Forthofer, 1998). The high comorbidity rate of anxiety with other disorders, such as alcohol abuse, also contributes to the increased burden on those with the condition (Brown, Campbell, et al., 2001).

In summary, anxiety disorders are among the most prevalent mental health problems and exact marked personal, familial, and economic costs. In fact, anxiety disorders cost about $42 billion annually in the United States, with the bulk of these costs attributable to nonpsychiatric medical treatment (Greenberg et al., 1999). In addition, despite the fact that the temporal stability of specific anxiety disorders in childhood is unclear, many anxiety problems have early developmental origins. In adulthood, these disorders are characterized by very low rates of spontaneous remission, and they often persist for many years. Existing treatments for anxiety, while often effective, fail to meet the needs of a substantial proportion of patients, both adults and children.

DEPRESSIVE DISORDERS

Descriptive Features of Depression

Although a transient negative mood state often accompanies psychological losses, frustrations, and disappointments (Gotlib & Hammen, 1992), depression, as a disorder, refers to a highly debilitating *constellation* of symptoms. These symptoms are associated with significant cognitive, behavioral, emotional, physiological, and interpersonal impairment (Dozois & Dobson, 2002).

There are many types of mental disorders that have depression as either a central or an associated feature. These disorders are highlighted in Table 2.3. Within the mood disorders, the *DSM–IV* (American Psychiatric Association, 1994, 2000) distinguishes conditions that involve depression only (major depressive disorder, dysthymia) from those that are cyclical in nature and also consist of elevations in affect (bipolar I and II, cyclothymia). As a syndrome, or cluster of symptoms, depression is also represented in other diagnostic categories. For example, schizoaffective disorder is included within the spectrum of psychotic disorders, and there are three types of adjustment disorders that relate to depressed mood. Other nosologies involving depression have also attained some empirical support but require further validation to determine whether they should be represented in the formal nomenclature. From a prevention perspective, these syndromes (e.g., mixed anxiety–depressive disorder) are important to consider as well because they are common, cause notable distress and impairment, and are predictive of more severe subsequent episodes (Angst, 1997b; Boulenger, Fournier, Rosales, & Lavallée, 1997). Most research findings and preventative programs emphasize unipolar depression as an entity or experience. Thus, although our review of depression is necessarily selective and focuses primarily on major depression, much of our discussion is also relevant to the construct of depression more generally and to these associated conditions.

Unipolar major depressive disorder is an etiologically and clinically heterogeneous condition (Kendler, Gardner, & Prescott, 1999) characterized by either depressed mood or significantly curtailed interest or pleasure in virtually all activities. In addition to these two primary symptoms, of which at least one must be present, major depressive disorder includes a number of other symptoms, including weight or appetite loss or gain, insomnia or hypersomnia, psychomotor retardation or agitation, loss of energy or fatigue,

TABLE 2.3

Psychiatric Disorders With Depression as a Central or Associated Feature

Mood disorders	Key features
Unipolar disorders	
Major depressive disorder	A major depressive episode defined by (1) the presence of significant depressed mood or loss of interest and (2) a minimum of four additional cognitive, behavioral, or somatic symptoms Symptoms must last 2 weeks or longer
Dysthymic disorder	Chronically depressed mood lasting for at least 2 years An alternative set of criteria has also been proposed and is presented in the appendix of *DSM-IV*
Bipolar disorders	
Bipolar I disorder	At least one manic or mixed episode Individuals with this disorder also typically have one or more major depressive episodes
Bipolar II disorder	One or more major depressive episodes, coupled with at least one hypomanic episode
Cyclothymic disorder	The presence of hypomanic symptoms and subsyndromal depressive symptoms for at least 2 years
Mood disorder due to a general medical condition	A significant disturbance in mood due to the physiological consequence of a medical condition
Substance-induced mood disorder	A significant disturbance in mood due to the physiological consequence of a drug, somatic intervention, or toxin
Related mood disturbances	
Adjustment disorder with depressed mood	Clinically significant depressed mood, tearfulness, or hopelessness in response to identifiable psychosocial stressors
Adjustment disorder with mixed anxiety and depressed mood	Clinically significant depressed mood, nervousness, and worry in response to identifiable psychosocial stressors
Adjustment disorder with mixed disturbance of emotions and conduct	Clinically significant emotional symptoms (e.g., depression) and a disturbance of conduct in response to identifiable psychosocial stressors
Schizoaffective disorder	A condition of active-phase symptoms of schizophrenia and a prominent mood disturbance (the former must precede the latter by at least 2 weeks).
Mood disorders in need of further validation	
Recurrent brief depression	Recurrent episodes of depression that are identical to a major depressive episode, but that are brief in duration (i.e., at least 2 days, but less than 2 weeks)
Minor depression	Depressive symptoms that last at least 2 weeks, but cause less impairment and have fewer symptoms than a major depressive episode has
Depressive personality disorder	A persistent and pervasive pattern of depressive thoughts and behaviors that begin by early adulthood, do not simply occur during a major depressive episode, and are not better accounted for by dysthymia

continues

TABLE 2.3 (Continued)

Mood disorders	Key features
Postpsychotic disorder of schizophrenia	A major depressive episode (including sad or depressed mood) that occurs during the residual phase of schizophrenia
Mixed anxiety— depressive disorder	Persistent and recurrent dysphoria, coupled with symptoms of anxiety (e.g., hypervigilance, worry)
Premenstrual dysphoric disorder	A cluster of symptoms, including depressed mood, anxiety, anhedonia, and affective lability, that occur consistently during the last week of the menstrual cycle's luteal phase

worthlessness or excessive guilt, impaired concentration, indecisiveness or difficulty thinking, and suicidal ideation, attempted suicide, or recurrent thoughts of death (American Psychiatric Association, 1994, 2000).

The diagnostic criteria for major depressive disorder require that at least five out of nine symptoms be present and that they cause significant distress or impairment nearly every day for two weeks or longer. Exclusionary criteria include the physiological effects of a substance or general medical condition that fully accounts for the profile of symptoms, and short-term (i.e., up to two months) bereavement that is not characterized by feelings of worthlessness, suicidal ideation, psychotic symptomatology, or psychomotor retardation (American Psychiatric Association, 2000).

There are also some specific age and cultural variations in the expression and classification of major depressive disorder (Garber & Flynn, 2001; Hammen & Rudolph, 2003). For example, somatic complaints, irritability, and social withdrawal are common symptoms in children. In contrast, psychomotor retardation, delusions, and hypersomnia are more typical in adolescents and adults than they are in children (American Psychiatric Association, 2000). Diagnostically, therefore, the mood may be manifested as irritation, rather than sadness, in children and adolescents.

Even when diagnostic criteria are not met, subsyndromal depressive symptoms nonetheless cause serious distress. Between 10% and 30% of adolescents exceed the cutoffs of high severity when self-report indices are used (Hammen & Rudolph, 1996), and a lifetime prevalence rate of 24% has been reported for depressive symptoms in adults (Horwath, Johnson, Klerman, & Weissman, 1992). Clinically significant first-onset depression among never-depressed individuals is rare and is usually preceded by a series of "subthreshold" episodes (Coyne, Pepper, & Flynn, 1999; Horwath et al., 1992; Pine, Cohen, Cohen, & Brook, 1999). Subthreshold depression is associated with significant functional impairment and appears to be an important risk factor for the development of major depressive disorder (Brent, Birmaher, Kolko, Baugher, & Bridge, 2001; Horwath et al., 1992).

Prevalence of Depression

A number of large-scale epidemiological studies have been conducted to assess the prevalence of depression in the general population. Two of the most well-known investigations, both conducted in the United States, are the Epidemiologic Catchment Area (ECA; Eaton & Kessler, 1985; Eaton et al., 1989; Regier et al., 1988; Regier et al., 1993) and the National Comorbidity Survey (NCS; Blazer, Kessler, McGonagle, & Swartz, 1994; Kessler et al., 1994). The former study assessed approximately 20,000 residents in five U.S. sites. Data were collected in two main waves, with the first involving a cross-sectional estimate of one-month, one-year, and lifetime prevalence rates. The second wave was conducted a year later to provide additional estimates of prevalence and to assess one-year incidence rates (i.e., the number of new cases). Almost 30% of the participants reported having experienced dysphoric mood for as long as two weeks during their lifetimes (Weissman, Bruce, Leaf, Florio, & Holzer, 1991). The annual incidence rate of major depressive disorder was 1.59% (Eaton et al., 1989). One-year and lifetime prevalence estimates were 2.7% and 4.9%, respectively. These estimates were slightly higher (one-year = 3.7%; lifetime = 6.3%) when major depressive episodes were examined (Weissman et al., 1991).

The NCS yielded higher prevalence estimates than did the ECA. For example, the one-year prevalence estimate was 10%, with a lifetime estimate of 17%. These disparities may have been due to a number of factors, including both population and methodological differences (for an excellent critique, see Kaelber, Moul, & Farmer, 1995). Although these differences may be problematic for the interpretation of the prevalence estimates and the identification of risk factors (Kaelber et al., 1995; Wakefield & Spitzer, 2002), both studies nonetheless indicate that depression is currently one of the most prevalent mental disorders.

A number of studies have also accumulated that provide international estimates of depression. Community-based epidemiological studies (e.g., De Marco, 2000; Murphy, Laird, Monson, Sobol, & Alexander, 2000; Ohayon, Priest, Guilleminault, & Caulet, 1999; Patten, 2000; Regier et al., 1988; Regier et al., 1993) suggest that there is considerable variability in the point prevalence, one-year, and lifetime estimates of the disorder. The mean point prevalence rate across the countries represented was 4.75%. The average one-year and lifetime prevalence estimates were 5.18% and 8.75%, respectively. The figures were higher, however, when North American countries were examined (one-year prevalence, M = 9.18%; lifetime prevalence, M = 13.98%). On the one hand, methodological differences among the studies (e.g., discrepancies in the diagnostic systems used, different periods over which the study took place, and potential cohort effects) may partially account for discrepancies in the estimated prevalence of major depressive disorder. On the other hand, the rates may reflect a true indication of differences across countries in the manifestation of depression.

The rate of major depressive disorder in children and adolescents, collapsed across ages, is quite consistent with figures given in the adult literature and ranges between 6% and 8%, although younger children have much lower rates than do adolescents (Hammen & Rudolph, 1996). Empirical data also suggest that the prevalence of depression may be increasing, particularly in children and adolescents (Garber & Flynn, 2001; Hammen & Rudolph, 2003). This rise in estimates may be due, in part, to increased awareness of the condition and enhanced sensitivity of the diagnostic instruments used (Angst, 1997b). The higher cumulative lifetime prevalence rates of major depressive disorder in younger than in older birth cohorts may also be related to changes in the social climate (e.g., reduced resources and support, family disruption; see Hammen & Rudolph, 2003).

From early to middle adolescence and throughout adulthood, females are consistently twice as likely as males to become depressed (Blazer et al., 1994; Eaton et al., 1989; Smith & Weissman, 1992; Garber & Flynn, 2001). A number of explanations have been proposed to account for these gender differences, including artifactual variables (e.g., reporting biases, differences in manifestation of the disorder), genetics, hormonal differences, personality factors that serve as gender-specific diatheses, sex role interpretations, "learned helplessness," differences in socialization, gender discrimination issues, differences in experienced trauma, and variation in ruminative styles.

Few of these single-factor explanations have received strong empirical support (for reviews, see Brems, 1995; Nolen-Hoeksema, 1987). One consistent finding, however, is that women are more likely to ruminate than are men, who tend to use distraction to cope with depressive mood states (see Nolen-Hoeksema, 1987). Rather than being a main effect, it is possible that various risk factors interact in dynamic ways to produce gender differences in the expression of depression, but research that has tested such complex etiological hypotheses is scant. For example, gonadal hormones and brain neurotransmitters might affect biological and emotional regulation processes in complex ways in vulnerable adolescents who experience stressful life events (see Hammen & Rudolph, 2003; Kendler & Prescott, 1999). Aside from the fact that the reasons for gender differences in depression are poorly understood, the identification and modification of these mechanisms have clear implications for prevention.

Course of Depression

The first onset of major depression most frequently occurs in mid- to late adolescence (Hammen, 2001). The risk associated with an initial episode of depression appears to be relatively low in childhood, considerably higher in adolescence, and at its pinnacle in middle adulthood, with decreased rates in elderly samples (Lewinsohn, Duncan, Stanton, & Hautzinger, 1986).

In the absence of treatment, major depressive disorder usually lasts between four months and one year (American Psychiatric Association, 2000). The rate of reduction of symptoms without treatment ranges between 10% and 15%, with approximately 20% of individuals experiencing spontaneous remission over an 8-week period (Posternak & Miller, 2001). However, most of what we know about the course of the disorder is based on treated samples, which are likely unrepresentative of the natural course of the condition (Gotlib & Hammen, 1992). This information is particularly limited, given that the majority of people with depressive disorders do *not* seek treatment (cf. Greenberg, Stiglin, Finkelstein, & Berndt, 1993). In individuals who have received antidepressant or psychological treatment, the average duration of major depressive disorder is 27 weeks (Coryell et al., 1994). Similar findings regarding the course of depression have been reported in children (Garber & Flynn, 2001). In some individuals, there is a complete remission of symptoms and a return to the premorbid level of functioning. However, enduring or fluctuating periods of residual symptoms persist for months to years in 20% to 30% of cases. This partial remission is associated with increased risk of relapse (Gotlib, Lewinsohn, & Seeley, 1995; Judd et al., 2000).

Within treated samples, the base rate of recovery is approximately 40% within three months, 60% within six months, and 80% within one year (Coryell et al., 1994). Notwithstanding these rates, a substantial proportion of individuals continue on a course that may involve chronic major depressive disorder, depression that is recurrent without full interepisodic recovery, dysthymia, or double depression (i.e., major depression superimposed on dysthymia; Rush & Thase, 1997; Rush et al., 1998). In fact, the rates of chronicity in treated samples are 20% at 2 years and between 7% and 12% after 5 to 10 years of follow-up (Keller & Boland, 1998; Rush et al., 1998).

Although numerous effective treatments are available for depression (Chambless & Ollendick, 2001; DeRubeis & Crits-Christoph, 1998), the recurrence of the disorder is problematic and debilitating (Duggan, 1997). On average, between 50% and 85% of depressed patients experience multiple subsequent episodes (Coyne et al., 1999), with an average of five throughout their life spans (Gotlib & Hammen, 1992). The chance of experiencing a recurrence also increases (Kessing, 1998), and the time for an episode to recur decreases (Keller & Boland, 1998), exponentially with each episode. Hoencamp, Haffmans, Griens, Huijbrechts, and Heycop ten Ham (2001) examined the long-term course of depression in 95 depressed outpatients treated with pharmacotherapy. These researchers found that 36% of the sample showed a chronic course, 25% experienced at least one recurrence, and only 39% recovered without recurrence at 3 1/2-year follow-up. Chronicity was associated with an earlier age of onset and with higher initial severity. Solomon et al. (2000) followed 318 individuals with major depressive disorder over a period of 10 years and reported that 64% of the sample suffered at least one recurrence. The number of lifetime episodes was significantly associated with the probability of recurrence, with a 16% increase in risk with each additional episode. Furthermore, when dropouts in psychotherapy trials, who range between 20% and 47%, are accounted for (McQuaid, Stein, Laffaye, & McCahill, 1999), and the criterion for response is eight weeks of minimal or no symptoms, the success rate of psychotherapy outcome trials is less favorable than previously thought (Duggan, 1997). Thus, depression is characterized by high relapse rates and a fairly chronic course (Hammen, 2001; Hoencamp et al., 2001; Judd et al., 2000), both of which have important implications for prevention.

Keller and Boland (1998) concluded that a history of frequent or multiple depressive episodes, double depression, onset after age 60, lengthy duration of individual episode or episodes, a family history of mood disorders, poor management of symptoms during continuation of pharmacotherapy, and comorbidity of anxiety or substance abuse were associated with higher rates of recurrence. Without question, the best predictor of future depression is past depression (e.g., Lewinsohn, Hoberman, & Rosenbaum, 1988), yet the mechanisms associated with first-onset depression may be very different from those accompanying repeated episodes (Hammen, 2001) and, accordingly, may need to be differentially targeted in preventative interventions. Further research is also necessary to address salient intervention issues such as resistance to treatment, refusal of treatment, dropping out, and the prediction and prevention of relapse and recurrence (National Institute of Mental Health, National Advisory Mental Health Council Workgroup on Child and Adolescent Mental Health Intervention Development and Deployment [NAMHC Workgroup], 2001).

Theorists have recently attempted to account for the increased risk of depression associated with each sequential episode. Some researchers have suggested, for instance, that depressed individuals may become more "sensitized" the longer they experience depression or the more frequently their episodes recur (Segal, Williams, & Teasdale, 2002; Segal, Williams, Teasdale, & Gemar, 1996; Teasdale et al., 2000). That is, the threshold for the reactivation of negative thinking patterns associated with dysphoric mood may be lowered the more an individual has experienced depression. Consistent with this idea is the finding by Dozois and Dobson (2001) that the organization of self-relevant negative content did not improve when depressed individuals went into remission, even though their information processing did shift significantly. These findings suggest that a negative self-schema remains in these individuals but has become (temporarily) deactivated. Individuals with a greater number of past episodes of depression also organized their cognitive content differently than did equally symptomatic individuals with fewer episodes (Dozois & Dobson, 2003). Depressed individuals may therefore benefit from strategies that help them to reallocate attention once they begin to experience dysphoric mood (see Segal et al., 2002).

Joiner (2000) has also discussed a model in which multiple interpersonal variables (e.g., generation of stress, seeking of negative feedback, excessive seeking of reassurance, avoidance of interpersonal conflict) may interact in reciprocal and dynamic ways to maintain the depressive process and increase the individual's vulnerability to the recurrence of depressive episodes. The various models have important implications for preventative interventions aimed at reducing the substantial rates of relapse in this disorder.

The Burden Associated With Depression

The symptomatology of depression, and the phenomenological devastation experienced by those individuals with the disorder, affect most aspects of everyday functioning (Judd et al., 2000; Lecrubier, 2001). Depressed individuals, for instance, experience considerable disruption in their occupational functioning (Broadhead, Blazer, George, & Tse, 1990; McQuaid et al., 1999). Several researchers have also reported a strong connection between depression and troubled parent–child relationships (e.g., Alloy et al., 2001; Ingram, 2001), marital distress (Dudek et al., 2001; Gotlib, Lewinsohn, & Seeley, 1998), and other interpersonal difficulties. Gotlib et al. (1998), for example, found that the experience of a major depressive episode during adolescence predicted higher subsequent rates of marital dissatisfaction. The effect appeared to be specific to depression and did not generalize to other psychiatric disorders. A 21-year longitudinal study of 1,265 children revealed significant long-term difficulties in the cohort that developed depression during adolescence (Fergusson & Woodward, 2002). Those individuals were significantly more likely than nondepressed adolescents to experience later depressive episodes, anxiety disorders, problems with alcohol and other substances, nicotine dependence, educational difficulties, and higher rates of recurrent unemployment.

Clearly, the specific developmental trajectories that ultimately lead to depression are complex, dynamic, and idiographic (see Mash & Dozois, 2003), but the Fergusson and Woodward (2002) study adds to a large literature attesting to the adverse impact of early depression. Obviously, depression may also result in loss of life: According to Blair-West, Cantor, Mellsop, & Eyeson-Annan (1999), the lifetime suicide risk for individuals with major depressive disorder is 3.4%, although other studies have reported rates between 10% and 15% (see Gotlib & Hammen, 1992).

In addition to the individual impact of depression are the costs to society. Major depressive disorder is one of the most common presenting complaints encountered by mental health professionals (Zheng et al., 1997) and among the most financially costly of disorders. In the United States alone, the total economic costs of depression are estimated at $44 billion annually (Greenberg et al., 1993). Researchers have, in fact, predicted that by the year 2020, depression will be second only to ischemic heart disease in terms of cost to society (Keller & Boland, 1998; Lecrubier, 2001).

By most accounts, the economic impact of depression may actually be *underestimated* because of medical morbidity (e.g., masking somatic symptoms of depression), underdiagnosis, and infrequent seeking of treatment (Panzarino, 1998). In addition, the financial costs of depression would escalate drastically if subclinical depression were also taken into account. A number of studies have shown that subclinical depression results in substantial impairment, confers a high rate of nonpsychiatric health care use on individuals, and is associated with elevated risk for severe psychiatric conditions (Boulenger et al., 1997; Gotlib et al., 1995). Gotlib et al. (1995), for instance, found that false positives (i.e., individuals with a high number of self-reported symptoms but who did not meet diagnostic criteria) (a) experienced significantly greater impairment than individuals who did not experience depression (true negatives) and (b) were more likely to succumb to a depressive episode within one year.

Unfortunately, the majority of individuals with depression receive no treatment (Mojtabai, Olfson, & Mechanic, 2002; Ohayon, Shapiro, & Kennedy, 2000; Young, Klap, Sherbourne, & Wells, 2001). This situation is particularly unfortunate, given that many effective interventions are available and that early detection and treatment may reduce the severity and course of the disorder and minimize subsequent episodes (McQuaid et al., 1999).

SYMPTOM COVARIANCE AND DIAGNOSTIC COMORBIDITY

Anxiety and depression both exhibit high rates of comorbidity with other Axis I and Axis II disorders, and with a number of medical conditions (Barlow, 2002; Dozois & Dobson, 2002; Hammen, 2001). Most striking, however, is the relationship between anxiety and depression itself. Several commonalities exist between the two disorders, and these mutual features have raised skepticism as to whether anxiety and depression are, in fact, empirically distinct entities (Barlow, 2002; Cole, Truglio, & Peeke, 1997; Dobson, 1985; Mineka, Watson, & Clark, 1998). At the symptom level, the correlation between anxiety and depression tends to be above .61 on self-report measures (e.g., Dobson, 1985). In both community and clinical samples, the average comorbidity rate of major depressive disorder and various anxiety disorders is over 50% (Brown, Campbell, Lehman, Grisham, & Mancill, 2001; Mineka et al., 1998). Brown and Barlow (2002), for example, reported that 55% of patients with an anxiety or mood disorder met the diagnostic criteria for an additional concurrent anxiety or depressive disorder. The rate was even higher (76%) when lifetime diagnoses were examined. Major depressive disorder, dysthymia, PTSD, and generalized anxiety disorder were the most highly comorbid disorders, whereas specific phobia had the lowest rate.

The comorbidity of anxiety and depression is associated with increased severity of symptoms, psychological distress, and overall impairment (Angst, 1997a; Brown, Schulberg, Madonia, Shear, & Houck, 1996; Roy-Byrne et al., 2000). Compared with individuals with either disorder alone, patients with depression and anxiety have greater functional disability, have more occupational and social disruptions, report more symptoms, and often have a poorer response to treatment (Lecrubier, 1998b; Nutt, 2000). In a recent study of a large European sample of 78,463 individuals, Tylee (2000) found that the patient group that made the most demands on health care consisted of individuals with depression and anxiety. Increased suicide rates are also found in individuals with comorbid depression and anxiety relative to those with either disorder alone (Lecrubier, 1998b).

In addition to concurrent comorbidity rates is evidence of "successive comorbidity" (Hammen & Rudolph, 2003, p. 240) between anxiety and depression. Clinical (Brown, Campbell, et al., 2001), community (Cole, Peeke, Martin, Truglio, & Seroczynski, 1998; Wetherell, Gatz, & Pedersen, 2001), and college (Whittal & Dobson, 1991) studies have supported the notion that anxiety is more likely to precede depression than the reverse. The temporal relationship between anxiety and depression does, however, appear to depend on which specific anxiety disorder the individual has. Social phobia and generalized anxiety disorder, for instance, are more likely to predate major depressive disorder, whereas panic disorder is most likely to occur concomitantly with or subsequent to depression (Brown, Campbell, et al., 2001; Fava et al., 2000).

There are several possible reasons that this temporal relationship between anxiety and depression may exist (see chap. 11, this volume). For example, the relationship may reflect the effects of chronic anxiety on self-esteem (see Brown et al., 1996); anxious avoidance leading to a reduction in reinforcements, which, in turn, contributes to depression (Brown, Campbell, et al., 2001); or the progression of a similar cognitive style, such as helplessness, which leads to hopelessness (Alloy, Kelly, Mineka, & Clements, 1990). Research has not yet delineated the specific reasons for the high covariance and diagnostic comorbidity between anxiety and depression, but it does not appear to be simply artifactual (Angold, Costello, & Erkanli, 1999). Instead, myriad overlapping mechanisms (see Mineka, Pury, & Luten, 1995) suggest that the two disorders may share a common pathogenesis (Barlow, 2002; Eley & Stevenson, 1999; Roy, Neale, Pedersen, Mathé, & Kendler, 1995; see also chap. 11, this volume). This temporal relationship of anxiety preceding depression, together with high comorbidity rates, has important ramifications for prevention.

IMPLICATIONS FOR PREVENTION

This review has demonstrated that clinical and subclinical anxiety and depression are highly prevalent and that the modal course of both disorders is marked by chronicity and relapse. Existing treatments, although effective, leave a substantial proportion of individuals only partially treated or non-responsive to treatment. In addition, epidemiological studies consistently reveal that the vast majority of individuals with anxiety, depression, or both fails to access treatment. In the NCS, for example, only 20% of individuals with a 12-month psychiatric disorder obtained any professional treatment in the year preceding the study (Kessler et al., 1994), and only 40% of those with a lifetime diagnosis ever received professional assistance (Wang, Demler, & Kessler, 2002). Together, these factors contribute to the observed high personal, societal, and financial burden exacted by anxiety and depression. These factors alone provide a compelling case for prevention efforts aimed at reducing the onset and recurrence of the two groups of disorders.

Throughout this chapter, we have also alluded to a number of syndromal features of anxiety and depression that may help inform prevention efforts. The following list summarizes six major themes, together with their implications for prevention research and intervention:

1. It is now apparent that most anxiety and mood disorders originate in childhood and adolescence and that poor childhood mental health is one of the strongest predictors of mental health problems in adulthood (van Os & Jones, 1999). Furthermore, early-onset disorders tend to be more severe and disabling than late-onset disorders(Hoehn-Saric, Hazlett, & McLeod, 1993), are associated with a high risk of comorbidity, and are predictive of adverse life events, including marital instability, failure in school, teenage childbearing and early marriage, and lower family income (Kessler, Olfson, & Berglund, 1998). Childhood anxiety and depression are undertreated, as fewer than 20% of all children who require mental health services receive necessary interventions (Tuma, 1989). These findings, together with the fact that the rate at which individuals seek treatment is highest in the year of onset and declines progressively thereafter (Kessler, Olfson, et al., 1998), suggest that early detection and intervention programs are critical.

2. The finding that anxiety typically precedes depression implies that enhanced efforts are needed to identify anxiety disorders. Of note, although treatment rates of all psychiatric disorders are low, anxiety disorders appear to be particularly undertreated. Ohayon et al. (2000), for instance, noted that 30% of individuals with a mood disorder, but only 11% of those

with an anxiety disorder, received treatment. Similarly, these investigators reported that only 4% and 18% of people with an anxiety and mood disorder, respectively, received appropriate pharmacotherapy. Prevention efforts to identify and manage anxiety disorders may be of particular importance in curbing the progression of emotional disorders.

3. Subclinical symptomatology is a reliable precursor to the development of clinical manifestations of emotional disorders, and a growing body of evidence suggests that anxiety and depression involve a prodromal accumulation of symptoms (Horwath et al., 1992; Rueter, Scaramella, Wallace, & Conger, 1999). Individuals with many subthreshold symptoms are most likely to meet the diagnostic criteria for a disorder at a later point in time (Dadds, Spence, Holland, Barrett, & Laurens, 1997). The reality, however, is that both clinical and subclinical manifestations of anxiety and depression are grossly underdetected. For example, a number of studies indicate that detection rates of anxiety and depression in primary care range from 15% to 36% (e.g., Klinkman & Okkes, 1998; Lecrubier, 1998a). The reasons for this underdetection likely include an amalgamation of patient (e.g., style of presentation, willingness to disclose symptoms, fear of stigma, presence of comorbid medical problems, cultural and geographic factors, stages of change), physician (e.g., knowledge of mental health problems, skill in recognizing symptoms indicative of mental illness, demands of practice, willingness to diagnose and treat mental health issues), and systemic (e.g., lack of integration of services for which individuals are most likely to present for treatment, failure to develop treatments compatible with natural change processes) factors (Christiana et al., 2000; Dozois & Dobson, 2002; Mojtabai et al., 2002). The circumstances underlying the underdetection of emotional disorders need to be addressed more systematically to enhance prevention efforts. Improved access to, and dissemination of, effective treatments is also critical (Olfson, Marcus, Druss, Tanielian, & Pincus, 2002). Davidson and Meltzer-Brody (1999), for example, estimated that the annual savings involved in the proper identification and treatment of depression would approach $4 billion annually in the United States alone. Arguably, increasing universal and selected preventative efforts would have an even more powerful impact.

4. Residual symptomatology and partial remission have been identified as strong predictors of future dysfunction and relapse (Paykel et al., 1995). There are compelling data that support

the prophylactic benefits of psychotherapy. For example, the use of cognitive–behavioral therapy in depression significantly reduces relapse rates over pharmacotherapy alone (30% relapse in cognitive–behavioral therapy, versus 60% in pharmacotherapy; Gloaguen, Cottraux, Cucherat, & Blackburn, 1998). Cognitive–behavioral therapy for anxiety disorders is now regarded as the treatment of choice, given its associations with long-lasting gains and reduced relapse rates over pharmacotherapy (Westra & Stewart, 1998). When one considers the highly recurrent nature of depression and the low probability of spontaneous remission in anxiety disorders, psychotherapies such as cognitive–behavioral therapy represent important and cost-effective options for anxiety and depression management. Moreover, models of relapse risk factors are emerging which will assist in the identification of vulnerabilities that can be targeted in relapse prevention programs. For instance, interventions aimed at preventing cognitive sensitization (Segal et al., 2002) and reducing the vicious interpersonal cycles associated with depression (Joiner, 2000; Hammen, 2001) may help prevent the recurrence that characterizes this disorder.

5. Comorbidity of anxiety and depression is common, and their co-occurrence is associated with a more severe and chronic course of illness. A notable hiatus in our knowledge base is why anxiety and depression are so highly related. Research is beginning to tease apart some of the unique and shared variance associated with these disorders, and it is clear that most, if not all, of the early risk factors are essentially the same (see chap. 11, this volume). Nevertheless, which disorder is manifested is likely based on multiple interacting variables. Researchers have yet to determine which particular risk or vulnerability factors are most important to target or how to maximize intervention at varying levels of prevention. Such research obviously requires costly longitudinal methodologies and complex statistical technologies to capture the dynamic interplay between and among the individual and the many risk and protective factors as they evolve and influence one another across time (see Mash & Dozois, 2003). Additional research is also needed to understand how to best treat the comorbidity of anxiety and depression and to prevent their relapse and recurrence.

6. The majority of the anxiety and depressive disorders occur more frequently in females than in males. A myriad of hypotheses has been purported to account for this gender discrepancy, but the true explanation for the prevalence data has remained

etiologically elusive. Identifying the causal factors that render females more susceptible to anxiety and depression will facilitate the development of foci for prevention programs with women and girls.

This chapter has highlighted a number of syndromal factors that may guide efforts directed at preventing anxiety and depression. Clearly, however, numerous other risk factors can be identified and are discussed in subsequent chapters. Among these risks are biological factors (e.g., behavioral inhibition), developmental factors (e.g., parental psychopathology, early loss of one or more parents, divorce, marital separation, a history of abuse or trauma), stressful life events (e.g., unemployment, high levels of family conflict, poverty, medical illnesses), and cognitive factors (e.g., a sense of hopelessness or helplessness; Kaelber et al., 1995; Lewinsohn, Hoberman, & Rosenbaum, 1988; Mrazek & Haggerty, 1994; NAMHC Workgroup, 2001; National Institute of Mental Health, NAMHC Workshop on Mental Disorders Prevention Research, 2001). Greater elucidation and understanding of the complex interplay of these variables in the development and maintenance of anxiety and depression will be important in facilitating effective prevention programs.

REFERENCES

Agras, W. S., Chapin, H. N., & Oliveau, D. C. (1972). The natural history of phobia. *Archives of General Psychiatry, 26*, 315–317.

Alloy, L. B., Abramson, L. Y., Tashman, N. A., Berrebbi, D. S., Hogan, M. E., Whitehouse, W. G., et al. (2001). Developmental origins of cognitive vulnerability to depression: Parenting, cognitive, and inferential feedback styles of the parents of individuals at high and low cognitive risk for depression. *Cognitive Therapy and Research, 25*, 397–423.

Alloy, L. B., Kelly, K. A., Mineka, S., & Clements, C. M. (1990). Comorbidity of anxiety and depressive disorders: A helplessness–hopelessness perspective. In J. D. Maser & C. R. Cloninger (Eds.), *Comorbidity of mood and anxiety disorders* (pp. 449–543). Washington, DC: American Psychiatric Press.

American Psychiatric Association. (1994). *Diagnostic and statistical manual of mental disorders* (4th ed.). Washington, DC: Author.

American Psychiatric Association. (2000). *Diagnostic and statistical manual of mental disorders* (4th ed., text revision). Washington, DC: Author.

Andrews, G. (1996). Comorbidity in neurotic disorders: The similarities are more important than the differences. In R. M. Rapee (Ed.), *Current controversies in the anxiety disorders.* New York: Guilford.

Angold, A., Costello, E. J., & Erkanli, A. (1999). Comorbidity. *Journal of Child Psychology and Psychiatry and Allied Disciplines, 40*, 57–87.

Angst, J. (1997a). Depression and anxiety: Implications for nosology, course, and treatment. *Journal of Clinical Psychiatry, 58*, 3–5.

Angst, J. (1997b). Epidemiology of depression. In A. Honig & H. M. van Praag (Eds.), Wiley Series on Clinical and Neurobiological Advances in Psychiatry, Vol. 3. *Depression: Neurobiological, psychopathological and therapeutic advances* (pp. 17–29). New York: Wiley.

Barlow, D. H. (2002). *Anxiety and its disorders: The nature and treatment of anxiety and panic* (2nd ed.). New York: Guilford.

Barlow, D. H., Chorpita, B. F., & Turovsky, J. (1996). Fear, panic, anxiety, and disorders of emotion. In D. A. Hope (Ed.), *Nebraska Symposium on Motivation: Vol. 43. Perspectives on anxiety, panic, and fear* (pp. 251–328). Lincoln: University of Nebraska Press.

Barrett, P. M., Dadds, M. R., Rapee, R. M., & Ryan, A. (1996). Family treatment of childhood anxiety disorders: A controlled trial. *Journal of Consulting and Clinical Psychology, 64*, 333–342.

Beidel, D. C. (1991). Social phobia and overanxious disorder in school-age children. *Journal of the American Academy of Child and Adolescent Psychiatry, 30*, 545–552.

Biederman, J., Rosenbaum, J. F., Bolduc-Murphy, E. A., Faraone, S. V., Chaloff, J., Hirshfeld, D. R., & Kagan, J. (1993). A three year follow-up of children with and without behavioral inhibition. *Journal of the American Academy of Child and Adolescent Psychiatry, 32*, 814–821.

Black, B., & Robbins, D. R. (1990). Panic disorder in children and adolescents. *Journal of the American Academy of Child and Adolescent Psychiatry, 29*, 36–44.

Blair-West, G. W., Cantor, C. H., Mellsop, G. W., & Eyeson-Annan, M. L. (1999). Lifetime suicide risk in major depression: Sex and age determinants. *Journal of Affective Disorders, 55*, 171–178.

Blazer, D. G., Kessler, R. C., McGonagle, K. A., & Swartz, M. S. (1994). The prevalence and distribution of major depression in a national community sample: The National Comorbidity Survey. *American Journal of Psychiatry, 151*, 979–986.

Boulenger, J. P., Fournier, M., Rosales, D., & Lavallée, Y. J. (1997). Mixed anxiety and depression: From theory to practice. *Journal of Clinical Psychiatry, 58*, 27–34.

Brems, C. (1995). Woman and depression: A comprehensive analysis. In E. E. Beckham & W. R. Leber (Eds.), *Handbook of depression* (2nd ed., pp. 539–566). New York: Guilford.

Brent, D. A., Birmaher, B., Kolko, D., Baugher, M., & Bridge, J. (2001). Subsyndromal depression in adolescents after a brief psychotherapy trial: Course and outcome. *Journal of Affective Disorders, 63*, 51–58.

Breton, J. J., Bergeron, L., Valla, J. P., Berthiaume, C., & Gaudet, N. (1999). Quebec child mental health survey: Prevalence of DSM-III-R mental health disorders. *Journal of Child Psychology and Psychiatry, 40*, 375–384.

Broadhead, W. E., Blazer, D. G., George, L. K., & Tse, C. (1990). Depression, disability days, and days lost from work in a prospective epidemiologic survey. *Journal of the American Medical Association, 264*, 2524–2529.

Brown, T. A., & Barlow, D. H. (1995). Long-term outcome in cognitive–behavioral treatment of panic disorder: Clinical predictors and alternative strategies for assessment. *Journal of Consulting and Clinical Psychology, 63,* 754–765.

Brown, T. A., & Barlow, D. H. (2002). Classification of anxiety and mood disorders. In D. H. Barlow (Ed.), *Anxiety and its disorders: The nature and treatment of anxiety and panic* (2nd ed., pp. 292–327). New York: Guilford.

Brown, T. A., Campbell, L. A., Lehman, C. L., Grisham, J. R., & Mancill, R. B. (2001). Current and lifetime comorbidity of the *DSM–IV* anxiety and mood disorders in a large clinical sample. *Journal of Abnormal Psychology, 110,* 585–599.

Brown, T. A., Di Nardo, P. A., Lehman, C. L., & Campbell, L. A. (2001). Reliability of *DSM–IV* anxiety and mood disorders: Implications for the classification of emotional disorders. *Journal of Abnormal Psychology, 110,* 49–58.

Brown, C., Schulberg, H. C., Madonia, M. J., Shear, M. K., & Houck, P. R. (1996). Treatment outcomes for primary care patients with major depression and lifetime anxiety disorders. *American Journal of Psychiatry, 153,* 1293–1300.

Candilis, P. J., McLean, R. Y., Otto, M. W., Manfro, G. G., Worthington, J. J., III, Penava, S. J., et al. (1999). Quality of life in patients with panic disorder. *Journal of Nervous and Mental Disease, 187,* 429–434.

Chakrabarti, S., Kulhara, P., & Verma, S. K. (1993). The pattern of burden in families of neurotic patients. *Social Psychiatry and Psychiatric Epidemiology, 28,* 172–177.

Chambless, D. L., & Ollendick, T. H. (2001). Empirically supported psychological interventions: Controversies and evidence. *Annual Review of Psychology, 52,* 685–716.

Christiana, J. M., Gilman, S. E., Guardino, M., Mickelson, K., Morselli, P. L., Olfson, M., & Kessler, R. C. (2000). Duration between onset and time of obtaining initial treatment among people with anxiety and mood disorders: An international survey of members of mental health patient advocate groups. *Psychological Medicine, 30,* 693–703.

Clark, D. M. (1997). Panic disorder and social phobia. In D. M. Clark & C. G. Fairburn (Eds.), *Science and practice of cognitive-behavioural therapy* (pp. 119–154). New York: Oxford University Press.

Cole, D. A., Peeke, L. G., Martin, J. M., Truglio, R., & Seroczynski, A. D. (1998). A longitudinal look at the relation between depression and anxiety in children and adolescents. *Journal of Consulting and Clinical Psychology, 66,* 451–460.

Cole, D. A., Truglio, R., & Peeke, L. (1997). Relation between symptoms of anxiety and depression in children: A multitrait–multimethod–multigroup assessment. *Journal of Consulting and Clinical Psychology, 65,* 110–119.

Cooper, M. (1996). Obsessive–compulsive disorder: Effects on family members. *American Journal of Orthopsychiatry, 66,* 296–304.

Coryell, W., Akiskal, H. S., Leon, A. C., Winokur, G., Maser, J. D., Mueller, T. I., & Keller, M. B. (1994). The time course of nonchronic major depressive disorder: Uniformity across episodes and samples. *Archives of General Psychiatry, 51,* 405–410.

atric disorders and their correlates: A primary
the American Academy of Child and Adolescent

Epidemiology. In J. S. March (Ed.), *Anxiety*
(pp. 109–124). New York: Guilford Press.

H. (1999). Significance of prior episodes of
is. *Journal of Consulting and Clinical Psychol-*

, & Barlow, D. H. (1990). A descriptive
d panic attacks in minimal and extensive
py, 28, 395–400.

Barrett, P. M., & Laurens, K. R. (1997).
anxiety disorders: A controlled trial.
ogy, 65, 627–635.

99). The underrecognition and under-
dth and depth of the problem? *Journal*

ology of major depression: Implications of
ess in a Canadian community sample. *Canadian*
iry, 45, 67–74.

ubeis, R. J., & Crits-Christoph, P. (1998). Empirically supported individual and group psychological treatments for adult mental disorders. *Journal of Consulting and Clinical Psychology, 66,* 37–52.

Dobson, K. S. (1985). The relationship between anxiety and depression. *Clinical Psychology Review, 5,* 307–324.

Dozois, D. J. A., & Dobson, K. S. (2001). A longitudinal investigation of information processing and cognitive organization in clinical depression: Stability of schematic interconnectedness. *Journal of Consulting and Clinical Psychology, 69,* 914–925.

Dozois, D. J. A., & Dobson, K. S. (2002). Depression. In M. M. Antony & D. H. Barlow (Eds.), *Handbook of assessment and treatment planning for psychological disorders* (pp. 259–299). New York: Guilford.

Dozois, D. J. A., & Dobson, K. S. (2003). The structure of the self-schema in clinical depression: Differences related to episode recurrence. *Cognition and Emotion, 17,* 933–941.

Dudek, D., Zieba, A., Jawor, M., Szymaczek, M., Opila, J., & Dattilio, F. M. (2001). The impact of depressive illness on spouses of depressed patients. *Journal of Cognitive Psychotherapy: An International Quarterly, 15,* 49–57.

Duggan, C. F. (1997). Course and outcome of depression. In A. Honig & H. M. van Praag (Eds.), Wiley Series on Clinical and Neurobiological Advances in Psychiatry: Vol. 3. *Depression: Neurobiological, psychopathological and therapeutic advances* (pp. 31–40). New York: Wiley.

Dweck, C. S. (1999). *Self-theories: Their role in motivation, personality and development.* Philadelphia: Psychology Press.

Eaton, W. W., & Kessler, L. G. (Eds.). (1985). *Epidemiologic field methods in psychiatry: The NIMH Epidemiologic Catchment Area program.* New York: Academic Press.

Eaton, W. W., Kramer, M., Anthony, J. C., Dryman, A., Shapiro, S., & Locke, B. Z. (1989). The incidence of specific DIS/DSM-III mental disorders: Data from the NIMH Epidemiologic Catchment Area program. *Acta Psychiatrica Scandinavica, 79,* 163–178.

Eisen, A. R., & Kearney, C. A. (1995). *Practitioner's guide to treating fear and anxiety in children and adolescents: A cognitive-behavioural approach.* Northvale: Jason Aronson.

Eley, T. C., & Stevenson, J. (1999). Using genetic analyses to clarify the distinction between depressive and anxious symptoms in children. *Journal of Abnormal Child Psychology, 27,* 105–114.

Ezpeleta, L., Keeler, G., Erkanli, A., Costello, J., & Angold, A. (2001). Epidemiology of psychiatric disability in childhood and adolescence. *Journal of Child Psychopathology, 42,* 901–914.

Fava, M., Rankin, M. A., Wright, E. C., Alpert, J. E., Nierenberg, A. A., Pava, J., & Rosenbaum, J. F. (2000). Anxiety disorders in major depression. *Comprehensive Psychiatry, 41,* 97–102.

Fergusson, D. M., & Woodward, L. J. (2002). Mental health, educational, and social role outcomes of adolescents with depression. *Archives of General Psychiatry, 59,* 225–231.

Figgitt, D. P., & McClellan, K. J. (2000). Fluvoxamine: An updated review of its use in the management of adults with anxiety disorders. *Drugs, 60,* 925–954.

Fisher, P. L., & Durham, R. C. (1999). Recovery rates in generalized anxiety disorder following psychological therapy: An analysis of clinically significant change in the STAI-T across outcome studies since 1990. *Psychological Medicine, 29,* 1425–1434.

Foa, E. B. (2000). Psychosocial treatment of post-traumatic stress disorder. *Journal of Clinical Psychiatry, 61,* 43–48.

Garber, J., & Flynn, C. (2001). Vulnerability to depression in childhood and adolescence. In R. E. Ingram & J. M. Price (Eds.), *Vulnerability to psychopathology: Risk across the lifespan* (pp. 175–225). New York: Guilford.

Gloaguen, V., Cottraux, J., Cucherat, M., & Blackburn, I. M. (1998). A meta-analysis of the effects of cognitive therapy in depressed patients. *Journal of Affective Disorders, 49,* 59–72.

Gotlib, I. H., & Hammen, C. L. (1992). *Psychological aspects of depression: Toward a cognitive-interpersonal integration.* Chichester, England: Wiley.

Gotlib, I. H., Lewinsohn, P. M., & Seeley, J. R. (1995). Symptoms versus a diagnosis of depression: Differences in psychosocial functioning. *Journal of Consulting and Clinical Psychology, 63,* 90–100.

Gotlib, I. H., Lewinsohn, P. M., & Seeley, J. R. (1998). Consequences of depression during adolescence: Marital status and marital functioning in early adulthood. *Journal of Abnormal Psychology, 107,* 686–690.

Greenberg, P. E., Sisitsky, T., Kessler, R. C., Finkelstein, S. N., Berndt, E. R., Davidson, J. R., Ballenger, J. C., & Fyer, A. J. (1999). The economic burden of anxiety disorders in the 1990s. *Journal of Clinical Psychiatry, 60,* 427–435.

Greenberg, P. E., Stiglin, L. E., Finkelstein, S. N., & Berndt, E. R. (1993). Depression: A neglected major illness. *Journal of Clinical Psychiatry, 54,* 419–424.

Hammen, C. (2001). Vulnerability to depression in adulthood. In R. E. Ingram & J. M. Price (Eds.), *Vulnerability to psychopathology: Risk across the lifespan* (pp. 226–257). New York: Guilford.

Hammen, C., & Rudolph, R. D. (1996). Childhood depression. In E. J. Mash & R. A. Barkley (Eds.), *Child psychopathology* (pp. 153–195). New York: Guilford.

Hammen, C., & Rudolph, R. D. (2003). Childhood mood disorders. In E. J. Mash & R. A. Barkley (Eds.), *Child psychopathology* (2nd ed., pp. 233–278). New York: Guilford.

Hirschfeld, R. M. A. (1996). Placebo response in the treatment of panic disorder. *Bulletin of the Menninger Clinic, 60*(2), A76–A86.

Hoehn-Saric, R., Hazlett, R. L., & McLeod, D. R. (1993). Generalized anxiety disorder with early and late onset of anxiety symptoms. *Comprehensive Psychiatry, 34,* 291–298.

Hoencamp, E., Haffmans, P. M. J., Griens, A. M. G. F., Huijbrechts, I. P. A. M., & Heycop ten Ham, B. F. (2001). A 3.5-year naturalistic follow-up study of depressed out-patients. *Journal of Affective Disorders, 66,* 267–271.

Horwath, E., Johnson, J., Klerman, G. L., & Weissman, M. M. (1992). Depressive symptoms as relative and attributable risk factors for first-onset major depression. *Archives of General Psychiatry, 49,* 817–823.

Ingram, R. E. (2001). Developing perspectives on the cognitive-developmental origins of depression: Back is the future. *Cognitive Therapy and Research, 25,* 497–504.

Jacobson, N. S., Wilson, L., & Tupper, C. (1988). The clinical significance of treatment gains resulting from exposure-based interventions for agoraphobia: A reanalysis of outcome data. *Behaviour Therapy, 19,* 539–554.

Joiner, T. E., Jr. (2000). Depression's vicious scree: Self-propagating and erosive processes in depression chronicity. *Clinical Psychology: Science and Practice, 7,* 203–218.

Judd, L. L., Akiskal, H. S., Zeller, P. J., Paulus, M., Andrew, C., Maser, J. D., et al. (2000). Psychosocial disability during the long-term course of unipolar major depressive disorder. *Archives of General Psychiatry, 57,* 375–380.

Juster, H. R., Brown, E. J., & Heimberg, R. G. (1996). Social phobia. In J. Margraf (Ed.), *Textbook of behaviour therapy* (pp. 43–59). Berlin: Springer-Verlag.

Kaelber, C. T., Moul, D. E., & Farmer, M. E. (1995). Epidemiology of depression. In E. E. Beckham & W. R. Leber (Eds.), *Handbook of depression* (2nd ed., pp. 3–35). New York: Guilford.

Kashani, J. H., & Orvaschel, H. (1990). A community study of anxiety in children and adolescents. *American Journal of Psychiatry, 145,* 960–964.

Kashani, J. H., Orvaschel, H., Rosenberg, T. K., & Reid, J. C. (1989). Psychopathology in a community sample of children and adolescents: A developmental perspective. *Journal of the American Academy of Child and Adolescent Psychiatry, 31,* 701–706.

Katschnig, H., & Amering, M. (1994). The long-term course of panic disorder. In B. E. Wolfe & J. D. Maser (Eds.), *Treatment of panic disorder: A consensus development conference* (pp. 73–81). Washington, DC: American Psychiatric Press.

Katzelnick, D. J., & Greist, J. H. (2001). Social anxiety disorder: An unrecognized problem in primary care. *Journal of Clinical Psychiatry, 62,* 11–15.

Keller, M. B., & Boland, R. J. (1998). Implications of failing to achieve successful long-term maintenance treatment of recurrent unipolar major depression. *Biological Psychiatry, 44,* 348–360.

Keller, M. B., Yonkers, K. A., Warshaw, M. G., Pratt, L. A., Golan, J., Mathews, A. O., et al. (1994). Remission and relapse in subjects with panic disorder and agoraphobia: A prospective short interval naturalistic follow-up. *Journal of Nervous and Mental Disorders, 182,* 290–296.

Kendall, P. C. (1994). Treating anxiety disorders in children: Results of a randomized clinical trial. *Journal of Consulting and Clinical Psychology, 62,* 100–110.

Kendler, K. S., Gardner, C. O., & Prescott, C. A. (1999). Clinical characteristics of major depression that predict risk of depression in relatives. *Archives of General Psychiatry, 56,* 322–327.

Kendler, K. S., & Prescott, C. A. (1999). A population-based twin study of lifetime major depression in men and women. *Archives of General Psychiatry, 56,* 39–44.

Kessing, L. (1998). Recurrence in affective disorder: II. Effect of age and gender. *British Journal of Psychiatry, 172,* 29–34.

Kessler, R. C., McGonagle, K. A., Zhao, S., Nelson, C. B., Hughes, M., Eshleman, S., et al. (1994). Lifetime and 12-month prevalence of DSM-III-R psychiatric disorders in the United States: Results from the National Comorbidity Survey. *Archives of General Psychiatry, 51,* 8–19.

Kessler, R. C., Olfson, M., & Berglund, P. A. (1998). Patterns and predictors of treatment contact after first onset of psychiatric disorders. *American Journal of Psychiatry, 155,* 62–69.

Kessler, R. C., Walters, E. E., & Forthofer, M. S. (1998). The social consequences of psychiatric disorders, III: Probability of marital stability. *American Journal of Psychiatry, 155,* 1092–1096.

Klinkman, M. S., & Okkes, I. (1998). Mental health problems in primary care. *Journal of Family Practice, 47,* 379–384.

Last, C. G., Perrin, S., Hersen, M., & Kazdin, A. E. (1996). A prospective study of childhood anxiety disorders. *Journal of the American Academy of Child and Adolescent Psychiatry, 35,* 1502–1510.

Lecrubier, Y. (1998a). Is depression under-recognized and undertreated? *International Clinical Psychopharmacology, 13,* 3–6.

Lecrubier, Y. (1998b). The impact of comorbidity on the treatment of panic disorder. *Journal of Clinical Psychiatry, 59*, 11–14.

Lecrubier, Y. (2001). The burden of depression and anxiety in general medicine. *Journal of Clinical Psychiatry, 62*, 4–9.

Leon, A. C., Portera, L., & Weissman, M. M. (1995). The social costs of anxiety disorders. *British Journal of Psychiatry, 166*, 19–22.

Lewinsohn, P. M., Duncan, E. M., Stanton, A. K., & Hautzinger, M. (1986). Age at first onset for nonbipolar depression. *Journal of Abnormal Psychology, 95*, 378–383.

Lewinsohn, P. M., Hoberman, H. M., & Rosenbaum, M. (1988). A prospective study of risk factors for unipolar depression. *Journal of Abnormal Psychology, 97*, 251–264.

Livingston-VanNoppen, B., Rasmussen, S. A., Eisen, J., & McCartney, L. (1990). Family function and treatment in obsessive-compulsive disorder. In M. Jenike, L. Baer, & W. E. Minichiello (Eds.), *Obsessive-compulsive disorder: Theory and treatment* (pp. 325–340). Chicago: Yearbook Medical Publisher.

Mash, E. J., & Dozois, D. J. A. (2003). Child psychopathology: A developmental-systems perspective. In E. J. Mash & R. A. Barkley (Eds.), *Child psychopathology* (2nd ed., pp. 3–71). New York: Guilford.

McGee, R., Freehan, M., Williams, S., Partridge, F., Silva, P. A., & Kelly, J. (1990). DSM-III disorders in a large sample of adolescents. *Journal of the American Academy of Child and Adolescent Psychiatry, 29*, 611–619.

McQuaid, J. R., Stein, M. B., Laffaye, C., & McCahill, M. E. (1999). Depression in a primary care clinic: The prevalence and impact of an unrecognized disorder. *Journal of Affective Disorders, 55*, 1–10.

Mendlowicz, M. V., & Stein, M. B. (2000). Quality of life in individuals with anxiety disorders. *American Journal of Psychiatry, 157*, 669–682.

Mineka, S., Pury, C. L., & Luten, A. G. (1995). Explanatory style in anxiety and depression. In G. M. Buchanan & M. E. P. Seligman (Eds.), *Explanatory style* (pp. 135–158). Hillsdale, NJ: Erlbaum.

Mineka, S., Watson, D., & Clark, L. A. (1998). Comorbidity of anxiety and unipolar mood disorders. *Annual Review of Psychology, 49*, 377–412.

Mojtabai, R., Olfson, M., & Mechanic, D. (2002). Perceived need and help-seeking in adults with mood, anxiety, or substance use disorder. *Archives of General Psychiatry, 59*, 77–84.

Moreau, D., & Follett, C. (1993). Panic disorder in children and adolescents. *Child and Adolescent Psychiatric Clinics of North America, 2*, 581–602.

Moreno, F. A., & Delgado, P. L. (2000). Living with anxiety disorders: As good as it gets…? *Journal of Anxiety Disorders, 64*, A4–A21.

Mrazek, P. J., & Haggerty, R. J. (Eds.). (1994). *Reducing risks for mental disorders: Frontiers for preventive intervention research*. Washington, DC: National Academy Press.

Muris, P., Merckelbach, H., Mayer, B., & Prins, E. (2000). How serious are common childhood fears? *Behaviour Research and Therapy, 38*, 217–228.

Murphy, J. M., Laird, N. M., Monson, R. R., Sobol, A. M., & Alexander, H. (2000). A 40-year perspective on the prevalence of depression: The Stirling County Study. *Archives of General Psychiatry, 57*, 209–215.

Nathan, P. E. (2001). Deny nothing, doubt everything: A comment on Westen & Morrison (2001). *Journal of Consulting and Clinical Psychology, 69*, 900–903.

National Institute of Mental Health, National Advisory Mental Health Council Workgroup on Child and Adolescent Mental Health Intervention Development and Deployment. (2001). *Blueprint for change: Research on child and adolescent mental health*. Washington, DC: Author.

National Institute of Mental Health, National Advisory Mental Health Council Workshop on Mental Disorders Prevention Research. (2001). Priorities for prevention research at NIMH. *Prevention and Treatment, 4*, NP. Retrieved September 15, 2002 from http://www.apa.org/pre0040017a.html

Nolen-Hoeksema, S. (1987). Sex differences in unipolar depression: Evidence and theory. *Psychological Bulletin, 101*, 259–282.

Noyes, R., Clancy, J., Hoenk, P. R., & Slymen, D. J. (1980). The prognosis of anxiety neurosis. *Archives of General Psychiatry, 37*, 173–178.

Nutt, D. (2000). Treatment of depression and concomitant anxiety. *European Neuropsychopharmacology, 10*(Suppl. 14), S433–S437.

Ohayon, M. M., Priest, R. G., Guilleminault, C., & Caulet, M. (1999). The prevalence of depressive disorders in the United Kingdom. *Biological Psychiatry, 45*, 300–307.

Ohayon, M. M., Shapiro, C. M., & Kennedy, S. H. (2000). Differentiating DSM-IV anxiety and depressive disorders in the general population: Comorbidity and treatment consequences. *Canadian Journal of Psychiatry, 45*, 166–172.

Olfson, M., Marcus, S. C., Druss, B., Tanielian, T., & Pincus, H. A. (2002). National trends in the outpatient treatment of depression. *Journal of the American Medical Association, 287*, 203–209.

Panzarino, P. J. (1998). The costs of depression: Direct and indirect; treatment versus nontreatment. *Journal of Clinical Psychiatry, 59*, 11–14.

Patten, S. B. (2000). Major depression prevalence in Calgary. *Canadian Journal of Psychiatry, 45*, 923–926.

Paykel, E. S., Ramana, R., Cooper, Z., Hayhurst, H., Kerr, J., & Barocka, A. (1995). Residual symptoms after partial remission: An important outcome in depression. *Psychological Medicine, 25*, 1171–1180.

Pine, D. S., Cohen, E., Cohen, P., & Brook, J. (1999). Adolescent depressive symptoms as predictors of adult depression: Moodiness or mood disorder? *American Journal of Psychiatry, 156*, 133–135.

Posternak, M. A., & Miller, I. (2001). Untreated short-term course of major depression: A meta-analysis of outcomes from studies using wait-list control groups. *Journal of Affective Disorders, 66*, 139–146.

Rachman, S. (1990). *Fear and courage (2nd ed.)*. San Francisco: Freeman.

Regier, D. A., Boyd, J. H., Burke, J. D., Rae, D. S., Myers, J. K., Kramer, M., et al. (1988). One-month prevalence of mental disorders in the United States: Based on five Epidemiologic Catchment Area sites. *Archives of General Psychiatry, 45,* 977–986.

Regier, D. A., Narrow, W. E., Rae, D. S., Mandersheid, R. W., Locke, B. Z., & Goodwin, F. K. (1993). The de facto U.S. mental and addictive disorders service system: Epidemiologic Catchment Area prospective 1-year prevalence rates of disorders and services. *Archives of General Psychiatry, 50,* 85–94.

Roy, M. A., Neale, M. C., Pedersen, N. L., Mathé, A. A., & Kendler, K. S. (1995). A twin study of generalized anxiety disorder and major depression. *Psychological Medicine, 25,* 1037–1049.

Roy-Byrne, P. P., Stang, P., Wittchen, H. U., Ustun, B., Walters, E. E., & Kessler, R. C. (2000). Lifetime panic–depression comorbidity in the National Comorbidity Survey: Association with symptoms, impairment, course and help-seeking. *British Journal of Psychiatry, 176,* 229–235.

Rubin, H. C., Rapaport, M. H., Levine, B., Gladsjo, J. K., Rabin, A., Auerbach, M., et al. (2000). Quality of well being in panic disorder: The assessment of psychiatric and general disability. *Journal of Affective Disorders, 57,* 217–221.

Rueter, M. A., Scaramella, L., Wallace, L. E., & Conger, R. D. (1999). First onset of depressive or anxiety disorders predicted by the longitudinal course of internalizing symptoms and parent-adolescent disagreements. *Archives of General Psychiatry, 56,* 726–732.

Rush, A. J., Koran, L. M., Keller, M. B., Markowitz, J. C., Harrison, W. M., Miceli, R. J., et al. (1998). The treatment of chronic depression, Part 1: Study design and rationale for evaluating the comparative efficacy of sertraline and imipramine as acute, crossover, continuation, and maintenance phase therapies. *Journal of Clinical Psychiatry, 59,* 589–597.

Rush, A. J., & Thase, M. E. (1997). Strategies and tactics in the treatment of chronic depression. *Journal of Clinical Psychiatry, 58,* 14–22.

Sanderson, W. C., & Barlow, D. H. (1990). A description of patients diagnosed with DSM-III-R generalized anxiety disorder. *Journal of Nervous and Mental Disease, 178,* 588–591.

Schneier, F. R., Heckelman, L. R., & Garfinkel, R. (1994). Functional impairment in social phobia. *Journal of Clinical Psychiatry, 55,* 322–331.

Segal, Z. V., Williams, J. M., & Teasdale, J. D. (2002). *Mindfulness-based cognitive therapy for depression: A new approach to preventing relapse.* New York: Guilford Press.

Segal, Z. V., Williams, J. M., Teasdale, J. D., & Gemar, M. (1996). A cognitive science perspective on kindling and episode sensitization in recurrent affective disorder. *Psychological Medicine, 26,* 371–380.

Sharp, D. M., Power, K. G., Simpson, R. J., Swanson, V., Moodie, E., Anstee, J. A., & Ashford, J. J. (1996). Fluvoxamine, placebo and cognitive behaviour therapy used alone and in combination in the treatment of panic disorder and agoraphobia. *Journal of Anxiety Disorders, 10,* 219–242.

Smith, A. L., & Weissman, M. M. (1992). Epidemiology. In E. S. Paykel (Ed.), *Handbook of affective disorders* (2nd ed., pp. 111–129). New York: Guilford.

Solomon, D. A., Keller, M. B., Leon, A. C., Mueller, T. I., Lavori, P. W., Shea, M. T., et al. (2000). Multiple recurrences of major depressive disorder. *American Journal of Psychiatry, 157,* 229–233.

Stein, M. B., Fuetsch, M., Muller, N., Hofler, M., Lieb, R., & Wittchen, H. U. (2001). Social anxiety disorder and the risk of depression. *Archives of General Psychiatry, 58,* 251–256.

Teasdale, J. D., Segal, Z. V., Williams, J. M., Ridgeway, V. A., Soulsby, J. M., & Lau, M. A. (2000). Prevention of relapse/recurrence in major depression by mindfulness-based cognitive therapy. *Journal of Consulting and Clinical Psychology, 68,* 615–623.

Tuma, J. (1989). Mental health services for children: The state of the art. *American Psychologist, 44,* 188–199.

Tylee, A. (2000). Depression in Europe: Experience from the DEPRES II survey. *European Neuropsychopharmacology, 10*(Suppl. 4), S445–S448.

van Os, J., & Jones, P. B. (1999). Early risk factors and adult person-environment relationships in affective disorder. *Psychological Medicine, 29,* 1055–1067.

Wakefield, J. C., & Spitzer, R. L. (2002). Lowered estimates—but of what? *Archives of General Psychiatry, 59,* 129–130.

Wang, P. S., Demler, O., & Kessler, R. C. (2002). Adequacy of treatment for serious mental illness in the United States. *American Journal of Public Health, 92,* 92–98.

Weissman, M. M., Bland, R., Canino, G., Greenwald, S., Hwo, H., Lee, C., et al. (1994). The cross-national epidemiology of obsessive compulsive disorder. *Journal of Clinical Psychiatry, 55,* 5–10.

Weissman, M. M., Bruce, M., Leaf, P., Florio, L., & Holzer, C. (1991). Affective disorders. In L. Robins & E. Regier (Eds.), *Psychiatric disorders in America* (pp. 53–80). New York: Free Press.

Westen, D., & Morrison, K. (2001). A multidimensional meta-analysis of treatments for depression, panic, and generalized anxiety disorder: An empirical examination of the status of empirically supported therapies. *Journal of Consulting and Clinical Psychology, 69,* 875–899.

Westra, H. A., & Stewart, S. H. (1998). Cognitive behavioural therapy and pharmacotherapy: Complementary or contradictory approaches to the treatment of anxiety? *Clinical Psychology Review, 18,* 307–340.

Wetherell, J. L., Gatz, M., & Pedersen, N. L. (2001). A longitudinal analysis of anxiety and depressive symptoms. *Psychology and Aging, 16,* 187–195.

Whitaker, A., Johnson, J., Shaffer, D., Rapoport, J., Kalikow, K., Walsh, B. T., et al. (1990). Uncommon troubles in young people: Prevalence estimates of selected psychiatric disorders in a nonreferred adolescent population. *Archives of General Psychiatry, 47,* 487–496.

Whittal, M., & Dobson, K. S. (1991). An investigation of the temporal relationship between anxiety and depression as a consequence of cognitive vulnerability to interpersonal evaluation. *Canadian Journal of Behavioural Science, 23,* 391–398.

Young, A. S., Klap, R., Sherbourne, C. D., & Wells, K. B. (2001). The quality of care for depressive and anxiety disorders in the United States. *Archives of General Psychiatry, 58,* 55–61.

Zheng, D., Macera, C. A., Croft, J. B., Giles, W. H., Davis, D., & Scott, W. K. (1997). Major depression and all-cause mortality among white adults in the United States. *Annals of Epidemiology, 7,* 213–218.

3

MEASUREMENT ISSUES IN PREVENTING ANXIETY AND DEPRESSION: CONCEPTS AND INSTRUMENTS

PETER J. BIELING, RANDI E. MCCABE,
AND MARTIN M. ANTONY

Reliable and valid measurement tools are a cornerstone for researchers and clinicians who are interested in the science and practice of prevention. As in other endeavors related to psychopathology and clinical psychology, measures operationalize critical theoretical constructs of interest and are the basis for answering research questions in a manner that is internally consistent and that can be generalized outside the context of the study in which they first appear. Broad questions such as "How do we prevent the onset of depression or anxiety disorders?" need to be answered with clear, unambiguous tools that accurately target the clinical phenomena of interest over extended periods and across developmental stages. In this sense, choosing measures in prevention work is no different than choosing measures for research on descriptive psychopathology or for measuring treatment outcomes. However, choosing good measures for prevention-related efforts is more complicated than choosing measures in other areas of psychopathology research for two reasons. First, depending on the level of prevention and the conceptual model of prevention at issue, different constructs are more or less relevant. For example, vulnerability factors are important in identifying "at risk" populations, but are much less important in achieving prevention at the population level. As a result, there is no one measure, or even a set of theoretical constructs, that is relevant to all prevention research or interventions. Second, the focus on prevention research in mood and anxiety disorders is relatively recent, and measurement tools do not necessarily live up to some of the new challenges posed by prevention-based research.

These challenges for measurement are both practical and conceptual. First, theories about vulnerability to depression and anxiety are not yet matched by reliable, valid, and efficient screening tools. Even where early risk factors are well known (e.g., a shy temperament is often associated with the risk of social phobia), we may not have sufficient information to specify an intervention that could be preventative. Second, prevention research is highly likely to involve repeated assessments over long periods, using a variety of longitudinal designs. By contrast, most measures of anxiety, depression, and related constructs have been examined in cross-sectional or short-term intervention studies. To what extent such measures will be sensitive in repeated administrations over the human life span is not clear. As prevention research matures, new measures and constructs no doubt will be created and tested, and methods that are currently considered experimental will become standard and widely implemented. Our intention in this chapter is to review measures and measurement issues that are relevant to different levels of prevention in mood disorders and anxiety disorders, both to facilitate accurate assessment of prevention-relevant constructs and to raise unresolved issues and measurement challenges related to prevention.

To facilitate our review, we first describe the different types of prevention and outline the constructs that are most relevant to each form of prevention. We focus on specific measurement issues that are most relevant to mood and anxiety disorders, as well as on the more general measurement issues that warrant consideration by those interested in the prevention of pathological anxiety and depression. Following this discussion, we review some of the more commonly used measures of anxiety and depression, giving details of their psychometric properties and offering suggestions as to how they might be used in research or practice that is focused on preventing depression and anxiety.

MEASUREMENT ISSUES IN PRIMARY, SECONDARY, AND TERTIARY PREVENTION

The most common method for conceptualizing the prevention of health problems is a tripartite approach involving primary, secondary, and tertiary prevention. Recently, however, this approach has been identified as potentially limiting (see chap. 4, this volume), and in its place the National Institute of Mental Health (NIMH) National Advisory Mental Health Council (NAMHC) Workgroup on Mental Disorders Prevention Research has proposed a new, expanded framework for prevention research (NIMH, 2001). Here we present both the traditional primary, secondary, and tertiary framework, as well as the perspective of NAMHC.

Briefly, *primary preventions* are population-based interventions designed to prevent the occurrence of a disorder or problem (e.g., immunization programs). In primary prevention, the intervention is universal, and there is no attempt to target particular types of individuals. *Secondary prevention* involves the identification and targeting of individuals who are vulnerable to developing a problem or disorder. In *tertiary prevention*, the targeted individual has already been diagnosed with a disorder, and the aim is to restore that person to the highest possible level of functioning or to prevent further disorders and complications from developing.

The NAMHC concluded that this primary–secondary–tertiary approach did not adequately address the broader notion of prevention in mental health (NIMH, 2001). As an alternative, the Council proposed a broader vision of prevention work, made up of three basic types of research: preintervention prevention research, preventive intervention research, and preventive service systems research. *Preintervention prevention research* consists of the examination of diverse topics ranging from basic etiological processes to risk and protective factors. *Prevention intervention research* encompasses efficacy and effectiveness trials at the population level or in selected groups that have a known or suspected risk of some mental disorder. *Preventive service systems research* involves research on the implementation and dissemination of preventive services, as well as investigations of the economic impact of prevention interventions and their delivery system.

The current debate about conceptual issues in prevention research and theory adds unique challenges for measurement in prevention. For example, the NAMHC report focuses specifically on protective factors—those aspects of a person or the environment that serve as a buffer to psychological dysfunction. At the same time, our knowledge and measurement of such protective factors is not nearly so advanced as our understanding of predictors of psychopathology or our ability to assess symptoms of disorders (Seligman & Csikszentmihalyi, 2000). Also, if the definition of prevention efforts is broadened to include intervention efficacy trials and basic psychopathology research, the task of addressing measurement concepts in prevention work becomes similarly broad. Thus, in this chapter, we have highlighted those aspects of assessment and measurement which are relatively unique to prevention research and therefore have used a three-component approach: (a) primary, or universal; (b) secondary, or selective–indicated; and (c) tertiary, or relapse and comorbidity.

In all three types of prevention, it is important to demonstrate that the intervention has been adequately implemented. It is also important to measure relevant symptoms (both for the purpose of screening and for the purpose of measuring outcomes) across all three types of prevention programs. For the assessment of anxiety disorders and depression, it is important to choose instruments that assess the core features of the specific disorder—for example, in panic disorder, the nature and frequency of panic attacks, interoceptive anxiety (i.e., anxiety over physical arousal sensations), panic-related cognitions, and agoraphobic avoidance behaviors. To ensure that an assessment is comprehensive, associated features of anxiety and mood disorders (e.g., comorbidity, functional impairment, the course of the disorder, and family factors) should also be examined.

Instruments that assess symptoms are of particular value in prevention research, because these continuous measures are able to assess subclinical or subsyndromal levels of symptoms (i.e., symptoms that are not severe enough to meet the threshold for formal diagnosis). Subclinical levels of symptoms have been identified as risk factors for developing full-blown depression and thus are increasingly recognized as important to assess accurately (Crum, Cooper-Patrick, & Ford, 1994; Horwath, Johnson, Klerman, & Weissman, 1992; Zonderman, Herbst, Schmidt, Costa, & McCrae, 1993). The discussion that follows examines measurement issues that arise in the context of primary, secondary, and tertiary prevention.

Primary–Universal Prevention

The aim of primary–universal, prevention is to "prevent the onset of a targeted condition" (United States Preventative Services Task Force, 1996). What are the critical issues pertaining to measurement in primary–universal intervention? Broadly, four questions need to be answered in assessing the outcome of primary prevention: (a) Are the prevention efforts being delivered as intended? (b) Does the intervention have its intended impact? That is, does it reduce the rate of illness and symptoms? (c) What is an appropriate sample size, given that the intervention is targeting a population that includes everyone, whether they are at risk or not? (d) Because primary or universal prevention will likely involve children or adolescents, what are the measurement implications thereof?

The first question is one of adherence to, and compliance with, a protocol or an intervention, and this issue is germane to secondary and tertiary prevention as well. The question of adherence in primary prevention is similar to the issue of adherence to treatment protocols used in psychotherapy outcome studies. Numerous scales exist for rating compliance with a specific psychotherapy, often as it relates to a specific disorder. It is now a matter of course that a psychotherapy efficacy trial includes an explicit analysis of the extent to which therapists taking part in the study adhered to the specified protocol (e.g., Jacobson et al., 2000). Failure to demonstrate adherence to the specified method in psychotherapy trials raises fundamental doubts about the validity of the findings (Waltz, Addis, Koerner, & Jacobson, 1993). Thus, prevention efforts should be articulated in a protocol or curriculum that is unambiguous, is clear, and has considerable specificity. Measuring adherence is not straightforward, and, like any psychometric instrument, adherence scales need to demonstrate reliability and validity. One promising method that can be used to measure adherence in a psychotherapeutic intervention is to use a "checklist" approach to ensure that all key components of the intervention are included and to rate the quality of the material presented. Although adherence scales could be developed in a self-report format (e.g., completed by those implementing the intervention), such an approach would likely be associated with substantial bias, because the intent of the scale would be obvious. Instead, a scale completed by independent, expert raters is likely to lead to more objective findings, especially if the raters are not involved in the research. It is critical to have multiple assessors of adherence to ensure that interrater reliability can be established for an adherence scale.

Equally important is the question of how well the prevention works; that is, does it decrease the occurrence of mood and anxiety difficulties? This outcome can be measured in two broad, but related, ways. The first approach is to measure depression or anxiety symptoms either by self-report scales or interviewer-rated scales. A second type of measure includes diagnostic instruments, which are necessary to make a determination about whether a "case" of depression or anxiety disorder exists. Together, symptom measures and diagnostic measures can be used to assess the outcome of a particular prevention strategy.

It is also important to address the issue of very large sample sizes in primary prevention. Since the interventions are intended to be universal, and studying the efficacy of such approaches will likely involve a very large number of individuals, the efficiency of measurement systems is paramount. Measurements would likely take place in large, randomly selected samples of individuals who are interviewed in a myriad of ways (e.g., in their homes, over the telephone, or over the Internet). In this context, self-report scales and screening tools that are short and as simple as possible are most desirable. It would be most cost effective to complete outcome assessments via a staged approach. For example, individuals who report a certain level of symptoms could be followed up with more in-depth interviews. Certainly, it is unlikely that a primary prevention study would allow for complete diagnostic interviews of all participants. Interviews or diagnostic tools that can be used by trained laypersons are probably preferable, although structured interviews are often complex and require high levels of skill (see Summerfeldt & Antony, 2002, for a detailed discussion of issues surrounding structured diagnostic interviews).

The final issue in measurement for primary, or universal, prevention is that the efforts are likely to involve children and, perhaps, adolescents. Most health-related primary prevention (e.g., immunization) is carried out at an early age, often in the context of existing social structures such as schools. This is likely to be the case in mental health prevention efforts as well, especially in light of the likely age of onset of mood and anxiety disorders. Primary prevention with adults, while technically possible, will obviously fail to prevent disorders that emerge in childhood or adolescence. Because of the need to assess children or adolescents in primary prevention, we have included some child and adolescent measures of symptoms and diagnostic interviews for children. However, a more difficult issue to resolve is how to measure the phenomenon of interest (i.e., by level of symptoms or onset of disorder) consistently over time. In most primary prevention research, populations are likely to be followed for a considerable length of time. Indeed, investigating a prevention-related hypothesis in a methodologically sound way would necessitate long term follow-up through different developmental epochs, ideally from the time the intervention occurs until well into adulthood, when the expected age of onset has been reached and passed. Researchers then face the dilemma of using one measure during childhood and adolescence and another measure when the population under investigation reaches adulthood. Thus, a researcher might be left with having to compare multiple measures on different metrics that may or may not measure the same construct. Alternatively, adult measures can be adapted to children and adolescents. However, without significant validation work to show that the construct of interest and the new instrument are meaningful in younger ages, scores may not have the same meaning at different ages, and this strategy, too, may not provide clear results. Finally, when assessing children, there is a need to have multiple informants and a number of sources of data, including perhaps parents' reports, peer ratings, teachers' ratings, and school records (American Psychiatric Association, 2000a). Drawing on multiple sources of material, however, poses significant challenges for studying population-based interventions. Unfortunately, too, the literature on assessment of mood and anxiety disorders is quite clearly divided between adult assessment and child assessment, likely reflecting research and assessment needs that are more focused on cross-sectional methods or relatively short term intervention studies. Thus, the issue of "translation" of measures in childhood to adulthood is an area of prevention-related assessment in which some conceptual and pragmatic issues will need to be resolved.

Secondary or Selected–Indicated Prevention

Secondary prevention efforts "identify and treat asymptomatic persons who have already developed risk factors or preclinical disease but in whom the condition is not clinically apparent" (United States Preventative

Services [USPS] Task Force, 1996; p. xli). There are difficulties in applying this definition of secondary prevention to psychiatric disorders such as depression or anxiety, because the diagnosis is made based on symptoms alone, rather than on an underlying pathophysiology (USPS Task Force, 1996). Thus, for mood and anxiety disorders, secondary prevention is more likely to be aimed at those individuals with subclinical levels of symptoms or at populations known to be at risk for developing depression and anxiety disorders. The NAMHC distinction between selective and indicated interventions may be less meaningful for depression and anxiety, because the distinction between risk and subclinical symptoms may be difficult to make. For example, the presence of negative automatic thoughts could be seen as both a sign of subclinical depression and a risk factor for the condition. Also, selective and indicated interventions for anxiety are likely to be similar to those for depression. Hence, the critical factor is identifying and ameliorating a vulnerability to a future disorder. The USPS Task Force has set out constructive criteria for evaluating secondary prevention efforts, and these can be readily extrapolated to mood and anxiety disorders. For example, the USPS Task Force specifies that a screening test must satisfy two major criteria to be considered useful. First, the test must be able to detect the condition of interest with enough accuracy to avoid producing large numbers of false positive and false negative results. Second, screening and treatment of those with early signs of disease should result in better health outcomes, compared with the outcomes of those people who are treated after developing the fully syndromal disease. The first set of criteria is explicitly related to the sensitivity and specificity of a vulnerability or risk factor. The second set of criteria requires that the intervention reduce the probability of symptoms and cases of the disorder in screened and treated individuals, compared with the likelihood of symptoms and cases in those individuals who are not screened and treated.

One reasonable strategy for treating depression and anxiety might be to identify individuals with certain vulnerability markers and then to apply an intervention to prevent the onset of the disorder. To date, a small number of such interventions have been examined empirically. For example, Swinson, Soulios, Cox, and Kuch (1992) found that a single session of behavioral treatment was associated with a significantly better outcome than an intervention involving reassurance for individuals presenting to the emergency room during a panic attack. Similarly, Foa, Hearst-Ikeda, and Perry (1995) found that a brief intervention involving cognitive–behavior therapy prevented the onset of posttraumatic stress disorder in a group of recent assault victims.

As in primary prevention, the questions surrounding delivery and implementation processes are paramount. Thus, our discussions concerning measuring adherence to treatment, reduction of symptoms, and change in diagnostic status in primary prevention apply to secondary prevention as well. Whatever screening procedures and prevention interventions are to be delivered must be assessed against standard criteria to ensure that those procedures and interventions are carried out adequately and consistently. Similarly, in secondary prevention, it is critical to examine the treated individuals longitudinally, as regards symptoms of disorder, its severity, and "caseness" (i.e., that a diagnosis is warranted). These symptom and diagnostic measures thus form the outcome (or dependent) variables for secondary prevention efforts.

What is unique about secondary, or selective, prevention and not relevant to primary prevention is the identification of vulnerability or risk markers. These can assume a number of forms, including biological factors, psychological factors, and sociologic variables. In addition, such risk factors may be identified through a variety of methods, including self-report, interview, behavioral observation, psychophysiological monitoring, and response to an experimental probe or challenge. A discussion of biological and historical risk factors is beyond the scope of this chapter, although issues of reliability and validity of measurement still apply—for example, whether a screening test is a self-report psychological instrument, a sociological categorization of socioeconomic class, some other demographic variable, or a test for a genetic marker. Moreover, extensive research programs are dedicated to identifying a host of vulnerabilities to future symptoms and disorders; thus, knowledge in this area is fluid and rapidly developing. We focus here on those measures and methods which have psychological variables as a central focus and for which some amount of empirical evidence has accumulated.

Several of the measures described later in the chapter have the potential to identify individuals at risk and have been shown to be useful in at least some research thus far. However, the ultimate criterion by which a vulnerability measure must be judged is the measure's specificity and sensitivity in making predictions within the population. These indices determine the accuracy of *any* screening test, not just tests to screen for psychological vulnerabilities. *Sensitivity* refers to the proportion of persons who are eventually shown to develop the condition of interest and who correctly test positive when screened. A test with inadequate sensitivity will miss cases (i.e., produce false negatives), suggesting that the person in question is unlikely to develop the disorder when he or she, in fact, does subsequently develop it. *Specificity* refers to the proportion of persons who will *not* develop the disorder and who correctly test negative when screened. Inadequate specificity means that many people will be identified as being at risk for developing the disorder when, in fact, they never will (false positives). For the measures and paradigms described later, sensitivity and specificity for predicting risk are not yet known. However, an examination of these issues is likely to be a central concern in any prevention research. Another important consideration in prediction by means of screening tests is the base rate of the problem in the population. For any given level of sensitivity and specificity, the value of a test in predicting a condition is a function of the prevalence of that condition in the population. All other things being equal, the higher the base rate of a disorder, the better is the predictive value of a screening test. Finally, and perhaps most important, it is not clear how accurate a test needs to be in order to be useful. Clearly, an efficient (easy to use and inexpensive) test with high accuracy is preferable to a test that is less efficient and less accurate. What is not clear is at what level concerns about accuracy give way to concerns about efficiency.

An important issue that is also related to sensitivity and specificity is the availability of normative data for vulnerability measures. Absence of adequate norms is a problem that is not restricted to vulnerability markers; indeed, even well-known markers of outcomes sometimes lack sufficient normative information to draw conclusions about the clinical significance of change with intervention (Dozois, Covin, & Brinker, 2003; Kendall & Sheldrick, 2000). In terms of vulnerability measures, a lack of norms makes it difficult to identify those at high and those at low risk in a population, although norms on vulnerability measures are becoming more available (e.g., Dozois et al., 2003).

Tertiary or Relapse–Comorbidity Prevention

Tertiary prevention activities involve the care of an individual with an established disease, with attempts made to restore the individual to his or her highest level of function, minimize the negative effects of disease (i.e., prevent relapse), and prevent disease-related complications (e.g., comorbidity). For anxiety disorders and mood disorders, tertiary prevention can take many forms, including effective treatment of the condition and prevention of relapse in an individual who has been treated successfully. Another area receiving attention in the literature is related to general health, adaptive functioning, and quality of life. Here, attempts are made to minimize the impact of a problem by focusing less on the symptoms or the disorder per se and more on broader domains important to the general health, well-being, and adjustment of the individual. Thus, to some extent, these prevention efforts might be seen to be palliative rather than curative. Therefore, outcomes for tertiary prevention may include diagnostic change and reduction in symptoms, as well as increase in subjective and objective measures of functioning and satisfaction with life. Unlike the state of research on primary and secondary prevention for depression and anxiety, the literature on tertiary prevention is quite advanced. In fact, there are hundreds of studies supporting various biological and psychological interventions for anxiety disorders and depression.

As with other forms of prevention, assessment of symptoms and "caseness" are relevant to tertiary prevention. Thus, the continuous measures of symptoms and diagnosis discussed in regard to primary and secondary prevention are relevant here as well. Uniquely, however, tertiary prevention instruments need to go beyond symptoms and signs of illness, and measurement needs to focus on the *consequences* of illness in a number of domains. The domain of general health is the overall state of an individual's health (i.e., not just his or her mental health) and takes into account the entirety of the individual's physical and psychological health. *Functioning* typically refers to the individual's ability to engage in and successfully negotiate the circumstances of daily living, including, but not limited to, one's ability to maintain satisfying relationships, be productively occupied with tasks, and complete activities of daily living (e.g., chores, cooking, cleaning). *Quality of life* refers to a more subjective sense of whether, judged in its entirety, the individual's life is deemed to be satisfying. Quality-of-life measures may be multidimensional and often combine an assessment of disorder-specific symptoms with an evaluation of one's functioning or ability to carry out specific behaviors, as well as one's overall sense of satisfaction.

It is important to note that many of the best-known measures of functioning, such as the Global Assessment Scale (GAS), Global Assessment of Functioning (GAF), and Social and Occupational Functioning Assessment Scale (SOFAS) of the *Diagnostic and Statistical Manual of Mental Disorders* (DSM–IV–TR; American Psychiatric Association, 2000a), that are frequently used in clinical settings and research are not purely measures of functioning. Indeed, these ratings specifically take into account both symptoms and severity of illness—and often do so in a manner that makes it impossible to determine whether a rating is due to symptoms or poor functioning. A guiding principle for some measures of functioning seems to be that the presence of psychiatric symptoms is de facto evidence of functional impairment. We disagree with this notion and suggest that measures of functioning will have more construct validity if they disentangle the experience of symptoms from impairments in functioning. In our review of measures that assess functioning, we have focused on the more *pure* measures of functioning.

A REVIEW OF RELEVANT MEASURES

In this section, we review a sample of commonly used measures that may be used in research or interventions related to the prevention of anxiety disorders and depression. The measures are listed in alphabetical order, organized along four broad categories: (a) measures for preventing depression and mood disorders, (b) measures for preventing anxiety disorders, (c) diagnostic interviews and general screening measures, and (d) measures of general health, functional impairment, and quality of life. For each measure, we included a basic reference and a description of its format and administration. Psychometric data on these measures are readily available in other comprehensive volumes, to which we refer the reader for specifics on reliability and validity.

Listing all existing symptoms of, and diagnostic measures for, mood and anxiety disorders is beyond the scope of this chapter. In fact, there are several hundred such scales. Readers who are interested in more comprehensive resources on the topic of anxiety and depression measures can consult a number of recent books on the topic (Antony & Barlow, 2002; Antony, Orsillo, & Roemer, 2001; Nezu, Ronan, Meadows, & McClure, 2000). We have chosen to describe instruments that are generally considered among the most reliable and valid, as well as being frequently used in other research, so that levels of generalizability are high. Additional criteria for our listing include efficiency in terms of length and breadth (e.g., measures that assess multiple constructs in a reasonable number of items), applicability for use in large populations, and applicability to adults and children.

Most of the scales described in this section are either self-report or interviewer-administered scales. In a self-report approach to measuring depression and anxiety symptoms, the participant answers the specific questions or endorses items on an inventory, typically using a paper-and-pencil format. This method has the advantage of being efficient (e.g., scales can be completed in a clinic or at home) and, usually, brief. However, there are important limitations to self-reports. For example, few of the instruments we describe were intended for idiographic assessment (Nezu et al., 2000). Moreover, the assumption is made that, on a self-report scale, the participant is openly, honestly, and nondefensively responding to items.

In contrast, interviewer-rated scales are typically administered by a trained individual who may be better able to judge the participant's symptoms, behavior, and interpersonal functioning than is the individual being assessed. This approach is especially valuable when there are doubts about the participant's motivations or ability to report symptoms accurately. However, interviewer-based scales also have limitations. First, they rely on the individual's report and therefore may be influenced by many of the same biases as self-report scales. In addition, not all interviewer measures specify exactly how the clinician is to arrive at a rating, so there is a possibility of rater bias (Petkova, Quitkin, McGrath, Stewart, & Klein, 2000). Therefore, clinician rating scales are best completed by trained raters who are blind to the research question being asked and who have no other knowledge of the respondent.

In light of the limitations inherent in using self-report and interviewer-based scales, research often combines the use of self-report scales with other methods, including diagnostic interviews, interviewer-rated severity scales, scales completed by those who know the individual (e.g., teachers, family members), psychophysiological assessment, and behavioral observation.

Measures for Preventing Depression and Mood Disorders

This subsection reviews instruments that are useful for assessing depression-related constructs in both adults and children. Details of the psychometric properties of these scales are available in Nezu et al. (2000). The scales listed here include popular scales for assessing the severity of depression symptoms (e.g., Beck Depression Inventory-II, Hamilton Rating Scale for Depression), as well as scales that are useful for identifying those at risk for developing depression (e.g., the Attributional Style Questionnaire).

Attributional Style Questionnaire

The Attributional Style Questionnaire (ASQ; Peterson et al., 1982) is a self-report measure that was designed to assess perceptions of causality with regard to negative and positive events (specifically, whether an event is perceived to be due to external vs. internal factors, whether the cause is viewed to be stable vs. fleeting, and whether the cause is seen to be global vs. specific). The measure uses six vignettes and asks the respondent to make four ratings for each vignette. Importantly, high ASQ scores do seem to predict the subsequent development of depressive disorder and symptoms in individuals who are asymptomatic; thus, the ASQ is an excellent candidate for secondary prevention studies as a marker of vulnerability (Alloy et al., 2000).

Beck Depression Inventory, Second Edition

This 21-item measure is perhaps the most frequently used measure of depressive symptom severity. The Beck Depression Inventory, Second Edition (BDI-II; Beck, Steer, & Brown, 1996) items are based on criteria from the *DSM–IV–TR*, including sadness, guilt, suicidal thoughts, loss of interest, and physical manifestations such as sleep, appetite, and energy difficulties. The measure takes only 5 to 10 minutes to complete, and cutoff scores are available to characterize the ranges of depression symptoms, although the instrument does not make a diagnosis per se (Beck et al., 1996). As a continuous measure of the severity of depression, the BDI-II would be useful in primary and secondary prevention research in which a determination is needed regarding the extent to which symptoms of depression exist in the population being studied.

Center for Epidemiological Studies Depression Scale

The Center for Epidemiological Studies Depression Scale (CES-D; Radloff, 1977) is a relatively brief scale (20 items, taking about 10 minutes to complete) designed expressly to measure symptoms of depression in epidemiological studies of the general population. Items are based on the most common symptoms of depression and are rated on Likert scales. The CES-D is most appropriate as a screening tool, but it also is useful in assessing outcomes in primary or secondary prevention, especially in research designs where brevity of a scale is a major concern.

Children's Depression Inventory

This 27-item self-report measure of depression symptoms is suitable for children and adolescents (ages 7–17). Children's Depression Inventory (CDI; Kovacs, 1992) items focus on the symptoms and consequences of depression that are specific to children and cover the domains of disturbed mood, anhedonia, negative self-evaluation, ineffectiveness, and interpersonal problems. The CDI, a continuous measure of depression symptoms, would be useful as a screening tool in prevention research—for example, to detect subsyndromal symptoms in children for secondary prevention studies or as an outcome variable in primary or secondary prevention research.

Depression Anxiety and Stress Scales

The Depression Anxiety and Stress Scales (DASS; Lovibond & Lovibond, 1995a, 1995b), available either in a 42-item version or a 21-item short form, has the advantage of assessing both depression and anxiety symptoms, as well as a more general stress dimension. Given comorbidity rates of anxiety and depression (see chap. 2, this volume), an efficient measure that assesses and distinguishes these two kinds of symptoms is particularly useful (Antony, Bieling, Cox, Enns, & Swinson, 1998). The measure could be used as a screening tool or an outcome measure in prevention research, particularly in studies examining primary or secondary prevention of both depression and anxiety.

Dysfunctional Attitude Scale

The Dysfunctional Attitude Scale (DAS; Weissman & Beck, 1978) was designed to assess maladaptive beliefs associated with depression. Many of the DAS items are explicitly written as "if...then" statements that, if held in an extreme way, are rigid, maladaptive, and likely to lead to the experiencing of difficult emotions, including depression. The DAS is actually available in three forms: a 100-item version and two more commonly used 40-item versions (Forms A and B). The DAS has frequently been used as a measure of vulnerability to psychopathology, since, in theory, individuals who display these self-defeating attitudes, even in the absence of actual symptoms, are more likely to have a depression in the future. For example, the DAS is an important component of mood-activation paradigms described below and thus is likely to be most useful in secondary prevention studies.

Hamilton Rating Scale for Depression

The Hamilton Rating Scale for Depression (HRSD; Hamilton, 1960) is a 21-item clinician-rated instrument on which 17 depression symptoms and features are considered for scoring. There are no direct probes for the items, although clinicians are encouraged to use a variety of methods to ascertain answers to each item (Hamilton, 1967). The HRSD is likely the most commonly used measure of severity of depression in psychiatric research and medication studies. Because it has an interview format, the instrument lends itself to research designs in which a thorough assessment of the severity of symptoms is of critical importance, such as tertiary prevention studies wherein illness severity needs to be understood in detail.

Mood-Cognition Activation Procedures

These experimental procedures do not yet represent a unitary measurement system or a set of standardized procedures that can reliably and efficiently assess vulnerability. However, there are sufficient research data to warrant that such paradigms be carefully considered, and they have the important benefit of being anchored in a well-elucidated theoretical model of depression (Clark & Beck, 1999). The activation paradigm is based on the notion that, even when nonsymptomatic, those who are likely to become depressed will demonstrate specific cognitive reactivity in the face of a challenge to their mood (Ingram, Miranda, & Segal, 1998). There is now evidence that this degree of cognitive reactivity does predict depressive relapse (Segal, Gemar, & Williams, 1999); thus, mood-cognition activation procedures may lend themselves to assessing vulnerability to future episodes of depression both in secondary and tertiary prevention research programs.

Reynolds Adolescent Depression Scale

The Reynolds Adolescent Depression Scale (RADS; Reynolds, 1987) is a 30-item self-report measure of common symptoms of depression for adolescents aged 13–18 years. The measure takes 5 to 10 minutes to complete and is identified as a measure "about myself," to reduce the possibility of negative mood induction. The RADS is a commonly used measure in adolescents and would therefore be useful in any prevention research in which a continuous measure of depression symptoms is needed in that age group.

Young Mania Rating Scale

The presence of manic symptoms could indicate the presence of bipolar disorder, a common, severe mood disorder that may or may not be a focus of prevention. Because of the nature of the symptoms, scales to assess mania tended to be interviewer based. The authors of the Young Mania Rating Scale (YMRS; Young, Biggs, Ziegler, & Meyer, 1978) intended to develop an efficient (17 items, taking 15 minutes to administer) measure of the severity of mania, and the scale was designed with the HRSD format in mind. In depression prevention studies, it is critical to know whether emerging symptoms of a mood disorder represent unipolar disorder or a variant of the bipolar disorders. Thus, the YMRS may be useful at all levels of prevention research in which mood disorders are the focus. However, because of its interview format, the YMRS would best be used as a follow-up to a briefer measure in large-scale prevention studies.

Measures for Preventing Anxiety Disorders

Because of space limitations (there are more than 200 evidence-based measures of anxiety disorders), this subsection provides a description of only a sample of measures used for the assessment of anxiety-related problems. In our review, we selected one or two examples of commonly used measures for each of the main anxiety disorders. Popular instruments that are not reviewed, but that would assist in screening for anxiety in the population and assessing outcomes in primary and secondary prevention research, include measures such as the State–Trait Anxiety Inventory (Spielberger, Gorsuch, Lushene, Vagg, & Jacobs, 1983), State–Trait Anxiety Inventory for Children (Spielberger, 1973), Agoraphobic Cognitions Questionnaire (Chambless, Caputo, Bright, & Gallagher, 1984), Body Sensations Questionnaire (Chambless et al., 1984), Fear Survey Schedule for Children—Revised (Ollendick, 1983), Fear Questionnaire (Marks & Mathews, 1979), Revised Children's Manifest Anxiety Scale (Reynolds & Richmond, 1978, 1985), Mobility Inventory for Agoraphobia (Chambless, Caputo, Jasin, Gracely, & Williams, 1985), Brief Social Phobia Scale (Davidson et al., 1991), Liebowitz Social Anxiety Scale (Liebowitz, 1987), Social Phobia and Anxiety Inventory (Turner, Beidel, Dancu, & Stanley, 1989; Turner, Beidel, & Dancu, 1996), Social Phobia Scale (Mattick & Clarke, 1998), Social Interaction Anxiety Scale (Mattick & Clarke, 1998), Obsessive Compulsive Inventory (Foa, Kozak, Salkovskis, Coles, & Amir, 1998), Padua Inventory—Washington State University Revision (Burns, Keortge, Formea, & Sternberger, 1996), Davidson Trauma Scale (Davidson et al., 1997), Mississippi Scale for Posttraumatic Stress Disorder (PTSD; Keane, Caddell, & Taylor, 1988), and Posttraumatic Diagnostic Scale (Foa, Cashman, Jaycox, & Perry, 1997), among others. For more information about these and other scales, the most comprehensive review of anxiety-related measures is in a recent book by Antony et al. (2001).

Anxiety Sensitivity Index

The Anxiety Sensitivity Index (ASI; Peterson & Reiss, 1993; Reiss, Peterson, Gursky, & McNally, 1986) is a well-researched 16-item self-report measure of anxiety sensitivity (i.e., fear of anxiety-related symptoms). Anxiety sensitivity is a vulnerability or risk factor for the development of anxiety disorders—in particular, panic disorder. Thus, the ASI is an excellent instrument for secondary prevention studies, in that it is a marker for vulnerability to developing panic attacks and panic disorder.

Beck Anxiety Inventory

The Beck Anxiety Inventory (BAI; Beck, Epstein, Brown, & Steer, 1988) is a widely used 21-item self-report measure of anxiety symptoms. The items on the instrument include symptoms that only minimally overlap with depression symptoms, with an emphasis on symptoms of physical hyperarousal. The BAI can be completed in 5 to 10 minutes. As a continuous measure of anxiety severity, the BAI would be useful in primary and secondary prevention research in which a decision is required about the extent to which anxiety symptoms exist in the population being studied.

Clinician-Administered PTSD Scale

The Clinician-Administered PTSD Scale (CAPS; Blake et al., 1990; Blake et al., 1995) is a clinician-rated scale used to diagnose and assess symptoms of PTSD on the basis of DSM–IV–TR criteria. The CAPS takes from 45 to 60 minutes to administer and assesses the frequency and intensity of 17 PTSD symptoms, including onset, duration, distress, impairment, and severity. The CAPS may be useful in all levels of prevention research in which PTSD is the focus. However, because of its interview format, it would best be used as a follow-up to a briefer measure in large-scale prevention studies.

Hamilton Anxiety Rating Scale

The Hamilton Anxiety Rating Scale (HARS; Hamilton, 1959) is a widely used clinician-administered scale (taking approximately 15 to 30 minutes to complete) that is designed to assess severity of general anxiety symptoms (phobic avoidance is not assessed). The HARS is one of the most commonly used measures of anxiety severity in psychiatric research and medication studies. With its interview format, the HARS is suitable for research designs necessitating a thorough assessment of severity of symptoms, as in tertiary prevention studies wherein an in-depth understanding of illness severity is required.

Looming Maladaptive Style Questionnaire-Revised

The Looming Maladaptive Style Questionnaire-Revised (LMSQ-R; Riskind, Williams, Gessner, Chrosniak, & Cortina, 2000) is a measure of looming maladaptive style, a cognitive style conferring specific vulnerability to anxiety on its recipients. The looming vulnerability model of anxiety states that an individual's perception of the changing intensity of threat plays a central role in the experience of anxiety, with anxiety associated with the perception of threat as rapidly intensifying and growing in risk (Riskind, 1997). The LMSQ-R consists of six short descriptions of potentially threatening situations. Each description is followed by a series of eight questions, three of which measure perceptions of increasing threat, making up the looming maladaptive style subscale. Thus, the LMSQ-R is a useful instrument in secondary prevention studies as a marker of vulnerability to anxiety.

Multidimensional Anxiety Scale for Children

The Multidimensional Anxiety Scale for Children (MASC; March, 1998) is a 39-item measure of anxiety symptoms consisting of four subscales derived from factor analysis: physical symptoms, social anxiety, avoidance of harm, and separation anxiety. Items are rated on a 4-point scale. Appropriate for children and adolescents aged 8 to 16 years, the MASC is a useful tool for primary and secondary prevention research in which a decision is required about the extent to which anxiety symptoms exist in a child population.

Panic Disorder Severity Scale

This seven-item clinician-administered scale that takes 10 to 15 minutes to administer is designed to assess the severity of panic disorder in patients already diagnosed with the condition. The Panic Disorder Severity Scale (PDSS; Shear et al., 1992) is a common assessment measure in treatment outcome studies of panic disorder. With its interview format, the PDSS is most suitable for research designs necessitating a thorough assessment of severity of symptoms, as in tertiary prevention studies wherein an in-depth understanding of illness severity is required.

Penn State Worry Questionnaire

The Penn State Worry Questionnaire (PSWQ; Meyer, Miller, Metzger, & Borkovec, 1990) is a commonly used, 16-item self-report measure of the general tendency to worry excessively. Taking just a few minutes to complete, the instrument assesses the intensity and excessiveness of worry without regard to its content. As a continuous measure of the severity of worry, the PSWQ would be useful in primary and secondary prevention research in which a decision is required about the extent to which excessive worry is present in the study population.

Screen for Child Anxiety Related Emotional Disorders

The Screen for Child Anxiety Related Emotional Disorders (SCARED; Birmaher et al., 1997) is a 38-item measure of specific anxiety symptoms, including somatic sensations of anxiety or panic, general anxiety, separation anxiety, social phobia, and school phobia. Items are rated on a 3-point scale. Appropriate for children and adolescents aged 9 to 18, the SCARED is a useful tool for primary and secondary prevention research in which a decision is required about the extent to which anxiety symptoms exist in a child population.

Social Phobia Inventory

The Social Phobia Inventory (SPIN; Connor et al., 2000) is a 17-item self-report measure of the fear, avoidance, and physiological arousal associated with social phobia. As a continuous measure of social anxiety, the SPIN is useful in primary and secondary prevention research examining social anxiety in the study population.

Social Phobia and Anxiety Inventory for Children

The Social Phobia and Anxiety Inventory for Children (SPAI-C; Beidel, Turner, & Morris, 1995), a 26-item measure of social anxiety, is appropriate for children and adolescents aged 8 to 17 years. Subscales assess assertiveness, traditional social encounters, and public performance. As a continuous measure of social anxiety, the SPAI-C would be useful in primary and secondary prevention research examining social anxiety in a child population.

Spence Children's Anxiety Scale

The Spence Children's Anxiety Scale (SCAS; Spence, 1997) was developed in accordance with the DSM–IV–TR criteria for anxiety disorders. This 45-item measure consists of five factors: panic–agoraphobia, social phobia, separation anxiety, obsessive–compulsive problems, generalized anxiety, and physical fears. Items are rated on a 4-point scale. The SCAS is appropriate for children aged 8 to 12 years and is useful in primary and secondary prevention research that examines anxiety disorders in a child population.

Yale–Brown Obsessive Compulsive Scale

The Yale–Brown Obsessive Compulsive Scale (Y-BOCS; Goodman, Price, Rasmussen, Mazure, Delgado et al., 1989; Goodman, Price, Rasmussen, Mazure, Fleischmann et al., 1989) is a 10-item clinician-administered semistructured interview that measures the severity and types of symptoms in obsessive–compulsive disorder. Severity scores for obsessions and compulsions, as well as an overall severity score, are obtained. The Y-BOCS is a useful measure at all levels of prevention research in which obsessive–compulsive disorder is the focus. However, because of its interview format, the instrument is best used as a follow-up to a briefer screening measure in large-scale prevention studies.

Diagnostic Interviews and General Screening Measures

This section lists some of the best-known and well-validated measures related to the identification of disorders or "cases." Instruments for both adults and children are listed, because prevention researchers are likely to focus on cases of disorder across different age ranges. We have attempted to describe measures that range from simple, efficient screening tools suitable for population-based work to structured clinical interviews that may be more readily used in tertiary prevention (e.g., to assess comorbidity). Additional details regarding these measures can be found elsewhere (e.g., Bufka, Crawford, & Levitt, 2002; Rogers, 2001; Summerfeldt & Antony, 2002).

Anxiety Disorders Interview Schedule for DSM–IV

The Anxiety Disorders Interview Schedule for *DSM–IV* (ADIS-IV; Brown, Di Nardo, & Barlow, 1994; Di Nardo, Brown, & Barlow, 1994), a semistructured interview measure for diagnosing anxiety-related problems, is commonly used, extensively researched, and appropriate for diagnosis in both psychological and medical settings. Coverage includes detailed diagnostic criteria for anxiety disorders, mood disorders, somatoform disorders, and substance use disorders, as well as screening for other disorders, such as psychotic disorders. Because of its level of detail, the ADIS-IV is probably most applicable to studies in which a thorough assessment of diagnosis, or "caseness," is critical. For example, the ADIS-IV could be used in tertiary prevention studies in which the focus is reduction in the development of comorbid diagnostic conditions.

Brief Psychiatric Rating Scale

The Brief Psychiatric Rating Scale (BPRS; Overall & Gorham, 1962) is a 24-item rating scale that takes into account five syndromes (thought disorder, withdrawal, anxiety–depression, hostility–suspicion, and activity) over the 2 weeks previous to the administration of the instrument. The interviewer uses both questions and behavioral observations during the interview to make the ratings. Because of its efficiency, the BPRS is useful in studies in which "caseness" needs to be evaluated in a larger population for example, primary or secondary intervention studies. The BPRS also lends itself to being a screening tool for diagnosis, followed up by a more detailed assessment.

Diagnostic Interview Schedule for Children

The Diagnostic Interview Schedule for Children (DISC; NIMH, 1991) covers 30 diagnostic categories consistent with the *DSM* and can be administered by both professionals and nonprofessionals. The interview takes between 90 and 120 minutes. The DISC is a highly detailed diagnostic instrument that is useful in prevention studies in children where the child's diagnostic status is an outcome variable or is necessary for screening prior to prevention intervention.

Mini International Neuropsychiatric Interview

The Mini International Neuropsychiatric Interview (MINI; Sheehan et al., 1999) is a clinician-administered structured interview that provides diagnoses for both *DSM–IV* and the 10th edition of the *International Classification of Diseases* (ICD-10; World Health Organization, 1993). Most anxiety and mood disorders, along with several other Axis I categories, are covered in this interview. The MINI is brief, taking 10–15 minutes to complete, and was designed with epidemiological studies and multicenter trials in mind (Summerfeldt & Antony, 2002). The advantage of the MINI is that it affords information about diagnosis, not just severity or presence of symptoms, and that it does so in a short period. The MINI would be most useful in larger population studies, both in primary or secondary prevention, to establish whether a case of disorder exists.

Primary Care Evaluation of Mental Disorders

The Primary Care Evaluation of Mental Disorders (PRIME-MD; Spitzer et al., 1994) was designed to assess five types of disorder (mood, anxiety, somatoform, alcohol, and eating disorders) commonly found in primary care. The instrument uses a two-stage process: a patient questionnaire containing yes–no screening questions and a clinician follow-up interview inquiring about 18 diagnostic categories. The entire process takes under 20 minutes (Spitzer et al., 1994). Like the MINI, the PRIME-MD is an efficient tool for establishing a diagnosis. The PRIME-MD could be used alone in population research, or, together with a structured clinical interview, as a screening tool to select individuals for more detailed diagnostic assessment.

Structured Clinical Interview for DSM–IV Axis I Disorders

The Structured Clinical Interview for *DSM–IV* Axis I Disorders (SCID; First, Spitzer, Gibbon, & Williams, 1996, 1997; American Psychiatric Association, 1994) is a semistructured interview designed to be consistent with the *DSM–IV* Axis I disorders. The interview consists of questions and decision rules aimed at arriving at a formal diagnosis; in essence, it operationalizes the

DSM. There are both clinician (First et al., 1997) and research (First et al., 1996) versions, the latter including more detailed questions about diagnostic criteria, subtypes, and specifiers that are often more important in collecting research data. The most frequently used structured clinical interview, the SCID has a level of detail and consistency with the *DSM–IV* that makes it one of the most desirable tools for purposes of generalizability. The SCID is likely to be most useful in programs of research in which highly detailed and specific information about diagnostic status is most relevant—for example, in tertiary prevention research or as a follow-up to a screening instrument in primary or secondary intervention.

Measures of General Health, Functional Impairment, and Quality of Life

This section lists measures of general health, impairment, and quality of life that are likely to be most germane in tertiary research. We have opted not to list similar measures for children and adolescents, since tertiary prevention is more likely to occur with adults. Detailed psychometric information on these scales can be found in the *Handbook of Psychiatric Measures* (American Psychiatric Association, 2000b).

Duke Health Profile

This 17-item self-report was designed to be a brief measure of health for use in outcome work. The Duke Health Profile (Parkerson, Broadhead, & Tse, 1990) uses five distinct scales: physical health, mental health, social health, perceived health, and disability. The instrument is likely to be most useful in prevention research in which broader determinants of health, beyond symptoms of psychiatric disorder, are a key focus for intervention.

Illness Intrusiveness Rating Scale

Illness intrusions are lifestyle and activity disruptions that arise as a result of an illness or its treatment (Devins, 1994). The construct of illness intrusiveness, as well as the Illness Intrusiveness Rating Scale (IIRS; Devins, 1994) used to assess it, has been used in a variety of both medical and psychiatric illnesses (Antony, Roth, Swinson, Huta, & Devins, 1998; Bieling, Rowa, Antony, Summerfeldt, & Swinson, 2001). In studies that focus on preventing functional impairment that is a result of psychiatric illness, the IIRS is an efficient and valid option.

Quality of Life Interview

The Quality of Life Interview (QOLI; Lehman, 1988) is available in long (158 items) and brief (78 items) versions and was designed to assess the quality of life of individuals with severe and persistent mental illness. Quality of life is defined as a combination of the individual's experience of general well-being, personal characteristics, objective life conditions, and subjective satisfaction with life (Rabkin, Wagner, & Griffin, 2000). The instrument would lend itself to research in which a detailed analysis of quality of life, broadly defined, is a focus of study.

SF-36 Health Survey

Developed as a measure of perceived health status, the SF-36 Health Survey (SF-36; Ware & Sherbourne, 1992) includes a number of domains that may be affected by illness, including physical, psychological, and social factors. This self-report measure has eight subscales (physical functioning, physical role functioning, bodily pain, general health, vitality, social functioning, emotional role functioning, and mental health). The SF-36 is likely the most widely used measure of health status, a feature that facilitates generalizability and comparisons across studies. The instrument also covers broad domains of functioning that may be targeted in tertiary prevention.

Sheehan Disability Scale

The Sheehan Disability Scale (SDS; Sheehan, 1983) is a composite of three self-rated items designed to measure the extent to which three major sectors in the patient's life (work, social life, and family life) are impaired by psychiatric symptoms. A highly efficient measure of impairment of functioning, the SDS is most useful in large-scale studies in which prevention researchers need to separate illness severity from the individual's level of functioning.

CONCLUDING REMARKS

In this chapter, we described the three types of prevention and important measurement issues within these different areas. A number of critical measurement issues were identified, including whether prevention efforts are delivered as intended, assessment of the impact of the prevention intervention, and adequate sensitivity and specificity of screening tools. It is notable that, despite the vast literature on assessment for anxiety and depression, there are as yet few resources that are specific to the issue of prevention. Indeed, although the measures described in the chapter are empirically supported and well established, none were designed expressly with prevention in mind.

In the future, it is highly probable that measures will be developed which have the specific purpose of assessing the implementation and outcome of prevention strategies. For example, measures that have parallel forms for different developmental epochs and measures that are sensitive to changes in an individual over a span of months or years will likely evolve as prevention research matures. Until then, the best practice may be to adapt current "gold-standard" instruments, such as those described in this chapter, for the intended purpose. For the foreseeable future, those instruments which are most frequently used in current treatment studies and have good psychometric properties are also likely to be the best tools to bring to bear in prevention research. However, prevention research designs do have some unique features that need to be considered in choosing instruments.

First, because most research designs in prevention focus on either populations or large samples, efficiency is likely to be a critical factor in choosing an existing instrument. Second, large-scale prevention research is likely to examine a broad range of outcome variables (e.g., symptoms, general health, functioning, quality of life), rather than a narrow band of outcomes (e.g., symptom reduction) that are typically examined in treatment efficacy trials. Thus, multidimensional measures are likely to take center stage in most prevention studies. At the same time, measuring a range of outcomes will require judicious choices about the level of detail that can be assessed within domains. For example, primary prevention will require diagnostic measures with properties very different from the diagnostic instruments that might be used to select patients for a treatment efficacy study. When entire populations are scrutinized, it may be necessary to sacrifice the "bandwidth" of diagnostic instruments (Summerfeldt & Antony, 2002) for the sake of efficiency. Also, time frames in prevention research are likely to involve years, not days or weeks, and outcome measures need to be able to measure changes and fluctuations accurately over extended periods.

Clearly, issues of measurement will be paramount in the development of prevention research and interventions. Indeed, the development of measures that are specific to prevention work should itself be a focus in prevention research programs. Such measures would need to be constructed to have reliability and validity, but also would have to emphasize efficiency and sensitivity to change and be applicable across a range of ages. Alongside current standard measures, researchers could implement or pilot new measures that attempt to combine these desirable properties. In this manner, the researchers could begin the process of validating new tools specific to prevention.

REFERENCES

Alloy, L. B., Abramson, L. Y., Hogan, M. E., Whitehouse, W. G., Rose, D. T., Robinson, M. S., et al. (2000). The Temple–Wisconsin Cognitive Vulnerability to Depression Project: Lifetime history of Axis I psychopathology in individuals at high and low cognitive risk for depression. *Journal of Abnormal Psychology, 109*, 403–418.

American Psychiatric Association. (1994). *Diagnostic and statistical manual of mental disorders* (4th ed.). Washington, DC: Author.

American Psychiatric Association. (2000a). *Diagnostic and statistical manual of mental disorders* (4th ed., text revision). Washington, DC: Author.

American Psychiatric Association. (2000b). *Handbook of psychiatric measures.* Washington, DC: Author.

Antony, M. M., & Barlow, D. H. (Eds.) (2002). *Handbook of assessment and treatment planning for psychological disorders.* New York, NY: Guilford.

Antony, M. M., Bieling, P. J., Cox, B. J., Enns, M. W., & Swinson, R. P. (1998). Psychometric properties of the 42-item and 21-item versions of the Depression Anxiety Stress Scales in clinical groups and a community sample. *Psychological Assessment, 10,* 176–181.

Antony, M. M., Orsillo, S. M., & Roemer, L. (2001). *Practitioner's guide to empirically based measures of anxiety.* New York, NY: Kluwer Academic/Plenum Publishers.

Antony, M. M., Roth, D., Swinson, R. P., Huta, V., & Devins, G. M. (1998). Illness intrusiveness in individuals with panic disorder, obsessive compulsive disorder, or social phobia. *Journal of Nervous and Mental Disease, 186,* 311–315.

Beck, A. T., Epstein, N., Brown, G., & Steer, R. A. (1988). An inventory for measuring clinical anxiety: Psychometric properties. *Journal of Consulting and Clinical Psychology, 56,* 893–897.

Beck, A. T., Steer, R. A., & Brown, G. K. (1996). *Beck Depression Inventory—Second Edition Manual.* San Antonio, TX: Psychological Corporation.

Beidel, D. C., Turner, S. M., & Morris, T. L. (1995). A new inventory to assess childhood social anxiety and phobia: The social phobia and anxiety inventory for children. *Psychological Assessment, 7,* 73–79.

Bieling, P. J., Rowa, K., Antony, M. M., Summerfeldt, L. A., & Swinson, R. P. (2001). Structure of Illness Intrusiveness Rating Scale in Anxiety Disorders. *Journal of Psychopathology and Behavioral Assessment, 23,* 223–230.

Birmaher, B., Khertarpal, S., Brent, D., Cully, M., Balach, L., Kaufman, J., & McKenzie-Neer, S. (1997). The screen for child-anxiety-related emotional disorders (SCARED): Scale construction and psychometric characteristics. *Journal of the American Academy of Child and Adolescent Psychiatry, 36,* 545–553.

Blake, D. D., Weathers, F. W., Nagy, L. M., Kaloupek, D. G., Gusman, F. D., Charney, D. S., & Keane, T. M. (1995). The development of a clinician-administered PTSD scale. *Journal of Traumatic Stress, 8,* 79–90.

Blake, D. D., Weathers, F. W., Nagy, L. M., Kaloupek, D. G., Klauminzer, G., Charney, D. S., & Keane, T. M. (1990). A clinician rating scale for assessing current and lifetime PTSD: The CAPS-1. *The Behavior Therapist, 13,* 187–188.

Brown, T. A., Di Nardo, P. A., & Barlow, D. H. (1994). *Anxiety Disorders Interview Schedule for DSM-IV (ADIS-IV).* San Antonio, TX: The Psychological Corporation.

Bufka, L. F., Crawford, J. I., & Levitt, J. T. (2002). Brief screening assessments for managed care and primary care. In M. M. Antony and D. H. Barlow (Eds.),

Handbook of assessment and treatment planning for psychological disorders (pp. 38–66). New York: Guilford.

Burns, G. L., Keortge, S. G., Formea, G. M., & Sternberger, L. G. (1996). Revision of the Padua Inventory of Obsessive Compulsive Disorder Symptoms: Distinctions between worry, obsessions and compulsions. *Behaviour Research and Therapy, 34,* 163–173.

Chambless, D. L., Caputo, G. C., Bright, P., & Gallagher, R. (1984). Assessment of 'fear of fear' in agoraphobics: The Body Sensations Questionnaire and the Agoraphobic Cognitions Questionnaire. *Journal of Consulting and Clinical Psychology, 52,* 1090–1097.

Chambless, D. L., Caputo, G. C., Jasin, S. E., Gracely, E. J., & Williams, C. (1985). The Mobility Inventory for Agoraphobia. *Behaviour Research and Therapy, 23,* 35–44.

Clark, D. A., & Beck, A. T. (with Alford, B.) (1999). *Scientific foundations of cognitive theory and therapy of depression.* New York: Wiley.

Connor, K. M., Davidson, J. R. T., Churchill, L. E., Sherwood, A., Foa, E., & Wesler, R. H. (2000). Psychometric properties of the Social Phobia Inventory (SPIN). *British Journal of Psychiatry, 176,* 379–386.

Crum, R. M., Cooper-Patrick, L., & Ford, D. E. (1994). Depressive symptoms among general medical patients: Prevalence and one year outcome. *Psychosomatic Medicine, 56,* 109–117.

Davidson, J. R. T., Book, S. W., Colket, J. T., Tupler, L. A., Roth, S., David, D., et al. (1997). Assessment of a new self-rating scale for post-traumatic stress disorder. *Psychological Medicine, 27,* 153–160.

Davidson, J. R. T., Potts, N. L. S., Richichi, E. A., Ford, S. M., Krishnan, R. R., Smith, R. D., & Wilson, W. (1991). The Brief Social Phobia Scale. *Journal of Clinical Psychiatry, 52*(11, suppl.), 48–51.

Devins, G. M. (1994). Illness intrusiveness and the psychosocial impact of lifestyle disruptions in chronic life-threatening disease. *Advances in Renal Replacement Therapy, 1,* 251–263.

Di Nardo, P. A., Brown, T. A., & Barlow, D. H. (1994). *Anxiety Disorders Interview Schedule for DSM–IV: Lifetime Version.* San Antonio, TX: Psychological Corporation.

Dozois, D. J. A., Covin, R., & Brinker, J. K. (2003). Normative data on cognitive measures of depression. *Journal of Consulting and Clinical Psychology, 71,* 71–80.

First, M. B., Spitzer, R. L., Gibbon, M., & Williams, J. B. W. (1996). *Structured Clinical Interview for Axis I DSM-IV Disorders Research Version-Patient Edition (SCID-I/P, ver. 2.0).* New York: New York State Psychiatric Institute, Biometrics Research Department.

First, M. B., Spitzer, R. L., Gibbon, M., & Williams, J. B. W. (1997). *Structured Clinical Interview for DSM-IV Axis I Disorders (SCID-I)–Clinician Version.* Washington, DC: American Psychiatric Press.

Foa, E. B., Cashman, L., Jaycox, L. H., & Perry, K. (1997). The validation of a self report measure of PTSD: The PTSD Diagnostic Scale (PDS). *Psychological Assessment, 9*, 445–451.

Foa, E. B., Hearst-Ikeda, D., & Perry, K. J. (1995). Evaluation of a brief cognitive–behavioral program for the prevention of chronic PTSD in recent assault victims. *Journal of Consulting and Clinical Psychology, 63*, 948–955.

Foa, E. B., Kozak, M. J., Salkovskis, P. M., Coles, M. E., & Amir, N. (1998). The validation of a new obsessive compulsive disorder scale: The Obsessive-Compulsive Inventory. *Psychological Assessment, 10*, 206–214.

Goodman, W. K., Price, L. H., Rasmussen, S. A., Mazure, C., Delgado, P., Heninger, G. R., & Charney, D. S. (1989). The Yale–Brown Obsessive Compulsive Scale II. Validity. *Archives of General Psychiatry, 46*, 1012–1016.

Goodman, W. K., Price, L H., Rasmussen, S. A., Mazure, C. Fleischmann, R. L., Hill, C. L., et al. (1989). The Yale–Brown Obsessive Compulsive Scale: I. Development, use, and reliability. *Archives of General Psychiatry, 46*, 1006–1011.

Hamilton, M. (1959). The assessment of anxiety states by rating. *British Journal of Medial Psychology, 32*, 50–55.

Hamilton, M. (1960). A rating scale for depression. *Journal of Neurology, Neurosurgery, and Psychiatry, 23*, 56–62.

Hamilton, M. (1967). Development of a rating scale for primary depressive illness. *British Journal of Social and Clinical Psychology, 6*, 278–296.

Horwath, E., Johnson, J., Klerman, G. L., & Weissman, M. M. (1992). Depressive symptoms as relative and attributable risk factors for first-onset major depression. *Archives of General Psychiatry, 49*, 817–823.

Ingram, R. E., Miranda, J., & Segal, Z. V. (1998). *Cognitive vulnerability to depression.* New York: Guilford Press.

Jacobson, N. S., Dobson, K. S., Truax, P. A., Addis, M. E., Koerner, K., Gollan, J. K., et al. (2000). A component analysis of cognitive–behavioral treatment for depression. *Journal of Consulting and Clinical Psychology, 64*, 295–304.

Keane, T. M., Caddell, J. M., & Taylor, K. L. (1988). Mississippi Scale for Combat-Related Posttraumatic Stress Disorder: Three studies in reliability and validity. *Journal of Consulting and Clinical Psychology, 56*, 85–90.

Kendall, P. C., & Sheldrick, R. C. (2000). Normative data for normative comparisons. *Journal of Consulting and Clinical Psychology, 68*, 767–773.

Kovacs, M. (1992). *Children's Depression Inventory Manual.* North Tonawanda, NY: Multi-Health Systems.

Lehman, A. F. (1988). A Quality of Life Interview for the chronically mentally ill. *Evaluation and Program Planning, 11*, 51–62.

Liebowitz, M. R. (1987). Social phobia. *Modern Problems in Pharmacopsychiatry, 22*, 141–173.

Lovibond, P. F., & Lovibond, S. H. (1995b). The structure of negative emotional states: Comparison of the Depression Anxiety Stress Scales (DASS) with the Beck Depression and Anxiety Inventories. *Behaviour Research and Therapy, 33*, 335–342.

Lovibond, S. H., & Lovibond, P. F. (1995a). *Manual for the Depression Anxiety Stress Scales, second edition*. Sydney, Australia: The Psychology Foundation of Australia.

March, J. S. (1998). *Manual for the Multidimensional Anxiety Scale for Children (MASC)*. North Tonawanda, NY: Multi-Health Systems.

Marks, I. M., & Mathews, A. M. (1979). Brief standard self-rating for phobic patients. *Behavior Research and Therapy, 17*, 263–267.

Mattick, R. P., & Clarke, J. C. (1998). Development and validation of measures of social phobia scrutiny fear and social interaction anxiety. *Behavior Research and Therapy, 36*, 455–470.

Meyer, T. J., Miller, M. L., Metzger, R. L., & Borkovec, T. D. (1990). Development and validation of the Penn State Worry Questionnaire. *Behavior Research and Therapy, 28*, 487–495.

National Institute of Mental Health. (1991). *NIMH Diagnostic Interview for Children, Version 2.3*. Rockville, MD: Author.

National Institute of Mental Health. (2001). National Advisory Mental Health Council Workgroup on Mental Disorders Prevention Research. Priorities for prevention research at NIMH. *Prevention & Treatment, 4*, NP. (Posted June 26, 2001).

Nezu, A. M., Ronan, G. F., Meadows, E. A., & McClure, K. (2000). *Practitioner's guide to empirically based measures of depression*. New York, NY: Kluwer Academic/Plenum Publishers.

Ollendick, T. H. (1983). Reliability and validity of the revised fear survey schedule for children (FSSC-R). *Behaviour Research and Therapy, 21*, 685–692.

Overall, J. E., & Gorham, D. R. (1962). The Brief Psychiatric Rating Scale. *Psychological Reports, 10*, 799–812.

Parkerson, G. R., Jr, Broadhead, W. E., & Tse, C. K. J. (1990). The Duke Health Profile: A 17-item measure of health and dysfunction. *Medical Care, 28*, 1056–1072.

Peterson, C., Semmel, A., von Baeyer, C., Abramson, L. Y., Metalsky, G. I., & Seligman, M. E. P. (1982). The Attributional Style Questionnaire. *Cognitive Therapy and Research, 6*, 287–300.

Peterson, R. A., & Reiss, S. (1993). *Anxiety Sensitivity Index Revised test manual*. Worthington, OH: IDS Publishing Corporation.

Petkova, E., Quitkin, F. M., McGrath, P. J., Stewart, J. W., & Klein, D. F. (2000). A method to quantify rater bias in antidepressant trials. *Neuropsychopharmacology, 22*, 559–565.

Rabkin, J., Wagner, G., & Griffin, K. W. (2000). Quality of life measures. In American Psychiatric Association (Eds.), *Handbook of psychiatric measures*, pp. 135–150. Washington, DC: American Psychiatric Association.

Radloff, L. S. (1977). The CES-D Scale: A self-report depression scale for research in the general population. *Applied Psychological Measurement, 1*, 385–401.

Reiss, S., Peterson, R. A., Gursky, D. M., & McNally, R. J. (1986). Anxiety sensitivity, anxiety frequency and the prediction of fearfulness. *Behaviour Research and Therapy, 24*, 1–8.

Reynolds, C. R., & Richmond, B. O. (1978). What I think and feel: A revised measure of children's manifest anxiety. *Journal of Abnormal Child Psychology, 6,* 271–280.

Reynolds, C. R., & Richmond, B. O. (1985). *Revised Children's Manifest Anxiety Scale.* Los Angeles: Western Psychological Service.

Reynolds, W. M. (1987). *Reynolds Adolescent Depression Scale: Professional manual.* Odessa, FL: Psychological Assessment Resources.

Riskind, J. H. (1997). Looming vulnerability to threat: A cognitive paradigm for anxiety. *Behaviour Research and Therapy, 35,* 685–702.

Riskind, J. H., Williams, N. L., Gessner, T. L., Chrosniak, L. D., & Cortina, J. M. (2000). The looming maladaptive style: Anxiety, danger, and schematic processing. *Journal of Personality and Social Psychology, 79,* 837–852.

Rogers, R. (2001). *Handbook of diagnostic and structured interviewing.* New York: Guilford.

Segal, Z. V., Gemar, M., & Williams, S. (1999). Differential cognitive response to a mood challenge following successful cognitive therapy or pharmacotherapy for unipolar depression. *Journal of Abnormal Psychology, 108,* 3–10.

Seligman, M. E. P., & Csikszentmihalyi, M. (2000). Positive psychology: An introduction. *American Psychologist, 55,* 5–14.

Shear, M. K., Brown, T. A., Sholomskas, D. E., Barlow, D. H., Gorman, J. M., Woods, S. W., & Cloitre, M. (1992). *Panic Disorder Severity Scale (PDSS).* Pittsburgh: Department of Psychiatry, University of Pittsburgh School of Medicine.

Sheehan, D. V. (1983). *The anxiety disease.* New York: Scribner's.

Sheehan, D.V., Janavs, R., Baker, R., Harnett-Sheehan, K., Knapp, E., & Sheehan, M. (1999). *Mini International Neuropsychiatric Interview.* University of South Florida, Tampa.

Spence, S. (1997). Structure of anxiety symptoms among children: A confirmatory factor analytic study. *Journal of Abnormal Psychology, 106,* 280–297.

Spielberger, C. D. (1973). *Manual for the State–Trait Anxiety Inventory for Children.* Palo Alto, CA: Mind Garden.

Spielberger, C. D., Gorsuch, R. L., Lushene, R., Vagg, P. R., & Jacobs, G. A. (1983). *Manual for the State–Trait Anxiety Inventory (Form Y).* Palo Alto, CA: Mind Garden.

Spitzer, R. L., Williams, J. B. W., Kroenke, K., Linzer, M., deGruy, F. V., Hahn, S. R., et al. (1994). Utility of a new procedure for diagnosing mental disorders in primary care: The PRIME-MD 1000 study. *Journal of the American Medical Association, 272,* 1749–1756.

Summerfeldt, L. J., & Antony, M. M. (2002). Structured and semistructured diagnostic interviews. In M. M. Antony and D. H. Barlow (Eds.), *Handbook of assessment and treatment planning for psychological disorders* (pp. 3–37). New York: Guilford.

Swinson, R. P., Soulios, C., Cox, B. J., & Kuch, K. (1992). Brief treatment of emergency room patients with panic attacks. *American Journal of Psychiatry, 149,* 944–946.

Turner, S. M., Beidel, D. C., & Dancu, C. V. (1996). *The Social Phobia and Anxiety Inventory Manual*. North Tonawanda, NY: Multi-Health Systems, Inc.

Turner, S. M., Beidel, D. C., Dancu, C. V., & Stanley, M. A. (1989). An empirically derived inventory to measure social fears and anxiety: The Social Phobia and Anxiety Inventory. *Psychological Assessment: A Journal of Consulting and Clinical Psychology, 1*, 35–40.

United States Preventative Services Task Force. (1996). *Guide to clinical preventative services* (2d ed.). Baltimore: Williams & Wilkins.

Waltz, J., Addis, M. E., Koerner, K., & Jacobson, N. S. (1993). Testing the integrity of a psychotherapy protocol: Assessment of adherence and competence. *Journal of Consulting and Clinical Psychology, 61*, 620–630.

Ware, J. E., & Sherbourne, C. D. (1992). The MOS 36-Item Short-Form Health Survey (SF-36), I: Conceptual framework and item selection. *Medical Care, 30*, 473–483.

Weissman, A. N., & Beck, A. T. (1978, November). *Development and validation of the Dysfunctional Attitude Scale*. Paper presented at the annual meeting of the Association for the Advancement of Behavior Therapy, Chicago.

World Health Organization. (1993). *International Classification of Diseases* (10th ed.). Geneva: Author.

Young, R. C., Biggs, J. T., Ziegler, V. E., & Meyer, D. A. (1978). A rating scale for mania: Reliability, validity, and sensitivity. *British Journal of Psychiatry, 133*, 429–435.

Zonderman, A. B., Herbst, J. H., Schmidt, C., Costa, P. T., & McCrae, R. R. (1993). Depressive symptoms as a non-specific, graded risk for psychiatric diagnoses. *Journal of Abnormal Psychology, 102*, 544–552.

4

DESIGN CONSIDERATIONS
IN PREVENTION RESEARCH

DAVID A. CLARK

In the health care field, few would argue against the merits of preventive research and intervention for the alleviation of disease and the promotion of health. The well-known adage "an ounce of prevention is worth a pound of cure" could be considered the watchword of public health policy and programs in the last century. Under the auspices of various public health disease prevention initiatives, including mass immunizations and the introduction of hygienic practices, impressive advances were made in the eradication of death and disability from infectious diseases. More recently, we have seen progress in the application of a prevention model to noninfectious disease and other forms of chronic illness and injury, such as risk for cardiovascular disease and accidental injury. This progress has been achieved through the introduction of primary prevention interventions—promotion of smoking cessation, improved dietary intake, promotion of physical exercise, mandatory use of seat belts, and similar practices (Mrazek & Haggerty, 1994). Given these successes within the public health domain, why has it taken so long to apply the prevention model to mental health?

In all fairness, research and intervention in the prevention of mental illness has been receiving higher priority in the last few years (Holden &

Black, 1999; Mrazek & Haggerty, 1994; Reiss & Price, 1996; Seligman, 1998). A significant impetus in this direction came with two commissioned reports, one from the Institute of Medicine (IOM; Mrazek & Haggerty, 1994), the other from the National Institute of Mental Health (NIMH) Prevention Research Steering Committee (1994). A more recent report by the NIMH National Advisory Mental Health Council Workgroup on Mental Disorders Prevention Research (NIMH, 2001) offers a more refined and elaborated definition and conceptual framework for prevention research in mental health. Indeed, we are beginning to see examples of the psychological knowledge base developed for the diagnosis and treatment of mental disorders being applied to issues of disease prevention and health promotion in mental disorders. The launch of the American Psychological Association's electronic journal *Prevention and Treatment*, as well as peer-reviewed journal articles and edited volumes devoted to the subject of disease prevention and health promotion, attests to the greater interest in prevention issues by clinical psychologists.

Mrazek and Haggerty (1994) highlighted a number of obstacles responsible for the lag in research on prevention in mental disorders: (a) the public stigma of such disorders, (b) public ignorance about the fact that effective treatment is available for many disorders, such as depression and anxiety, (c) lack of an organizing theoretical framework for prevention of mental disorders, (d) limited understanding of the mechanisms that link risk and protective factors with outcomes, (e) problems in identifying, defining, and classifying mental disorders, and (f) confusion and lack of agreement on basic definitions, such as what constitutes prevention and prevention research. Holden and Black (1999) argue that the relatively recent alliance of psychology with the medical model has led to an emphasis on the diagnosis and treatment of disorder at the expense of research and interventions on prevention and health promotion. This state of affairs has left us in the awkward situation of possessing a relatively advanced knowledge base regarding psychopathology and its treatment, together with a limited understanding and background in prevention research and intervention. As a result, research and intervention programs that attempt to generalize the concepts, models, measures, and treatments relating to disorder to risk reduction and health promotion in mental disorders dominate current psychological research on prevention. The extent that such a generalization is valid remains to be seen.

This chapter focuses on conceptual issues that confront mental health professionals interested in research and intervention in the prevention of anxiety and depression. The first section explores the definitional problems that have emerged from efforts to apply disease prevention and health promotion concepts to mental disorder. The second section focuses on specific conceptual issues that arise in the context of preintervention and intervention prevention research in anxiety and depression. The chapter concludes with a summary and suggestions for future directions.

DEFINITION OF PREVENTION AND RELATED CONCEPTS

What Is Prevention?

In order to identify the boundaries of prevention research and intervention in anxiety and depression, one must first define the term *prevention*. Even at this starting point, however, there is considerable confusion, disagreement, and fuzziness over what constitutes prevention research, intervention, and service within the mental health field (Cowen, 1997; Mrazek & Haggerty, 1994; NIMH, 2001). Drawing sharp boundaries between prevention and treatment can be most difficult. In an effort to provide greater clarity, the IOM Committee on Prevention of Mental Disorders (Mrazek & Haggerty, 1994) recommended that the term *prevention* be "reserved for only those interventions that occur before the initial onset of a disorder" (p. 23). Once an individual meets the criteria for being diagnosed with a disorder, an intervention is no longer considered preventive, but rather falls within the category of treatment (Muñoz, Mrazek, & Haggerty, 1996). Thus, at the heart of the concept of prevention is the notion of risk reduction.

According to the IOM Report, *risk factors* are "those characteristics, variables, or hazards that, if present for a given individual, make it more likely that this individual, rather than someone selected from the general population, will develop a disorder" (Mrazek & Haggerty, 1994, p. 6). Risk factors can encompass a broad range of genetic, biological, psychological, and social variables that probably interact in a complex, multifactorial fashion to heighten susceptibility to an episodic disorder. Note that a distinction must be drawn between risk and vulnerability: *Risk* refers to all factors associated with an increased likelihood of experiencing an onset or exacerbation of symptoms or the disorder itself, whereas vulnerability refers to a subset of risk factors that are thought to have a causal effect on the disorder (chap. 9, this volume).

A second important focus within mental health prevention centers on the enhancement of *protective factors*—that is, "positive behaviors or features of the environment that lessen the likelihood of negative outcomes or increase the possibility [i.e., probability] of positive outcomes" (Durlak & Wells, 1997, p. 116). Research and intervention programs that emphasize protective factors in persons without a diagnosable disorder fall within the health promotion domain. Although the IOM Committee recognized that a better understanding of the interaction between risk and protective factors is important to the development of effective prevention intervention programs, it decided to exclude mental health promotion from the spectrum of mental health prevention. The committee reasoned that health promotion is driven, not by an emphasis on illness, but rather by the enhancement of well-being (Mrazek & Haggerty, 1994). In a disease-oriented model of prevention, the goal is to decrease risk and increase protection or resistance to the onset of disorder, whereas the primary focus of health promotion programs is the attainment of optimal states of wellness (Muñoz et al., 1996). Given our limited understanding of what constitutes mental health and optimal emotional well-being, one could argue that it is expedient to exclude health promotion from a preventive science of mental disorder.

This exclusive focus on risk and protective factors as precursors to dysfunction, however, is not without its critics (see Heller, 1996). One criticism is that the distinction between promotion and prevention may be more semantic than real, because intervention programs often use health promotion strategies to improve competencies, with the aim of reducing risk for both onset of, and disability from, the disorder (Cowen, 1997; Koretz & Mościcki, 1997). In their meta-analytic review of 177 primary prevention programs, Durlak and Wells (1997) included primary prevention programs that reflected health promotion goals. The IOM primary prevention research overview, however, excluded programs with a predominantly health promotion outcome. Currently, the pendulum appears to be swinging toward including positive health behaviors within a broader definition of prevention research. The NAMHC report (NIMH, 2001), for example, characterized prevention research as "seeking to understand and influence the developmental trajectory from the earliest formation of the nervous system throughout the course of life in order to prevent mental disorders and *promote mental health*" [italics added] (p. 11). This new definition of prevention research is more palatable to professionals and researchers who are interested in prevention, because most of the factors that reduce susceptibility to disorder (e.g., the role of high self-esteem in protection against depression) are also important variables for enhancing well-being. Often, the line between disease prevention and health promotion cannot be clearly drawn.

Prevention research in mental disorders has also struggled with the distinction between *treatment* and *prevention*. The IOM report (Mrazek & Haggerty, 1994) identified treatment as intervention offered to individuals with a disorder for the purpose of achieving an immediate therapeutic effect. Prevention, on the other hand, is held to be intervention intended to prevent later symptoms or disability and offered to asymptomatic individuals who exhibit clinically significant abnormality. Koretz and Mościcki (1997) note that this distinction is blurred when it is considered within a developmentally oriented etiological model in which many disorders show an early onset. Also, there are high rates of comorbidity in mental disorders, so an intervention could be introduced that prevents the occurrence of secondary disorders in diagnosed populations. Thus, a treatment that could have preventive effects in terms of reduced comorbidity and relapse rates could be offered to diagnosed individuals. Within the broader definition of a preventive science advocated by the NAMHC report (NIMH, 2001), the distinction between treatment and prevention is not as sharp.

Domains of Prevention

The NAMHC report (NIMH, 2001) describes three major domains that it deems constitute a preventive science of mental disorders. First, there is a body of *preintervention research* that includes "basic social, behavioral, and biological, pre-clinical, clinical, and epidemiologic/public health studies that form the building blocks for preventive intervention research" (p. 11). This domain includes studies of basic and clinical etiological processes of a disorder. In addition, the research performed identifies the risk and protective factors or processes that underlie biological, behavioral, and psychological change in a disorder and that increase or decrease the likelihood of developing particular outcomes. Preintervention research also focuses on the development and evaluation of mediation or moderation models that describe how risk is translated into the course and consequences of disorder. Research in this domain can also focus on intervention development by promoting innovative intervention methods and pilot testing, refining, and analyzing new prevention intervention strategies before efficacy trials are run. In sum, preintervention prevention research should be the basis for developing new prevention intervention programs. Such research plays a vital role in the development of innovative, theoretically driven, and empirically grounded efficacious preventive interventions for at-risk populations.

The heart of a preventive science of mental disorders is *preventive intervention research*, because of its potential for directly improving the lives of the public (NIMH, 2001). This research involves both efficacy (whether an intervention produces positive results under controlled conditions) and effectiveness (whether an intervention has beneficial effects in the natural setting) trials. Preventive intervention research can involve asymptomatic individuals, those with subclinical symptoms, and persons with a past or current diagnosis for whom the focus is on reducing the chances of relapse, recurrence, comorbidity, or disability (NIMH, 2001). This chapter focuses on conceptual issues that relate to preintervention and intervention prevention research in anxiety and depression.

A third domain acknowledged within the preventive literature is *preventive service systems research*. This research focuses on the effectiveness of preventive interventions within organizational aspects of the service environment by investigating (a) polices and procedures that encourage or thwart the implementation or adoption of preventive strategies, (b) variables that influence access and availability of preventive interventions, and (c) costs associated with the delivery of preventive services (NIMH, 2001). Prevention research in anxiety and depression is not sufficiently developed to the point where variables that impede the implementation and delivery of prevention programs have been considered. This will be an area for future research, but in the present volume the emphasis is on preintervention and intervention prevention research.

Classification of Prevention Interventions

The original public health classification of disease prevention proposed three types of intervention: primary, secondary, and tertiary (Mrazek & Haggerty, 1994). *Primary prevention* seeks to reduce the number of new cases of a disorder. The intervention is applied widely to large samples or to populations without targeting specific, at-risk individuals. More recently, the IOM report (Mrazek & Haggerty, 1994) suggested that the term *universal prevention* be adopted instead of primary prevention (a recommendation reiterated in the NAMHC report). Universal prevention emphasizes that the intervention is desirable for everyone in an eligible population and can often be applied without professional assistance. Thus, universal prevention interventions target the general public or a whole population group, regardless of risk for the disorder (NIMH, 2001). As Ingram et al. (chap. 9, this volume) note, primary (universal) prevention is the preferred mode of intervention, but it is used less frequently than secondary or tertiary intervention in the mental health field. The development and implementation of primary prevention interventions for anxiety and depression are difficult because one needs a sound scientific understanding of risk and resistance factors to disorder or healthy functioning, as well as the technical skills to develop low-cost, easily disseminated, and effective preventive intervention (Holden & Black, 1999). Neither of these conditions is satisfied in our knowledge base regarding anxiety and depression, so preventive researchers have tended to focus on secondary or targeted intervention (for exceptions, see Clarke, Hawkins, Murphy, & Sheeber, 1993; Rice & Meyer, 1994).

Secondary prevention seeks to lower the rate of established cases of a disorder (Mrazek & Haggerty, 1994). Within the mental health field, secondary prevention involves the identification of individuals who are at risk for the onset of a disorder and the provision of an intervention designed to prevent such onset or reduce the severity or duration of relevant symptoms. As discussed by Ingram et al. (chap. 9, this volume), secondary prevention can operate at two levels. First, targeted individuals can be identified who are asymptomatic for a disorder, but who possess a risk factor that is thought to increase the likelihood that symptoms or the disorder itself will occur. The second approach targets individuals who show subclinical symptoms, and the aim of the intervention is to reduce the progression of those symptoms into a full-blown clinical disorder. However, the IOM and NAMHC reports recommend that the term *selective prevention* be adopted to refer to interventions that target individuals whose risk of developing a disorder is greater than average within the general population (NIMH, 2001). An example of selected preventive intervention was reported by Seligman, Schulman, DeRubeis, and Hollon (1999) in which intervention was offered to a sample of university students considered at high risk for depression or anxiety because they exhibited a dysfunctional attributional style toward positive and negative events.

Tertiary prevention seeks to decrease the amount of disability stemming from an existing disorder (Mrazek & Haggerty, 1994). Here, individuals targeted for interventions have been diagnosed with a disorder. The aim of the intervention is to prevent future relapse of a new episode of the disorder or to reduce the amount of disability resulting from the disorder. The distinction between secondary and tertiary intervention can be fuzzy, because it can be difficult to determine whether a person is having a relapse or a recurrence of symptoms (see chap. 9, this volume). If a person is fully recovered or asymptomatic, and the intervention is delivered to prevent future episodes (i.e., recurrences), then the intervention would be considered secondary. However, if the person is not fully recovered from an episode and the intervention is designed to reduce an exacerbation or recurrence of symptoms, then it would be tertiary intervention. More recently, the term *indicated prevention* has been recommended in lieu of tertiary prevention. *Indicated prevention* refers to interventions that target high-risk individuals who have minimal, but detectable, symptoms of a disorder or who exhibit vulnerability markers which indicate that they have a predisposition to a disorder, but who do not currently meet the criteria for being diagnosed with the disorder. As noted in the NAMHC report (NIMH, 2001), this classification excludes all individuals with a full-blown disorder and thus appears more restrictive than the tertiary prevention classification (see chap. 1, this volume). Mrazek and Haggerty (1994) noted that, over time, there has been a "simplistic" blending of these two classification systems; in this volume, most authors assume that both tertiary and indicated prevention interventions target individuals who have been diagnosed with a disorder.

Not only does the conceptual framework for prevention research offered by the IOM report exclude individuals who meet the criteria for being diagnosed with a disorder, but it also excludes preintervention prevention research. For this reason, the NAMHC report (NIMH, 2001) recommended that a preventive science of mental health include preintervention, intervention, and preventive service systems research. In addition, the report suggested that the focus of preventive research be expanded to include not only universal, selective, and indicated prevention strategies, but also prevention interventions aimed at reducing relapse and comorbidity. The latter additions make prevention research with diagnosed individuals part of a broader mandate that prescribes a preventive science for mental disorders in general.

CONCEPTUAL ISSUES IN PREVENTION OF ANXIETY AND DEPRESSION

Most of the key conceptual issues that present challenges for research into the psychopathology and treatment of anxiety and depression are also highly relevant to prevention research. Readers who are well informed of the quantitative and experimental psychological research and psychotherapy outcome studies of anxiety disorders and depression will recognize many of the issues discussed in this section. A number of detailed critical reviews have been published on these issues within the context of psychopathology or psychotherapy (e.g., Alloy, Hartlage, & Abramson, 1988; Barlow, 2002; Barnett & Gotlib, 1988; Clark & Beck, 1999; Clark & Watson, 1991; Coyne, 1994; Coyne & Whiffen, 1995; Depue & Monroe, 1978; Flett, Vredenburg, & Krames, 1997; Garber & Hollon, 1991; Ingram, Miranda, & Segal, 1998; Monroe & Simons, 1991; Price & Ingram, 2001; Vredenburg, Flett, & Krames, 1993). The discussion herein offers a different perspective by examining the impact of these issues on the development of preintervention and intervention prevention research in anxiety and depression.

Case Identification

In order to provide preventive intervention, one must first possess an ability to identify the targeted mental disorder or problem in a reliable and valid manner (Mrazek & Haggerty, 1994). If the disorder can be assessed and diagnosed accurately, then the prevention researcher can move on to the problem of identifying risk and resistance factors. Thus, all of the issues in prevention discussed in the paragraphs that follow are predicated on the ability to identify or diagnose the occurrence of disorder.

Many characteristics of anxious and depressive disorders make their assessment and diagnosis more complicated. The apparent consensus in the use of structured diagnostic interviews and *DSM–IV* criteria (American Psychiatric Association, 1994) gives the appearance that anxious and depressive disorders can be detected in a reliable and accurate fashion. One might assume that case identification in the prevention of anxiety and depression is easily resolved by employing *DSM–IV* criteria to determine the presence or absence of a disorder. However, this is not a straightforward matter, especially in an asymptomatic general population.

Continuum of Anxiety and Depression

On the one hand, there is considerable empirical evidence that depressive and anxious disorders may form a continuum, with one end defined by milder states in the nonclinical general population and the other end composed of more severe variants of the disorder in clinical samples (Cox, Enns, Borger, & Parker, 1999; Flett et al., 1997; Ruscio & Ruscio, 2000; Vredenburg et al., 1993). Furthermore, symptoms such as panic attacks, social anxiety, and specific fears are clearly evident in nonclinical samples (Antony & Barlow, 2002; Stein, Walker, & Forde, 1994; Wilson et al., 1992). On the other hand, there is an equally prominent group of researchers who argue that diagnosable anxiety and depression are qualitatively different and distinct from subclinical variants of these disorders in the nonclinical population (e.g., Coyne, 1994; Coyne & Whiffen, 1995; Depue & Monroe, 1978; Santor & Coyne, 2001). This discontinuity, or categorical, view of anxiety and depression fits well within the *DSM–IV* framework which assumes that sharp boundaries can be drawn between those individuals who have a disorder and those who do not.

If the symptoms making up the criteria that define depressive and anxious disorders are dimensional in nature, then the threshold for defining "caseness" may be more arbitrary than is often assumed, which will present particular difficulties for prevention research. In addition, there is considerable evidence that subthreshold states of depression and anxiety are frequently encountered in the nonclinical population and that these very conditions can be risk factors for later disorder (e.g., Horwath, Johnson, Klerman, & Weissman, 1992). Together, these two factors make it particularly difficult to determine whether a person is asymptomatic and therefore eligible for primary or secondary preventive intervention. Where does one place the cutoff for determining that a person is symptomatic or asymptomatic? If subclinical depression or anxiety is a risk factor for a diagnosable disorder, it will be difficult to differentiate these milder conditions, given their continuous distribution in the general population.

The continuity of anxiety and depression can complicate tertiary intervention programs whose goal is to prevent new episodes of the disorder. *Recurrence* refers to the onset of a new episode of a disorder after a prolonged period of remission, whereas *relapse* is the return of clinically significant symptoms from an existing episode after a relatively short period of remission (Abramson, Alloy, & Metalsky, 1988). In reality, the distinction between relapse and recurrence can be difficult to make (chap. 9, this volume). If a person who was previously depressed now presents with some symptoms of depression, does this indicate a relapse, a recurrence of a new episode, or a continuing state of remission? How much remission of symptoms is needed to constitute a state of recovery from a previous episode? The dimensional nature of anxiety and depression makes it difficult to clearly identify which stage of a disorder is present. As a result, the most appropriate candidates for a secondary or tertiary prevention intervention program may be overlooked, whereas others may be included who are not in fact appropriate for the program. If the empirical evidence continues to point in the direction of a continuous distribution of anxious and depressive symptoms and disorders in the nonclinical and clinical populations, prevention research on depression and anxiety will be hindered by unreliable and inaccurate identification of both symptomatic and asymptomatic cases.

Comorbidity Rates

Dozois and Westra (chap. 2, this volume) discuss the considerable empirical evidence that documents a high comorbidity rate (over 50%)

between anxiety and depression. If one also considers the co-occurrence of anxiety and depression with other disorders, such as substance abuse, psychotic conditions, and the like, one readily sees that comorbidity rates can exceed 80% (Clark, Watson, & Reynolds, 1995). Within the anxiety disorders, high rates of diagnostic co-occurrence are evident, with a significant number of clinical individuals meeting the criteria for two or more anxiety disorders (Brown, Campbell, Lehman, Grisham, & Mancill, 2001). In addition, comorbid anxiety and depression is associated with a greater severity of symptoms, higher chronicity, and greater impairment (see chap. 2, this volume, for further discussion). A number of reasons have been cited for the high comorbidity rates: (a) Anxiety and depression have a number of symptoms in common, (b) they may share common genetic, biological, and psychological vulnerabilities, (c) measures of anxiety and depression are highly correlated, and (d) the *DSM–IV* diagnostic system encourages interpretations of comorbidity by allowing multiple diagnoses (see Clark & Beck, 1999, for further discussion).

The presence of comorbidity will complicate prevention intervention and research. For example, as regards primary prevention of depression, should individuals who meet the criteria for being diagnosed with an anxiety disorder, such as social phobia, be excluded, even though they have never experienced a full-blown depressive episode? Similarly, given the high co-occurrence of anxiety and depression, should individuals with a previous anxiety disorder be offered tertiary prevention intervention for depression, with the understanding that their risk for depression is high because they have had a previous anxiety disorder? The NAMHC report (NIMH, 2001) recommended that prevention researchers also target a reduction in comorbid conditions as one of their aims. However, our ability to identify these conditions and measure change to a reasonable degree of accuracy is hampered by the high correlation between anxious and depressive measures.

Another factor that complicates comorbidity is the close *temporal* relationship between anxiety and depression. Dozois and Westra (chap. 2, this volume) referred to this relationship as "successive comorbidity." There is considerable evidence that anxiety precedes depression, although this may depend on the specific anxiety disorder under consideration (Brown et al., 2001). A tertiary prevention program could aim for a reduction in comorbid depression in those with a previous anxiety disorder, although such a strategy might be relevant only for social phobia or generalized anxiety disorder. Clearly, the presence of current and lifetime comorbidity in anxiety and depression presents special challenges in identifying who is the most appropriate target for a prevention intervention program.

Base Rates

Prevention intervention and research programs are greatly influenced by the base rate of the targeted disorder within the general population.

Disorders with relatively high base rates (e.g., cardiovascular disease and accidental injury) are especially good candidates for primary prevention. However, the lower the base rate for a particular disorder, the less efficient and effective is the prevention intervention. This is especially true for primary prevention interventions that are given to unselected samples of the general population. If few—possibly even none—of the sample will develop the disorder, then there is no justification for providing primary prevention. This problem can be circumvented to some extent by offering secondary or tertiary intervention. However, low base rates can weaken the association between risk factors and outcome, thereby making it difficult to establish the effectiveness of an intervention.

In discussing the problem of base rate in reference to diagnosable depression, Coyne (1994) noted that the actual rate of diagnosable depression within community samples over a 1-year period may be around 4%. Twelve-month prevalence rates for anxiety disorders vary from 9% for specific phobias to 2.3% for panic disorder (Kessler et al., 1994). Overall, these base rates are relatively low in comparison to some of the illness and injury problems targeted for prevention intervention, such as substance abuse, tobacco consumption, motor vehicle accidents, occupational injury, and the like. The problem of a low base rate will be particularly severe if certain disorders, such as obsessive–compulsive disorder, are targeted. A couple of problems emerge in attempting prevention of a disorder with a low base rate. First, with such disorders, a weaker relationship exists between risk factors and outcome. In depression, for example, the majority of at-risk individuals never develop the disorder (Coyne, 1994). Consequently, in a secondary prevention program, the majority of individuals will show no benefit from the intervention (in terms of preventing the onset of a disorder), because they would not develop the disorder anyway. This means that there is less opportunity to demonstrate the effectiveness of an intervention in terms of reducing the onset of disorder. It follows that any change in risk factors has less of an opportunity to influence a low rate of disorder.

A second problem with low base rates is that the follow-up period for determining the effectiveness of a prevention intervention will have to be extended over many years in order to ensure a rate of onset of the disorder sufficient that differences can be measured. A lower base rate also tends to reduce the predictive utility, sensitivity, and specificity of measures used to assess risk factors and outcome (chap. 3, this volume; see also Coyne, 1994, for a discussion of this point with reference to the Beck Depression Inventory).

Risk Identification

Identification of the risk and protective factors that lead to a reduction in susceptibility to a disorder is a critical component of the preventive intervention research cycle (Mrazek & Haggerty, 1994). There is widespread recognition that the risk and protective factors involved in mental disorders, including anxiety and depression, are multiple and span a broad spectrum of genetic, biological, social, environmental, and psychological domains. However, there is a dearth of knowledge about the mechanisms that link these risk and protective factors to the initial onset of symptoms. Therefore, in designing a preventive intervention, the researcher must rely on the identification of particular risk and protective factors, rather than be guided by a more sophisticated theoretical model of prevention that specifies mediatory causal relationships. With this in mind, Mrazek and Haggerty (1994) recommended that investigators base their preventive interventions on the *risk reduction model*, in which the goal is to reduce the risk factors or enhance the protective factors (or both) implicated in a disorder. Mrazek and Haggerty (1994) suggested employing one or more of the following considerations in selecting risk and protective factors for prevention intervention: (a) Select risk and protective factors whose presence or absence, respectively, correlates with the disorder and that can be altered by an intervention, (b) determine the mechanisms that link the risk and protective factors to the onset of symptoms, (c) identify the triggers (e.g., life events) that activate mediatory mechanisms, (d) indicate the processes that mediate between the triggering event and the onset of symptoms, and (e) specify which processes are set in motion once symptoms have developed. There are, however, a number of issues that will complicate the selection of risk and protective factors for the development of prevention interventions for anxiety and depression.

Risk Status

Risk factors vary in the degree of their direct relation to a disorder and in their level of conceptual specificity. The risk factors for anxiety and depression that constitute vulnerability will be more useful in prevention intervention programs than will other factors that are merely correlates of the disorder. Also, broadly defined and widely distributed risk factors (e.g., female gender, poverty, divorce) make poorer candidates for a secondary or tertiary prevention intervention than do more specific factors (e.g., low self-esteem, perfectionism, social dependency; see chap. 9, this volume, for a discussion of the subject in relation to depression).

The type of prevention intervention will also determine which risk and protective factors should be targeted in an intervention program. For secondary preventive intervention, vulnerability factors implicated in anxiety or depression would be the best candidates. Ingram et al. (chap. 9, this volume) suggest that certain cognitive vulnerabilities, such as sociotropy, autonomy, perfectionism, and a negative inferential style, might be appropriate targets for secondary prevention intervention in depression. With anxiety, low perceived control, heightened anxiety sensitivity in panic disorder, and excessive responsibility in obsessive–compulsive disorder are vulnerability factors that could be included in secondary prevention intervention (Barlow, 2002; McNally, 2001). With tertiary prevention interventions, the critical risk factors targeted in preventing relapse or reducing comorbidity might be different from the variables leading to the initial onset of symptoms. In depression, for example, negative life events appear to play a more critical role in the initial episode than in subsequent relapse and recurrences, whereas depressed mood and dysfunctional thinking may be more influential in recurrent depression (Lewinsohn, Allen, Gotlib, & Seeley, 1999). In sum, which risk factors should be targeted in preventive intervention depends on their conceptual specificity, their causal involvement, and the prevention domain under investigation (i.e., secondary vs. tertiary).

Level of Specificity

There is increasing recognition that anxiety and depression share some common risk factors and symptoms, whereas other variables are more specific to one disorder than to the other (e.g., Mineka, Watson, & Clark, 1998). Moreover, it may be that risk factors more distal to episodic anxiety or depression (e.g., genetic vulnerability, early childhood experiences) tend to be common factors, whereas risk factors more proximal to an episode may have greater specificity (see chap. 11, this volume). However, Garber and Hollon (1991) remind us that a common, or nonspecific, variable can still play a causal role in the etiology of a disorder if such a variable is one of several interacting causal factors in the disorder. Thus, prevention researchers should not exclude a risk factor simply because it is common to both anxiety and depression.

A number of twin studies suggest that the anxiety disorders and major depression may share a common underlying diathesis. For example, Eley and Stevenson (1999) assessed 395 pairs of same-sex twins and found that most of the variance in the correlation between anxiety and depression was due to genetic factors and that specificity to each disorder was related more to environmental influences. In terms of a common psychological diathesis, studies indicate that high negative affect (Clark & Watson, 1991; Mineka et al., 1998) and a diminished sense of personal control (Barlow, 2002) are evident in anxiety and depression. In fact, Barlow (2002) argues that early developmental experiences of uncontrollability or unpredictable events may lead to a "generalized psychological vulnerability" or neurotic temperament, as indicated by low perceptions of control and increased neurobiological activity (e.g., increased activity in Gray's behavioral inhibition system).

Other risk factors appear to be more specific to each type of disorder. The content of negative self-referent cognition can be highly specific, with thoughts of personal loss and failure more characteristic of depression and cognitions of threat and danger specific to anxiety, albeit to a lesser extent

(Beck & Perkins, 2001; Clark & Beck, 1999). Low positive affect appears to be specific to depression, and autonomic hyperarousal may be specific only to panic disorder (Mineka et al., 1998). Empirical evidence supporting the construct validity of trait Positive and Negative Affect (Watson & Walker, 1996) indicates that low Positive Affect and high Negative Affect can be viewed as risk factors, as well as distinct symptom or mood descriptors, in anxiety and depression (Watson & Clark, 1984; Watson & Tellegen, 1985). Negative life events may have both common and specific characteristics in anxiety and depression. Whereas the presence of negative life stress is clearly a risk factor for both types of disorder, the nature of the stressor may differ between conditions. For example, negative events involving interpersonal loss may be one of the best predictors of depressive relapse and chronicity (Joiner, 2000).

Another feature of risk factors that is related to level of specificity is whether the variable is necessary or sufficient (or both) for episodic anxiety or depression. Abramson et al. (1988) defined an etiological factor a *necessary cause* if it must be present in order for symptoms to occur, whereas *sufficient cause* refers to whether the presence of the risk factor guarantees the occurrence of symptoms. A *contributory cause* refers to whether a risk factor increases the likelihood of symptoms, but is neither necessary nor sufficient therefor. Abramson et al. (1988) proposed that a negative attributional style is a proximal sufficient cause for hopelessness depression. More recently, Hammen (2001) concluded that cognitive vulnerability research has failed to demonstrate that its constructs make a necessary, substantial, and specific contribution to the onset of depression.

A final consideration under specificity of risk concerns whether a variable is a cause or an effect of a disorder. In many cases, a variable may both contribute to a disorder and be influenced by the occurrence of symptoms. That is, it can be both cause and effect of the disorder. A prime example is negative life events. A large research base shows that major negative life events contribute to the development of depression (e.g., Brown & Harris, 1989), but more recently evidence indicates that stress can be generated by the presence of depression and anxiety (Hammen, 1991; Harkness & Luther, 2001). Moreover, a first episode of a disorder such as depression may alter certain risk factors so that they play an even stronger contributory role in future recurrences of the disorder. As an example, Lewinsohn et al. (1999) found that depressed mood and dysfunctional attitudes were significant predictors of recurrent depressive episodes, but not of the initial episode of depression. This finding suggests that an initial episode of depression leaves a "scar" on depressed mood and dysfunctional thinking, such that these constructs became more closely associated with recurrent depression.

A number of issues should be considered in selecting risk factors for a preventive intervention program in anxiety or depression. Is the risk factor common or specific to the disorder under consideration? Targeting common risk factors may lead to treatment effects that are broader and more diffuse than desired. In addition, practically all of the vulnerability factors in anxiety and depression are neither necessary nor sufficient causes of the onset of symptoms. Accordingly, risk factors should be viewed as possible contributory causes of disorder. Further, it is likely that the presence of the disorder will modify the contributory status of a risk factor. Thus, tertiary prevention interventions may need to target a set of risk factors different from those proposed for primary or secondary intervention. Given the state of our knowledge of risk factors in anxiety and depression, the prevention researcher might be advised to target risk factors that are more proximal, specific, contributory causes of the onset of symptoms.

Activating Triggers

A diathesis–stress perspective on vulnerability has become increasingly recognized as the most appropriate conceptual framework for understanding the etiology of depression and, to a lesser extent, anxiety. Monroe and Simons (1991) noted, "the basic premise is that a stress activates a diathesis, transforming the potential of predisposition into the presence of psychopathology" (p. 406). The diathesis is an enduring, endogenous predisposition to illness, such as a personality factor, that becomes activated by events which are perceived to be stressful, thereby leading to an onset of a disorder (Ingram et al., 1998). For example, although the diathesis to depression was originally considered a constitutional predisposition, more recently researchers have generalized the model to psychological diatheses (Monroe & Simons, 1991). One of the best known is the cognitive vulnerability model of depression offered by Aaron T. Beck (Beck, 1987; Clark & Beck, 1999). Susceptibility to the onset of symptoms is apparent only when there is a match or congruence between the life event and underlying cognitive or personality vulnerability (e.g., sociotropy and negative social events or autonomy and negative achievement events).

The probability that vulnerability or other risk factors may lead to the onset of symptoms only in the presence of an activating event presents special problems for the development of preventive intervention programs. First, most diathesis–stress models assume that an underlying vulnerability marker is latent (i.e., not easily observable), until activated by a triggering event (Ingram et al., 1998). Research involving latent psychological variables is most difficult, requiring some form of challenge or priming stimulus to ensure that the vulnerability factor has been activated for observation and measurement (Segal & Ingram, 1994). In prevention research, one might offer an intervention for a risk factor that had no observable manifestation until it was activated by a priming manipulation. Would someone be motivated, for example, to participate in a prevention program aimed at ameliorating, say, the need to please others when such a need does not become manifest until one actually experiences the loss of a valued relationship? Could we accurately and reliably select such a vulnerable person for preventive intervention in the absence of a real-life activating event?

Second, a more precise definition of the type of stress involved in the activation of anxiety or depression is needed when one is employing a diathesis–stress model (Monroe & Simons, 1991). Not all types of stress present equal risk factors for depression or anxiety. For example, significant life events involving the loss of a valued relationship may be more potent in triggering major depression than an accumulation of minor daily hassles will be (Coyne & Whiffen, 1995). As already stated, the content of the event may play a role, so that only certain types of life events will activate a disorder. Finally, the perception of the life event may be more important than the actual occurrence of the event. That is, only when the event is perceived as threatening the loss of a valued personal resource will it constitute a risk for a particular disorder (Clark & Beck, 1999). If a diathesis–stress model is adopted, the prevention researcher will want to design interventions that inoculate individuals against the negative effects of events that are likely to activate the disorder. However, which type of events should be the target of the intervention? Should the intervention emphasize the modification of *perceptions* of events, or should one focus on teaching skills for coping with the events *themselves*?

Finally, diathesis–stress models require that the diathesis and stress constitute separate and distinct concepts. The diathesis should be quite distinct from the disorder that it predicts, it should not depend exclusively on the social context (i.e., the stressor), and it should show considerable temporal stability (Coyne & Whiffen, 1995). For example, self-criticism as a vulnerability factor for depression has been criticized because increased self-criticism is also a symptom of depression (Clark & Beck, 1999). Highly sociotropic individuals should exhibit this vulnerability over time and across a variety of situations. If the vulnerability were apparent only when, for example, the person was excluded from a social encounter, this would suggest that the personality assessment merely reflects involvement in a particular type of social context (Coyne & Whiffen, 1995). In sum, the development of prevention interventions for anxiety and depression must take into account the complex interplay of issues connected with diathesis–stress models of psychopathology.

Risk Factor Interactions

A final issue to consider in the selection of risk factors for a prevention intervention program concerns the nature of the relationship between risk factors, on the one hand, and the onset of symptoms or the outcome of intervention, on the other. Given that most vulnerability models of anxiety and depression assume a diathesis–stress perspective, certain assumptions prevail on the nature of the diathesis–stress interaction in its relation to the onset of symptoms. Much of the diathesis–stress research assumes simple additivity or interaction between diathesis and stress (Monroe & Simons, 1991). These two views assume that the degree of stress and loading of the diathesis summate to increase susceptibility to disorder or that a synergism occurs between the diathesis and stress so that their combined effect is greater than their separate effects. However, Monroe and Simons (1991) posit that the diathesis–stress interaction could be complex, so that certain thresholds of the diathesis must be reached before the interaction becomes manifest. Thus, individuals with a very high diathesis loading would require only minimal stress to precipitate symptoms, whereas individuals with low diathetic loading would require more extreme levels of stress to activate the diathesis.

If further research indicates that the diathesis–stress interaction is nonlinear, then that would present a considerable challenge to prevention research in anxiety and depression. For secondary prevention intervention, the results suggest that individuals who exceed a particular threshold for a risk factor should be targeted. At this point, none of the psychological vulnerability measures in anxiety or depression have established cutoff scores for identifying high vulnerability. Moreover, the existence of threshold values for a diathesis indicates that the diathesis–stress relationship differs at varying levels of the diathesis, a fact one would want to consider when designing preventive interventions. Finally, the possibility that different relationships exist between risk factors in a manner that can affect their impact on outcomes of intervention or the onset of symptoms needs to be understood. Kraemer, Stice, Kazdin, Offord, and Kupfer (2001) identified five different conceptual relationships that can exist between risk factors, including the mediator–moderator distinction. Given the complexity of these relationships, which can activate stress and precipitate symptoms, it is important that prevention research take into consideration the possible pathways from diathesis to stress and then on to the onset of anxiety or depression.

Developing Effective Prevention Interventions

Once the population has been targeted and the risk or protective factors identified, the next step in the preventive intervention research cycle is the design, implementation, and analysis of pilot and large-scale trials of the preventive intervention program (Mrazek & Haggerty, 1994). Many of the issues that face the development of efficacious and effective treatments for anxiety and depression are also applicable to the design of preventive interventions. Given the various issues that were raised in this chapter concerning the identification of a problem and risk factors, one may wonder whether effective preventive intervention for anxiety and depression is even possible. However, the NAMHC report (NIMH, 2001) reminds us that there are a number of examples of prevention studies in the community and clinical settings in which specific, well-characterized interventions have been effective in preventing the onset and relapse of depressive episodes and in reducing disability to anxiety disorders. Notwithstanding these successes, a number of additional intervention issues that must be considered in implementing a prevention program for anxiety or depression are summarized next.

First, one must consider the activities and technologies that will be used in the intervention program to effect behavioral change in a risk factor and bring about a reduction in the probability of onset of symptoms (Mrazek & Haggerty, 1994). The empirical literature on the etiology and treatment of anxiety and depression provides considerable guidance on the ingredients of a preventive intervention. However, our understanding of how treatments work often lags far behind demonstrations of their effectiveness (Dimidjian & Dobson, in press). For example, there is considerable evidence that Beck's cognitive therapy of depression leads to significant reductions in symptoms during an acute episodic phase of the disorder (see reviews by DeRubeis, Tang, & Beck, 2001; Dobson, 1989; Oei & Free, 1995). Yet there is also considerable debate and uncertainty over which ingredients of cognitive therapy are most active and whether a reduction in symptoms is due to change in dysfunctional cognition (Dimidjian & Dobson, in press). Thus, if a tertiary prevention intervention were planned that aimed to reduce the likelihood of relapse into depression, and if the risk factor targeted for change were dysfunctional self-referential schemas, then cognitive therapy process research is inconclusive on which of the various therapeutic ingredients should be included in the intervention to effect schematic change. No doubt one would include instruction in the identification of negative automatic thoughts, verbal disputation of negative beliefs, and empirical-hypothesis-testing assignments. However, the empirical research would not be very helpful in determining how much emphasis should be placed on each of these components of treatment.

A second set of issues focuses on who should receive the preventive intervention and in what setting. Issues surrounding case or problem identification have already been discussed. For secondary and tertiary preventive intervention, those at highest risk for onset or relapse of depression or anxiety should be targeted. However, other issues include ensuring that there is broad representation of different cultural and ethnic groups, age levels, comorbid disorders or conditions, socioeconomic levels, and geographic locations. Then, in addition to considering these characteristics of participants in an intervention program, the researcher also needs to consider whether the recipient is an individual or a group of peers, families, schools, or communities (NIMH, 2001).

A third set of issues revolves around the implementation of the preventive intervention. How many sessions of intervention should be offered over what period? Mrazek and Haggerty (1994) recommend that the intervention be short enough to be practical, but long enough to effect long-term behavioral change. Obviously, the potential benefits must justify the cost of the intervention. Thus, a cost–benefit analysis will be critical to determining the efficacy of a prevention intervention. Also, issues of noncompliance and attrition are major concerns in prevention research (Mrazek & Haggerty, 1994). Because participants are often asymptomatic, they may be less motivated to put the necessary effort into the intervention program. High noncompliance and dropout rates will undermine the effectiveness of the intervention. The very people who terminate the intervention prematurely may be the ones at highest risk for onset of symptoms. Consequently, special efforts are needed to promote compliance. Mrazek and Haggerty (1994) recommend that intervention activities be designed around the targeted population's daily routine and that their motives, feelings, and meanings associated with the intervention be directly addressed in the program. "Selling" the preventive intervention to the targeted population may be one of the greatest challenges facing prevention researchers of anxiety and depression.

Assessing Effectiveness in Prevention Research

The success of the preventive intervention research cycle depends, in the final analysis, on our ability to measure the effects of the intervention reliably and accurately. Many of the issues raised here were discussed in chapter 3 (this volume). A few of the main issues involved in the design of preventive intervention programs are highlighted next.

In preventive intervention research, one must assess change in the targeted risk factors, as well as in the onset of symptoms or disorder. Both sets of variables must be measured in order to determine whether an intervention has resulted in a change to a risk factor that is then responsible for a reduction in the likelihood of onset or relapse of anxious or depressive symptoms or disorder. In addition, measures of general functioning or quality of life should be included to assess the consequences of any onset of symptoms or disorder, especially in tertiary prevention. It is also recommended that researchers include measures of positive behaviors or emotional well-being, so that the health promotion aspects of a preventive intervention can be assessed. The adequacy of preventive intervention research will depend on utilizing observer ratings, interviews, and self-reports with high sensitivity and specificity for the various constructs under investigation (see chap. 11, this volume).

In order to demonstrate causal relations between changes in risk factors and prevention of onset of symptoms or relapse into a disorder, longitudinal research designs are necessary. The question then arises as to the optimal interval for the follow-up period. Mrazek and Haggerty (1994) state that, because the goal of preventive intervention is a decrease in the incidence of a disorder, the longer the follow-up period, the greater will be the power to detect statistically significant differences. Follow-up periods should be long enough to exceed the age of risk of onset. One of the recommendations of the NAMHC report (NIMH, 2001) is that long-term follow-up be encouraged in prevention research. The report notes that two-thirds of NIMH-funded community-based preventive intervention follow-up assessments ranged from 1 to 6 years, whereas the most desired effects may be observed 15 years after an intervention. Of course, long follow-up periods are very costly and create their own scientific difficulties, including the twin challenges of tracking, over time, both participants and changes in the status of measures and research questions used in the study (Holden & Black, 1999; Mrazek & Haggerty, 1994). In addition, after the initial baseline assessment, one must decide how often to conduct further assessments. Obviously, the more frequent the observations, the more precise is the measurement of the onset and course of the disorder (Mrazek & Haggerty, 1994). However, if assessments are too frequent, the cost of the research escalates and participants may become annoyed by the intrusion of the study into their lives. Clearly, some compromise is needed in planning the follow-up period and frequency of assessments.

Finally, randomized controlled trials in which a target population is randomly assigned to an experimental or a control condition are the preferred experimental design for testing hypotheses, especially in secondary (selective) and tertiary (indicated) preventive intervention trials (Mrazek & Haggerty, 1994). However, there are some practical and ethical issues that arise with random assignment in prevention research. For example, is it ethical to maintain high-risk participants in a control condition throughout a long follow-up period in order to demonstrate stronger intervention effects? Also, is it ethically defensible to offer low-risk participants a prevention intervention that they probably do not need and that will not confer on them any added advantage against the onset of illness? Although quasi-experimental designs are an alternative form of investigation, Mrazek and Haggerty (1994) concluded that randomized controlled designs are the best way to document the effects of a preventive intervention. Once again, the researcher is faced with having to balance the inherent costs and benefits of various research parameters in order to implement a preventive intervention program.

SUMMARY AND CONCLUSION

Prevention of anxiety and depression is an emerging area of research that holds great potential for reducing the human suffering, disability, and economic burden associated with those conditions. The knowledge base that currently exists in the psychopathology and treatment of anxiety and depression provides an excellent vantage point for the development and implementation of preventive intervention programs. From the empirical literature on the causal factors and correlates of anxiety and depression, a number of excellent candidates emerge as potential psychological risk or vulnerability factors that could be targeted in preventive intervention. In addition, the anxiety and depression psychotherapy outcome and process research provides examples of active therapeutic ingredients that should be included in a prevention intervention. Although preventive research in anxiety and depression is only a few years old, our more advanced understanding of the psychological, social, and behavioral basis of these disorders means that researchers have a large knowledge base on which to build a preventive science for anxiety and depression.

To what extent can the knowledge gained in the psychopathology and treatment of anxiety and depression be easily generalized to the prevention of those disorders? This chapter discussed a number of conceptual issues that characterize preventive research and intervention and that researchers of anxiety and depression should be cognizant of in designing preventive pre-intervention or intervention research programs. Without due consideration to these issues, we risk a naïve approach that will result in suboptimal interventions and weak research designs that could lead to erroneous conclusions about the ineffectiveness of preventing anxiety and depression.

The first section of the chapter reviewed basic definitions in the emerging field of preventive science in mental disorders. More precise definitions of *risk*, *vulnerability*, and *protective factors* were offered, and a distinction was drawn between treatment and prevention. It was noted that the development of a preventive science of anxiety and depression requires research at the preintervention, intervention, and service systems levels. This led to a discussion of the current debate on the classification of preventive research into primary, secondary, and tertiary interventions versus universal, selective, and indicated interventions. It was suggested that preventive research in anxiety and depression not restrict itself to these more familiar types of preventive intervention, but instead adopt the expanded view on prevention recommended in the NAMHC report (NIMH, 2001). That is, prevention should not be restricted to those persons who are asymptomatic for a disorder, but should also include intervention research focused on reductions in the probability of relapse, comorbid conditions, and the disability associated with disorders.

The remainder of the chapter discussed a variety of conceptual issues that fall under the rubric of case or problem identification, selection of risk and protective factors, development of prevention interventions, and assessment of effectiveness of interventions. Among the various features of anxiety and depressive disorders that complicate the selection of the most appropriate population for a prevention intervention are the probable dimensional nature of anxiety and depression, the high rate of comorbidity of disorders, and the relatively low base rate of disorders in the nonclinical population, especially in relation to a number of specific anxiety disorders. In order to select the most appropriate risk and protective factors for a preventive intervention, one should consider the causal status of the risk factors, the nature of their relation to episodic anxiety or depression, the presence of diathesis–stress vulnerability, and the type of interaction between multiple risk factors, on the one hand, and onset of symptoms, on the other. In designing a preventive intervention, decisions must be made on which activities and technologies to include in the intervention, who should receive the intervention and in what setting, the number of intervention sessions and the duration of intervention, and how to deal with issues of noncompliance and attrition. Finally, the assessment of an intervention's efficacy will depend on the sensitivity and specificity of the outcome measures, the use of longitudinal research designs with a sufficient follow-up period, and the implementation of randomized control trials that allow one to directly test specific hypotheses about differential effectiveness.

The development of a preventive intervention research cycle for anxiety and depression is an important initiative for a better understanding and treatment of anxious and depressive disorders. However, progress in this enterprise depends on research that leads to a better understanding of the etiological constructs and their interrelations and that connects these constructs with the onset and exacerbation of symptoms. Effective prevention strategies, especially at the universal, or primary, level, depend on a scientific understanding of risk and resistance factors to the onset of disorder or to healthy functioning and of the technical skills required to deliver low-cost, easy to disseminate, and empirically based preventive interventions (Holden & Black, 1999).

REFERENCES

Abramson, L. Y., Alloy, L. B., & Metalsky, G. I. (1988). The cognitive depression onset theories of depression: Toward an adequate evaluation of the theories' validities. In L. B. Alloy (Ed.), *Cognitive processes in depression* (pp. 3–30). New York: Guilford.

Alloy, L. B., Hartlage, S., & Abramson, L. Y. (1988). Testing the cognitive diathesis–stress theories of depression: Issues of research design, conceptualization and assessment. In L. B. Alloy (Ed.), *Cognitive processes in depression* (pp. 31–73). New York: Guilford.

American Psychiatric Association (1994). *Diagnostic and statistical manual of mental disorders* (4th ed.). Washington, DC: Author.

Antony, M. M., & Barlow, D. H. (2002). Specific phobias. In D. H. Barlow (Ed.), *Anxiety and its disorders: The nature and treatment of anxiety and panic* (2nd ed., pp. 380–417). New York: Guilford.

Barlow, D. H. (2002). *Anxiety and its disorders: The nature and treatment of anxiety and panic* (2nd ed.). New York: Guilford.

Barnett, P. A., & Gotlib, I. H. (1988). Psychosocial functioning and depression: Distinguishing among antecedents, concomitants and consequences. *Psychological Bulletin, 104*, 97–126.

Beck, A. T. (1987). Cognitive models of depression. *Journal of Cognitive Psychotherapy: An International Quarterly, 1*, 5–37.

Beck, R., & Perkins, T. S. (2001). Cognitive content-specificity for anxiety and depression: A meta-analysis. *Cognitive Therapy and Research, 25*, 651–663.

Brown, G. W., & Harris, T. O. (1989). Depression. In G. W. Brown & T. O. Harris (Eds.), *Life events and illness* (pp. 49–93). New York: Guilford.

Brown, T. A., Campbell, L. A., Lehman, C. L., Grisham, J. R., & Mancill, R. B. (2001). Current and lifetime comorbidity of the *DSM–IV* anxiety and mood disorders in a large clinical sample. *Journal of Abnormal Psychology, 110*, 585–599.

Clark, D. A., & Beck, A. T., with Alford, B. (1999). *Scientific foundations of cognitive theory and therapy of depression*. New York: Wiley.

Clark, L.A., & Watson, D. (1991). A tripartite model of anxiety and depression: Psychometric evidence and taxometric considerations. *Journal of Abnormal Psychology, 100*, 316–336.

Clark, L. A., Watson, D., & Reynolds, S. (1995). Diagnosis and classification of psychopathology: Challenges to the current system and future directions. *Annual Review of Psychology, 46*, 121–153.

Clarke, G. N., Hawkins, W., Murphy, M., & Sheeber, L. (1993). School-based primary prevention of depressive symptomatology in adolescents: Findings from two studies. *Journal of Adolescent Research, 8*, 183–204.

Cowen, E. L. (1997). On the semantics and operations of primary prevention and wellness enhancement (or will the real primary prevention please stand up?). *American Journal of Community Psychology, 25*, 245–255.

Cox, B. J., Enns, M. W., Borger, S. C., & Parker, J. D. A. (1999). The nature of the depressive experience in analogue and clinically depressed samples. *Behaviour Research and Therapy, 37*, 15–24.

Coyne, J. C. (1994). Self-reported distress: Analog or ersatz depression? *Psychological Bulletin, 116*, 29–45.

Coyne, J. C., & Whiffen, V. E. (1995). Issues in personality as diathesis for depression: The case of sociotropy-dependency and autonomy-self-criticism. *Psychological Bulletin, 118*, 358–378.

Depue, R. A., & Monroe, S. A. (1978). Learned helplessness in the perspective of the depressive disorders: Conceptual and definitional issues. *Journal of Abnormal Psychology, 87*, 3–20.

DeRubeis, R. J., Tang, T. Z., & Beck, A. T. (2001). Cognitive therapy. In K. S. Dobson (Ed.), *Handbook of cognitive–behavioral therapies* (2nd ed., pp. 349–392). New York: Guilford.

Dimidjian, S., & Dobson, K. S. (in press). Processes of change in cognitive therapy. In M. A. Reinecke & D. A. Clark (Eds.), *Cognitive therapy across the lifespan: Theory, research and practice*. Cambridge, UK: Cambridge University Press.

Dobson, K. S. (1989). A meta-analysis of the efficacy of cognitive therapy for depression. *Journal of Consulting and Clinical Psychology, 57*, 414–419.

Durlak, J. A., & Wells, A. M. (1997). Primary prevention mental health programs for children and adolescents: A meta-analytic review. *American Journal of Community Psychology, 25*, 115–152.

Eley, T. C., & Stevenson, J. (1999). Using genetic analyses to clarify the distinction between depressive and anxious symptoms in children. *Journal of Abnormal Child Psychology, 27*, 105–114.

Flett, G. L., Vredenburg, K., & Krames, L. (1997). The continuity of depression in clinical and nonclinical samples. *Psychological Bulletin, 121*, 395–416.

Garber, J., & Hollon, S. D. (1991). What can specificity designs say about causality in psychotherapy research? *Psychological Bulletin, 110*, 129–136.

Hammen, C. L. (1991). Generation of stress in the course of unipolar depression. *Journal of Abnormal Psychology, 100*, 555–561.

Hammen, C. L. (2001). Vulnerability to depression in adulthood. In R. E. Ingram & J. M. Price (Eds.), *Vulnerability to psychopathology: Risk across the lifespan* (pp. 226–257). New York: Guilford.

Harkness, K. L., & Luther, J. (2001). Clinical risk factors for the generation of life events in major depression. *Journal of Abnormal Psychology, 110*, 564–572.

Heller, K. (1996). Coming of age of prevention science: Comments on the 1994 National Institute of Mental Health–Institute of Medicine Prevention Reports. *American Psychologist, 51*, 1123–1127.

Holden, E. W., & Black, M. M. (1999). Theory and concepts of prevention science as applied to clinical psychology. *Clinical Psychology Review, 19*, 391–401.

Horwath, E., Johnson, J., Klerman, G. L., & Weissman, M. M. (1992). Depressive symptoms as relative and attributable risk factors for first-onset major depression. *Archives of General Psychiatry, 49*, 817–823.

Ingram, R. E., Miranda, J., & Segal, Z. V. (1998). *Cognitive vulnerability to depression.* New York: Guilford.

Joiner, T. E., Jr. (2000). Depression's vicious scree: Self-propagating and erosive processes in depression chronicity. *Clinical Psychology: Science and Practice, 7*, 203–218.

Kessler, R. C., McGonagle, K. A., Zhao, S., Nelson, C. B., Hughes, M., Eshleman, S., et al. (1994). Lifetime and 12-month prevalence of DSM–III–R psychiatric disorders in the United States: Results of the National Comorbidity Survey. *Archives of General Psychiatry, 51*, 8–19.

Koretz, D. S., & Mościcki, E. K. (1997). An ounce of prevention research: What is it worth? *American Journal of Community Psychology, 25*, 189–195.

Kraemer, H. C., Stice, E., Kazdin, A., Offord, D., & Kupfer, D. (2001). How do risk factors work together? Mediators, moderators, and independent, overlapping and proxy risk factors. *American Journal of Psychiatry, 158*, 848–856.

Lewinsohn, P. M., Allen, N. B., Gotlib, I. H., & Seeley, J. R. (1999). First onset versus recurrence of depression: Differential processes of psychosocial risk. *Journal of Abnormal Psychology, 108*, 483–489.

McNally, R. J. (2001). Vulnerability to anxiety disorders in adulthood. In R. E. Ingram & J. M. Price (Eds.), *Vulnerability to psychopathology: Risk across the lifespan* (pp. 304–321). New York: Guilford.

Mineka, S., Watson, D., & Clark, L. A. (1998). Comorbidity of anxiety and unipolar mood disorders. *Annual Review of Psychology, 49,* 377–412.

Monroe, S. M., & Simons, A. D. (1991). Diathesis–stress theories in the context of life stress research: Implications for the depressive disorders. *Psychological Bulletin, 110,* 406–425.

Mrazek, P. J., & Haggerty, R. J. (Eds.). (1994). *Reducing risks for mental disorders: Frontiers for preventive intervention research.* Washington, DC: National Academy Press.

Muñoz, R. F., Mrazek, P. J., & Haggerty, R. J. (1996). Institute of Medicine Report on Prevention of Mental Disorders: Summary and commentary. *American Psychologist, 51,* 1116–1122.

National Institute of Mental Health. (2001). National Advisory Mental Health Council Workgroup on Mental Disorders Prevention Research. Priorities for prevention research at NIMH. *Prevention and Treatment, 4,* NP. (Posted June 26, 2001, pre0040017a.html)

National Institute of Mental Health, Prevention Research Steering Research Committee. (1994). *The prevention of mental disorders: A national research agenda.* Washington, DC: Author.

Oei, T. P. S., & Free, M. L. (1995). Do cognitive behavior therapies validate cognitive models of mood disorder? A review of the empirical evidence. *International Journal of Psychology, 30,* 145–179.

Price, J. M., & Ingram, R. E. (2001). Future directions in the study of vulnerability to psychopathology. In R. E. Ingram & J. M. Price (Eds.), *Vulnerability to psychopathology: Risk across the lifespan* (pp. 455–466). New York: Guilford.

Reiss, D., & Price, R. H. (1996). National Research Agenda for Prevention Research: The National Institute of Mental Health Report. *American Psychologist, 51,* 1109–1115.

Rice, K. G., & Meyer, A. L. (1994). Preventing depression among young adolescents: Preliminary process results of a psycho-educational intervention program. *Journal of Counseling & Development, 73,* 145–152.

Ruscio, J., & Ruscio, A. M. (2000). Informing the continuity controversy: A taxometric analysis of depression. *Journal of Abnormal Psychology, 109,* 473–487.

Santor, D. A., & Coyne, J. C. (2001). Evaluating the continuity of symptomatology between depressed and nondepressed individuals. *Journal of Abnormal Psychology, 110,* 216–225.

Segal, Z. V., & Ingram, R. E. (1994). Mood priming and construct activation on tests of cognitive vulnerability to unipolar depression. *Clinical Psychology Review, 14,* 663–695.

Seligman, M. E. P. (1998, January). President's column: Building human strength: Psychology's forgotten mission. *Monitor on Psychology, 29,* 2.

Seligman, M. E. P., Schulman, P., DeRubeis, R. J., & Hollon, S. D. (1999). The prevention of depression and anxiety. *Prevention and Treatment, 2*, NP. (Posted December 21, 1999, pre0020008a.html)

Stein, M. B., Walker, J. R., & Forde, D. R. (1994). Setting diagnostic thresholds for social phobia: Considerations from a community survey of social anxiety. *American Journal of Psychiatry, 151*, 408–412.

Vredenburg, K., Flett, G. L., & Krames, L. (1993). Analogue versus clinical depression: A critical reappraisal. *Psychological Bulletin, 113*, 327–344.

Watson, D., & Clark, L. A. (1984). Negative affect: The disposition to experience aversive emotional states. *Psychological Bulletin, 96*, 465–490.

Watson, D., & Tellegen, A. (1985). Toward a consensual structure of mood. *Psychological Bulletin, 98*, 219–235.

Watson, D., & Walker, L. M. (1996). The long-term stability and predictive validity of trait measures of affect. *Journal of Personality and Social Psychology, 70*, 567–577.

Wilson, K. G., Sandler, L. S., Asmundson, G. J. G., Ediger, J. M., Larsen, D. K., & Walker, J. R. (1992). Panic attacks in the nonclinical population: An empirical approach to case identification. *Journal of Abnormal Psychology, 101*, 460–468.

II

PREVENTION AND INTERVENTION STRATEGIES

5

PRIMARY PREVENTION OF ANXIETY DISORDERS

JENNIFER L. HUDSON, ELLEN FLANNERY-SCHROEDER,
AND PHILIP C. KENDALL

Recent research attention has shifted from the treatment of mental disorders to prevention. Evidence for this shift comes from recommendations and reports of federal agencies (e.g., National Advisory Mental Health Council Workgroup on Mental Disorders Prevention Research, 2001; U.S. Department of Health and Human Services, 1991, 1999). In line with these initiatives, numerous researchers (e.g., Dadds, Holland, Barrett, Laurens, & Spence, 1997; Donovan & Spence, 2000; Greenberg, Domitrovich, & Bumbarger, 2001; Spence, 2001) have suggested the need for prevention and early identification for individuals at risk for the development of anxiety. The importance of such research has been underscored by numerous theoretical articles, chapters in books, and special sections of journals (e.g., *Prevention and Treatment*, Volume 2); however, empirical prevention and early intervention studies aimed at reducing the prevalence of anxiety disorders are few in number.

Anxiety is frequently perceived as a less interfering problem in comparison to school violence and suicide and hence has received less attention in the past. However, the need for prevention research on anxiety disorders is manifold. Anxiety disorders often go unnoticed by parents and teachers, tend to persist into adulthood (Kovacs & Devlin, 1998), may be associated with both later depression and substance use (e.g., Brady & Kendall, 1992; Cole, Peeke, Martin, Truglio, & Seroczynski, 1998), and frequently cause secondary difficulties such as peer and academic problems (e.g., Benjamin, Costello, & Warren, 1990; Hartup, 1983; King & Ollendick, 1989; Strauss, Forehand, Smith, & Frame, 1986). In addition, the societal costs stemming from anxiety disorders are enormous: The annual economic burden of anxiety disorders in the United States was estimated at $42.3 billion, or $1,542 per individual with an anxiety disorder, in 1990 (Greenberg et al., 1999). Treatments have been developed that have been found to be effective in reducing anxiety once a disorder develops (e.g., Barlow, 2001; Kendall, 1994; Rapee, Wignall, Hudson, & Schniering, 2000). Interventions that occur prior to the onset of a diagnosable anxiety disorder may be instrumental in preventing not only the disorder itself, but concomitant problems as well (Kendall & Kessler, 2002). Furthermore, successful preventative interventions will serve to lessen personal and societal costs resulting from treatment efforts aimed at anxiety and associated problems.

Prevention efforts, however, require a solid knowledge of both risk and protective factors related to the disorder. To intervene prior to the onset of clinical disorder, the therapist must first possess the knowledge to identify the factors that place individuals at risk for, or that protect individuals against, the development of disorder. In this chapter, we review both risk and protective factors associated with the anxiety disorders and discuss the benefits of choosing primary prevention strategies for dealing with those disorders. One of the key issues in deciding the most effective method of preventing mental health problems is whether prevention should be aimed at the general population (universal prevention), at individuals at risk for disorder (selective prevention), or at individuals who exhibit subclinical symptoms of disorder (indicated prevention). Our review focuses on primary prevention programs aimed either directly or indirectly at anxiety or associated problems. Consideration is also given to the components of an ultimate, if not slightly idealistic, primary prevention program that would truly be populationwide, rather than offered just to isolated groups. Finally, some cautions are raised regarding the implementation of primary prevention programs for anxiety.

RISK FACTORS

Research has identified several risk or maintaining factors for anxiety disorder: individual characteristics (e.g., child temperament, cognitive vulnerability, and attachment style), parental characteristics (e.g., parental anxiety and certain parenting variables), peer influences (e.g., sociometric status), and stressful life events, among others. Much of the research reviewed in this section focuses on childhood risk factors, because less attention has been paid to risk factors specifically occurring in adolescence and adulthood. When available, however, studies from across the life span are reviewed.

Individual Characteristics

Individuals who possess certain temperaments appear to be at increased risk for the development of an anxiety disorder. Child temperament has been the focus of both retrospective and prospective studies of the etiology of anxiety. In a retrospective study of children aged 7–16 years, Rapee and Szollos (1997) found that, compared with mothers of nonanxious children, mothers of anxious children reported that their children had experienced significantly more bouts of crying, sleep difficulties, pain, and gas in the first year of life. In addition, mothers of anxious children reported that their children were more fearful from birth to age 2 and had greater difficulties calming themselves after distress. No differences among anxiety disorder diagnoses (e.g., separation anxiety, social phobia, generalized anxiety) were found for these temperamental characteristics (i.e., difficult or colicky and fearful disposition).

Behavioral inhibition, a temperamental feature characterized by irritability in infancy, fearfulness in toddlerhood, and shyness, wariness, and withdrawal in childhood, has also been associated with an increased vulnerability to anxiety disorders (e.g., Biederman et al., 1993; Kagan, 1989, 1997; Rosenbaum et al., 1993). Kagan and colleagues found that approximately 15% of White American children exhibited this temperamental trait (Kagan, 1989). Biederman, Rosenbaum, Chaloff, and Kagan (1995) found that the rates of anxiety disorders were highest among children who had been identified as behaviorally inhibited throughout childhood. Prospective studies have also demonstrated that children identified as behaviorally inhibited at 21 months were more likely than uninhibited children to develop anxiety disorders over the next 5 to 10 years (Biederman et al., 1993; Hirshfeld et al., 1992). In addition, inhibited children have a greater likelihood of having a parent with an anxiety disorder (Biederman et al., 1995; Rosenbaum et al., 1993). Collectively, the research is strongly suggestive of a relationship between behavioral inhibition and increased risk for anxiety disorder.

Anxiety disorders in general, and generalized anxiety disorder particularly, appear to be related to a specific cognitive vulnerability: abnormalities in threat perception (e.g., Butler & Mathews, 1983; Muris, Mayer, & Meesters, 2000). Several researchers have suggested that individuals with anxiety disorders tend to overestimate the likelihood and exaggerate the effects of dangerous events. Rapee (1991) has suggested that generalized anxiety disorder, for example, involves not only a biased perception of threat, but also a low perception of control over one's situation or environment. Other researchers have proposed that individuals with anxiety disorders fail to perceive indexes of safety. Woody and Rachman (1994) theorize that increased perception of threat results in an inability to identify safety signals that, in turn, perpetuate the continued experience or maintenance of anxiety.

Attachment style has also been identified as a potential risk factor for childhood anxiety (e.g., Erickson, Sroufe, & Egeland, 1985; Lewis, Feiring, McGafey, & Jaskir, 1984; Sroufe, Egeland, & Kreutzer, 1990). Bowlby (1982) suggested that anxiety in adulthood may be related to an insecure attachment in childhood. According to Bowlby, attachment is the child's attempt to ensure safety and security in his or her world. If the attachment figure is perceived as unavailable, the child may come to experience the world as dangerous and threatening. An anxious–resistant attachment style at 12 months of age appears to be associated with a greater incidence of an anxiety disorder at 18 years of age (Warren, Huston, Egeland, & Sroufe, 1997). Cassidy (1995) examined the role of childhood attachment as a precursor of generalized anxiety disorder, specifically. In both analogue and clinical samples, Cassidy investigated the relationship between attachment (as measured by the Inventory of Adult Attachment [INVAA]; Lichtenstein & Cassidy, 1991) and a diagnosis of generalized anxiety disorder. In the analogue sample, participants with symptoms of the disorder reported experiencing significantly higher rejection and either role reversal or enmeshment in childhood and greater anger and vulnerability related to their mothers in adulthood than did the nonanxious participants. In the clinical sample, participants with generalized anxiety disorder reported greater role reversal or enmeshment in childhood, more anger and vulnerability related to their mothers in adulthood, and fewer childhood memories than controls reported. Although the attachment measure (i.e., the INVAA) used by Cassidy does not measure secure versus insecure attachment, it is suggestive of a connection between attachment and generalized anxiety disorder and provides an impetus and direction for future studies.

Parental Characteristics

Parental anxiety has been demonstrated to be predictive of anxiety disorders. Anxious individuals are more likely than their nonanxious peers to have an anxious parent (Last, Hersen, Kazdin, Francis, & Grubb, 1987; Turner, Beidel, & Costello, 1987; Weissman, Leckman, Merikangas, Gammon, & Prusoff, 1984). Also, parents with anxiety disorders are more likely to have offspring who are at increased risk for anxiety (Rosenbaum et al., 1993). However, parental anxiety is likely to be a factor that is not directly, but indirectly, linked to offspring anxiety via genetics (e.g., temperament) or environmental factors (e.g., parenting style; Donovan & Spence, 2000). In a similar vein, research has suggested a familial link among anxiety disorders in adulthood. Numerous twin studies have demonstrated that genetics account for 30 to 40% of the variance in anxious symptomatology and anxiety disorder (e.g., Andrews, Stewart, Allen, & Henderson, 1990; Andrews, Stewart, Morris-Yates, Holt, & Henderson, 1990; Jardine, Martin, & Henderson, 1984; Kendler, Neale, Kessler, Heath, & Eaves, 1992; Torgersen, 1983; Tyrer, Alexander, Remington, & Riley, 1987). Several studies appear to suggest the inheritance of a general predisposition rather than the heritability of any one or more individual disorders (e.g., Andrews, Stewart, Morris-Yates, et al., 1990; Torgersen, 1983).

Several parenting variables have also been associated with the anxiety disorders. For example, Barrett, Dadds, Rapee, and Ryan (1996) found that parents of anxious children were more likely to reinforce avoidant strategies than were other parents. In this study, children were presented with ambiguous scenarios (e.g., approaching a group of laughing children) and asked about their likely response to the situation. The children were again asked about their likely response after a 5-minute family discussion of the scenario. Following the discussion, anxious children were significantly more likely to provide an avoidant response than were oppositional and control children. Thus, it appears that parents of anxious children may encourage or support avoidant behaviors (Dadds, Barrett, Rapee, & Ryan, 1996).

Some research evidence suggests that, compared with nonanxious control participants, adults with social phobia recalled less family socializing (Rapee & Melville, 1997). Retrospective questionnaire studies have indicated that parental characteristics such as overcontrol are associated with anxiety (see Rapee, 1997, for a review). In an investigation of parental rearing behaviors and anxiety symptoms in nonclinical children, Muris and Merckelbach (1998) found that both child perceptions of parental control and anxious rearing were correlated with increases in anxious symptomatology, especially symptoms of generalized anxiety disorder. Observational studies of parent–child interactions have revealed some clear differences between the interactions of parents of anxiety-disordered children and parents of nonclinical controls (Khrone & Hock, 1991; Siqueland, Kendall, & Steinberg, 1996). For example, Hudson and Rapee (2001) found that parents of anxious children were more involved and more intrusive during a difficult cognitive task than were parents of nonclinical children. Rapee (2001) has suggested that this style of parenting may occur partially in response to the child's inhibited nature and, additionally, may serve to reinforce the child's inhibited temperament.

Peer Influences

Children's peer relations and interactions provide the basis for the development of important skills (e.g., assertiveness, social competence, and altruism; Hartup, 1978) and are related to current and future behavioral adjustment (Kupersmidt, Coie, & Dodge, 1990). Peers often serve as "control agents" for one another, punishing or ignoring undesirable and nonnormative behaviors and promoting socially and culturally appropriate ones through reinforcement (see Harris, 1995, for a review of the importance of peer groups in child and adolescent development). Many behaviors (e.g., prosocial, aggressive) may be shaped and modified through exposure to peers who serve as models and "cognitive and behavioral change agents" (Harris, 1995; Rubin, LeMare, & Lollis, 1990; Rubin & Mills, 1988). Thus, anxious children who befriend anxious peers may not be pressured to take risks, whereas anxious peers who associate with nonanxious peers may, in fact, be shaped to behave more courageously. Similarly, anxious adults who associate with low-risk-taking peer groups may be molded toward more avoidant and anxious behavior.

Numerous research studies demonstrate that social withdrawal is correlated with anxiety (e.g., Rubin, 1985; Strauss et al., 1986). Similarly, social reservedness has been found to be associated with anxiety, vulnerability, submissiveness, lack of adventuresomeness, and negative self-perceptions of social, cognitive, physical, and general attributes (Hartup, 1983; Rubin, 1985). Hartup speculated that these negative self-perceptions may generalize to the social realm, resulting in impaired peer interactions. Given the importance of peer interactions and the link between social withdrawal and anxiety, some researchers (e.g., Morris, Messer, & Gross, 1995) have begun to investigate the utility of pairing peer-neglected children with popular children in order to improve neglected children's sociometric status and social interactions. Neglected peers were paired with popular peers and participated in twelve 15-minute play sessions over 4 weeks. Outcome and one-month maintenance analyses demonstrated that, relative to controls, the neglected peers experienced significant improvements in sociometric status and positive peer interactions (Morris et al., 1995). This research underscores the relationship between social withdrawal and anxiety and lends support to the notion that peers may indeed shape the behaviors of anxious children.

Traumatic and Stressful Life Events

Traumatic and stressful life events have been identified as factors that may precipitate anxious distress throughout the life span. Individuals have been found to demonstrate increases in anxiety, somatic complaints, sleep disturbance, intrusive thoughts, and avoidance behaviors (Dollinger, 1986; Dollinger, O'Donnell, & Staley, 1984), as well as increases in the incidence of anxiety disorders (Dollinger et al., 1984; Maes, Mylle, Delmeire, & Janca 2001; Terr, 1981; Yule & Williams, 1990), in the aftermath of traumatic events such as earthquakes, fires, and storms. Several researchers have suggested that anxiety-disordered individuals may experience significantly more stressful life events (e.g., parental separations or divorce, death of a family member) than do non-anxiety-disordered individuals (Bandekow et al., 2002; Benjamin et al., 1990; Goodyer & Altham, 1991; Rapee & Szollos,

1997), and the occurrence of stressful life events has been found to be associated with an increased risk of anxiety disorder across the life span (e.g., Blazer, Hughes, & George, 1987; deBeurs et al., 2001; Tiet et al., 1998). However, some research has found that the perceived impact, and *not* the number of stressful life events per se, is predictive of an anxiety disorder (Rapee, Litwin, & Barlow, 1990).

Classical conditioning has been suggested as the primary means for the development of such pathological anxiety (Spence, 1996; Spielberger, Pollans, & Worden, 1984). However, not all individuals who experience traumatic or stressful life events go on to develop anxious distress or anxiety disorders. Thus, research has begun to identify the protective or buffering influences that serve to moderate the development of anxiety.

PROTECTIVE FACTORS

In addition to factors that place an individual at risk for anxiety are factors that may protect him or her against the development of an anxiety disorder. Research on protective factors is scarce in comparison to research on risk factors. Two bodies of research have emerged: (a) research on the protective effects of social support and (b) research on the relationship between coping style and anxiety.

Social Support

Social support appears to moderate the relationship between negative life events and the development of anxiety (e.g., Cowen, Pedro-Carroll, & Alpert-Gillis, 1990; Hill, Levermore, Twaite, & Jones, 1996; White, Bruce, Farrell, & Kliewer, 1998). For example, social support appears to be a protective factor in the development of posttraumatic stress disorder (PTSD). In a study of combat veterans, for instance, those diagnosed with the condition reported significantly less social support (e.g., more problems with self-disclosure and expressiveness to significant others, physical aggression against partners, and difficulty adjusting to relationships) than both combat veterans without PTSD and noncombat veterans reported (Carroll, Rueger, Foy, & Donahoe, 1985). Thus, greater available social support may result in a reduced incidence of symptomatology of the disorder or of the disorder itself. Barlow (2001) has suggested that social support may be a protective factor in *all* anxiety disorders.

Coping Style

Coping has been defined as "constantly changing cognitive and behavioral efforts to manage specific external or internal demands that are appraised as taxing or exceeding the resources of the person" (Lazarus & Folkman, 1984, p. 141). Coping is a process purported to mediate the relationship between stressful events and psychological well-being (Folkman, Lazarus, Gruen, & DeLongis, 1986). Coping "styles" (i.e., individual differences in the psychological and physiological reactions to objective stressors) have been, and continue to be, defined in the research literature. Folkman and Lazarus (1980) have distinguished between emotion-focused coping (attempts to reduce emotional distress, often by avoidance or distraction) and problem-focused coping (attempts to change the source of the problem). These coping styles have been investigated in relation to anxiety disorders and symptomatology. Generally, the means by which one attempts to cope with an anxiety-eliciting situation (often, by emotion-focused or avoidant coping) is associated with anxious symptomatology and disorder (e.g., Jeavons, Horne, & Greenwood, 2000; Warman & Kendall, 2000; Whatley, Foreman, & Richards, 1998; Zeidner & Ben-Zur, 1994). The use of problem-focused coping may serve as an important protective factor; however, additional research is needed to fully elucidate the importance of this style of coping. Similarly, cognitive appraisals have been investigated as important determinants of anxious distress. One type of appraisal, perception of the controllability of events, appears to modulate the risk for both anxious distress and disorder. More specifically, Chorpita and Barlow (1998) postulate that a lack of control in one's early environment may create a psychological vulnerability that places one at risk for later anxiety.

It is likely that these risk and protective factors do not exert independent or mutually exclusive effects on anxiety. In fact, interactive effects are deemed probable and are ill researched (Coie et al., 1993; Donovan & Spence, 2000; Greenberg et al., 2001). Several etiological theories have recently emerged in the literature that attempt to explain the multiple and interactive pathways leading to anxiety disorder (e.g., Chorpita & Barlow, 1998; Hudson & Rapee, in press; Manassis & Bradley, 1994; Rubin & Mills, 1991). Donovan and Spence (2000) suggest that future research should "examine both the combinations of risk factors and the processes involved in order to achieve a more holistic understanding of the etiological processes involved" (p. 513).

WHY PRIMARY PREVENTION
OF ANXIETY?

The aim of primary prevention is to promote general mental health rather than to target specific disorders or categories of disorder. However, now that research has begun to find causal and maintaining factors for specific disorders, primary prevention efforts can be more focused and disorder specific. Given the relatively high rates of anxiety symptomatology and disorders (e.g.,

Verhulst, van der Ende, Ferdinand, & Kasius, 1997), primary prevention of anxiety appears warranted.

Prevention programs aimed at reducing the prevalence of anxiety disorders in the general population have advantages over selective and indicated preventions. First, prevention aimed at the general public avoids the stigmatization potentially associated with interventions that select certain individuals from the population. Despite community education about mental disorder and psychological intervention, receiving mental health services continues to be associated with weakness in today's society. Universal programs that provide intervention at a population level prevent individuals from being labeled in such ways. Second, because our knowledge of risk and protective factors relating to anxiety is just developing and is by no means exhaustive, no one can be sure that any particular selective or indicated prevention program is targeting all individuals who would otherwise develop an anxiety disorder. Prevention programs frequently identify individuals as at risk when they obtain a particular score on a given screening instrument. In a recent school-based survey of ninth-grade students, Dierker et al. (2001) evaluated the ability of a number of self-report questionnaires to detect children with anxiety and depressive disorders. A random sample of students who scored below the 80th percentile on the questionnaire was interviewed with structured diagnostic techniques designed to assess anxiety and depressive disorders (Ambrosini, Metz, Prabucki, & Lee, 1989; Silverman & Albano, 1997). Thirty-five percent of those children not identified by elevated scores on the self-reported anxiety measures met the criteria for a disorder, with 17% diagnosed with more than one anxiety disorder. These results indicate that anxious or "at-risk" children may be missed through such selection methods.

Population-based interventions, however, can be both time consuming and costly. Much of the resources go to waste on individuals who, without intervention, would remain free of disorder. Nevertheless, fear and anxiety are universal human experiences, and learning to manage these emotions more effectively may produce benefits populationwide. Moreover, some studies have reported 12-month prevalence rates of anxiety disorders in children, adolescents, and adults that range from 12% to 17% (Anderson, Williams, McGee, & Silva, 1987; Benjamin et al., 1990; Fergusson, Horwood, & Lynskey, 1993; Kessler et al., 1994). With such high rates of disorder and elevated distress, it may be worthwhile to "immunize" against this disorder, given its cost to society.

Despite the prevalence and cost, there have been very few primary prevention studies specifically designed to target anxiety disorders. There have, however, been numerous primary prevention programs designed to target (a) general mental health or emotional functioning, (b) problems associated with anxiety (e.g., substance abuse), (c) stress, and (d) traumatic stress. Following an examination of these areas of research, studies specifically targeting anxiety will be reviewed.

Primary Prevention Aimed at General Mental Health or Emotional Functioning

Given the high rates of comorbidity of disorders, particularly in children, it is possible that targeting general emotional or mental health functioning can prevent multiple forms of psychopathology, including anxiety. Unfortunately, however, many of the interventions designed to target general mental health and emotional functioning have failed to measure anxious symptomatology either pre- or posttreatment (e.g., Greenberg, Kusche, Cook, & Quamma, 1995). Hence, one can only speculate about the potential benefits one would reap from these types of programs aimed at preventing anxiety symptoms or disorders.

Most primary prevention studies have occurred in schools and are aimed at preventing psychopathology in childhood and throughout the life span. These prevention programs have components that overlap with anxiety interventions (e.g., problem solving, relaxation training, social competence). Targeting problem-solving skills, for example, is likely to have an impact on anxiety: A child who is able to choose among alternatives, rather than either worrying about the situation or feeling limited to an avoidant response, is likely to experience less anxiety. Also, a child who develops increased confidence in social situations is likely to be more able to confront anxiety-provoking events, resulting in lower anxiety.

Durlak and Wells (1997) conducted a meta-analysis of primary prevention mental health programs for children and adolescents and concluded that "most interventions significantly reduced problems and significantly increased competencies, and affected functioning in multiple adjustment domains" (p. 137). Further, the improvements that occurred as a result of primary prevention efforts were maintained over time (see Durlak, 1998). For example, the Promoting Alternative Thinking Strategies (PATHS; Greenberg et al., 1995) program is a general program for school-aged children that teaches cognitive skill building to promote social and emotional competence. For the majority of the school year, a classroom teacher administers the program, which is not aimed specifically at internalizing symptoms, but includes some components that would be expected to affect anxiety symptoms. For example, the program teaches children to recognize and regulate their emotions and also teaches social problem solving. Evaluated with second- and third-grade students, the program demonstrated that children experienced significant changes in emotional understanding and expression by the end of the school year. Greenberg and colleagues also found that significant improvements in self-reported conduct problems and teacher reports of adaptive behavior and social problem solving were maintained 1 and 2 years after the intervention (Greenberg et al., 2001). The success of this program, while providing some good evidence regarding the efficacy of programs designed to promote social problem-solving abilities, affords only limited information regarding the prevention of anxiety disorders.

Primary Prevention Aimed at Problems Associated With Anxiety

There have been a number of primary prevention efforts that target disorders other than anxiety, such as depression and substance abuse. Within school-based primary prevention programs, most of the studies have focused on childhood externalizing problems, with very few studies examining the prevention of internalizing symptoms (see Greenberg et al., 2001, for a review). Nevertheless, these programs may have a secondary impact on anxiety. For example, aspects of the programs involve problem-solving skills and relaxation exercises, both of which may help to reduce anxiety symptoms as well as the targeted behaviors (i.e., externalizing behaviors). We discuss the anxiety-relevant components of these programs. We do not, however, review universal prevention programs that are targeted specifically at depression (e.g., Klingman & Hochdorf, 1993; Orbach & Bar-Joseph, 1993), because these programs are covered in chapter 8 (this volume). Given the established high levels of co-occurrence of the symptoms of anxiety and depression, we assume that these programs could also be helpful in reducing anxiety.

Shure and Spivack (1982) designed and evaluated an interpersonal cognitive problem-solving program titled "I Can Problem Solve" (ICPS). This program is taught within the classroom and is intended to prevent impulsive and socially inhibited behaviors in Black 4- and 5-year-olds. Children were categorized as impulsive, inhibited, or adjusted, using teacher ratings of behavior. Inhibited children were those who, according to the teacher, rarely expressed impatience, aggression, anger, or distress. The study compared children who received no treatment with children who completed the ICPS intervention in preschool, kindergarten, or both. The results of the comparison showed that all children in the treatment condition—even those identified as inhibited and impulsive—improved their cognitive problem-solving abilities and peer relationships (e.g., cooperation) significantly and decreased their impulsivity and inhibition, regardless of whether they were trained in preschool, kindergarten, or both. Gains were maintained at the 1-year follow-up. In addition, a prevention effect was clearly shown, with adjusted children who completed 1 or 2 years of the program being less likely to show signs of impulsivity or inhibition at 1- and 2-year follow-ups, compared with controls (Shure & Spivack, 1979, 1982, Spivack & Shure, 1974). Although this study did not measure anxiety symptoms or pathology, inhibition has been linked with anxiety disorders.

Botvin, Baker, Dusenbury, Tortu, and Botvin (1990) implemented the Life Skills Training (LST) program for 4,466 junior high school students. The LST, aimed at preventing substance abuse, includes a section on anxiety management that involves teaching children anxiety recognition and relaxation strategies. The program also includes a 15-unit intervention for 1 year, with additional booster sessions in the second and third years. In addition to measuring changes in attitude, knowledge, skill use, substance use, self-esteem, and self-efficacy, Botvin and colleagues' study measured social anxiety. Fifty-six schools were randomized to one of three conditions: (a) no treatment, (b) intervention with teachers who received a 1-day workshop and supervision or feedback regarding each session, and (c) intervention with teachers who received a 2-hour training video and no session-by-session feedback. Although several significant improvements (e.g., reductions in substance use) were evident in both of the intervention conditions, no significant differences were found between the control and intervention groups in the use of relaxation skills, social anxiety, or self-efficacy. This finding is disappointing with respect to the ability of substance use prevention programs to reduce anxiety symptoms. However, given the small number of studies measuring anxiety symptoms in prevention programs aimed at general mental health (or problems associated with anxiety), further research is important to substantiate the findings.

Primary Prevention of Stress

Numerous primary prevention studies have attempted to reduce general stress levels in both children and adults. *Stress* is a ubiquitous term used to describe elevated levels of anxiety and depression. More specifically, stress is similar to symptoms of generalized anxiety disorder (i.e., worry about performance, health, minor matters, etc.). Although stress and generalized anxiety disorder are not identical, there is some overlap. Thus, primary prevention programs aimed at reducing general stress are reviewed.

Children and Adolescents

Dubow, Schmidt, McBride, Edwards, and Merk (1993) evaluated a 13-session school-based prevention developed to teach fourth-grade children coping skills to deal with stressful situations. The program was referred to as the "I CAN DO" program. Children were taught skills to deal with specific stressful experiences, such as parental separation or divorce, loss of a loved one, moving to a new home or school, self-care, and feeling different. A psychoeducational component of the program entails learning its acronym, which involves Identifying the problem; generating Choices that are available to deal with the problem; paying Attention to the information and consequences; Narrowing down the choices; Doing what needs to be done; and Observing the outcome. Video material, group discussions, and games are also used to help the children apply the coping skills they learn to different stressors. In addition, the program encourages children to seek out social support networks to help deal with various stressors. The program was evaluated in a sample of 92 fourth-grade children, half of whom received the intervention immediately and half of whom were in the control group, which experienced a delay in intervention. After the intervention, significant changes were observed in the children's ability to generate effective solutions to hypothetical stressful situations. Children's self-efficacy in enacting positive coping responses to the hypothetical stressors was also improved compared with that of the control group. The effects were maintained at a 5-month follow-up. It is important to note, however, that this evaluation was based on the children's reports and not actual observed behavior.

Stress management programs have also been implemented within the school setting. For example, Lohaus, Klein-Hessling, and Shebar (1997) compared psychoeducation only, relaxation only, problem solving only, and a combined group (psychoeducation, relaxation, and problem solving) intervention to a wait-list condition in a sample of third- and fourth-graders. The results showed that the interventions led to significant increases in knowledge about stress symptoms or coping strategies and improvements in somatic and psychological well-being, whereas those on the wait list experienced no such gains. On the basis of all of the assessment measures, the problem-solving program showed the greatest improvement, followed by the combined version, the psychoeducation condition, and the relaxation-only condition. Similarly, Hiebert, Kirby, and Jaknavorian (1989) compared progressive muscular relaxation with an attention control condition (career education) in a group of eighth graders. Both conditions showed improvements on self-reported stress levels. No changes in state anxiety were observed for either condition; however, those participating in progressive muscular relaxation showed a significant improvement in trait anxiety that was not observed in the control condition. Furthermore, the progressive muscular relaxation group showed greater increases in academic self-concept than was evident in the control condition. The study also compared the progressive muscular relaxation program with health fitness programs in eleventh- and twelfth-graders. The results showed that the progressive muscular relaxation program produced greater improvements in stress symptoms and in state and trait anxiety, compared with the health fitness programs. The authors noted that the older children (eleventh- and twelfth-graders) showed greater compliance with the program, compared with children in the eighth grade, and hence demonstrated more favorable results.

Adults

Numerous primary prevention stress management programs are implemented in the workplace to reduce work-related stress, yet few have been evaluated with the use of randomized clinical trials. In a review of the primary prevention programs aimed at decreasing employee stress, Godfrey, Bonds, Kraus, Wiener, and Toth (1990) concluded that strategies such as time management, coping strategies, goal setting, and problem resolution were effective in reducing stress in the workplace. In addition, the authors' meta-analysis showed that other strategies, such as scheduled staff meetings, relaxation techniques, and aerobic exercise, can also reduce employee stress. In another meta-analysis, Kaluza (1997) reported that the interventions produced mean effect sizes from .38 to .53 on subjective health status and mood states after treatment and even greater effect sizes at long-term follow-up.

Other studies have implemented stress management courses as part of college curricula or the workplace, but without a controlled or randomized controlled design (e.g., Kline & Snow, 1994; Romano, 1984). Although these programs frequently show significant changes in anxiety, coping responses, or symptomatology, it is difficult to draw conclusions regarding the efficacy of the programs because of their limited designs. In addition, the measures used to evaluate improvements following stress management programs tend to focus on constructs such as coping styles or general emotional functioning; hence, the efficacy of these programs in preventing anxiety symptoms and disorders is unclear. Future research examining their efficacy in preventing disorders and associated symptoms is warranted.

Primary Prevention of Anxiety in High-Risk Situations

Interventions designed to prevent anxiety or stress during stressful and traumatic situations (e.g., medical or dental procedures, the transition to a new school, dealing with war) are also considered primary prevention, in that the intervention occurs prior to the specific occurrence of a stressful event. Research examining primary prevention efforts prior to specific developmental stages and traumatic events (e.g., war) will be reviewed.

Specific Developmental Stages

Several general programs have targeted children at particular stages in their development, with the understanding that specific transitions may in fact elevate levels of stress across the age group (Barrios & Shigetomi, 1980). Elias and colleagues (Bruene-Butler, Hampson, Elias, Clabby, & Schuyler, 1997; Elias et al., 1986; Elias, Gara, Schuyler, Branden-Muller, & Sayette, 1991) developed a program (Improving Social Awareness—Social Problem Solving) for children making the transition to middle school. The program was developed to enable children to handle imminent transitions by enhancing the children's decision-making skills, self-control skills, group participation, and social awareness. Since its inception, the program has been adapted for use across all grades and has accrued empirical support in controlled trials (cited in Bruene-Butler et al., 1997). Children in the intervention groups showed significantly more effectiveness in dealing with stressors than did children in the control group (Elias et al., 1986). Although no anxiety symptoms were measured, children in the prevention groups showed lower rates of alcohol use, violent behavior in boys, and tobacco use and vandalism in girls when they were followed up in high school 4 to 6 years later (Elias et al., 1991).

Another program, the School Transitional Environment Project (STEP), was developed to prevent stress and psychopathology during the transition to middle school and to high school (Felner & Adan, 1988; Felner et al., 1993; Felner, Gitner, & Primavera, 1982). Rather than teaching specific skills, the STEP program focuses more on developing ecological change. Learning communities were established within the school, and students were grouped into cohorts. The homeroom teacher played the role of advisor, administrator, supporter, and counselor. Several randomized, controlled studies have evaluated the program. Felner et al. (1982) reported that, whereas the control students showed a decline in self-concept over the period of the intervention, those in the program exhibited significant improvements in their level of stress.

Posttraumatic Stress

As mentioned earlier in the chapter, experiencing one or more traumatic events is a known risk factor for anxiety disorders. Primary prevention includes programs aimed at PTSD that take place before the trauma occurs. A review of combat stress disorders in the U.S. Air Force indicated that rest periods, intervals between missions, control of risk, and length of tour are several measures the Air Force takes in the primary prevention of combat stress (Rundell, Holloway, Ursano, & Jones, 1990). There is a dearth of literature on pretrauma prevention for high-risk occupations other than the army. As Melançon and Boyer (1999) point out, there is limited evidence regarding the usefulness of "identified risk factors" for the primary prevention of PTSD. Those authors also emphasized the importance of focusing on protective factors (e.g., social support). Given that the majority of research in the prevention of posttraumatic stress has focused on prevention *following* the traumatic event, increasing the individual's protective factors *prior to* the trauma may prove to be a worthwhile endeavor.

Primary Prevention of Anxiety

Only a handful of studies have been devoted to the primary prevention of anxiety and its disorders (Barrett & Turner, 2001; Cradock, Cotler, & Jason, 1978; Lowry-Webster, Barrett, & Dadds, 2001). Prevention programs aimed specifically at anxiety disorders are likely to affect the incidence and prevalence not only of anxiety, but also of comorbid conditions. Several studies have suggested that anxiety predates depression (e.g., Brady & Kendall, 1992; Dobson, 1985); thus, implementing a prevention program that reduces anxiety disorders will likely also affect the formation of new cases of depression. Recently, research has indicated that child anxiety is associated with later substance abuse (Kendall & Kessler, 2002). Thus, targeting anxiety in prevention efforts will likely affect later substance-use problems as well. The few studies that have evaluated primary prevention programs for anxiety will be reviewed.

Recently, Barrett and Turner (2001) published the first primary prevention program designed specifically to prevent anxiety disorders in children. The FRIENDS program was developed from a cognitive–behavioral intervention for anxiety-disordered youth and includes 10 weekly sessions, four parent education sessions, and two booster sessions conducted 1 and 3 months following the program's end. Using FRIENDS as an acronym, the children are taught how to manage their anxiety: Feeling worried; Relax and feel good; Inner thoughts; Explore plans of action; Nice work, reward yourself; Don't forget to practice; Stay cool. Barrett and Turner (2001) evaluated the program with sixth-grade (10–12 years) children in 10 schools. Two intervention conditions were used (one delivered by a psychologist, one by a teacher) and compared with a monitoring-only condition. There were 188 children in the psychologist-led intervention, 263 in the teacher-led intervention, and 137 in the control condition. Significant improvements in self-reported anxiety were evident in both intervention conditions relative to the control condition. The program also demonstrated slight improvements in self-reported depression symptoms in the psychologist-led intervention and in the control condition, but not in the teacher-delivered intervention.

One of the arguments against primary prevention is that a universal program may not be focused enough to have an impact on those children who are at risk, because the "dosage" of effective treatment may be too low. Hence, Barrett and Turner (2001) performed a post hoc analysis of children who scored in the clinical range on self-reported anxiety measures. Although the sample size was too small to conduct statistical comparisons, the data hint that high-risk children in the intervention group were more likely to move into the healthy range than were high-risk children in the monitoring condition.

In a similar study, Lowry-Webster et al. (2001) conducted a teacher-delivered FRIENDS program for children aged 10 to 13 years. Children either were assigned to an intervention group or were placed on a wait list on the basis of the school that they attended. Both children in the intervention group and children in the monitoring group showed significant changes on one self-report measure of anxiety (Spence Children's Anxiety Scale [SCAS]; Spence, 1998), but not another (Revised Children's Manifest Anxiety Scale [RCMAS]). The changes from pre- to postintervention on the SCAS were significantly greater for those receiving the intervention than those in the control group. Significant changes in the SCAS were evident regardless of whether the child exhibited high levels of anxiety at pretreatment. The intervention was effective only in reducing symptoms of depression in children reporting high levels of anxiety prior to treatment. Children identified as being at risk for anxiety (i.e., those who scored in the clinical range on the SCAS) were more likely to move into the clinical range if they were on the wait list.

The two programs just described have shown promise with respect to the prevention of anxiety disorders in children. Another study, however, has produced less positive results. The study followed a prevention program aimed at public-speaking anxiety in a group of 40 ninth-grade high school students (Cradock et al., 1978). The study compared both a gradual-exposure group and a cognitive-rehearsal group with a control group. No significant differences on any of the behavioral measures of anxiety before and after intervention were found for the intervention or control group; however, children in the cognitive-rehearsal group reported more confidence following the intervention. The limited sample size of the study, however, suggests the need for replication.

Taken together, the preceding studies provide preliminary evidence that cognitive–behavioral interventions aimed at the primary prevention of anxiety disorders are beneficial in reducing anxiety in the general population, as well as in those children who are at risk for anxiety disorders. Future research should conduct longitudinal assessments to determine the long-term benefits of primary prevention. Another direction for further research is to determine the optimal time to intervene with such programs as the FRIENDS program.

The Ultimate Primary Prevention Program

At present, primary prevention programs are offered to isolated groups of individuals. Ultimately, primary prevention should be provided populationwide and across the life span in order to truly make an impact on all individuals. This effort would entail the interventions being routinely implemented as part of (a) prenatal parenting classes, (b) the school curriculum, and (c) workplace health and safety. In addition, the media (e.g., television, radio, the Internet, the printed press, cinema) can be used as a vital tool in relaying the information to the masses. Just as the media are currently being used to educate parents and children about the dangers of smoking, media campaigns that promote the identification of anxiety and the implementation of skills to face and conquer anxiety or fear could be promoted.

Nevertheless, it may be premature to begin implementing populationwide programs without additional knowledge of the efficacy of such programs, gained through methodologically rigorous evaluations. Research to date is highly limited in this regard, with only a few studies having utilized randomized controlled designs or measured symptomatology of anxiety before and after the intervention. Future research, aimed at improving our understanding of risk and protective factors, is also essential to developing more effective primary prevention programs.

Given our current knowledge of risk and protective factors for the development of anxiety disorders, what components would likely be incorporated into an ultimate prevention program? Donovan and Spence (2000) outline a proactive developmental–ecological prevention paradigm developed by Winett (1998) and apply the paradigm to childhood anxiety. In their analysis, they provide prevention suggestions on the personal, interpersonal, organizational or environmental, and institutional levels. In addition to using preventative programs that teach both child coping skills and parenting skills, the paradigm outlines the need for government and other organizational policies that emphasize the importance of children's mental health by allocating funding to mental health prevention.

An ultimate primary prevention program would be designed to target specific risk and protective factors associated with anxiety. Two possible methods of preventing the development of anxiety disorders would be to remove the genetic vulnerability of anxiety and to remove or reduce threats from the environment. Since such methods are not currently possible, a primary prevention program must work to modify other factors in the environment that are known to either increase or decrease the likelihood of anxiety disorder. Table 5.1 lists a number of potential interventions, derived from our current knowledge of risk, protective, and maintaining factors, that could be utilized in the primary prevention of anxiety and implemented via the mechanisms described in this chapter. The list is by no means exhaustive: There is a multitude of selective and indicated prevention efforts that could also be implemented in the ultimate prevention of anxiety, such as providing education or intervention for individuals who are at risk (e.g., children of parents with an anxiety disorder).

CAUTIONS TO CONSIDER:
DOES PREVENTION HAVE A DOUBLE EDGE?

On the positive side, prevention is consistent with a humane philosophy. Prevention rests on a well-articulated argument and can satisfy society's general desire to be proactive and helpful. Indeed, how can there be cautions when one wants to reduce distress and disorder by intervening in a positive manner for large groups of people and improve lives by minimizing the unwanted and deleterious effects of anxiety? In an idealized sense, intervening and educating the population could prevent unnecessary emotional problems. Optimism aside, however, are there less positive, or even negative, consequences that may be associated with the primary prevention of anxiety? Although our conclusion is consistent with the overall merits of prevention, there are concerns that are worthy of consideration.

TABLE 5.1
Primary Prevention Strategies Designed to Target
Specific Risk and Protective Factors

Factors	Main finding	Primary prevention strategy
Individual characteristics	Cognitive bias toward threat	Provide education about anxiety in order to increase an individual's ability to recognize anxious affect and associated somatic symptoms to avoid misinterpretation of symptoms; teach skills to challenge unrealistic threat interpretations and consider realistic alternative explanations to situation; provide skills to adequately assess threat in one's environment; provide skills increase perceived ability to cope with and control environment.
	Temperamental style of avoiding rather than approaching novel or potentially threatening situations	Teach skills to increase ability to generate multiple solutions to a situation and choose approach and avoidance strategies when appropriate; education about managing anxiety to conquer an unrealistic fear one must face.
	Avoidant or emotion-focused coping style	Teach skills that utilize problem-solving approaches to cope with fear.
Family, peer, and other environmental factors	Insecure attachment	Educate parents to promote secure parent–child attachments.
	Parental anxiety	Teach parents skills to manage their own anxiety.
	Environmental support of avoidance behavior	Teach skills that allow individuals to provide support for anxious family members, friends, or colleagues; skills that promote approach not avoidant behavior.
	Peer influences via shaping	Make ecological changes within the school and workplace environment, routinely pairing anxious, inhibited individuals with adjusted individuals.
	Peer victimization	Encourage acceptance of differences (e.g., within schools) to reduce the potential for victimization of anxious individuals.
	Lack of social support	Provide education regarding the benefits of increased social support—in particular, how to develop and make use of such support in times of stress.

For example, will universal prevention, if effective, not only do what it is intended to do, namely, reduce anxious distress among those so disposed, but also do what it is *not* intended to do, homogenize the emotional experiences of youth? Variability—in performance, skills, emotional reaction, and life in general—is to be applauded. Is it possible that a universal intervention program will truncate variability and place limits on the human emotional experience? One might, in an extreme case, try to make such an argument; however, a more plausible outcome lies in the homogeneity of managing unwanted arousal, not in an overflattening of all affective experience.

Are there risks associated with making people anxious by exposing them to feared stimuli? One consistent finding from the literature on the treatment of anxiety disorders in both children (e.g., Kendall et al., 1997) and adults (e.g., Borkovec & Costello, 1993; Hope, Heimberg, & Bruch, 1995) is that exposure tasks contribute meaningfully to the beneficial gains linked to intervention. Note that, by design, the exposure tasks create anxiety for the participants. Exposure tasks not only provide opportunities to learn and apply coping skills, but also offer multiple opportunities to begin to overcome unwanted avoidance. The exposure tasks can thus be said to lead to mastery. Is such mastery the product of success for an individual who is anxiously aroused and facing a challenge? If so, then can we produce a truly preventive effect without at times making participants genuinely anxious? Do we need to create and face genuine emotional arousal in order for it to be mastered, and if so, would such arousal be able to be a part of a prevention program?

Are there potential iatrogenic effects of prevention programs? Consider the primary prevention applied against a different condition—say, childhood impulsivity. Parents and professionals can observe the undesirable consequences of impulsivity in a child's school, peer, and social situations, and, consistent with normal development, there is a naturally occurring trajectory toward less impulsivity over the years. The prevention of impulsivity would be a desirable intervention, because it would be prosocial and would advance development. Such an intervention would be designed to help youths control their impulses, be more aware of the effects of their behavior, and use more forethought in their action plans. However, an intervention that is designed to prevent impulsivity and is applied universally would teach more cautious, step-by-step-approach thinking not only to those impulsive youths in the program, but also (being universal) to youths who may be somewhat obsessive in their style of thinking. One would want to see more caution in the actions of impulsive youths, of course, but one would not want to see more caution being taught to obsessive children. For such children, *less* caution may be the prescription. Although this example is about impulsivity and not anxiety, it nevertheless illustrates that a universally applied program can have iatrogenic effects.

Now, what about the universal prevention of anxiety? Are such programs open to criticism based on iatrogenic effects? If one considers anxious youths to be overcontrolled and unwilling to take reasonable risks, then part of an intervention directed at reducing anxiety would be to encourage increased risk taking. Note, however, that this preferred component of a program for anxiety may have unwanted effects on children who are already predisposed to take risks. Fortunately, not all of the skills that would be universally taught to manage anxiety have as great a negative edge: Whether they be taught to persons who warrant a diagnosis, to persons who may or may not experience transient distressing anxiety, or to persons within the normative range, it is likely that all of the recipients of the preventive intervention can use skills to manage instances of unwanted anxious arousal. As mentioned before, fear is a universal human experience. The goal of intervention is not the *removal* of all anxious arousal, but the imparting of information and skills that empower one to be able to *manage* distressing levels of anxiety when they occur.

In sum, a number of risk factors and protective factors are likely to be the focus of prevention programs aimed at reducing the incidence of anxiety disorders. Although numerous risk factors have been identified, the research on protective factors is sparse. Research has begun to give attention to prevention efforts. However, the few primary prevention interventions that have been conducted have limitations that make generalizing them to primary prevention of anxiety disorders difficult at best. Still, a handful of primary prevention programs specifically targeting anxiety provide preliminary support for the utility of cognitive–behavioral approaches. Future research is needed to investigate the long-term effects of primary prevention of anxiety and to explore the advantages, limitations, and potential iatrogenic effects associated with such programs.

REFERENCES

Ambrosini, P. J., Metz, C., Prabucki, K., & Lee, J. C. (1989). Videotape reliability of the third revised edition of the K-SADS. *Journal of the American Academy of Child and Adolescent Psychiatry, 28,* 723–728.

Anderson, J. C., Williams, S., McGee, R., & Silva, P. A. (1987). DSM-III disorders in preadolescent children. Prevalence in a large sample from a general population. *Archives of General Psychiatry, 44,* 69–76.

Andrews, G., Stewart, G. W., Allen, R., & Henderson, A. S. (1990). The genetics of six neurotic disorders: A twin study. *Journal of Affective Disorders, 19,* 23–29.

Andrews, G., Stewart, G. W., Morris-Yates, A., Holt, P., & Henderson, A. S. (1990). Evidence for a general neurotic syndrome. *British Journal of Psychiatry, 157,* 6–12.

Bandekow, B., Spaeth, C., Alvarez Tichauer, G., Broocks, A., Hajak, G., & Ruether, E. (2002). Early traumatic life events, parental attitudes, family history, and birth risk factors in patients with panic disorder. *Comprehensive Psychiatry, 43,* 269–278.

Barlow, D. H. (2001). Anxiety and its disorders: The nature and treatment of anxiety and panic (2nd ed.). New York: Guilford.

Barrett, P., & Turner, C. (2001). Prevention of anxiety symptoms in primary school children: Preliminary results from universal school-based trial. *British Journal of Clinical Psychology, 40,* 399–410.

Barrett, P. M., Dadds, M. R., Rapee, R. M., & Ryan, S. M. (1996). Family enhancement of cognitive style in anxious and aggressive children. *Journal of Abnormal Child Psychology, 24,* 187–203.

Barrios, B. A., & Shigetomi, C. C. (1980). Coping skills training: Potential for prevention of fears and anxieties. *Behavior Therapy, 11,* 431–439.

Benjamin, R. S., Costello, E. J., & Warren, M. (1990). Anxiety disorders in a pediatric sample. *Journal of Anxiety Disorders, 4,* 293–316.

Biederman, J., Rosenbaum, J. F., Bolduc-Murphy, E. A., Faraone, S. V., Chaloff, J., Hirshfeld, D. R., & Kagan, J. (1993). A 3-year follow-up of children with and without behavioral inhibition. *Journal of the American Academy of Child and Adolescent Psychiatry, 32,* 814–821.

Biederman, J., Rosenbaum, J. F., Chaloff, J., & Kagan, J. (1995). Behavioral inhibition as a risk factor for anxiety disorders. In J. S. March (Ed.), *Anxiety disorders in children and adolescents* (pp. 61–81). New York: Guilford.

Blazer, D., Hughes, D., & George, L. K. (1987). Stressful life events and the onset of a generalized anxiety syndrome. *American Journal of Psychiatry, 144,* 1178–1183.

Borkovec, T., & Costello, E. (1993). Efficacy of applied relaxation and cognitive–behavioral therapy in the treatment of generalized anxiety disorder. *Journal of Consulting and Clinical Psychology, 61,* 611–619.

Botvin, G. J., Baker, E., Dusenbury, L., Tortu, S., & Botvin, E. M. (1990). Preventing adolescent drug abuse through a multimodal cognitive–behavioral approach: Results of a 3-year study. *Journal of Consulting and Clinical Psychology, 58,* 437–446.

Bowlby, J. (1982). Attachment and loss: Retrospect and prospect. *American Journal of Orthopsychiatry, 52*(4), 664–678.

Brady, E. U., & Kendall, P. C. (1992). Comorbidity of anxiety and depression in children and adolescents. *Psychological Bulletin, 111,* 244–255.

Bruene-Butler, L., Hampson, J., Elias, M., Clabby, J., & Schuyler, T. (1997). Improving Social Awareness–Social Problem Solving Project. In G. W. Albee & T. P. Gullotta (Eds.), *Primary prevention works: Issues in children's and families' lives* (pp. 239–267). Thousand Oaks, CA: Sage.

Butler, G., & Mathews, A. (1983). Cognitive process in anxiety. *Advances in Behaviour Research and Therapy, 5,* 51–62.

Carroll, E. M., Rueger, D. B., Foy, D. W., & Donahoe, C. P. (1985). Vietnam combat veterans with posttraumatic stress disorder: Analysis of marital and cohabitating adjustment. *Journal of Abnormal Psychology, 94,* 329–337.

Cassidy, J. (1995). Attachment and generalized anxiety disorder. In D. Cicchetti & S. L. Toth (Eds.), *Emotion, cognition, and representation* (pp. 343–370). Rochester, NY: University of Rochester Press.

Chorpita, B. F., & Barlow, D. H. (1998). The development of anxiety: The role of control in the early environment. *Psychological Bulletin, 124,* 3–21.

Coie, J. D., Watt, N. F., West, S. G., Hawkins, J. D., Asarnow, J. R., Markman, H. J., et al. (1993). The science of prevention: A conceptual framework and some directions for a national research program. *American Psychologist, 48,* 1013–1022.

Cole, D. A., Peeke, L. G., Martin, J. M., Truglio, R., & Seroczynski, A. D. (1998). A longitudinal look at the relation between depression and anxiety in children and adolescents. *Journal of Consulting and Clinical Psychology, 66,* 451–460.

Cowen, E. L., Pedro-Carroll, J. L., & Alpert-Gillis, L. J. (1990). Relationships between support and adjustment among children of divorce. *Journal of Child Psychology and Psychiatry and Allied Disciplines, 31,* 727–735.

Cradock, C., Cotler, S., & Jason, L. A. (1978). Primary prevention: Immunization of children for speech anxiety. *Cognitive Therapy and Research, 2,* 389–396.

Dadds, M. R., Barrett, P. M., Rapee, R. M., & Ryan, S. M. (1996). Family process and child anxiety and aggression: An observational analysis of the FEAR effect. *Journal of Abnormal Child Psychology, 24,* 715–734.

Dadds, M. R., Holland, D. E., Barrett, P. M., Laurens, K. R., & Spence, S. H. (1997). Prevention and early intervention for anxiety disorders: A controlled trial. *Journal of Consulting and Clinical Psychology, 65,* 627–635.

deBeurs, E., Beekman, A., Geerlings, S., Deeg, D., van Dyck, R., & van Tilburg, W. (2001). On becoming depressed or anxious in late life: Similar vulnerability factors but different effects of stressful life events. *British Journal of Psychiatry, 179,* 426–431.

Dierker, L. C., Albano, A. M., Clarke, G. N., Heimberg, R. G., Kendall, P. C., Merikangas, K. R., et al. (2001). Screening for anxiety and depression in early adolescence. *Journal of American Academy of Child and Adolescent Psychiatry, 40,* 929–936.

Dobson, K. (1985). The relationship between anxiety and depression. *Clinical Psychology Review, 5,* 307–324.

Dollinger, S. J. (1986). The measurement of children's sleep disturbances and somatic complaints following a disaster. *Child Psychiatry and Human Development, 16,* 148–153.

Dollinger, S. J., O'Donnell, J. P., & Staley, A. A. (1984). Lightning-strike disaster: Effects on children's fears and worries. *Journal of Consulting and Clinical Psychology, 52,* 1028–1038.

Donovan, C. L., & Spence, S. H. (2000). Prevention of childhood anxiety disorders. *Clinical Psychology Review, 20,* 509–531.

Dubow, E. F., Schmidt, D., McBride, J., Edwards, S., & Merk, F. L. (1993). Teaching children to cope with stressful experiences: Implementation and evaluation of a primary prevention program. *Journal of Clinical Child Psychology, 22,* 428–440.

Durlak, J. A. (1998). Primary prevention mental health programs for children and adolescents are effective. *Journal of Mental Health—UK, 7,* 463–469.

Durlak, J. A., & Wells, A. M. (1997). Primary prevention mental health programs for children and adolescents: A meta-analytic review. *American Journal of Community Psychology, 25,* 115–151.

Elias, M. J., Gara, M. A., Schuyler, T. F., Branden-Muller, L. R., & Sayette, M. A. (1991). The promotion of social competence: Longitudinal study of a preventive school-based program. *American Journal of Orthopsychiatry, 61,* 409–417.

Elias, M. J., Gara, M. A., Ubriaco, M., Rothbaum, P., Clabby, J., & Schuyler, T. (1986). Impact of a preventive social problem solving intervention on children's coping with middle school stressors. *American Journal of Community Psychology, 14,* 259–275.

Erickson, M. F., Sroufe, L. A., & Egeland, B. (1985). The relationship between quality of attachment and behaviour problems in preschool and a high-risk sample. *Monographs of the Society for Research in Child Development, 50,* 147–166.

Felner, R. D., & Adan, A. M. (1988). The school transition project: An ecological intervention and evaluation. In R. H. Price, E. L. Cowen, R. P. Lorion, & J. Ramos-McKay (Eds.), *14 ounces of prevention: A casebook for practitioners* (pp. 112–122). Washington, DC: American Psychological Association.

Felner, R. D., Brand, S., Adan, A. M., Mulhall, P. F., Flowers, N., Sartain, B., & Dubois, D. L. (1993). Restructuring the ecology of the school as an approach to prevention during school transitions: Longitudinal follow-ups and extensions of the school transitional environment project (STEP). *Prevention in Human Services, 10,* 103–156.

Felner, R. D., Gitner, M., & Primavera, J. (1982). Primary prevention during school transitions: Social support and environmental structure. *American Journal of Community Psychology, 10,* 277–290.

Fergusson, D. M., Horwood, L. J., & Lynskey, M. T. (1993). Prevalence and comorbidity of DSM-III-R diagnoses in a birth cohort of 15 year olds. *Journal of the American Academy of Child and Adolescent Psychiatry, 32,* 1127–1134.

Folkman, S., & Lazarus, R. S. (1980). An analysis of coping in a middle-aged community sample. *Journal of Health and Social Behavior, 21,* 219–239.

Folkman, S., Lazarus, R. S., Gruen, R. J., & DeLongis, A. (1986). Appraisal, coping, health status, and psychological symptoms. *Journal of Personality and Social Psychology, 50,* 571–579.

Godfrey, K. J., Bonds, A. S., Kraus, M. E., Wiener, M. R., & Toth, C. S. (1990). Freedom from stress: A meta-analytic view of treatment and intervention programs. *Applied H.R.M. Research, 1,* 67–80.

Goodyer, I. M., & Altham, P. M. (1991). Lifetime exit events and recent social and family adversities in anxious and depressed school-aged children. *Journal of Affective Disorders, 21,* 219–228.

Greenberg, M. T., Domitrovich, C., & Bumbarger, B. (2001). The prevention of mental disorders in school-aged children: Current state of the field. *Prevention and Treatment, 4,* 1–63.

Greenberg, M. T., Kusche, C. A., Cook, E. T., & Quamma, J. P. (1995). Promoting emotional competence in school-aged deaf children: The effects of the PATHS curriculum. *Development and Psychopathology, 7,* 117–136.

Greenberg, P. E., Sisitsky, T., Kessler, R. C., Finkelstein, S. N., Berndt, E. R., Davidson, J. R. T., et al. (1999). The economic burden of anxiety disorders in the 1990s. *Journal of Clinical Psychiatry, 60,* 427–435.

Harris, J. R. (1995). Where is the child's environment? A group socialization theory of development. *Psychological Review, 102*(3), 458–489.

Hartup, W. W. (1978). Children and their friends. In H. McGurk (Ed.), *Issues in childhood social development*. London: Methuen.

Hartup, W. W. (1983). Peer relations. In P. Mussen (Ed.), *Handbook of child psychology* (pp. 103–196). New York: John Wiley.

Hiebert, B., Kirby, B., & Jaknavorian, A. (1989). School-based relaxation: Attempting primary prevention. *Canadian Journal of Counselling, 23,* 273–287.

Hill, H. M., Levermore, H., Twaite, J., & Jones, L. P. (1996). Exposure to community violence and social support as predictors of anxiety and social and emotional behaviour among African American children. *Journal of Child and Family Studies, 5,* 399–414.

Hirshfeld, D. R., Rosenbaum, J. F., Biederman, J., Bolduc, E. A., Faraone, S. V., Snidman, N., et al. (1992). Stable behavioral inhibition and its association with anxiety disorder. *Journal of the American Academy of Child and Adolescent Psychiatry, 31,* 103–111.

Hope, D. A., Heimberg, R. G., & Bruch, M. A. (1995). Dismantling cognitive–behavioral group therapy for social phobia. *Behaviour Research and Therapy, 33,* 637–650.

Hudson, J. L., & Rapee, R. M. (2001). Parent–child interactions and the anxiety disorders: An observational analysis. *Behaviour Research and Therapy, 39,* 1411–1427.

Hudson, J. L., & Rapee, R. M. (in press). From Anxious Temperament to Disorder: An etiological model of Generalized Anxiety Disorder. In R. Heimberg, C. Turk, & D. Menin (Eds.), *Generalized Anxiety Disorder: Advances in research and practice*. New York: Guilford.

Jardine, R., Martin, N. G., & Henderson, A. S. (1984). Genetic covariance between neuroticism and the symptoms of anxiety and depression. *Genetics Epidemiology, 1,* 89–107.

Jeavons, S., Horne, D., & Greenwood, K. (2000). Coping style and psychological trauma after road accidents. *Psychology, Health and Medicine, 5*(2), 213–221.

Kagan, J. (1989). Temperamental contributions to social behavior. *American Psychologist, 44*(4), 668–674.

Kagan, J. (1997). Temperament and the reactions to unfamiliarity. *Child Development, 68,* 139–143.

Kaluza, G. (1997). Evaluation of stress management interventions in primary prevention—a meta-analysis of (quasi-)experimental studies. *Zeitschrift für Gesundheitspsychologie, 5,* 149–169.

Kendall, P. C. (1994). Treating anxiety disorders in children: Results of a randomized clinical trial. *Journal of Consulting and Clinical Psychology, 62,* 100–110.

Kendall, P. C., Flannery-Schroeder, E., Panichelli-Mindel, S., Southam-Gerow, M. Henin, A., & Warman, M. (1997). Therapy for youth with anxiety disorders: A second randomized clinical trial. *Journal of Consulting & Clinical Psychology, 65,* 366–380.

Kendall, P. C., & Kessler, R. C. (2002). The impact of childhood psychopathology interventions on subsequent substance abuse: Comments and recommendations. *Journal of Consulting and Clinical Psychology, 70*, 1303–1306.

Kendler, K. S., Neale, M. C., Kessler, R. C., Heath, A. C., & Eaves, L. J. (1992). Major depression and generalized anxiety disorder: Same genes, (partly) different environments? *Archives of General Psychiatry, 49*, 716–722.

Kessler, R. C., McGonagle, K. A., Zhao, S., Nelson, C. B., Hughes, M., Eshleman, S., et al. (1994). Lifetime and 12-month prevalence of DSM-III-R psychiatric disorders in the United States. *Archives of General Psychiatry, 51*, 8–19.

Khrone, H. W., & Hock, M. (1991). Relationships between restrictive mother–child interactions and anxiety of the child. *Anxiety Research, 4*, 109–124.

King, N. J., & Ollendick, T. H. (1989). Children's anxiety and phobic disorders in school settings: Classification, assessment, and intervention issues. *Review of Educational Research, 59*, 431–470.

Kline, M. L., & Snow, D. L. (1994). Effects of a worksite coping skills intervention on the stress, social support, and health outcomes of working mothers. *Journal of Primary Prevention, 15*, 105–121.

Klingman, A., & Hochdorf, Z. (1993). Coping with distress and self-harm: The impact of a primary prevention program for adolescents. *Journal of Adolescence, 16*, 121–140.

Kovacs, M., & Devlin, B. (1998). Internalizing disorders in childhood. *Journal of Child Psychology and Psychiatry and Allied Disciplines, 39*(1), 47–63.

Kupersmidt, J. B., Coie, J. D., & Dodge, K. A. (1990). The role of poor peer relationships in the development of disorder. In S. R. Asher & J. D. Coie (Eds.), *Peer rejection in childhood* (pp. 274–305). New York: Cambridge University Press.

Last, C. G., Hersen, M., Kazdin, A. E., Francis, G., & Grubb, H. J. (1987). Psychiatric illness in the mothers of anxious children. *American Journal of Psychiatry, 144*, 1580–1583.

Lazarus, R. S., & Folkman, S. (1984). *Stress, appraisal, and coping*. New York: Springer.

Lewis, M., Feiring, C., McGafey, C., & Jaskir, J. (1984). Predicting psychopathology in six-year-olds from early social relations. *Child Development, 55*, 123–136.

Lichtenstein, J., & Cassidy, J. (1991, April). *The Inventory of Adult Attachment: Validation of a new measure*. Paper presented at the meeting of the Society for Research in Child Development, Seattle, WA.

Lohaus, A., Klein-Hessling, J., & Shebar, S. (1997). Stress management for elementary school children: A comparative evaluation of different approaches. *Revue Européenne de Psychologie Appliquée, 47*, 157–161.

Lowry-Webster, H. M., Barrett, P. M., & Dadds, M. R. (2001). A universal prevention trial of anxiety and depressive symptomatology in childhood: Preliminary data from an Australian study. *Behaviour Change, 18*, 36–50.

Maes, M., Mylle, J., Delmeire, L., & Janca, A. (2001). Pre- and post-disaster negative life events in relation to the incidence and severity of posttraumatic stress disorder. *Psychiatry Research, 105*, 1–12.

Manassis, K., & Bradley, S. J. (1994). The development of childhood anxiety disorders: Toward an integrated model. *Journal of Applied Developmental Psychology, 15,* 345–366.

Melançon, G., & Boyer, R. (1999). Comment prévenir l'apparition d'un trouble de stress post-traumatique avant un traumatisme? [How do we prevent the onset of posttraumatic stress disorder before trauma occurs?] *Canadian Journal of Psychiatry, 44,* 253–258.

Morris, T. L., Messer, S. C., & Gross, A. M. (1995). Enhancement of the social interaction and status of neglected children: A peer-pairing approach. *Journal of Clinical Child Psychology, 24*(1), 11–20.

Muris, P., Mayer, B., & Meesters, C. (2000). Self-reported attachment style, anxiety, and depression in children. *Social Behavior and Personality, 28,* 157–162.

Muris, P., & Merckelbach, H. (1998). Perceived parental rearing behaviour and anxiety disorders symptoms in normal children. *Personality and Individual Difference, 25,* 1199–1206.

National Advisory Mental Health Council Workgroup on Mental Disorders Prevention Research. (2001, June 26). Priorities for prevention research at NIMH. *Prevention and Treatment, 4,* Article 17. Retrieved June 27, 2001, from http://journals.apa.org/prevention/volume4/pre0040017a.html

Orbach, I., & Bar-Joseph, H. (1993). The impact of a suicide prevention program for adolescents on suicidal tendencies, hopelessness, ego identity, and coping. *Suicide and Life-Threatening Behavior, 23,* 120–129.

Rapee, R. M. (1991). Generalized anxiety disorder: A review of clinical features and theoretical concepts. *Clinical Psychology Review, 11,* 419–440.

Rapee, R. M. (1997). The potential role of childrearing practices in the development of anxiety and depression. *Clinical Psychology Review, 17,* 47–67.

Rapee, R. M. (2001). The development of generalized anxiety. In M. W. Vasey & M. R. Dadds (Eds.), *The developmental psychopathology of anxiety* (pp. 481–503). New York: Oxford University Press.

Rapee, R. M., Litwin, E. M., & Barlow, D. H. (1990). Impact of life events on subjects with panic disorder and on comparison subjects. *American Journal of Psychiatry, 147,* 640–644.

Rapee, R. M., & Melville, L. F. (1997). Recall of family factors in social phobia and panic disorder: Comparison of mother and offspring reports. *Depression and Anxiety, 5,* 7–11.

Rapee, R. M., & Szollos, A. (1997, November). *Early life events in anxious children.* Paper presented at the 31st Annual Association for the Advancement of Behavior Therapy Convention, Miami, FL.

Rapee, R. M., Wignall, A., Hudson, J. L., & Schniering, C. A. (2000). *Evidence-based treatment of child and adolescent anxiety disorders.* Oakland, CA: New Harbinger.

Romano, J. L. (1984). Stress management and wellness: Reaching beyond the counselor's office. *Personnel and Guidance Journal, 62,* 533–537.

Rosenbaum, J. F., Biederman, J., Bolduc-Murphy, E. A., Faraone, S. V., Chaloff, J., Hirshfeld, D. R., & Kagan, J. (1993). Behavioral inhibition in childhood: A risk factor for anxiety disorders. *Harvard Review of Psychiatry, 1*, 2–16.

Rubin, K. H. (1985). Socially withdrawn children: An "at risk" population? In B. H. Schneider, K. H. Rubin, & J. E. Ledingham (Eds.), *Peer relationships and social skills in childhood: Issues in assessment and training* (pp. 125–139). New York: Springer-Verlag.

Rubin, K. H., LeMare, L. J., & Lollis, S. (1990). Social withdrawal in childhood: Developmental pathways to rejection. In S. R. Asher & J. D. Coie (Eds.), *Peer rejection in childhood* (pp. 217–252). New York: Cambridge University Press.

Rubin, K. H., & Mills, R. S. (1988). The many faces of social isolation in childhood. *Journal of Consulting and Clinical Psychology, 56*(6), 916–924.

Rubin, K. H., & Mills, R. S. L. (1991). Conceptualizing developmental pathways to internalizing disorders in childhood. *Canadian Journal of Behavioural Science, 23*, 300–317.

Rundell, J. R., Holloway, H. C., Ursano, R. J., & Jones, D. R. (1990). Combat stress disorders and the U.S. Air Force. *Military Medicine, 155*, 515–518.

Shure, M. B., & Spivack, G. (1979). Interpersonal cognitive problem solving and primary prevention: Programming for preschool and kindergarten children. *Journal of Clinical Child Psychology, 8*, 89–94.

Shure, M. B., & Spivack, G. (1982). Interpersonal problem solving in young children: A cognitive approach to prevention. *American Journal of Community Psychology, 10*, 341–356.

Silverman, E., & Albano, A. M. (1997). *The Anxiety Disorders Interview Schedule for Children (DSM-IV)*. San Antonio: Psychological Corporation.

Siqueland, L., Kendall, P. C., & Steinberg, L. (1996). Anxiety in children: Perceived family environments and observed family interaction. *Journal of Clinical Child Psychology, 25*, 225–237.

Spence, S. (1996). The prevention of anxiety disorders in childhood. In P. Cotton & H. Jackson (Eds.), *Early intervention and prevention in mental health* (pp. 87–107). Carlton South Victoria, Australia: Australian Psychological Society.

Spence, S. H. (1998). A measure of anxiety symptoms among children. *Behaviour Research and Therapy, 36*, 545–566.

Spence, S. H. (2001). Prevention strategies. In M. W. Vasey and M. R. Dadds (Eds.), *The developmental psychopathology of anxiety* (pp. 325–351). New York: Oxford University Press.

Spielberger, C. D., Pollans, C. H., & Worden, T. (1984). Anxiety disorders. In S. M. Turner & M. Hersen (Eds.), *Adult psychopathology: A behavioral perspective* (pp. 613–630). New York: John Wiley.

Spivack, G., & Shure, M. B. (1974). *Social adjustment of young children: A cognitive approach to solving real-life problems*. San Francisco: Jossey-Bass.

Sroufe, L. A., Egeland, B., & Kreutzer, T. (1990). The fate of early experience following developmental change: Longitudinal approaches to individual adaptation in childhood. *Child Development, 61*, 1363–1373.

Strauss, C. C., Forehand, R., Smith, K., & Frame, C. L. (1986). The association between social withdrawal and internalizing problems of children. *Journal of Abnormal Child Psychology, 14,* 525–535.

Terr, L. C. (1981). Psychic trauma in children: Observations following the Chowchilla school bus kidnapping. *American Journal of Psychiatry, 138,* 14–19.

Tiet, Q. Q., Bird, H. R., Davies, M., Hoven, C., Cohen, P., Jensen, P. S., & Goodman, S. (1998). Adverse life events and resilience. *Journal of American Academy of Child and Adolescent Psychiatry, 37,* 1119–1200.

Torgersen, S. (1983). Genetic factors in anxiety disorders. *Archives of General Psychiatry, 40,* 1085–1089.

Turner, S. M., Beidel, D. C., & Costello, A. (1987). Psychopathology in the offspring of anxiety disordered patients. *Journal of Consulting and Clinical Psychology, 55,* 229–235.

Tyrer, P., Alexander, J., Remington, M., & Riley, P. (1987). Relationship between neurotic symptoms and neurotic diagnosis: A longitudinal study. *Journal of Affective Disorders, 13,* 13–21.

U.S. Department of Health and Human Services. (1991). *Healthy People 2000* (Publication No. 91-50212). Washington, DC: Government Printing Office.

U.S. Department of Health and Human Services. (1999). *Mental health: A report of the Surgeon General.* Rockville, MD: Author.

Verhulst, F. C., van der Ende, J., Ferdinand, R. F., & Kasius, M. C. (1997). The prevalence of DSM-III-R diagnoses in a national sample of Dutch adolescents. *Archives of General Psychiatry, 54,* 329–336.

Warman, M. J., & Kendall, P. C. (2000). *Ideas about coping among anxious and nonanxious youth: The role of controllability.* Unpublished doctoral dissertation, Temple University, Philadelphia, PA.

Warren, S. L., Huston, L., Egeland, B., & Sroufe, L. A. (1997). Child and adolescent anxiety disorders and early attachment. *Journal of the American Academy of Child and Adolescent Psychiatry, 36,* 637–644.

Weissman, M. M., Leckman, J. F., Merikangas, K. R., Gammon, G. D., & Prusoff, B. A. (1984). Depression and anxiety disorders in parents and children: Results from the Yale Family Study. *Archives of General Psychiatry, 41,* 845–852.

Whatley, S. L., Foreman, A. C., & Richards, S. (1998). The relationship of coping style to dysphoria, anxiety, and anger. *Psychological Reports, 83*(3), 783–791.

White, K. S., Bruce, S. E., Farrell, A. D., & Kliewer, W. (1998). Impact of exposure to community violence on anxiety: A longitudinal study of family social support as a protective factor for urban children. *Journal of Child and Family Studies, 7,* 187–203.

Winett, R. A. (1998). Prevention: A proactive–developental–ecological perspective. In T. H. Ollendick & M. Hersen (Eds.), *Handbook of child psychopathology* (3rd ed., pp. 637–671). New York: Plenum.

Woody, S., & Rachman, S. (1994). Generalized anxiety disorder (GAD) as an unsuccessful search for safety. *Clinical Psychology Review, 14,* 743–753.

Yule, W., & Williams, R. (1990). Post-traumatic stress reactions in children. *Journal of Traumatic Stress, 3*, 279–295.

Zeidner, M., & Ben-Zur, H. (1994). Individual differences in anxiety, coping, and post-traumatic stress in the aftermath of the Persian Gulf War. *Personality and Individual Differences, 16*(3), 459–476.

6

SECONDARY PREVENTION OF ANXIETY DISORDERS

TYLER J. STORY, BONNIE G. ZUCKER,
AND MICHELLE G. CRASKE

Anxiety disorders are chronic, widespread conditions that generate considerable emotional, social, and economic burdens for individuals and society at large. Data from the National Comorbidity Survey indicated that 25% of respondents chosen randomly from the community met the criteria for at least one anxiety disorder in their lifetime, with 17% meeting the criteria in the 12 months prior to the survey (Kessler et al., 1994). Posttraumatic stress disorder (PTSD) and obsessive–compulsive disorder (OCD), however, were not included in the survey, suggesting even higher lifetime and 12-month prevalence rates. In 1990, anxiety disorders generated a $42.3 billion economic burden, with panic disorder and posttraumatic stress disorder accounting for the highest health care costs (Greenberg et al., 1999). Although responsive to treatment, untreated anxiety disorders usually have a poor prognosis, because of their chronicity in adult samples. Rates of remission without treatment range from 15% to 42%, depending on the severity and type of disorder. In addition, individuals with anxiety disorders typically avoid seeking treatment, perhaps because of the impairment resulting from the disorder itself (Craske, 1999). The data suggest a pressing need to intervene earlier in the development of these disorders, before their personal impact reduces the likelihood that the person will seek treatment and before their economic impact is fully established.

In 1994, the NIMH Prevention and Research Steering Committee and the Institute of Medicine's Committee on Prevention of Mental Disorders stressed the crucial role of malleable risk and protective factors in the understanding and prevention of mental disorders (Mrazek & Haggerty, 1994). Moreover, in identifying target populations, research endeavors in secondary prevention may address early symptoms of a disorder. In an effort to integrate research in prevention that includes both risk factors and early signs of a disorder, this chapter discusses the secondary prevention of anxiety disorders in terms of interventions that are implemented prior to the onset of a diagnosable disorder and that target at-risk groups, with the intention of reducing the occurrence of new cases. Therefore, early signs of a disorder, such as recurrent panic attacks prior to developing panic disorder, are considered identifying risk factors for secondary prevention. As we discuss, even subclinical symptoms do not correlate perfectly with the development of an anxiety disorder, supporting the use of more integrated models of risk and prevention.

Research in the secondary prevention of anxiety must also consider childhood risk factors and interventions as they relate to broader mental health vulnerability. Left untreated, childhood anxiety typically becomes chronic, resulting in adverse effects on school performance, social skills, and mood (e.g., Dadds et al., 1999; Hayward, Killen, Kraemer, & Taylor, 2000; Spence, 2001). Epidemiological data suggest that 21% of children and adolescents have an anxiety disorder of some kind (Kashani & Orvaschel, 1990). Of even more concern is the evidence that anxiety disorders in childhood seem to show a chronic course, possibly predisposing individuals to additional anxiety and mood disorders as adults (Dadds et al., 1999; Spence, 2001). In addition, a significant number of children with anxiety disorders (30%–40%) do not exhibit robust responses to treatment, still meeting the criteria for the disorder following the intervention (Spence, 2001). Interestingly, however, Hayward and colleagues (1997, 2000) have demonstrated that anxiety symptoms in early adolescence do not always develop into specific adult anxiety disorders, but rather predispose individuals to a wide range of anxiety and mood disorders. Therefore, secondary prevention efforts targeting children and adolescents might focus on general vulnerabilities to anxiety disorders, as opposed to predisposition to specific disorders.

We begin by presenting research on the identification and understanding of general risk factors for anxiety disorders. The etiology of anxiety as a maladaptive cognitive, emotional, and behavioral response will be reviewed briefly. Then, we present distinctions between adult and child secondary prevention research on anxiety as a general condition. Next, we review research specific to each disorder, highlighting specific risk and protective factors, theoretical models of prevention, and empirically supported models of secondary prevention for those disorders. A brief discussion of the implications of these findings closes the review of each disorder. Finally, the topic of secondary prevention of anxiety disorders is discussed in terms of the strengths and weaknesses of the extant literature and directions for future research in this area.

RISK FACTORS

As with most psychological conditions, the etiologies of anxiety disorders originate from both biological and environmental factors. Some risk factors common to most, if not all, of the anxiety disorders include gender, temperament (negative affectivity), family history of psychiatric illness, threatening or stressful life events, cognitive style, and lack of social support (Craske & Zucker, 2001; Davey, Burgess, & Rashes, 1995; Eaton, Badawi, & Melton, 1995; Eysenck, 1985; Kennerley, 1996; Kessler et al., 1994; Norton, Cox, & Malan, 1992). Heritability estimates of childhood anxiety disorders vary considerably. Although twin studies have reported heritability estimates between 30% and 44% (Kendler, Heath, Martin, & Eaves, 1986; Kendler, Neale, Kessler, Heath, & Eaves, 1992), these rates pertain mostly to *symptoms* of anxiety, not actual diagnoses. To date, the most robust risk factors for childhood anxiety include anxious-resistant attachment, parental anxiety, behaviorally inhibited temperament, traumatic or stressful life events, and parenting style (see Donovan & Spence, 2000, for a review). In the next section, we undertake a closer examination of these risk factors as they pertain to general vulnerabilities to anxiety.

Gender

Epidemiological data implicate gender as a risk factor for the development of anxiety disorders. The National Comorbidity Survey found that women were two times as likely as men to develop most anxiety disorders, although gender differences observed in social phobia and OCD were less robust (Kessler et al., 1994). Some research suggests that these findings may also reflect aspects of chronicity and response to treatment (Breslau & Davis, 1992), such that women may show poorer treatment outcomes than men (Noyes, Holt, & Woodman, 1996). In addition to biologically driven differences in susceptibility to anxiety, it is possible that men underreport anxiety symptoms or choose to self-medicate with drugs or alcohol instead of seeking treatment. Nevertheless, women are typically exposed to greater social stereotypes (e.g., regarding coping skills), life stressors, and socialized patterns of responding to fearful situations (Craske & Zucker, 2001). These factors may affect both women's subjective experiences with stress and anxiety and their coping skills and self-efficacy.

Neuroticism and Temperament

Research on the genetic transmission of anxiety has focused primarily on general, higher order risk factors such as personality temperament and traits that typically appear during early childhood and predispose individuals to multiple mental health concerns. From this research, two models in particular have received considerable attention as etiological risk factors of anxiety disorders: Eysenck's (1960) neuroticism personality trait and Kagan and colleagues' "inhibited temperament" (Kagan, Reznick, & Snidman, 1988).

Eysenck (1960) originally extended the classification of human personality from a single extraversion–introversion axis to include an orthogonal dimension of neuroticism–stability. Eysenck equated neuroticism with emotional instability. Individuals who were high on the neuroticism trait exhibited lifelong or episodic anxiety, neurotic traits in childhood, unsatisfactory early life experiences, lifelong or episodic symptoms of hysteria, and anxiety symptoms for over 12 months. They also showed signs of unsatisfactory adjustment during adolescence, a family history of neuroses, obsessive symptoms, low energy output, and a poor work record (Eysenck, 1960).

Whereas introverts represented individuals who showed higher baseline cortical arousal, thus avoiding situations for fear of (cognitive or "psychic") overstimulation, neurotics exhibited a specific sensitivity to autonomic arousal (Eysenck, 1985). This autonomic reactivity placed individuals at greater risk for conditioned anxiety responses to perceived threats. Empirical support for such a predisposition, however, is mixed, a fact that Walsh, Eysenck, Wilding, and Valentine (1994) attribute to differences between self-reported and actual physiological experiences. That is, individuals high on neuroticism may be hypervigilant and thus more likely to misperceive physiological changes. Also, neuroticism has been implicated as a risk factor in response to stress, predisposing individuals to anxiety disorders following stressful life experiences and traumatic events (Timmerman, Emmelkamp, & Sanderman, 1998).

Kagan and colleagues (e.g., Kagan, 1999; Kagan, Reznick, & Snidman, 1987, 1988) have developed a body of research on inhibited temperament, a distinct innate factor that shares some features with neuroticism and is characterized by a predictable pattern of behavioral inhibition in certain environments. An inhibited temperament might emerge as irritability and sleeplessness during infancy, anxious behavior in early childhood, and hypervigilance and withdrawal beginning in childhood and continuing through adulthood (Kashdan & Herbert, 2001). Behaviors associated with inhibited temperament can be observed before 12 months of age and are typically exhibited in reaction to unfamiliar stimuli, people, or environments. Although shyness around adults and strangers is considered a hallmark of inhibited children, it is not a prerequisite, and inhibition may be evoked by unfamiliar events or places for some children (Kagan, 1999). Estimates for heritability of behavioral inhibition range from .42 to .70, indicating a modest to high genetic influence (Oosterlaan, 2001).

Several studies have found strong associations between behaviorally inhibited children and a predisposition for developing anxiety disorders. Biederman et al. (1990) reported that inhibited children have an increased risk for anxiety disorders compared with controls and exhibit higher rates of multiple anxiety disorders, multiple psychiatric disorders, oppositional defiant disorder, and overanxious disorder. Similar longitudinal findings reveal that inhibited children were more likely to meet the criteria for comorbid anxiety disorders, comorbid psychiatric disorders, avoidant disorder, separation anxiety disorder, and agoraphobia at 3-year follow-up (Biederman et al., 1993). Children who remain inhibited over time exhibit higher rates of any anxiety disorder and multiple anxiety disorders, as do their siblings and parents (Hirshfeld et al., 1992).

Biological Factors

The mental and physical health of mothers during pregnancy has been studied with respect to biological risk factors for childhood anxiety disorders. Anxious mothers typically have newborns who demonstrate more active and irritable behavior, and elevated levels of anxiety during pregnancy are associated with lower fetal body movement during active sleep (Monk, 2001). The hyperactive HPA axis in anxious mothers is posited to affect central nervous system development in the fetus. In a study eliciting stress in pregnant women while assessing maternal and fetal physiological reactivity, the anxious group differed from the nonanxious group in systolic blood pressure, diastolic blood pressure, and fetal heart rate. Although this research is relatively new, stress during pregnancy may have implications for neurobiological substrates to emotion regulation in newborns (Monk, 2001).

Neurobiological research suggests a strong relationship between early life stressors and increases in the secretion of corticotropin-releasing factor (CRF), the primary neurotransmitter governing the endocrinologic, autonomic, immunologic, and behavioral stress response systems. Increased CRF leads to elevated reactivity to stress, with effects resembling depression and acute stress response (Heim & Nemeroff, 1999). The behavioral effects of CRF are similar to those of the behavioral inhibition system and suggest a strong relationship to anxiety (see Heim & Nemeroff, 1999).

Effects of Parental Anxiety

In addition to biological factors, parental anxiety contributes to risk for child and adult anxiety disorders, through the impact of anxiety on family environment and parenting skills. The basic tenets of learning theory as it relates to anxiety in children suggest that parents model anxious behavioral responses to specific stimuli, thereby prompting and reinforcing anxious responses in their children (Donovan & Spence, 2000). For example, children of anxious parents typically respond anxiously to ambiguous cues and use avoidant coping strategies based on their parents' instructions (Barrett, Dadds, & Rapee, 1996). Similarly, parental overcontrol, overprotection, and criticism appear to place children at risk for developing anxiety disorders, partly because those traits have been found to contribute to the stability of behavioral inhibition in children (Krohne & Hock, 1991). These parental factors also may influence children's abilities to formulate adequate problem-solving strategies, ingraining a sense of low self-efficacy and low coping ability by teaching them that they cannot adequately cope with adverse experiences.

Parental behaviors and parental psychopathology can be especially powerful influences on a child's anxiety, as are early traumatic or stressful life experiences (Spence, 2001), presumably because they can affect several other risk factors (e.g., attachment style, coping strategies, etc.). Considering that children are likely to learn most of their early coping skills from their parents, maladaptive strategies modeled by parents could create a domino effect and lead to susceptibility to other risk factors (e.g., poor coping skills might lead to avoidant behavior in challenging social situations or to low self-efficacy with respect to emotion regulation). In addition, traumatic and stressful experiences during childhood may occur before adequate coping and problem-solving strategies are established, in which case the children may not recover as easily and fail to engage in activities that are likely to mitigate, as opposed to exacerbate, the effects. For instance, children exposed to early traumas are more likely to show PTSD symptoms if their mothers are anxious and overprotective following the event (McFarlane, 1987; Spence, 2001).

Classical conditioning may hold a more powerful influence on the development of phobias in children than in adults (Rachman, 1997). One explanation is children's lack of alternative experiences to which they can compare a specific incident. For instance, if a child's first encounter with a dog results in a severe bite on her leg, that child is more likely to develop a phobia than an adult who has interacted with hundreds of dogs, but happens to be painfully bitten on one occasion. This example embodies the concept of *latent inhibition*, according to which exposure to a stimulus that results in either the absence of an outcome or a positive outcome may inhibit subsequent pairing of that stimulus with a negative outcome (Mackintosh, 1983).

Life Transitions

Significant transitions during childhood and adolescence—particularly, unexpected or uncontrollable events, such as parental divorce—appear to have a considerable impact on mental health. In the case of divorce, the most substantial impacts of the separation appear to surface during the first year or two following the divorce, in which the child's attachment to each parent may be changed or reevaluated (Hess & Camara, 1979). Divorce also places a new emotional burden on children, in that they must now negotiate sensitive emotional topics with each parent. In a study comparing both marital status (intact vs. divorced) and quality of family interactions, Hess and Camara (1979) found that process variables (e.g., how the parents relate to the children) within the family were more predictive of childhood problems than marital status. More specifically, the parent–child relationship was most influential, with parental harmony also contributing. Interestingly, although school and social adjustment are more influenced by the parent–child relationship, level of stress on the child was predicted most by parental harmony in both divorced and intact families.

Developmentally Specific Risk

Donovan and Spence (2000) have advanced the understanding of risk factors and appropriate prevention in children by discussing them in the context of specific developmental periods. For example, the authors posit that genetics and parental psychopathology are highly relevant during prenatal periods, when parental skills training and treatment of parental anxiety may be the primary means of prevention. During infancy, insecure attachment, behavioral inhibition, parental anxiety, and anxious parenting are posited to contribute to greater risk, again requiring parent training and treatment of parental anxiety as a means of preventing anxiety disorders in the children. In childhood, preventive interventions should incorporate child training in coping skills, in addition to parent training and treatment, because risk factors in childhood include an overprotective or critical parenting style, behavioral inhibition, school-related events, parental anxiety, and early symptoms of anxiety. Finally, during adolescence, vulnerabilities include the transition to high school, parental anxiety, and symptoms of anxiety; preventive interventions for adolescents would incorporate the same procedures as those employed during childhood, but with more emphasis on teaching coping skills (Donovan & Spence, 2000; Spence, 2001).

GENERAL PREVENTION

Although the developmental model presented by Donovan and Spence (2000) has not been empirically validated, LaFreniere and Capuano (1997) provided support for developmentally appropriate anxiety prevention and treatment. In their study of anxious–withdrawn preschool children, a 20-session treatment intervention was administered to the mothers (the children themselves did not receive any direct intervention), emphasizing the developmental needs of preschoolers, promoting competent parenting, alleviating parental stress, and providing social support. The intervention demonstrated significant benefits for the children's social competence and problem-solving cooperation. Decreases in overcontrolling behavior by the mother were observed in the experimental group (LaFreniere & Capuano, 1997). That the children were not targeted directly emphasized the importance of parental intervention in this population.

The Queensland Early Intervention and Prevention of Anxiety Project, a longitudinal study conducted by Dadds and colleagues (1997, 1999), has contributed considerably to research investigating the prevention of childhood anxiety disorders. In the project, the authors outlined three major points in the development of a prevention strategy: an accurate identification (i.e., screening) procedure, accessibility to screening and identification, and an intervention that is cost effective for the mental health system (Dadds, Spence, Holland, Barrett, & Laurens, 1997). The preventive intervention consisted of the *Coping Koala: Prevention Manual* paradigm, modeled after Kendall et al's *Coping Cat* treatment manual (see Kendall & Treadwell, 1996), together with parent training sessions. Although posttreatment effects were negligible, 54% of the children in the control group developed an anxiety disorder by 6-month follow-up, compared with 16% in the treatment group. There were no significant effects for age, gender, or pretreatment diagnostic status for either group (Dadds et al., 1997). After 12 months, the treatment and control groups converged with respect to overall rates of anxiety disorders (37% in the treatment group, versus 42% in the control group). The analyses, however, included children who met the criteria for anxiety disorders at baseline, as well as those who did not. The 2-year follow-up assessment again indicated a treatment group advantage, with 20% meeting the criteria for an anxiety disorder diagnosis, versus 39% in the control group. In addition to group status (treatment vs. control), internalizing scores and diagnostic severity at baseline predicted diagnostic status at the 2-year follow-up (Dadds et al., 1999). The implications of these initial results are twofold. First, one out of every two children in the at-risk group who did not receive treatment developed an anxiety disorder within 6 months, suggesting that identification of risk by self-report and corroborating sources (i.e., teacher ratings) may be an important combination for identifying at-risk children. Second, children who received the preventive intervention were half as likely to develop an anxiety disorder by 24-month follow-up.

In sum, several risk factors (e.g., gender, neuroticism, behavioral inhibition, family history, life transitions) appear to increase general vulnerability to anxiety disorders in children and adults. Despite extensive research on these etiological factors, few studies have attempted to intervene prior to the onset of an anxiety disorder. The limited research on secondary prevention of anxiety disorders has, in general, emphasized intervention during childhood with successful results (e.g., Dadds et al., 1997, 1999; LaFreniere & Capuano, 1997).

SPECIFIC PHOBIA

Risk Factors

The onset of most specific phobias occurs during childhood, although some situational phobias have a second peak during early adulthood (Craske, 1999). For that reason, research on risk factors and age-appropriate preventions focus primarily on childhood intervention. The most salient vulnerabilities to developing specific phobias result from experiences with aversive events or stimuli that may lead to conditioning. This may be especially true with certain stimuli that are associated with an innate "preparedness" for fearful behavior that was necessary to the survival of our ancestors (for more on "biological preparedness" see Seligman, 1971, and Cook & Mineka, 1989). The intensity of the traumatic event may also influence the strength of conditioned fear (Craske, 1999). For instance, Dollinger, O'Donnell, and Staley (1984) found that children who experienced a severe lightning strike subsequently had increased fears of storms. The researchers also found that fears relating to noise, dark, death, and dying were most pronounced in "traumatized" children specifically when those fears were associated with storms; the control group did not show this relationship.

Despite the intuitive relationship between specific phobias and traumatic experiences, individuals who experience an aversive or traumatic event do not always develop phobias. As discussed earlier, the concept of latent inhibition suggests that prior learning experiences may inhibit the conditioning of fear (Mackintosh, 1983). Similarly, not all individuals with specific phobias report a traumatic or conditioning experience with that stimulus. Vicarious observation and informational transmission also appear to contribute significantly to the development of fear (Craske, 1999). Research suggests that parental behavior and modeling may instill unrealistic fears in children. Studies examining children's responses to painful medical procedures, for example, indicate that youngsters gauge their responses to the reaction of their parents (Spence, 1994).

Physiological factors also appear to influence vulnerability to specific phobias. Children with inhibited temperaments may be at greater risk for developing specific phobias because of the physiological correlates of behavioral inhibition. Such children show specific changes in heart rate and pupillary dilation, higher salivary cortisol, greater muscle tension, and higher levels of norepinephrine in their urine (Spence, 1994). This biological response may intensify fear sensations and inhibit the development of coping skills in fearful situations. Individuals with blood and injection phobias appear to have a unique physiological risk factor that predisposes them to fainting. In response to fearful stimuli, they exhibit initial sympathetic arousal (as is common with many anxiety disorders), followed by parasympathetic hypotension and bradycardia that may lead to loss of consciousness (Craske, 1999).

Prevention

Of the specific phobias, fears of dental procedures are among the most prevalent, with 10%–20% of children and adolescents having such fears. Weinstein (1990) reviewed methods for preventing dental phobias, including providing the child with as much control over the procedure as possible, preexposing the child to the treatments in a non-traumatic manner, and having the child observe videos of other children coping with the procedure. In a similar vein, Melamed, Yurcheson, Fleece, Hutcherson, and Hawes (1978) conducted a prevention study dealing with fears of dental procedures. Children in the experimental group watched a videotape of peers coping with the procedure. The control group watched a demonstration video, with the dentist providing an explanation of the process without a child model actually undergoing the procedure. While watching the videos, the children in the peer model group showed a deceleration in heart rates compared with those in the control group, who exhibited higher heart rates. In addition, children who observed peer models undergoing the procedure reported fewer dental fears, cooperated more with the dentist, and were less disruptive during the procedure than the control participants were (Melamed et al., 1978).

Other research on the prevention of fears of dental or medical procedures suggests that modeling alone does not suffice when a procedure is invasive or painful. In this regard, training in coping skills, in conjunction with modeling, reduces anticipatory distress more effectively than does modeling alone (Peterson & Shigetomi, 1981). Jay, Elliott, Katz, and Siegel (1987) investigated the prevention and reduction of anxiety during a painful medical procedure by comparing cognitive–behavioral therapy intervention with pharmacological intervention and no treatment (the control groups). Leukemia patients aged 3–13 years old were recruited prior to undergoing bone marrow aspiration. The cognitive–behavioral therapy intervention was conducted 30–45 minutes prior to the procedure with approximately one third of the participants. The treatment included peer modeling via videotape, breathing exercises, positive incentives, imagery and distraction, and behavioral rehearsal. A second group of children received 0.3mg/kg of Valium 30 minutes before the procedure, and the control (no cognitive–behavioral therapy treament) group watched cartoons for 30 minutes before the procedure. Children who received cognitive–behavioral therapy reported significantly lower behavioral distress, pulse rate, and (self-reported) pain. The group that received Valium showed lower blood pressure and decreased anticipatory distress prior to (but not during) the procedure, but otherwise did not differ from the controls (Jay et al., 1987).

SOCIAL ANXIETY DISORDER/SOCIAL PHOBIA

Risk Factors

As with the other anxiety disorders, the presence of behavioral inhibition in childhood has been linked with later social anxiety disorders (e.g., Kagan et al., 1988; Schwartz, Snidman, & Kagan, 1999). For example, Schwartz and colleagues (1999) found that 61% of those who were classified as inhibited at age 2 had social anxiety at age 13, whereas 27% of uninhibited 2-year-olds developed later social anxiety. Interestingly, the authors also found that girls who were inhibited at age 2 were more likely to have generalized social anxiety at age 13 than were adolescent boys who exhibited similar temperament patterns at age 2. The authors concluded that this sex difference might be a result of biological factors or of differences in the socialization of boys and girls.

The characteristic fearfulness of individuals with elevated behavioral inhibition in novel social situations is similar to the construct of shyness. Individuals who label themselves as shy are more likely to be self-deprecating when they feel shy, which leads to a constellation of problems, including social isolation; feelings of shame, frustration, and inadequacy; and lowered self-confidence. This is not the case with individuals who do not identify themselves as being shy, but who feel shy in certain situations (Ishiyama, 1984). Negative beliefs associated with being shy might lead to the development of more severe pathology, such as social phobia. In a longitudinal study of shy-inhibited temperament, Prior, Smart, Sanson, and Oberklaid (2000) found that 42% of children who were persistently shy from infancy to early adolescence exhibited anxiety problems in early adolescence. However, of adolescents with anxiety problems, only one-fifth were persistently shy throughout childhood. Thus, an association between shyness and social phobia appears modest.

Additional research also suggests that traumatic social conditioning contributes to the development of social phobia (e.g., Ost & Hugdahl, 1981). Hofmann, Ehlers, and Roth (1995), however, found that, in a sample of 30 individuals with public-speaking phobia, no one reported experiencing a traumatic speaking event prior to the onset of the phobia, and only 15% reported having a traumatic speaking event that coincided with the phobia's onset. In fact, more of the participants attributed their phobia to panic attacks, as opposed to a traumatic event. Clearly, more research is needed, particularly on the relationship between traumatic conditioning and generalized social phobia.

Family dynamics and upbringing may also contribute to risk for social phobia. For example, Boegels, van Oosten, Muris, and Smulders (2001) found that socially anxious children were more likely than controls to judge their parents as rejecting. Socially anxious children and their parents both reported less family sociability than controls, and maternal social anxiety was associated with social anxiety in their children. Although constrained by a retrospective design, Bruch and Heimberg (1994) found that adults with generalized social phobia were more likely to perceive their parents as having isolated them from other people, compared with individuals with nongeneralized social phobia and healthy controls. Similarly, both patients with generalized social phobia and patients with nongeneralized social phobia were more likely to report that their parents were overly concerned with other people's opinions and used shame as a method of discipline. Finally, a diagnosis of social phobia in a parent is associated with psychological morbidity in a child: In a study of 26 outpatients with social phobia, 49% of their children had a lifetime anxiety disorder diagnosis. Overanxious disorder was the most common (30%), followed by social phobia (23%) and separation anxiety disorder (19%). Overall, the path between risk and onset has not been clearly delineated for social phobia, but recent research suggests some promising areas for longitudinal study and, eventually, secondary prevention.

Prevention

Efforts to prevent social phobia might prove most successful if they are directed at children and adolescents, because signs of behavioral inhibition can be identified at a very young age (e.g., Kagan, 1988). Furthermore, deficits in social skills can be targeted before they become pervasive and dysfunctional. Although there are currently no published prevention programs directed specifically at social phobia, group cognitive–behavioral treatments for children and adolescents with the disorder have been efficacious (e.g., Barrett, 1998). Further modification of these treatments for prevention seems appropriate. As previously mentioned, Dadds et al. (1997, 1999) implemented a school-based cognitive–behavioral early intervention program for a constellation of anxiety problems. To maximize their dissemination and also to alleviate stigmatization issues, these treatments could be delivered in a universal prevention format via the school system (see Barrett & Turner, 2001; Lowry-Webster, Barrett, & Dadds, 2001).

OBSESSIVE–COMPULSIVE DISORDER

Risk Factors

The hallmark characteristics of OCD—intrusive thoughts (obsessions) and compulsive behaviors—are also seen in the general population.

Research has shown that between 80% and 99% of the general population have at least occasional intrusive thoughts or impulses (e.g., Rachman & de Silva, 1978). Compulsive behaviors are common as well. Muris, Merckelbach, and Clavan (1997) found that 55% of their sample of normal participants reported performing compulsive behaviors similar to those observed in obsessive–compulsive patients. Moreover, Freeston, Ladouceur, Thibodeau, and Gagnon (1991) found that 92% of a university sample that endorsed having intrusive thoughts used a neutralization strategy at least some of the time. An understanding of the pathway from nonclinical to clinical symptoms is important in identifying risk factors for the disorder.

Cognitive theorists suggest that catastrophic misinterpretations of these "normal" intrusive thoughts can contribute to the development of clinically significant obsessions (e.g., Rachman, 1997, 1998; Salkovskis, 1985). According to Rachman (1997), those individuals with abnormal obsessions mistakenly interpret their thoughts as being very important, personally relevant, and threatening in nature, whereas persons with "normal" obsessions do not make these types of appraisals. In turn, individuals prone to making these catastrophic misinterpretations will have more frequent and distressing obsessions than those who deem the thoughts less significant.

Feelings of guilt, increased responsibility, scrupulosity, and superstition attached to distressing intrusive thoughts can give rise to catastrophic misinterpretations, as can engaging in thought action fusion (the belief that one's thoughts can somehow influence outside events or that immoral thoughts are tantamount to an immoral character) and thought suppression (see Rachman 1997, 1998). Indeed, researchers have found that these characteristics are often elevated in individuals with OCD, compared with other populations (e.g., Frost et al., 1993; Rachman, 1993, 1997; Shafran, Thordarson, & Rachman, 1996; Shafran, Watkins, & Charman, 1996). In addition, experimental manipulation of such characteristics can elicit obsessive–compulsive behaviors (e.g., Rachman, Shafran, Mitchell, Trant, & Teachman, 1996; Salkovskis & Campbell, 1994; Wegner, Schneider, Carter, & White, 1987; Zucker, Craske, Barrios, & Holguin, 2002).

Perhaps unique to OCD is the fact that families may become involved in the affected member's rituals, which may encourage both the onset and maintenance of the disorder. For example, Shafran, Ralph, and Tallis (1995) found that 60% of family members of individuals with obsessive or compulsive symptoms were involved in the rituals of the affected person, with 90% of family members reporting at least some interference in their own lives due to their relative's symptoms. However, because a diagnostic interview was not used, the accuracy of this study as it relates to family members of individuals with a diagnosis of OCD is in question. Similarly, Calvocoressi and colleagues (1995) evaluated family members of patients diagnosed with OCD and found that 88% reported engaging in at least mild accommodation of their relatives' symptoms. Moreover, such accommodation was associated with greater distress and dysfunction in the family. These two studies speak to the importance of involving family members in interventions.

Few prospective studies of OCD have aided in identifying risk factors. Recently, Peterson, Pine, Cohen, and Brook (2001) found that tics and attention deficit hyperactivity disorder (ADHD) in childhood were each significant predictors of OCD in later adolescence and adulthood. In addition, these researchers found that the presence of OCD in late adolescence also predicted tics and ADHD in adulthood.

Subclinical OCD—the manifestation of some obsessions and compulsions, but not at a severe enough level to reach clinical significance—also has been hypothesized to confer an increased risk for the clinical disorder on the individual (Flament et al., 1988; Thomsen, 1993). However, studies with children and adolescents with subclinical OCD did not find it to be a significant risk factor for the clinical disorder (see Berg et al., 1989). Currently, there are no published prospective studies with adult populations with subclinical OCD.

Prevention Studies

No studies on the prevention of OCD have yet been published. Recently, Zucker, Craske, Barrios, and Holguin (2002) were able to demonstrate the effectiveness of a brief educational intervention to offset anxiety associated with an intrusive thought. Participants who endorsed high levels of thought action fusion listened either to a brief educational audiotape about the fallacy of thought action fusion or to a "placebo" tape about stress. Participants were then asked to write the sentence "I hope _____ is in a car accident," inserting a loved one's name in the blank. Those who heard the educational tape were significantly less anxious after writing the sentence than those who heard the "placebo." This finding indicates the importance of education in correcting maladaptive thoughts. However, since a follow-up period was not included in the protocol, it is impossible to speculate on the longevity of the intervention. Zucker and Craske are currently investigating a brief (3-hour) cognitive–behavioral group intervention for university students with subclinical OCD. The intervention's efficacy is currently under investigation in terms of its ability to prevent obsessive–compulsive symptoms and full onset of the disorder, as well as its effect on comorbid conditions.

Although the current data on the transition from subclinical OCD to its clinical counterpart are inconclusive, the presence of subclinical symptomatology might confer an increased risk for the disorder and might be an appropriate target for prevention efforts. In general, prospective research is warranted to elucidate the relationship between psychosocial risk factors and the onset of the disorder. In addition, opportunities to prevent OCD exist in both childhood and adulthood, given the range of onset of the condition.

PANIC DISORDER

Risk Factors

Panic disorder is characterized by brief, intense surges of anxiety or fear and related physiological sensations that occur repeatedly and unexpectedly, generating distress, worry, and interference (American Psychiatric Association, 1994). Physiological sensations, such as a racing heart and shortness of breath, are typically perceived as threatening because of their unexplainable and unpredictable onset and because those with panic disorder are hypersensitive to sensations of arousal (Ehlers, 1993, 1995).

This fear of physiological sensations of anxiety and arousal has received considerable attention with respect to vulnerability to panic disorder and other anxiety disorders. Reiss, Peterson, Gursky, and McNally (1986) have identified a cognitive predisposition—*anxiety sensitivity*—that refers to the tendency to perceive symptoms of anxiety or arousal as harmful. Anxiety sensitivity is considered distinct from trait anxiety, although it is thought to be stable over time (Messenger & Shean, 1998). From a developmental perspective, anxiety sensitivity may be fostered throughout childhood by recurrent exposure to significant illness (directly or vicariously) and general hypochondriacal concerns within the family (Craske, 1999; Stewart & Watt, 2000). Presumably, individuals learn that slight physiological discomfort or symptoms may signify impending threat, whereupon they become hypervigilant.

Several studies have demonstrated that heightened anxiety sensitivity differentiates clinical from subclinical panickers, predicts future attacks, and predicts the development of panic disorder (Ehlers, 1995; Maller & Reiss, 1992; Norton et al., 1992; Schmidt, Lerew, & Jackson, 1999). For instance, anxiety sensitivity was lower in a group of nonclinical panickers (individuals with recurrent panic attacks who did not meet the criteria for panic disorder) than in those with panic disorder (Norton et al., 1992). Schmidt et al. (1999) conducted a prospective study of the relationship between anxiety sensitivity and the development of unexpected panic attacks in response to stress. In their study, anxiety sensitivity and trait anxiety at baseline predicted the onset of "spontaneous" panic attacks during basic training in the military, and the relationship between trait anxiety and panic attacks appeared to be mediated by anxiety sensitivity. Although history of panic attacks was also a predictor, anxiety sensitivity showed a unique influence on the development of panic attacks (Schmidt et al., 1999). Despite their significance, these findings are limited by the absence of diagnostic assessment at baseline, so that some participants may have had panic disorder prior to starting basic training. Other research confirms that anxiety sensitivity influences responses to stress independently of panic attacks (e.g., Messenger & Shean, 1998).

As suggested by the nature of the disorder, experience with panic attacks is a risk factor for developing panic disorder. The Epidemiological

Catchment Area project found that approximately 10% of individuals report the occurrence of multiple panic attacks over their lifetime, although some reports indicate that percentage might be an underestimate (Eaton et al., 1995). These epidemiological data also revealed that a prodromal period may exist for panic disorder, lasting anywhere from 10–15 years before the condition actually develops. Panic attacks that occurred in the year preceding the interviews were strong predictors of panic disorder (Eaton et al., 1995).

Ehlers (1995) followed a group of individuals who had experienced at least one spontaneous panic attack, but never met the criteria for panic disorder, and compared them with a group of controls with no history of panic attacks. She found that, in the infrequent panickers group, 15% were diagnosed with panic disorder at a 1-year follow-up. In comparison, only 2% of those who had never experienced a panic attack developed panic disorder within the year. The maintenance of panic attacks was related to accurate perception of heartbeat, increased avoidance behaviors, elevated anxiety sensitivity, and the presence of comorbid diagnoses. Fifty percent of the infrequent panickers continued to have panic attacks at follow-up (Ehlers, 1995).

Prevention

There have been only two prevention studies in the treatment of panic disorder. Swinson, Soulios, Cox, and Kuch (1992) provided a brief intervention to individuals who sought help at an emergency room because of a panic attack. Most participants had attributed the symptoms to a heart attack and thus sought medical attention. The members of the randomized-treatment group were first reassured that they had experienced a panic attack with sensations that were harmless. These individuals were then educated about the role of exposure in overcoming these fears and were encouraged to practice exposure on their own. The control group simply received reassurance that they had experienced a panic attack with harmless sensations. One week following the intervention, panic attack frequencies dropped in the exposure group from 2.53 to 0.76 and increased in the control group from 2.50 to 3.38. The exposure group continued to show improvement on all measures of anxiety and panic at 3- and 6-month follow-ups. Unfortunately, 40% of the sample already had met the criteria for panic disorder at intake, and diagnostic assessments were not conducted during the follow-up interviews. Thus, whereas the intervention decreased the frequency and severity of panic attacks, it did not necessarily prevent the onset of panic disorder (Swinson et al., 1992).

More recently, Gardenswartz and Craske (2001) conducted a secondary preventive study with psychology undergraduates who reported at least moderate anxiety sensitivity and a history of at least one panic attack in the previous 12 months, but who did not meet the criteria for a diagnosis of panic disorder. Of 121 students participating in the study, 55 were randomly assigned to a 5-hour workshop group. The preventive workshop was modeled after a standard cognitive–behavioral protocol for panic disorder treatment, providing psychoeducation about panic, cognitive skills training (e.g., restructuring), psychoeducation about agoraphobia, and education about confronting their fears.

The workshop yielded robust results, with nine (14%) participants in the control group developing panic disorder by 6-month follow-up, versus only one (2%) participant in the workshop group. Individuals who attended the workshop also exhibited more decreases in frequency and severity of panic and less agoraphobia than the control group, who nevertheless also showed modest improvement during the follow-up period (Gardenswartz & Craske, 2001). These results are particularly promising, because the use of a workshop format for administering treatment is both cost and time efficient. Unfortunately, neither the assessors nor the participants were blind to conditions, so the results may be biased.

POSTTRAUMATIC STRESS DISORDER

Risk Factors

Relative to other anxiety disorders, PTSD may be the most amenable to timely secondary prevention, because of its onset subsequent to a specific traumatic event or events. Estimates of the incidence of PTSD following a traumatic event vary widely and range from 5% to 51% of those developing full-blown PTSD at some point following a trauma (e.g., Epstein, Fullerton, & Ursano, 1998; Shalev, Peri, Canetti, & Schreiber, 1996; Yule et al., 2000). These discrepancies in PTSD incidence are attributable to a number of factors, including varying methods of diagnostic assessment, severity of disaster assessed, and participant recruitment issues.

PTSD risk factors can be divided into three categories: pretrauma factors, factors specific to the trauma itself, and posttrauma factors. Pretrauma factors that have been found to be associated with a diagnosis of PTSD or symptomatology of the disorder are female gender, previous exposure to trauma (childhood abuse in particular), personal and family history of mental illness, lower education and intelligence, lower socioeconomic status, and younger age at time of exposure to trauma (e.g., Brewin, Andrews, & Valentine, 2000; Epstein et al., 1998; Fontana & Rosenheck, 1994; Zlotnick, Bruce, Shea, & Keller, 2001). Greater severity of trauma, perceived threat to one's life, and dissociation during the trauma are risk factors specific to the trauma itself that have been shown to be associated with the onset of PTSD (Brewin et al., 2000; Shalev et al., 1996). Finally, posttrauma dissociative symptoms, anxiety, depression, lack of social support, additional life events, and increased arousal have been implicated as predictors of PTSD (e.g., Brewin, Andrews, Rose, & Kirk, 1999; Brewin et al., 2000; Fontana & Rosenheck, 1994; Shalev et al., 1996). In the special case of war veterans, postwar societal rejection at homecoming also has been demonstrated to contribute to PTSD pathology (e.g., Fontana & Rosenheck, 1994). Although some of these risk factors, such as severity of the trauma itself, cannot be addressed through prevention efforts, other factors can be addressed at different levels of prevention. Some of the pretrauma risk factors might be addressed in primary, nonspecific anxiety prevention efforts, whereas many risk factors are more easily targeted in selective PTSD prevention efforts.

The diagnosis of acute stress disorder is a useful tool for targeting individuals at risk for PTSD, because acute stress disorder can be assessed soon after exposure to the trauma. The criteria include a constellation of symptoms, including dissociation, increased anxiety and arousal, persistent reexperiencing of the trauma, and avoidance of trauma-related stimuli (American Psychiatric Association, 1994). The presence of acute stress disorder has been found to be a strong predictor of a later diagnosis of PTSD (e.g., Brewin et al., 1999; Harvey & Bryant, 2000). For example, one study found that 73% of motor vehicle accident survivors diagnosed with acute stress disorder met the criteria for PTSD 2 years after the accident (Harvey & Bryant, 2000). Nonetheless, the onset of PTSD might be delayed for long periods subsequent to exposure to trauma (Zlotnick et al., 2001), so an initial diagnosis of acute stress disorder cannot be relied on as a singular predictor of PTSD.

Prevention

According to Rachman (1980), emotional processing after a trauma or some other type of emotional event is necessary to reduce subsequent fear and emotional disturbances, such as nightmares, unpleasant intrusive thoughts, and subjective distress, because many fears and trauma-related distress reactions develop through inadequate emotional processing. To facilitate posttrauma emotional processing, the military and other groups have utilized an intervention called *critical incident stress debriefing*. This process of immediate psychological debriefing is believed to allow trauma victims to "process" a trauma both cognitively and emotionally, before maladaptive behaviors and cognitions are established (Deahl, Gillham, Thomas, Searle, & Srinivasan, 1994). Critical incident stress debriefing is delivered in a group setting within a few hours or days of the event. The intervention includes education about normal poststress reactions, instructions for managing stress, a reconstruction of the traumatic event, and the opportunity to share thoughts and emotions associated with the event. Participants are encouraged to seek follow-up assistance if desired (e.g., Mitchell, 1983; Wollman, 1993).

Unfortunately, there is a paucity of well-controlled empirical studies of psychological debriefings, and there have been mixed findings about the efficacy of the procedure. Although some reports of debriefing are promising, (e.g., Fitzgerald et al., 1993; Wollman, 1993), others are not. For example, in a study of British Gulf War veterans, wherein some received a debriefing and others did not, researchers found no significant effects of the debriefing (Deahl et al., 1994). Two limiting factors were that the debriefing was not conducted in a timely fashion and that no standardized debriefing curriculum was ever used; thus, the generalizability of the findings is compromised (Deahl et al., 1994). However, other studies have found debriefing to be associated with worse outcomes than those of individuals who are not debriefed (Bisson, Jenkins, Alexander, & Bannister, 1997; Mayou, Ehlers, & Hobbs, 2000). Given these conflicting results, it is difficult to draw scientific conclusions regarding the efficacy of debriefing in preventing PTSD.

Other PTSD prevention studies have also failed to yield significant results. For example, Brom, Kleber, and Hofman (1993) did not find any effects of their intervention on victims of motor vehicle accidents (the intervention was administered at least 1 month after the accident) relative to a group that was monitored only. However, the authors did not describe their intervention, and it is impossible to determine whether the absence of effects was due to delays in providing the intervention, to characteristics of the intervention itself, or to both. Foa, Zoellner, Feeny, Meadows, and Jaycox (2000) compared four weekly 2-hour sessions of cognitive–behavioral intervention or supportive counseling with a wait list for victims of a recent assault. Because a majority of the victims recovered from the trauma regardless of treatment, participants from the two groups did not differ 3 months or 6 months after the assault.

In sum, although research in this area is limited, the relationship of the disorder to a discrete event makes PTSD particularly amenable to prevention efforts. Timing, however, is clearly crucial to the interventions. It is not yet clear whether PTSD preventative interventions should be implemented immediately following the trauma. However, the failure of the Deahl et al. (1994) and Brom et al. (1993) studies to find significant results of an intervention could be due to delay between the time of exposure to trauma and that of delivery of treatment. Emergency rooms, crisis centers, and military bases may be the most appropriate venues for expedient PTSD prevention efforts. Group intervention may also be efficacious, cost effective, and feasible, especially when large groups are exposed to the same trauma.

GENERALIZED ANXIETY DISORDER

Risk Factors

Studies of generalized anxiety disorder (GAD) have been greatly underrepresented in the literature, and from 1980 to 1997 fewer studies of GAD have been published than for panic disorder, OCD, or PTSD (Dugas, 2000).

As a result of this paucity of empirical (especially longitudinal) investigation of the disorder, our knowledge of specific risk factors is largely speculative. General risk factors, such as neuroticism and maladaptive parenting, may combine with dysfunctional use of worry to increase an individual's risk for GAD.

Muris and Merckelbach (1998) found that parental control and anxious rearing were significantly related to symptoms of GAD in children 8 to 12 years old. The authors also assessed children's perceptions of parenting in an attempt to eliminate the issue of retrospective reporting by parents. The correlational nature of their study, however, limits generalizability considerably. Similarly, Siqueland, Kendall, and Steinberg (1996) observed that parents of children with anxiety disorders granted less psychological autonomy than did parents of control children. On self-report measures, the children with anxiety disorders rated their parents as significantly less accepting than the control children rated their parents. Interestingly, no differences emerged between the two groups of parents on self-reports of their own parenting style in the areas of psychological control or acceptance.

Other research specific to GAD has examined the role of worry as a method of avoiding emotionally difficult issues. In support of this hypothesis, Borkovec and Roemer (1995) found that undergraduates who met DSM–III–R criteria for the disorder used worry as a distraction from emotional topics significantly more frequently than did nonanxious and nonworried anxious controls. One interpretation of this finding is that worry enables individuals with GAD to process emotional topics in an abstract way, permitting them to avoid intense emotions and autonomic arousal (Borkovec, Alcaine, & Behar, in press). Subsequent experiences with emotional material, however, typically become more troublesome, and the use of worry is further reinforced.

Research in metacognition may provide another explanation for the development of pathological worry. Metabeliefs about worry—beliefs about the act and function of worrying itself—can be positive (e.g., worry is a coping mechanism) or negative (e.g., worry is dangerous) in nature (e.g., Cartwright-Hatton & Wells, 1997; Wells, 1995). According to Wells (1995), what differentiates normal worry from pathological worry is the presence of metabeliefs in pathological worriers, but not in normal worriers. Worry becomes problematic only when metaworry is developed—that is, when "worry itself becomes the focus of rumination and of efforts at control" (p. 306). Thus, efforts at targeting metacognitive beliefs about worry could be an important element in GAD prevention, especially when other risk factors are present.

Prevention Programs

Cognitive–behavior therapy appears to be the preferred modality of intervention for GAD. In a review of 13 controlled treatment outcome studies, Borkovec and Ruscio (2001) found that cognitive–behavior therapy was more efficacious than waitlist control or nonspecific therapy conditions. Nonetheless, GAD remains the least successfully treatable anxiety disorder (Brown, Barlow, & Liebowitz, 1994), which speaks to the need to investigate prevention efforts for this disorder. To date, there have been no published studies of prevention programs for the disorder, although preventative interventions designed to target stress, anxiety, and other related problems may offer important directions for future research.

In one community-based intervention, Timmerman et al. (1998) selected individuals who were deemed to be at risk for developing serious mental health problems. The criteria for defining at risk involved social anxiety, poor coping strategies, dissatisfaction with social support, the presence of life events in the past year, and high scores on at least three measures of neuroticism. Participants in the experimental group attended eight weekly 2 1/2-hour stress management group sessions that focused on changes in lifestyle, relaxation techniques, problem solving, and social skills training. Compared with a control group that received no treatment, the treatment group reported significantly less distress, fewer somatic complaints, more assertiveness, and more satisfaction with social support after treatment and at 6-month follow-up. Improvements in problem-solving ability observed after treatment, however, were not maintained at the 6-month follow-up. Unfortunately, interpretations of these findings are seriously limited because of the absence of diagnostic assessments and nonrandom assignment of participants to the two groups.

Prevention of GAD has also been investigated in the context of a prevention program aimed at targeting depression (Seligman, Schulman, DeRubeis, & Hollon, 1999). Participants in this study were defined as at risk for depression on the basis of a pessimistic explanatory style. The intervention was composed of eight 2-hour group workshop sessions based largely on cognitive–behavioral techniques developed for depression, including stress management and relaxation training. In addition to experiencing less depressive symptomatology, the treatment group had significantly fewer anxiety symptoms and fewer diagnoses of GAD at 3-year follow-up than an assessment-only group had.

Although the Seligman et al. study was not specifically designed for the prevention of GAD, the investigators were able to offset cases with the disorder by treating depression. Treatment studies have demonstrated this phenomenon: Successful treatment targeted at one disorder can reduce comorbid conditions (e.g., Brown & Barlow, 1995; Tsao, Mystkowski, Zucker, & Craske, 2002). The issue of comorbidity prevention is particularly salient in the case of GAD, for which lifetime rates of comorbidity are as high as 90% (Wittchen, Zhao, Kessler, & Eaton, 1994). Thus, one might posit that successful prevention of GAD will aid in offsetting other disorders. Similarly, studying the prevention of GAD will aid in further identifying risk factors for the disorder, informing those who may be vulnerable how to cope with distressing emotions.

CONCLUSIONS AND FUTURE DIRECTIONS

Secondary prevention is a burgeoning area in treatment outcome research for anxiety disorders. With many disorders, little is understood about the most effective strategies for early identification and intervention. Because knowledge of specific causal and mediating factors is limited for some disorders, risk factors that are sensitive enough to identify those who will develop a disorder, yet specific enough to rule out those who will not, are difficult to establish. For instance, the etiologies of GAD and OCD remain relatively vague, limiting our ability to identify specific risk factors. PTSD and panic disorder, however, have specific individual factors and stressors that predict their onset with considerable accuracy, thus making these disorders more amenable to preventive treatment approaches. The specificity of criteria for identifying those who are at risk is an important concept in developing prevention programs, because high false positive rates limit our ability considerably to identify the effective aspects of an intervention. For this reason, Story and Craske are conducting a prospective study of vulnerability to panic disorder, and additional prospective investigations are warranted in anxiety disorders.

The current literature also suggests that the application of preventive strategies should be developmentally appropriate, such that the age at intervention becomes a critical variable. Interventions with younger samples, for instance, need elements that address parenting skills and familial factors, as is consistent with current cognitive–behavioral therapy interventions. Similarly, prevention strategies that target at-risk children and adolescents may be more effective at reducing general vulnerabilities to anxiety and mood disorders, as opposed to preventing the onset of specific conditions. By contrast, secondary prevention in adults may be most effective if it is aimed at predispositions for specific anxiety disorders, because these factors appear more stable in adulthood. Initial prevention studies employing this approach (e.g., Gardenswartz & Craske, 2001) have yielded promising results.

Considerations for future research should address some notable absences in the extant body of literature. Surprisingly, researchers have directed little attention toward buffering factors as they relate to vulnerability to anxiety disorders. Latent inhibition was discussed as one potential buffer, although this has not been examined empirically and needs further specification for individual disorders. For instance, exercise is one potential buffer for anxiety disorders that deserves consideration, given that physiological arousal is a central feature of anxiety, particularly panic disorder. Regular positive experiences with physiological arousal through exercise may mitigate negative interpretations of arousal during anxiety-provoking situations. In addition, there is a clear and present need to expand and develop cross-cultural research in this area. Convenience samples make up a large portion of today's findings, limiting the external validity of this body of research. Finally, as mentioned, more prospective work with at-risk samples is necessary to improve both the current understanding of developmental pathways of anxiety disorders and possible methods of early intervention. Though secondary prevention of clinical anxiety is still in its infancy, future work in the area may diminish the debilitating impact of this family of disorders.

REFERENCES

American Psychiatric Association. (1994). *Diagnostic and statistical manual of mental disorders* (4th ed.). Washington, DC: Author.

Barrett, P. M. (1998). Evaluation of cognitive–behavioral group treatments for childhood anxiety disorders. *Journal of Clinical Child Psychology, 27,* 459–486.

Barrett, P. M., Dadds, M. R., & Rapee, R. M. (1996). Family treatment of childhood anxiety: A controlled trial. *Journal of Consulting and Clinical Psychology, 64,* 333–342.

Barrett, P., & Turner, C. (2001). Prevention of anxiety symptoms in primary school children: Preliminary results from a universal school-based trial. *British Journal of Clinical Psychology, 40,* 399–410.

Berg, C. Z., Rapoport, J. L., Whitaker, A., Davies, M., Leonard, H., Swedo, S. E., et al. (1989). Childhood obsessive compulsive disorder: A two-year prospective follow-up of a community sample. *Journal of the American Academy of Child and Adolescent Psychiatry, 28*(4), 528–533.

Biederman, J., Rosenbaum, J. F., Bolduc-Murphy, E. A., Faraone, S. V., Chaloff, J., Hirschfeld, D. R., & Kagan, J. (1993). A 3-year follow-up of children with and without behavioral inhibition. *Journal of the American Academy of Child and Adolescent Psychiatry, 32,* 814–821.

Biederman, J., Rosenbaum, J. F., Hirshfeld, D. R., Faraone, S. V., Bolduc, E. A., Gersten, M., et al. (1990). Psychiatric correlates of behavioral inhibition in young children of parents with and without psychiatric disorders. *Archives of General Psychiatry, 47,* 21–26.

Bisson, J. I., Jenkins, P. L., Alexander, J., & Bannister, C. (1997). Randomised controlled trial of psychological debriefing for victims of acute burn trauma. *British Journal of Psychiatry, 171,* 78–81.

Boegels, S. M., van Oosten, A., Muris, P., & Smulders, D. (2001). Familial correlates of social anxiety in children and adolescents. *Behaviour Research and Therapy, 39,* 273–287.

Borkovec, T. D., Alcaine, O., & Behar, E. (in press). Avoidance theory of worry and generalized anxiety disorder. In R. G. Heimberg, C. L. Turk, & D. S. Mennin (Eds.), *Generalized anxiety disorder: Advances in research and practice.* New York: Guilford.

Borkovec, T. D., & Roemer, L. (1995). Perceived functions of worry among general-ized anxiety disorder subjects: Distraction from more emotionally distressing topics? *Journal of Behavior Therapy and Experimental Psychiatry, 26,* 25–30.

Borkovec, T. D., & Ruscio, A. M. (2001). Psychotherapy for generalized anxiety disorder. *Journal of Clinical Psychiatry, 62*(Suppl. 11), 37–42.

Breslau, N., & Davis, G. C. (1992). Posttraumatic stress disorder in an urban popula-tion of young adults: Risk factors for chronicity. *American Journal of Psychiatry, 149,* 671–675.

Brewin, C. R., Andrews, B., Rose, S., & Kirk, M. (1999). Acute stress disorder and posttraumatic stress disorder in victims of violent crime. *American Journal of Psychiatry, 156*(3), 360–366.

Brewin, C. R., Andrews, B., & Valentine, J. D. (2000). Meta-analysis of risk factors for posttraumatic stress disorder in trauma-exposed adults. *Journal of Consulting and Clinical Psychology, 68,* 748–766.

Brom, D., Kleber, R. J., & Hofman, M. C. (1993). Victims of traffic accidents: Incidence and prevention of post-traumatic stress disorder. *Journal of Clinical Psychology, 49,* 131–140.

Brown, T. A., & Barlow, D. H. (1995). Long-term outcome in cognitive behavioral treatment of panic disorder: Clinical predictors and alternative strategies for assessment. *Journal of Consulting and Clinical Psychology, 63*(5), 754–765.

Brown, T. A., Barlow, D. H., & Liebowitz, M. R. (1994). The empirical basis of gen-eralized anxiety disorder. *American Journal of Psychiatry, 151,* 1272–1280.

Bruch, M. A., & Heimberg, R. G. (1994). Differences in perceptions of parental and personal characteristics between generalized and nongeneralized social phobics. *Journal of Anxiety Disorders, 8,* 155–168.

Calvocoressi, L., Lewis, B., Harris, M., Trufan, S. J., Goodman, W. K., McDougle, C. J., & Price, L. H. (1995). Family accommodation in obsessive–compulsive disorder. *American Journal of Psychiatry, 152,* 441–443.

Cartwright-Hatton, S., & Wells, A. (1997). Beliefs about worry and intrusions: The Meta-Cognitions Questionnaire and its correlates. *Journal of Anxiety Disorders, 11,* 279–296.

Cook, M., & Mineka, S. (1989). Observational conditioning of fear to fear-relevant versus fear-irrelevant stimuli in rhesus monkeys. *Journal of Abnormal Psychology, 98,* 448–459.

Craske, M. G. (1999). *Anxiety disorders: Psychological approaches to theory and treat-ment.* Boulder, CO: Westview.

Craske, M. G., & Zucker, B. G. (2001). Prevention of anxiety disorders: A model for intervention. *Applied and Preventive Psychology, 10,* 155–175.

Dadds, M. R., Holland, D. E., Laurens, K. P., Mullins, M., Barrett, P. M., & Spence, S. H. (1999). Early intervention and prevention of anxiety disorders in chil-dren: Results at two-year follow-up. *Journal of Consulting and Clinical Psychology, 65,* 627–635.

Dadds, M. R., Spence, S. H., Holland, D. E., Barrett P. M., & Laurens, K. P. (1997). Prevention and early intervention for anxiety disorders: A controlled trial. *Journal of Consulting and Clinical Psychology, 65,* 627–635.

Davey, G., Burgess, I., & Rashes, R. (1995). Coping strategies and phobias: The relationship between fears, phobias and methods of coping. *British Journal of Clinical Psychology, 34*, 423–434.

Deahl, M. P., Gillham, A. B., Thomas, J., Searle, M. M., & Srinivasan, M. (1994). Psychological sequelae following the Gulf War: Factors associated with subsequent morbidity and the effectiveness of psychological debriefing. *British Journal of Psychiatry, 165*(1), 60–65.

Dollinger, S. J., O'Donnell, J. P., & Staley, A. A. (1984). Lighting-strike disaster: Effects on children's fears and worries. *Journal of Consulting and Clinical Psychology, 52*, 1028–1038.

Donovan, C. L., & Spence, S. H. (2000). Prevention of childhood anxiety disorders. *Clinical Psychology Review, 20*, 509–531.

Dugas, M. J. (2000). Generalized anxiety disorder publications: So where do we stand? *Journal of Anxiety Disorders, 14*, 31–40.

Eaton, W. W., Badawi, M., & Melton, B. (1995). Prodromes and precursors: Epidemiologic data for primary prevention of disorders with slow onset. *American Journal of Psychiatry, 152*, 967–972.

Ehlers, A. (1993). Interoception and panic disorder. *Behavioral Research and Therapy, 15*, 3–21.

Ehlers, A. (1995). A 1-year prospective study of panic attacks: Clinical course and factors associated with maintenance. *Journal of Abnormal Psychology, 104*, 164–172.

Epstein, R. S., Fullerton, C. S., & Ursano, R. J. (1998). Posttraumatic stress disorder following an air disaster: A prospective study. *American Journal of Psychiatry, 155*(7), 934–938.

Eysenck, H. (1960). *The structure of human personality* (2nd ed.). New York: Wiley.

Eysenck, H. (1985). *Personality and individual differences.* New York: Plenum.

Fitzgerald, M. L., Braudaway, C. A., Leeks, D., Padgett, M. B., Swartz, A. L., Samter, J., et al. (1993). Debriefing: A therapeutic intervention. *Military Medicine, 158*(8), 542–545.

Flament, M. F., Rapoport, J. L., Berg, C. Z., Sceery, W., Whitaker, A., et al. (1988). Obsessive–compulsive disorder in adolescence: An epidemiological study. *Journal of the American Academy of Child and Adolescent Psychiatry, 27*, 764–771.

Foa, E. B., Zoellner, L. A., Feeny, N. C., Meadows, E. A. & Jaycox, Z. H. (2000, November). *Evaluation of a brief cognitive-behavioral program for the prevention of chronic PTSD in recent assault victims.* Paper presented at Annual Convention for the Association for the Advancement of Behavior Therapy, New Orleans, LA.

Fontana, A., & Rosenheck, R. (1994). Posttraumatic stress disorder among Vietnam theater veterans: A causal model of etiology in a community sample. *Journal of Nervous and Mental Disease, 182*(12), 677–684.

Freeston, M. H., Ladouceur, R., Thibodeau, N., & Gagnon, F. (1991). Cognitive intrusions in a non-clinical population: i. Response style, subjective experience, and appraisal. *Behaviour Research and Therapy, 29*, 585–597.

Frost, R. O., Krause, M. S., McMahon, M. J., Peppe, J., Evans, M., McPhee, A. E., & Holden, M. (1993). Compulsivity and superstitiousness. *Behaviour Research and Therapy, 31*(4), 423–425.

Gardenswartz, C. A., & Craske, M. G. (2001). Prevention of panic disorder. *Behavior Therapy, 32*, 725–737.

Greenberg, P. E., Sisitsky, T., Kessler, R. C., Finkelstein, S. N., Berndt, E. R., Davidson, J. R. T., et al. (1999). The economic burden of anxiety disorders in the 1990s. *Journal of Clinical Psychiatry, 60*, 427–435.

Harvey, A. G., & Bryant, R. A. (2000). Two-year prospective evaluation of the relationship between acute stress disorder and posttraumatic stress disorder following mild traumatic brain injury. *American Journal of Psychiatry, 157*(4), 626–628.

Hayward, C., Killen, J. D., Kraemer, H. C., Blair-Greiner, A., Strachowski, D., Cunning, D., & Taylor, C. B. (1997). Assessment and phenomenology of nonclinical panic attacks in adolescent girls. *Journal of Anxiety Disorders, 11*, 17–32.

Hayward, C., Killen, J. D., Kraemer, H. C., & Taylor, C. B. (2000). Predictors of panic attacks in adolescents. *Journal of the American Academy of Child and Adolescent Psychiatry, 39*, 207–214.

Heim, C., & Nemeroff, C. B. (1999). The impact of early adverse experiences on brain systems involved in the pathophysiology of anxiety and affective disorders. *Society of Biological Psychiatry, 46*, 1509–1522.

Hess, R. D., & Camara, K. A. (1979). Post-divorce family relationships as mediating factors in the consequences of divorce for children. *Journal of Social Issues, 35*, 79–96.

Hirshfeld, D. R., Rosenbaum, J. F., Biederman, J., Bolduc, E. A., Faraone, S. V., Sandman, N., et al. (1992). Stable behavioral inhibition and its association with anxiety disorder. *Journal of the American Academy of Child and Adolescent Psychiatry, 31*, 103–111.

Hofmann, S. G., Ehlers, A., & Roth, W. T. (1995). Conditioning theory: A model for the etiology of public speaking anxiety? *Behaviour Research and Therapy, 33*, 567–571.

Ishiyama, F. I. (1984). Shyness: Anxious social sensitivity and self-isolating tendency. *Adolescence, 19*, 903–911.

Jay, S. M., Elliott, C. H., Katz, E., & Siegel, S. E. (1987). Cognitive–behavioral and pharmacologic interventions for children's distress during painful medical procedures. *Journal of Consulting and Clinical Psychology, 55*, 860–865.

Kagan, J. (1999). The concept of behavioral inhibition. In Louis A. Schmidt & Jay Schulkin (Eds.), *Extreme fear, shyness, and social phobia* (pp. 3–13). New York: Oxford University Press.

Kagan, J., Reznick, J. S., & Snidman, N. (1987). The physiology and psychology of behavioral inhibition in children. *Child Development, 58*, 1459–1473.

Kagan, J., Reznick, J. S., & Snidman, N. (1988). Biological bases of childhood shyness. *Science, 240*(4849), 167–171.

Kashani, J. H., & Orvaschel, H. (1990). A community study of anxiety in children and adolescents. *American Journal of Psychiatry, 147*, 313–318.

Kashdan, T. B., & Herbert, J. D. (2001). Social anxiety disorder in childhood and adolescence: Current status and future directions. *Clinical Child and Family Psychology Review, 4*, 37–61.

Kendall, P. C., & Treadwell, K. R. (1996). Cognitive–behavioral treatment for childhood anxiety disorders. In E. D. Hibbs & P. S. Jensen (Eds.). *Psychosocial treatments for child and adolescent disorders: Empirically based strategies for clinical practice* (pp. 23–42). Washington, DC: American Psychological Association.

Kendler, K. S., Heath, A. C., Martin, N. G., & Eaves, L. J. (1986). Symptoms of anxiety and depression in a volunteer twin population. *Archives of General Psychiatry, 43*, 213–221.

Kendler, K. S., Neale, M. C., Kessler, R. C., Heath, A. C., & Eaves, L. J. (1992). Generalised anxiety disorder in women: A population-based twin study. *Archives of General Psychiatry, 49*, 267–272.

Kennerley, H. (1996). The prevention of anxiety disorders. In T. Kendrick, A. Tylee, & P. Freeling (Eds.), *The prevention of mental illness in primary care* (pp. 188–206). New York: Cambridge University Press.

Kessler, R., McGonagle, K., Zhao, S., Nelson, C., Hughes, M., Eshleman, S., et al. (1994). Lifetime and 12-month prevalence of DSM–III–R psychiatric disorders in the United States: Results from the National Comorbidity Survey. *Archives of General Psychiatry, 51*, 8–19.

Krohne, H. W., & Hock, M. (1991). Relationships between restrictive mother/child interactions and anxiety of the child. *Anxiety Research, 4*, 109–124.

LaFreniere, P. J., & Capuano, F. (1997). Preventive intervention as means of clarifying direction of effects of socialization: Anxious withdrawn preschoolers case. *Development and Psychopathology, 9*, 551–564.

Lowry-Webster, H. M., Barrett, P. M., & Dadds, M. R. (2001). A universal prevention trial of anxiety and depressive symptomatology in childhood: Preliminary data from an Australian study. *Behaviour Change, 18*(1), 36–50.

Mackintosh, N. (1983). *Conditioning and associative learning*. New York: Oxford University Press.

Maller, R., & Reiss, S. (1992). Anxiety sensitivity in 1984 and panic attacks in 1987. *Journal of Anxiety Disorders, 6*, 241–247.

Mayou, R. A., Ehlers, A., & Hobbs, M. (2000). Psychological debriefing for road traffic accident victims: Three-year follow-up of a randomized controlled trial. *British Journal of Psychiatry, 176*, 589–593.

McFarlane, A. C. (1987). Family functioning and overprotection following a natural disaster: The longitudinal effects of post-traumatic morbidity. *Australian and New Zealand Journal of Psychiatry, 21*, 210–218.

Melamed, B. G., Yurcheson, R., Fleece, E. L., Hutcherson, S., & Hawes, R. (1978). Effects of film modeling on the reduction of anxiety-related behaviors in individuals varying in level of previous experience in the stress situation. *Journal of Consulting and Clinical Psychology, 46*, 1357–1367.

Messenger, C., & Shean, G. (1998). The effects of anxiety sensitivity and history of panic on reactions to stressors in a non-clinical sample. *Journal of Behavior Therapy and Experimental Psychiatry, 29*, 279–288.

Mitchell, J. T. (1983). When disaster strikes: The critical incident stress debriefing process. *Journal of Emergency Medical Services, 8,* 36–39.

Monk, C. (2001). Stress and mood disorders during pregnancy: Implications for child development. *Psychiatric Quarterly, 72,* 347–357.

Mrazek, P. J., & Haggerty, R. J. (1994). *Reducing risks for mental disorders: Frontiers for preventive intervention research.* Washington, DC: National Academy Press.

Muris, P., & Merckelbach, H. (1998). Perceived parental rearing behavior and anxiety disorders symptoms in normal children. *Personality and Individual Differences, 25,* 1199–1206.

Muris, P., Merckelbach, H., & Clavan, M. (1997). Abnormal and normal compulsions. *Behavior Research and Therapy, 35,* 249–252.

Norton, R., Cox, B., & Malan, J. (1992). Nonclinical panickers: A critical review. *Clinical Psychology Review, 12,* 121–139.

Noyes, R., Holt, C., & Woodman, C. L. (1996). *Natural course of anxiety disorders.* Washington, DC: American Psychiatric Association.

Oosterlaan, J. (2001). Behavioral inhibition and the development of childhood anxiety disorders. In W. K. Silverman & P. D. A. Treffers (Eds.), *Anxiety disorders in children and adolescents: Research, assessment and intervention* (pp. 45–71). New York: Cambridge University Press.

Ost, L.-G., & Hugdahl, K. (1981). Acquisition of phobias and anxiety response patterns in clinical patients. *Behaviour Research and Therapy, 19,* 439–447.

Peterson, B. S., Pine, D. S., Cohen, P., & Brook, J. S. (2001). Prospective, longitudinal study of tic, obsessive–compulsive, and attention deficit/hyperactivity disorders in an epidemiological sample. *Journal of the American Academy of Child and Adolescent Psychiatry, 40,* 685–695.

Peterson, L., & Shigetomi, C. (1981). The use of coping techniques to minimize anxiety in hospitalized children. *Behavior Therapy, 12,* 1–14.

Prior, M., Smart, D., Sanson, A., & Oberklaid, F. (2000). Does shy-inhibited temperament in childhood lead to anxiety problems in adolescence? *Journal of the American Academy of Child and Adolescent Psychiatry, 39,* 461–468.

Rachman, S. (1980). Emotional processing. *Behavior Research and Therapy, 18,* 51–60.

Rachman, S. (1993). Obsessions, responsibility and guilt. *Behavior Research and Therapy, 31,* 149–154.

Rachman, S. (1997). A cognitive theory of obsessions. *Behavior Research and Therapy, 35*(9), 793–802.

Rachman, S. (1998). A cognitive theory of obsessions: Elaborations. *Behavior Research and Therapy, 36,* 385–401.

Rachman, S., & de Silva, P. (1978). Abnormal and normal obsessions. *Behavior Research and Therapy, 16,* 233–248.

Rachman, S., Shafran, R., Mitchell, D., Trant, J., & Teachman, B. (1996). How to remain neutral: An experimental analysis of neutralization. *Behavior Research and Therapy, 34,* 889–898.

Reiss, S., Peterson, R., Gursky, D., & McNally, R. (1986). Anxiety sensitivity, anxiety frequency and the predictions of fearfulness. *Behavior Research and Therapy, 24*, 1–8.

Salkovskis, P. M. (1985). Obsessional–compulsive problems: A cognitive–behavioural analysis. *Behavior Research and Therapy, 23*, 571–583.

Salkovskis, P. M., & Campbell, P. (1994). Thought suppression induces intrusion in naturally occurring negative intrusive thoughts. *Behavior Research and Therapy, 32*, 1–8.

Schmidt, N. B., Lerew, D. R., & Jackson, R. J. (1999). Prospective evaluation of anxiety sensitivity in the pathogenesis of panic: Replication and extension. *Journal of Abnormal Psychology, 108*, 532–537.

Schwartz, C. E., Snidman, N., & Kagan, J. (1999). Adolescent social anxiety as an outcome of inhibited temperament in childhood. *Journal of the American Academy of Child and Adolescent Psychiatry, 38*(8), 1008–1015.

Seligman, M. E. (1971). Phobias and preparedness. *Behavior Therapy, 2*, 307–320.

Seligman, M. E. P., Schulman, P., DeRubeis, R. J., & Hollon, S. D. (1999). The prevention of depression and anxiety. *Prevention and Treatment, 2.* Retrieved January 18, 2002 from http://journals.apa.org/prevention/volume2/pre0020008a.html

Shafran, R., Ralph, J., & Tallis, F. (1995). Obsessive–compulsive symptoms and the family. *Bulletin of the Menninger Clinic, 59*(4), 472–479.

Shafran, R., Thordarson, D. S., & Rachman, S. (1996). Thought–action fusion in obsessive compulsive disorder. *Journal of Anxiety Disorders, 10*(5), 379–391.

Shafran, R., Watkins, E., & Charman, T. (1996). Guilt in obsessive–compulsive disorder. *Journal of Anxiety Disorders, 10*(6), 509–516.

Shalev, A. Y., Peri, T., Canetti, L., & Schreiber, S. (1996). Predictors of PTSD in injured trauma survivors: A prospective study. *American Journal of Psychiatry, 153*(2), 219–225.

Siqueland, L., Kendall, P. C., & Steinberg, L. (1996). Anxiety in children: Perceived family environments and observed family interaction. *Journal of Clinical Child Psychology, 25*, 225–237.

Spence, S. H. (1994). Preventative strategies. In T. Ollendrick, N. J. King, & W. Yule (Eds.), *International handbook of phobic and anxiety disorders in children and adolescents* (pp. 453–474). New York: Plenum.

Spence, S. H. (2001). Prevention strategies. In Michael W. Vasey & Mark R. Dadds (Eds.), *The developmental psychopathology of anxiety* (pp. 325–351). New York: Oxford University Press.

Stewart, S. H., & Watt, M. C. (2000). Illness Attitudes Scale dimensions and their associations with anxiety-related constructs in a nonclinical sample. *Behaviour Research and Therapy, 38*, 83–99.

Swinson, R., Soulios, C., Cox, B., & Kuch, K. (1992). Brief treatment of emergency room patients with panic attacks. *American Journal of Psychiatry, 149*, 944–946.

Thomsen, P. H. (1993). Obsessive–compulsive disorder in children and adolescents: Self-reported obsessive–compulsive behaviour in pupils in Denmark. *Acta Psychiatrica Scandinavica, 88,* 212–217.

Timmerman, I. G., Emmelkamp, P. M., & Sanderman, R. (1998). The effects of a stress-management training program in individuals at risk in the community at large. *Behaviour Research and Therapy, 36,* 863–875.

Tsao, J. C. I., Mystkowski, J. L., Zucker, B. G., & Craske, M. G. (2002). Effects of cognitive–behavioral therapy for panic disorder on comorbid conditions: Replication and extension. *Behavior Therapy, 33,* 493–509.

Walsh, J. M., Eysenck, M. W., Wilding, J., & Valentine, J. (1994). Type A, neuroticism, and physiological functioning (actual and reported). *Journal of Personality and Individual Differences, 16,* 959–965.

Wegner, D. M., Schneider, D. J., Carter, S. R., & White, T. L. (1987). Paradoxical effects of thought suppression. *Journal of Personality and Social Psychology, 53,* 5–13.

Weinstein, P. (1990). Breaking the worldwide cycle of pain, fear and avoidance: Uncovering risk factors and promoting prevention for children. *Annals of Behavioral Medicine, 12,* 141–147.

Wells, A. (1995). Metacognition and worry: A cognitive model of generalized anxiety disorder. *Behavioral and Cognitive Psychotherapy, 23,* 301–320.

Wittchen, H.-U., Zhao, S., Kessler, R. C., & Eaton, W. W. (1994). DSM-III-R generalized anxiety disorder in the national comorbidity survey. *Archives of General Psychiatry, 51,* 355–364.

Wollman, D. (1993). Critical incident stress debriefing and crisis groups: A review of the literature. *Group, 17*(2), 70–83.

Yule, W., Bolton, D., Udwin, O., Boyle, S., O'Ryan, D., & Nurrish, J. (2000). The long-term psychological effects of a disaster experienced in adolescence: I: The incidence and course of PTSD. *Journal of Child Psychology and Psychiatry and Allied Disciplines, 41,* 503–511.

Zlotnick, C., Bruce, S. E., Shea, M. T., & Keller, M. B. (2001). Delayed posttraumatic stress disorder (PTSD) and predictors of first onset of PTSD in patients with anxiety disorders. *Journal of Nervous and Mental Disease, 189*(6), 404–406.

Zucker, B. G., Craske, M. G., Barrios, V., & Holguin, M. (2002). Thought action fusion: Can it be corrected? *Behaviour Research and Therapy, 40,* 653–664.

7

TERTIARY INTERVENTION FOR ANXIETY AND PREVENTION OF RELAPSE

MICHEL J. DUGAS, ADAM S. RADOMSKY,
AND PASCALE BRILLON

Although the field of prevention is relatively young, it is marked by considerable conceptual controversy. *Tertiary intervention* in particular has been defined in a number of ways. Some experts in prevention even claim that tertiary intervention is not prevention at all and should be termed *treatment* or *rehabilitation* (Price, Bader, & Ketterer, 1980). Because tertiary intervention is often aimed at individuals who meet the diagnostic criteria for a given disorder, one can certainly understand how tertiary intervention and treatment may appear to be one and the same. The distinction between the two, however, is real and conceptually important: Whereas the main goal of treatment is the alleviation of symptoms and remission of a given disorder, the principal objective of tertiary intervention is the prevention of the reoccurrence of the disorder following successful treatment. Tertiary intervention, therefore, is akin to what the treatment literature refers to as *relapse prevention*. Although some would argue that tertiary intervention and

161

relapse prevention represent different constructs, they will be considered synonymous in this chapter.

Given the high prevalence rates of the anxiety disorders (Kessler et al., 1994) and their serious consequences for society and the individual (Greenberg et al., 1999), research on the treatment of anxiety disorders and the prevention of relapse represents a top priority in the area of mental health. Although there is accumulating evidence for the efficacy of different treatments for anxiety disorders, evidence that these treatments lead to lasting change is more limited. In a recent meta-analysis of treatments for selected anxiety disorders, Westen and Morrison (2001) conclude that "one of the most striking things . . . is the sheer lack of data on follow-up at 12 months or longer." Certainly, their statement reflects the current state of the literature, but it is encouraging to note that an increasing number of treatment studies are now including long-term follow-up data. In fact, recent studies often include follow-up assessments ranging from 1 to 2 years, and many scientific journals now require that follow-up data be included in treatment studies. Further strides must be made, however, before such data are given the importance they clearly deserve. Follow-up data are often treated as a secondary feature of a study, typically addressed in a small section of the manuscript. Moreover, predictors of long-term success are rarely investigated in treatment studies. Demonstrating that some individuals stay well following treatment is one aspect of efficacy research; knowing why they stay well is a separate, but equally important, aspect.

This chapter seeks to answer three questions: (a) How efficacious are different psychosocial treatments at preventing the relapse of anxiety disorders in successfully treated patients? (b) What are the most promising treatments for preventing the relapse of anxiety disorders? and (c) What are the predictors of the maintenance of treatment gains in successfully treated patients? To address these questions, we will review the literature on tertiary intervention and on the prevention of relapse for each anxiety disorder: specific phobia, social anxiety disorder, obsessive–compulsive disorder, posttraumatic stress disorder, panic disorder, and generalized anxiety disorder. The review, however, will be restricted in three ways. First, in an effort to provide a relatively detailed picture of the state of the literature, we will focus on studies carried out in adult populations. Second, we will examine mainly psychosocial interventions for the different anxiety disorders (although some studies that include pharmacological interventions will be presented). The reason for this restriction is that clinical trials of pharmacological treatments typically do not include follow-up data. When follow-up data are included, it is often for a brief period of no longer than 3 months. Third, we will consider chiefly empirically supported treatments, as originally defined by the American Psychological Association's Division 12 Task Force on Psychological Interventions and later revisited by Diane Chambless and colleagues (1998). Although some other treatments will be examined, we have included all empirically supported treatments identified by Chambless et al. that are relevant to the issues addressed in this chapter.

TERTIARY INTERVENTION FOR
SPECIFIC ANXIETY DISORDERS

Specific Phobia

Among empirically supported treatments for psychological problems, the first support for effective and durable therapy came from investigations of behavior therapy for specific phobia. Based on early therapeutic models and approaches (e.g., Wolpe, 1958), the application of systematic desensitization, modeling, and exposure techniques to populations with a variety of specific phobias have consistently produced robust positive findings in both the short and long term.

One early investigation of behavior therapy for specific phobia, which was carried out by Bandura, Blanchard, and Ritter (1969), compared the effects of four types of treatment on participants with snake phobia. Participants were randomly assigned to imaginal desensitization, symbolic modeling (watching a film of a model therapist), modeling in vivo, or no treatment. The study produced a couple of important findings: First, all treatments were more effective than the absence of treatment, and all of these essentially behavioral approaches were equally effective in reducing snake phobia symptoms, as assessed by self-report and behavioral measures. Second, the improvement achieved through the various treatments was maintained at 1-month follow-up. This investigation was an early demonstration of how behavioral techniques can lead not only to immediate gains, but also to sustained gains over a period during which no treatment is administered. Since 1969, several other investigations have demonstrated the capacity of behavior therapy to prevent relapse over longer follow-up periods (see Öst, 1996).

More recent advances in the improvement of treatment outcomes and relapse prevention include investigations of massed (one-session) behavior therapy and, increasingly, cognitive–behavioral approaches to treating specific phobias. There is growing evidence that intensive one-session exposure therapy can be highly effective against several manifestations of specific phobia after treatment (e.g., Öst, Salkovskis, & Hellström, 1991) and, more impressively, that treatment gains can be maintained after a lengthy (1-year) follow-up (Öst, Alm, Brandberg, & Breitholtz, 2001). In addition, many behavioral treatments for specific phobia are becoming increasingly cognitive–behavioral and even cognitive (Craske & Rowe, 1998), with similar long-term benefits (Öst et al., 2001). This development probably stems from the fact that theoretical conceptualizations of phobias are becoming increasingly cognitive (e.g., Radomsky, Rachman, Thordarson, Teachman, & McIsaac, 2001) and easily lend themselves to cognitive–behavioral treatment approaches. Because early developments in behavior therapy for specific phobia were extremely influential in devising behavioral treatments for other anxiety disorders, research on issues such as the cognitive components of treatment and massed vs. gradual treatments is expected to have important applications in cognitive–behavioral approaches to treating other anxiety disorders and in the prevention of relapse after successful treatment.

Social Anxiety Disorder/Social Phobia

A review of empirically supported treatments for social anxiety disorder yields overall findings similar to the outcome and follow-up data associated with specific phobia. Given the complex nature of social anxiety disorder, however, theoretical models are somewhat more multifaceted than are models of specific phobia (see Rapee & Heimberg, 1997). Psychological treatments have also developed into more complex packages, which, in addition to exposure, often include elements of role play, behavioral experiments, cognitive exercises, homework exercises, reductions of safety behaviors, and a growing emphasis on components designed to prevent relapse (Radomsky & Otto, 2001).

One of the earliest long-term studies examining an empirically supported treatment for social anxiety disorder (though well before that specific diagnostic term was used) compared modified systematic desensitization, insight-oriented psychotherapy, an attention-placebo control, and a no-treatment condition after treatment and at 2-year follow-up (Paul, 1967). At the time, participants complained of "interpersonal anxiety," and the primary theoretical arguments against the use of behavioral techniques were strong concerns about relapse and symptom substitution. At that early stage in the development of empirically supported treatments, the results were extremely encouraging. For the systematic desensitization group, "significant improvement" was found in 85% of participants 2 years after the end of treatment. This percentage was markedly better than that of any of the other groups (50% were significantly improved in both the insight-oriented therapy group and the attention–placebo control, while only 22% of the no-treatment participants showed significant improvement). Although the initial focus of this long-term outcome study was to look for signs of relapse or symptom substitution, no evidence of either was found. It appeared that behavior therapy for social anxiety could produce not only treatment gains, but long-term maintenance of these gains and a reduction, or, in this case, a prevention, of relapse.

A more recent advance in delivering effective and lasting treatment for social anxiety disorder is the growing use of group cognitive–behavioral treatments. A group format for treating this disorder has certain advantages—in particular, that in-session exposure is readily accessible and that hypothesis testing about feared social interactions can be carried out with almost instant feedback (Radomsky & Otto, 2001). In one controlled study examining outcome and follow-up data from group cognitive–behavioral therapy for social anxiety disorder (Heimberg et al., 1990), 12 sessions of either group cognitive–behavioral therapy or a credible control therapy were provided to 49 individuals seeking treatment for social anxiety disorder. Although both groups improved, participants in the group cognitive–behavioral therapy condition were rated as more improved than controls and reported significantly less anxiety before and during the behavioral test portion of the posttreatment assessment. Furthermore, participants in the group cognitive–behavioral therapy condition reported fewer negative self-statements and more positive self-statements at 3- and 6-month follow-ups. This investigation demonstrates that group cognitive–behavioral therapy not only is highly effective for social anxiety disorder in the short term, but also produces lasting gains, resulting in a reduced likelihood of relapse.

Neither of the foregoing studies, however, makes any specific statement about the mechanisms involved in preventing relapse or the best method for maintaining treatment gains during extended follow-up periods. Some insight into these issues may come from two related studies comparing group cognitive–behavioral therapy for social anxiety disorder with pharmacotherapy. In the first study, each of 133 participants from two sites was assigned to one of four groups: a group that received cognitive–behavioral therapy, one that was given phenelzine therapy, a group that got a pill placebo, and a group that received educational–supportive therapy (an attention–placebo control; Heimberg et al., 1998). The authors found that, after 12 sessions, both phenelzine therapy and group cognitive–behavioral therapy were associated with significant, comparable gains. After the same 12 sessions, the pharmacotherapy condition produced stronger gains on some measures, and both active treatments were significantly more effective than the control conditions. The most interesting findings, however, come from a follow-up study conducted on the responders from the initial outcome study.

In the follow-up study (Liebowitz et al., 1999), participants from the Heimberg et al. (1998) treatment outcome research who responded to either psychotherapy or pharmacotherapy were placed in a maintenance program for 6 months. Those participants who continued to show gains through the maintenance period were placed in an additional 6-month no-treatment phase of the study. The authors found that, whereas the recipients of pharmacotherapy entered the maintenance phase of the study more improved than the recipients of group psychotherapy, there were no differences in relapse during the maintenance phase. Furthermore, pharmacotherapy resulted in a trend toward higher relapse than did psychotherapy. The authors concluded that the two treatments may differ significantly in their long-term effects and recommended group cognitive–behavioral therapy as a treatment both for the short term and for sustaining gains during the maintenance and treatment-free periods.

Although psychotherapy (in this case, group cognitive–behavioral therapy) does seem to result in reliably durable prevention of relapse, we have yet to discover why that is the case. Clearly, someone who benefits from treatment does not necessarily also have a low probability of experiencing relapse (see Liebowitz et al., 1999). Because of the relatively low number of long-term outcome studies of social anxiety disorder, it is difficult to address this issue on the basis of the data alone. However, reviews of the literature comparing various short-term or immediate treatment outcomes may provide some clues about the mechanisms involved in maintaining treatment gains over longer periods.

One meta-analysis that compared outcome studies using cognitive–behavioral therapy with studies using exposure alone (behavior therapy) for social anxiety disorder (Feske & Chambless, 1995) may shed light on the mechanisms involved in preventing relapse. These authors' review, which examined a total of 21 outcome studies, found that cognitive–behavioral therapy and behavior therapy were equally effective at posttest. Furthermore, cognitive–behavioral therapy was found to be no more effective at reducing self-reports of social anxiety, cognitive symptoms, or depressed or anxious mood than behavioral treatments were. In addition, the meta-analysis showed that, although more exposure was generally related to better outcomes, more sessions (i.e., the duration of treatment) were not. The findings in this review of immediate outcomes, together with some of the preceding observations, give rise to certain hypotheses about the mechanisms involved in promoting both short- and long-term positive treatment outcomes.

It seems likely that, overall, different mechanisms may be involved in short- and long-term gains. Clearly, a comparison of psychological and pharmacological interventions supports this idea. However, it is entirely possible that factors promoting gains in psychological treatments for social anxiety disorder also promote the maintenance of these gains in the long term. That is, if behavior therapy and cognitive–behavioral therapy lead to changes in maladaptive cognitions, reduction in the use of safety behaviors, reduced avoidance behavior, and increased exposure both during sessions and afterwards, it is quite possible that these factors, believed to be responsible for improvement, may also be responsible for maintaining that improvement. Whereas earlier models of behavior change included the idea that maladaptive associations are extinguished through successful treatment, it may be more appropriate to think of effective behavior therapy and cognitive–behavioral therapy for social anxiety disorder as promoting the acquisition of new adaptive learning, rather than erasing or replacing old learning (Radomsky & Otto, 2001). If so, these empirically supported approaches to treatment may have twofold effects. The first and most obvious result of effective treatment is that symptoms of social anxiety disorder are reduced (probably through learning a new adaptive set of behaviors and cognitions), leading to more adaptive beliefs about oneself and others. The second, more subtle, result may be that recipients of effective psychological treatments for social anxiety disorder are also learning a new way of learning. That is, developing the skill to test hypotheses about anxiety and using more objective information to evaluate those hypotheses may produce gains beyond the short term. This is, of course, a hypothesis in itself and would benefit from further investigation.

Obsessive–Compulsive Disorder

Obsessive–compulsive disorder (OCD) is one of the more difficult anxiety disorders to treat and may provide some of the most complex issues relating to enhancing both short- and long-term outcomes. This complexity may be due to the inherently reinforcing nature of compulsions and other neutralizing behaviors and the subsequently difficult task of encouraging patients to reduce or eliminate these maladaptive, yet anxiety-reducing coping mechanisms (Rachman & Hodgson, 1980). It is also probable that negative beliefs and other cognitive biases make a large contribution to the maintenance of this disorder, with beliefs related to perceived responsibility playing a central role (Salkovskis, 1985). Thus, a treatment that successfully reduces the symptoms of OCD and prevents relapse following treatment not only must weaken the connection between anxiety and compulsive actions, but also must provide credible and sustainable alternative beliefs about coping with perceived risk and danger.

The first empirically supported treatment study of OCD was a comparison of cognitive–behavioral therapy and behavior therapy (exposure and response prevention; van Oppen et al., 1995). In this study, 28 participants received 16 sessions of cognitive–behavioral therapy based on the prevailing cognitive–behavioral model of OCD (Salkovskis, 1985). The other 29 participants received 16 sessions of "self-controlled exposure in vivo with response prevention," a behavior therapy approach based on early behavioral interventions for OCD (Meyer, 1966). Results showed that the cognitive–behavioral therapy condition produced significantly better outcomes than did the exposure condition, particularly when patients were rated on a "recovered" dimension. Patients were considered "recovered" when their assessment scores dropped below clinical levels and when their change on these measures was deemed to be clinically significant. The authors concluded that, although both behavior therapy and cognitive–behavioral therapy were effective in the short term, there were reasons to favor the latter in the treatment of OCD. However, the authors also stated that the long-term effects of cognitive–behavioral treatments for OCD were in need of further investigation.

To extend these findings, McLean et al. (2001) conducted a study comparing group cognitive–behavioral therapy, group exposure and response prevention, and a wait-list control condition after a 12-week treatment and at 3 months following treatment. The results of this study are somewhat inconsistent with the preceding findings. Whereas both treatments were superior to the wait-list control in terms of reducing symptoms, exposure and response prevention was marginally more effective than cognitive–behavioral therapy both after treatment and at 3-month follow-up. In terms of clinically significant improvement, the authors reported that the two treatments were equivalent at the conclusion of treatment, but that there were significantly more "recovered" patients in the exposure and response prevention group than in the cognitive–behavioral therapy group at 3-month follow-up. These results not only are inconsistent with the advantages of cognitive–behavioral therapy over behavior therapy reported previously, but also are inconsistent with the advantages of group therapy seen in the cognitive–behavioral treatment of social anxiety disorder (see earlier). This difference may be due to several factors. In the first place, although it is apparent that the authors made every attempt to maximize the benefits of a group format, group behavior therapy for OCD is likely to present fewer complications than group cognitive–behavioral therapy for OCD. In addition, unless the particular fears of individual clients or patients are related to interacting with others, the group format is not likely to produce the same added benefits that it does for social anxiety disorder. One could argue that group treatments for OCD that focus on changes in beliefs and cognition probably lack the specificity required to be maximally effective. Furthermore, it may be that the heterogeneous groups treated in the study were unable to benefit from the specific distinctions and subtleties only now being made explicit in new theories and models of OCD.

One of the most encouraging advances in the prevention of relapse following successful treatment of OCD comes from the study of a relapse prevention program created especially for that purpose (Hiss, Foa, & Kozak, 1994). In this investigation, all participants underwent 3 weeks of intensive behavior therapy (exposure and response prevention). The treatment led to significant reductions in OCD symptoms on all five assessment measures used in the study. Following intensive exposure and response prevention, participants were assigned to either a relapse prevention program or an "associative therapy" program, which served as an attention-placebo control. After treatment, there were no differences between the groups on any of the assessment measures. The relapse prevention program was also intensive, involving four 90-minute sessions conducted over a 1-week period. During these sessions, participants received training in self-exposure and cognitive restructuring, and in planning for changes in their lifestyle that might be associated with fewer OCD symptoms. The "associative therapy" control program involved four intensive sessions over a 1-week period in which participants completed progressive muscle relaxation exercises followed by free association. After a 6-month follow-up period during which no intervention was offered to either group, a number of significant differences emerged between the two groups. On four of the five assessment measures, the relapse prevention group had significantly less symptomatology than the attention-placebo control. An examination of clinically significant change also demonstrated that the relapse prevention group was more effective at maintaining gains after a follow-up period with no treatment.

Of course, a central question raised by the foregoing study is how the relapse prevention program achieved its results. In this specific case, there are two likely possibilities. The first is that, through continued self-administered exposure and newly self-administered cognitive restructuring, patients in the relapse prevention group were able to continue active treatment beyond the end of the formal treatment period. The second possibility is that the response prevention program had specific effects on how participants approached and dealt with their obsessive–compulsive problems during the ensuing follow-up period. If the result of the relapse prevention program was that participants had learned a new way to approach their anxiety (through behavioral and cognitive exercises), it is entirely possible that associated adaptive beliefs were also acquired. These beliefs may have been related to perceptions of self-efficacy, but possibly also to new ways of conceptualizing risk and threat and new ways of coping within the context of obsessions and compulsions. Although these constructs were not measured in the study carried out by Hiss and colleagues (1994), it is consistent with their findings that the relapse prevention program led to alternative, productive anxiety management styles that no longer included immediately engaging in compulsions.

While behavioral treatments for OCD (e.g., exposure and response prevention) are based primarily on models and theories developed long before the advent of cognitive approaches (see Wolpe, 1958), even recent cognitive–behavioral approaches to treating OCD (e.g., Salkovskis, 1985) could benefit from some adjustment. As we learn more about specific manifestations of OCD (e.g., compulsive hoarding, compulsive checking, compulsive washing, obsessions without compulsions), new, focused theories are being developed to account for the specific phenomena associated with each (Frost & Hartl, 1996; Rachman, 1998). These different manifestations of OCD probably have differential response patterns to treatment, and further refinement of our approaches is necessary. The new models are promising and are likely to produce modifications in cognitive–behavioral approaches that will better enable clinicians to assess and address the cognitions, behavior, and emotions associated with the various manifestations of OCD. With a better understanding of the psychopathology associated with OCD, our short- and long-term treatments are certain to become more effective. Current results of long-term outcome trials involving OCD indicate that both behavioral and cognitive–behavioral therapies can lead to excellent outcomes and prevent relapse. In addition, supplementary relapse prevention programs may enhance these treatments. The further refinement of our models and treatments is bound to improve upon this already encouraging state of affairs and add to the successful treatment and prevention of relapse associated with this (for now) often intractable condition.

Panic Disorder

Controlled treatment outcome studies for panic disorder began in the mid-1960s. Since then, numerous studies have assessed the efficacy of in vivo exposure, relaxation, cognitive restructuring, and, more recently, interoceptive exposure in the treatment of panic disorder with agoraphobia (PDA). Despite the abundance of treatment studies for panic disorder, the inclusion of long-term follow-up data is a relatively new phenomenon.

In one such study, Fava, Zielezny, Savron, and Grandi (1995) found that a treatment based on behavioral exposure homework was effective for PDA in the long term. Ninety-three patients completed 12 sessions of psychotherapy that included behavioral exposure homework (each therapy session lasted 30 minutes, once every 2 weeks). At each session, the need for exposure to the feared object or event was emphasized, and patients discussed their exposure diaries and the ensuing steps to be taken. Following treatment, 81 patients were panic free for at least 1 month. Long-term follow-up evaluations were performed for these panic-free patients, while the remaining 12 were excluded. Of the 81 initially panic-free patients, only 19% had a relapse of PDA at some time during the 9-year follow-up. Furthermore, the estimated cumulative percentage of patients remaining in remission during the 2–9 year follow-up was 96% for at least 2 years, 78% for at least 5 years, and 67% for at least 7 years.

The long-term impact of applied relaxation, in vivo exposure, and cognitive therapy was assessed by Öst, Westling, and Hellstrom (1993). Therapy sessions of 60 minutes were held weekly for 12 weeks, with all 45 patients receiving self-exposure instructions. The results showed no significant between-group differences at follow-up, suggesting that the three treatment strategies were equally effective in promoting the maintenance of treatment gains. This result, however, may in part have been due to the self-exposure instructions that participants in each condition received. Between-group differences were observed on only two measures, both showing better results for relaxation than for cognitive therapy: One criterion of clinically significant improvement, behavioral avoidance, was fulfilled by 85% of relaxation patients, 79% of exposure patients, and 67% of cognitive therapy patients at 1-year follow-up; the other criterion of clinically significant change, self-reported avoidance, was fulfilled by 47% of relaxation patients, 50% of exposure patients, and 47% of cognitive patients.

Barlow, Craske, Cerny, and Klosko (1989), as well as Clark et al. (1994), also included a relaxation condition in their treatment studies; however, they did not find relaxation superior to other treatment strategies. Barlow et al. assessed 60 patients with panic disorder without agoraphobia who were randomly assigned to one of four treatment conditions: progressive relaxation, exposure and cognitive restructuring, relaxation combined with exposure and cognitive restructuring, and wait-list control. Each of the active-treatment groups exhibited significant and essentially equivalent reductions in general anxiety, whereas the wait-list group scores remained largely unchanged. Because insufficient data were available, between-group differences at 24-month follow-up could not be analyzed, and data from the three treatment groups were combined. The results showed that none of the outcome variables changed significantly from posttest to follow-up, although daily functioning evidenced a positive trend: Sixty-eight percent of clients demonstrated improvement in the areas of work, social life, and leisure. This change accounts, in part, for the increase in high end-state functioning from 48% just after treatment to 60% at follow-up.

Clark et al. (1994) assigned 64 patients to cognitive therapy, applied relaxation, imipramine, or a wait-list condition. Cognitive therapy and applied relaxation were administered over 12 weekly sessions and included elements of exposure. Results indicated that cognitive therapy, applied relaxation, and imipramine all differed significantly from the wait-list condition. Comparisons between the treatments showed that, at 3-month follow-up, cognitive therapy was superior to both relaxation and imipramine on most measures. At 6 months, however, cognitive therapy results did not differ from imipramine results, and both were superior to relaxation on several measures. However, when imipramine was gradually withdrawn after the 6-month assessment, patients tended to deteriorate, with 40% of the imipramine group experiencing relapse. At 15-month follow-up, cognitive therapy was superior to both relaxation and imipramine: Eighty-five percent of the cognitive therapy patients were panic free, whereas 47% of relaxation patients and 60% of imipramine patients reported having no more panic attacks. Overall, cognitive therapy was the superior treatment, and at no point was applied relaxation more effective than either cognitive therapy or imipramine. The percentage of patients who experienced a relapse at 15-month follow-up and required further treatment was 5% for the cognitive treatment, 26% for the relaxation treatment, and 40% for the imipramine treatment. This set of outcomes may rest on the fact that the cognitive strategy used in the study included interoceptive exposure, which could well have enhanced the treatment.

The mechanisms underlying treatments for PDA have yet to be clearly defined, a situation that limits our ability to explain why certain treatments are more effective in the long term. A consideration of these treatments in light of current theoretical perspectives, however, may generate some useful hypotheses. One such perspective proposes that panic can be seen as the result of chronic hyperventilation (Ley, 1985). According to this perspective, relaxation techniques may operate through mechanisms such as a reduction in breathing rate, which is part of relaxation training. A second perspective attributes panic to the catastrophic misinterpretation of normal somatic sensations. Cognitive theory consequently proposes that sustained improvement after treatment depends on cognitive change occurring during the course of treatment. Thus, cognitive theory predicts that a person's long-term outcome depends on the extent to which his or her interpretations of bodily sensations have changed during treatment. Clark et al. (1994) tested this hypothesis and found that misinterpretations of bodily sensations at the end of the cognitive treatment were significant predictors of subsequent symptoms and relapse in individuals who had been panic free at the end of the treatment. Finally, a third conceptualization posits that improvement is associated with habituation to somatic cues and the prevention of escape behaviors. In vivo exposure and interoceptive exposure focus directly on this mechanism (Barlow et al., 1989), and relaxation training may also operate via this mechanism by producing exposure to anxiety-producing interoceptive cues.

Posttraumatic Stress Disorder

In general, well-controlled treatment studies for posttraumatic stress disorder (PTSD) have been carried out more recently than those for other anxiety disorders. Indeed, over the past decade, research on the treatment of PTSD has flourished and produced highly encouraging results. In one of the earlier examinations of treatment for PTSD, 24 Vietnam veterans were randomly assigned to an implosive therapy group or a wait-list control group (Keane, Fairbank, Caddell, & Zimmering, 1989). The implosive therapy condition involved 14 individual sessions that included 10 minutes of relaxation training and 45 minutes of flooding (gradual presentation of the traumatic scene, with details regarding the patient's behavioral, cognitive, and physiological responses). At the end of therapy, the treatment group showed significant decreases in the reexperiencing dimension of PTSD that were maintained at 6-month follow-up. Moreover, implosive therapy led to a significant reduction in startle responses and increases in memory and concentration, improvements that were also sustained at follow-up. However, the results indicated that the sole use of imaginal exposure did not have an impact on the numbing-and-social-avoidance characteristic of PTSD.

Questions concerning the capacity of imaginal exposure to decrease all PTSD symptoms gave rise to studies combining in vivo and imaginal exposure (Marks, Lovell, Noshirvani, Livanou, & Thrasher, 1998; Richards, Lovell, & Marks, 1994). This strategy of combining both types of exposure has generally led to a significant reduction in PTSD symptoms, with gains being maintained over time. For example, using both in vivo and imaginal exposure, Marks et al. assessed a 10-session, 90-minute treatment involving 5 sessions of imaginal exposure followed by 5 sessions of in vivo exposure. The results from this study indicated that 75% of participants who met the PTSD criteria before treatment no longer met them at 3-month follow-up. Furthermore, results from a study conducted by Richards et al. (1994) suggest that the order of delivery of imaginal and in vivo exposure produces no significant difference in the rate or magnitude of recovery from PTSD. The only difference between in vivo and imaginal exposure in this study was that in vivo exposure was more effective in reducing phobic avoidance than imaginal exposure was, regardless of the order of presentation of the two treatments. The magnitude of improvement was also considerable, ranging from 75% to 80% across PTSD-specific measures and from 65% to 75% for measures of depression, fear, general health, and social adjustment. Interestingly, not only were these improvements maintained, but they actually increased from posttreatment to 12-month follow-up, with 7 out of 12 measures showing further statistically significant improvement.

More recently, a new method of delivering exposure therapy has been introduced. *Eye movement desensitization and reprocessing* (EMDR) treatment requires that participants read a description of the trauma they experienced, visualize the trauma, think about a negative cognition associated with it, engage in eye movements, and pair a positive cognition with the memory of the trauma. A study that compared the impact of three 90-minute sessions of EMDR with a delayed-treatment condition found a significant decrease in anxiety and an increase in positive cognitions among 80 participants with PTSD (Wilson, Becker, & Tinker, 1995). Moreover, the size of the effect of the treatment was strong (1.82) for trauma-specific measures at 3-month follow-up. The results also showed additional improvement in three measures of general psychopathology at 3-month follow-up, and none of the scales showed a worsening of symptoms at 3-month follow-up. Nevertheless, some important questions remain, even though EMDR appears to lead to considerable change in trauma-specific and associated symptoms. Specifically, do the unique elements of EMDR actually add to the efficacy of traditional exposure treatments for PTSD? Is EMDR effective because it taps the same underlying mechanisms as does imaginal exposure? Is the sole use of EMDR sufficient to decrease behavioral avoidance, which was not specifically measured in the Wilson et al. (1995) study? More research is needed to provide adequate answers to these questions.

Cognitive treatments for PTSD have also been tested, often with excellent results. For instance, a study by Resick and Schnicke (1992) showed that cognitive-processing therapy produced significant improvement in PTSD symptoms at 6-month follow-up assessment. In this study, cognitive-processing therapy involved 12 weekly sessions of 90 minutes each, during which maladaptive beliefs related to the trauma were identified and challenged. All patients treated with cognitive-processing therapy no longer met diagnostic criteria for PTSD at 6-month follow-up. Measures chosen for their standardized norms were used to examine clinical change on self-report scales. Prior to therapy, 60% of the participants scored at least two standard deviations above the normative mean on a measure of PTSD symptoms. From pretreatment to 6-month follow-up, 68% of the sample had improved at least one full standard deviation, and 81% had improved at least one-half standard deviation, on the measure of PTSD symptoms. There were no significant changes from posttreatment to 3-month follow-up, except that depression scores continued to show improvement. From posttreatment to 6-month follow-up, there were no significant changes on any of the measures, indicating that gains achieved during treatment were maintained.

Is cognitive therapy more efficient than exposure therapy in the long term? Marks et al. (1998) compared cognitive restructuring strategies, exposure strategies, a combined treatment (cognitive restructuring and exposure), and relaxation in 87 victims with chronic PTSD. The results showed that the cognitive–restructuring strategies were effective from pretreatment to 6-month follow-up. The results also showed that cognitive and exposure strategies, alone or combined, produced a similar degree of improvement; furthermore, these strategies led to better outcomes on most measures than did relaxation at 6-month follow-up. Still, despite the separate effectiveness of exposure and cognitive strategies, combining them yielded no clear synergy.

Taken all together, the various research endeavors on empirically supported treatments for PTSD lead to a number of conclusions. First, while empirically supported treatments are effective, they are not effective for everyone: Approximately one-third of victims with PTSD do not improve significantly after treatment. However, when treatment is effective, gains tend to be maintained over time, even though gains generally do not increase from posttreatment to follow-up. Another interesting point is that in vivo and imaginal exposure, as well as cognitive restructuring, seem to result in similar improvements in the long term. Furthermore, combined strategies do not seem to be superior to each type of treatment alone. One possible explanation for this last point is that combined treatment studies might not have included enough sessions that each separate technique could be adequately learned. Alternatively, processes common to exposure and cognitive restructuring may have been responsible for treatment gains, so that duplicating these processes in combined treatments conferred no added value on the combination.

The literature on the long-term efficacy of empirically supported treatments for PTSD is quite recent, and further research in this area is needed. In particular, the underlying mechanisms responsible for efficacious treatment are just beginning to be explored. However, these underlying factors can be conceptualized in terms of corrections made to pathological elements of the fear structure, which are likely to be related to long-term change. Two necessary conditions for this type of correction have been proposed: First, the fear structure must be activated, and second, new information must be provided, including information about elements that are incompatible with existing pathological elements, so that the latter can be corrected. In vivo and imaginal exposure are examples of methods that elicit these specific changes in the fear structure. However, the most salient mechanisms at work during exposure may be the correction of erroneous probability estimates of danger and habituation of the fearful response to trauma-relevant stimuli. Cognitive therapy may also elicit a correction of the fear structure, by facilitating a search for meaning and an examination of the conflict between the event and prior beliefs and by restoring a sense of safety and control.

Generalized Anxiety Disorder

Although generalized anxiety disorder (GAD) is a relatively common anxiety disorder (Kessler et al., 1994), only a handful of randomized controlled clinical trials have included data on the prevention of relapse following treatment. In one of these studies, Power, Simpson, Swanson, and Wallace (1990) randomly assigned each of 101 patients with GAD to cognitive–behavioral therapy, pharmacotherapy (diazepam), pill placebo, cognitive–behavioral therapy plus diazepam, or cognitive–behavioral therapy plus placebo. Treatments lasted 10 weeks, and data were collected after the treatment and at 6-month follow-up. The results showed that all cognitive–behavioral therapy conditions (especially cognitive–behavioral therapy alone and cognitive–behavioral therapy plus diazepam) were superior to the other conditions at both posttest and follow-up. Moreover, not only did the cognitive–behavioral therapy conditions produce the greatest improvements in the study's main outcome measures, but they also were associated with a lower incidence of receiving further treatment over the 6-month follow-up period. Although new molecules have been developed for the treatment of GAD since Power and colleagues carried out their study (e.g., selective serotonin reuptake inhibitors), their data nonetheless show that cognitive–behavioral therapy leads to sustained improvement in patients with GAD.

Butler, Fennell, Robson, and Gelder (1991) compared behavior therapy, cognitive–behavioral therapy, and wait-list control. A total of 57 patients with GAD participated in the study, and therapy lasted anywhere from 4 to 12 sessions. Behavior therapy included applied relaxation, graded exposure, and reengagement in pleasurable activities, whereas cognitive–behavioral therapy involved cognitive reevaluation and the testing of behavioral hypotheses. Posttest results showed that both treatment conditions were superior to wait-list control and that cognitive–behavioral therapy was superior to behavior therapy on a wide range of measures. At 6-month follow-up, patients in the cognitive–behavioral therapy condition continued to fare better than those who received behavior therapy. In fact, follow-up data showed that the between-group differences increased at 6 months and that patients in the cognitive–behavioral therapy group were more resistant to early relapse. The authors concluded that greater cognitive change was attained with cognitive–behavioral therapy and that cognitive change might predict the prevention of relapse in GAD.

Barlow, Rapee, and Brown (1992) compared three treatments for GAD with wait-list control and collected data after treatment and at 6-, 12-, and 24-month follow-ups. Sixty-five patients with GAD were randomly allocated to applied relaxation, cognitive therapy, a combination of applied relaxation and cognitive restructuring, or wait-list control. All treatments were administered over 15 1-hour sessions. Immediately after treatment, patients in all three treatment conditions were more improved than those on the wait list. There were no notable differences, however, between the three treatment conditions, and gains were modest on some of the study measures. Because of the small number of participants available at each follow-up point, analyses of follow-up data were performed by collapsing the three treatment conditions. Overall, the results showed that the recurrence of GAD symptoms over the 2-year follow-up period was limited.

In 1993, Borkovec and Costello published what has become a widely cited study comparing nondirective therapy, applied relaxation, and cognitive–behavioral therapy in the treatment of GAD. Fifty-five patients with GAD were randomly allocated to one of the three treatment conditions (12 sessions, twice a week) and were assessed after treatment and at 6- and 12-month follow-ups. The posttreatment assessment showed that applied relaxation and cognitive–behavioral therapy yielded similar results and that both were superior to nondirective therapy. Follow-up assessments revealed that treatment gains were maintained in the applied relaxation and cognitive–behavioral therapy conditions, whereas further losses were noted in the nondirective therapy condition, despite the fact that more patients in this condition received subsequent treatment over the follow-up period. Moreover, the cognitive–behavioral therapy condition was associated with the highest end-state functioning at 1-year follow-up. The authors concluded that the cognitive factors and imagery processes associated with cognitive–behavioral therapy may be conducive to the prevention of the recurrence of GAD.

In an attempt to disentangle the long-term effects of different types of psychotherapy for GAD, Durham and colleagues (1999) reported 1-year follow-up data on 110 patients receiving either cognitive therapy or analytic psychotherapy. (Although some patients received anxiety management training, the authors focused on the first two treatment conditions for their analyses.) The results of the study showed that cognitive therapy was clearly superior to analytic psychotherapy at 1-year follow-up and that only a minority of patients who received analytic psychotherapy improved significantly.

Furthermore, cognitive therapy, but not analytic psychotherapy, was associated with reductions in the use of medication. Given the considerable between-group differences observed by Durham et al., this study argues strongly for the superiority of cognitive therapy for GAD with respect to long-term gains. The findings also lend support to the notion that cognitive therapy may be superior in preventing relapse into GAD.

In a recently published study, Ladouceur and colleagues (2000) compared 16 sessions of cognitive–behavioral therapy with a wait-list control condition. Cognitive–behavioral therapy was based on a model of GAD that has intolerance of uncertainty as its underlying feature (see Dugas, Gagnon, Ladouceur, & Freeston, 1998). The treatment targets intolerance of uncertainty via reevaluation of the usefulness of worrying, training in solving current problems, and imaginal exposure to core fears. In all, 26 patients with GAD were randomly allocated to either cognitive–behavioral therapy or wait-list control and were assessed both at treatment and at 6- and 12-month follow-ups. Posttest data showed that cognitive–behavioral therapy was superior to being on a wait list on all study measures. Following the 16-week waiting period, patients on the wait list received cognitive–behavioral therapy, and posttest analyses were rerun for all study participants. The results demonstrated that the majority of patients reached high responder status and high end-state functioning and that 77% of participants were in full remission following treatment. Overall, treatment gains were maintained at 6- and 12-month follow-ups. Furthermore, at 1-year follow-up, 77% of the original sample continued to be in full remission. The authors suggested that change in tolerance for uncertainty may be an important factor in explaining both the success of the treatment and the prevention of relapse following treatment.

Dugas and colleagues (2003) further tested the cognitive–behavioral treatment used by Ladouceur et al. (2000) by adapting it to the treatment of GAD in small groups (four to six patients). Fifty-two patients with GAD were randomly allocated to 14 sessions of group cognitive–behavioral therapy or wait-list control. As in the Ladouceur et al. study, results showed that group cognitive–behavioral therapy was superior to the wait list on all measures. After those from the wait list had received group cognitive–behavioral therapy, posttest analyses were conducted on all study participants. Results showed strong treatment gains, with effect sizes ranging from 0.72 for the measure of social adjustment to 1.62 for the measure of pathological worry. One important feature of the Dugas et al. study is that participants were assessed over a 2-year period (at 6, 12, and 24 months) following treatment. Maintenance of treatment gains was examined by conducting a growth curve analysis which revealed that treatment gains were maintained for all study variables and that worry scores decreased significantly at follow-up. These findings suggest that group cognitive–behavioral therapy may be effective in preventing the recurrence of the disorder over extended periods of time. In an attempt to explain the maintenance of treatment gains (and continued improvement in dealing with worry), Dugas (2002) examined the relationship between change in tolerance for uncertainty over the course of treatment and symptoms of the disorder at each follow-up. The results of the analyses showed that change in tolerance of uncertainty predicted symptoms at 2-year follow-up, even when nonspecific therapy factors (characteristics of the therapist, expectations of the participant, and motivation for treatment) were statistically controlled. These findings thus lend further support to the idea that changes in cognitive variables specifically related to an anxiety disorder may be a key factor in preventing the recurrence of generalized anxiety disorder.

The review of treatment studies that have included follow-up assessments suggests that cognitive–behavioral therapy for GAD leads not only to marked improvement, but also to lasting change. Furthermore, the data indicate that cognitive–behavioral therapy has specific components that contribute to both the remission and nonrecurrence of the disorder over periods of at least 2 years. Thus, it appears that these components play a key role in the tertiary prevention of GAD.

GENERAL CONCLUSIONS

It is somewhat difficult to draw general conclusions from the literature reviewed in this chapter; instead, different conclusions may be drawn for each specific anxiety disorder. This "potpourri" is not surprising, however, when one considers the breadth and heterogeneity of the diagnostic category of the anxiety disorders. For example, PTSD is conceptually very different from the other anxiety disorders, being the only one that includes a precipitating event (i.e., trauma) in its diagnostic criteria. Another example of the heterogeneity of the anxiety disorders is illustrated by the fact that PDA is characterized by somatic activation whereas GAD appears to be characterized by decreased flexibility in autonomic responsiveness. With this caveat in mind, we will nevertheless attempt to draw conclusions about the research that has been presented.

The first question posed at the outset of this chapter was "How efficacious are different psychosocial treatments at preventing the relapse of anxiety disorders in successfully treated patients?" Overall, the answer to this question appears to be that different forms of behavior therapy and cognitive–behavioral therapy are quite effective in preventing relapse into anxiety disorders. Follow-up data ranging from 1 month to 9 years indicate that, for the most part, patients who are successfully treated for an anxiety disorder with either behavior therapy or cognitive–behavioral therapy will continue to benefit from these treatments. Of course, successful treatment does not guarantee that patients will continue to fare well over long periods, but the data certainly suggest that patients with an anxiety disorder who are treated with behavior therapy or cognitive–behavioral therapy have a reasonable chance of remaining well. As new and more sophisticated forms of these therapies are developed, one can hope that relapse rates will continue to dwindle. In addition, as more treatment studies begin to include long-term follow-ups, we will be in a better position both to address the issue of relapse prevention and, indeed, to prevent relapse.

The second question posed at the beginning of the chapter, namely, "What are the most promising treatments for preventing the relapse of anxiety disorders?" can also be addressed, albeit with certain reservations. When psychotherapy is compared with pharmacotherapy, emerging data suggest that behavior therapy and cognitive–behavioral therapy are superior to pharmacotherapy in terms of preventing relapse (Clark et al., 1994; Liebowitz et al., 1999; Power et al., 1990). Although new and promising molecules are constantly being developed, the current state of the literature indicates that both behavior therapy and cognitive–behavioral therapy are more effective than pharmacotherapy in preventing the reoccurrence of anxiety disorders following treatment. The literature also suggests that not all forms of psychotherapy are equally effective in preventing the reoccurrence of anxiety disorders. Specifically, behavior therapy and cognitive–behavioral therapy appear to be superior to other forms of psychotherapy, such as insight-oriented therapy (Paul, 1967), nondirective therapy (Borkovec & Costello, 1993), and analytic psychotherapy (Durham et al., 1999).

When behavior therapy and cognitive–behavioral therapy are compared with each other, however, the picture is not as clear. Some studies suggest that behavior therapy is superior to cognitive–behavioral therapy in terms of preventing relapse (e.g., McLean et al., 2001); other studies suggest that behavior therapy and cognitive–behavioral therapy are equally effective in preventing relapse (e.g., Marks et al., 1998); still other studies suggest that cognitive–behavioral therapy is superior to behavior therapy in this regard (e.g., Borkovec & Costello, 1993; Butler et al., 1991; Clark et al., 1994). How can these mixed results be explained? First, as noted at the beginning of this section, the anxiety disorders form a broad and heterogeneous class of mental disorders. It may be, therefore, that purely behavioral approaches are more effective in preventing relapse with some disorders, while approaches that are both cognitive and behavioral are more effective in preventing relapse with others. Second, behavior therapy and cognitive–behavioral therapy include different treatment strategies in different studies. For example, behavior therapy in the Butler et al. (1991) study consisted of three components—applied relaxation, graded exposure, and reengagement in pleasurable activities—whereas behavior therapy in the Borkovec and Costello (1993) study consisted of only one component (applied relaxation). In this sense, "behavior therapy" and "cognitive–behavioral therapy" may not be the most informative descriptors for the treatments actually being tested. Finally, an important distinction must be drawn between a treatment strategy and the process by which it operates. Although a strategy such as in vivo exposure would be considered by most to be a behavioral treatment strategy, the process by which exposure leads to change may, in fact, be fundamentally cognitive. In the same way, a cognitive intervention such as the reevaluation of automatic thoughts via a four-column spreadsheet may owe much of its effectiveness to the fact that it leads to behavioral change. Thus, the distinction between behavioral and cognitive treatment strategies may not be highly useful in the clinical or empirical sense, because the processes involved in the patient's improvement are certainly not restricted to separate cognitive, behavioral, or emotional domains. In light of these arguments, it is not surprising that the effects of behavior therapy and cognitive–behavioral therapy are difficult to disentangle empirically.

The third and final question posed at the outset of the chapter was "What are the predictors of maintenance of treatment gains in successfully treated patients?" Again, the data seem to present a mixed picture. There is, however, some evidence that both general and specific cognitive changes are important predictors of relapse prevention. More precisely, there are three types of cognitive change that may predict the prevention of relapse. First, anxiety disorder patients acquire new ways of learning over the course of behavior therapy and cognitive–behavioral therapy (Radomsky & Otto, 2001), and such new avenues may affect those individuals' ability to ward off future occurrences of their disorder. For example, an individual who learns to test his or her beliefs via behavioral experiments would certainly be less likely to validate anxiety-producing automatic thoughts that might lead to relapse. Second, those with an anxiety disorder may experience a change in their fundamental beliefs about themselves and the world over the course of therapy, which would further protect them from a recurrence of the disorder. Finally, over the course of treatment, people may experience a change in cognitive biases that are specifically related to their disorder. For example, there is emerging data that persons with GAD who become more tolerant of uncertainty over treatment may do better in the long term than those who do not (Dugas, 2002).

Taken together, the studies reviewed in this chapter suggest that therapy can be effective for the tertiary prevention of anxiety disorders, that behavior therapy and cognitive–behavioral therapy may be particularly effective at preventing relapse, and that cognitive change is a key factor in preventing relapse. Finally, cognitive variables have received considerable attention in the anxiety literature over the past two decades, as research inquiry has shifted toward cognitive treatment strategies and cognitive processes. As our ability to measure complex factors increases, so should our capacity to relate complex interactions among cognitive, behavioral, physiological, and affective systems to the prediction and prevention of relapse.

REFERENCES

Bandura, A., Blanchard, E. B., & Ritter, B. (1969). Relative efficacy of desensitization and modeling approaches for inducing behavioral, affective, and attitudinal changes. *Journal of Personality and Social Psychology, 13*, 173–199.

Barlow, D. H., Craske, M. G., Cerny, J. A., & Klosko, J. S. (1989). Behavioral treatment of panic disorder. *Behavior Therapy, 20*, 261–282.

Barlow, D. H., Rapee, R. M., & Brown, T. A. (1992). Behavioral treatment of generalized anxiety disorder. *Behavior Therapy, 23*, 551–570.

Borkovec, T. D., & Costello, E. (1993). Efficacy of applied relaxation and cognitive behavioral therapy in the treatment of generalized anxiety disorder. *Journal of Consulting and Clinical Psychology, 61*, 611–619.

Butler, G., Fennell, M., Robson, P., & Gelder, M. (1991). A comparison of behavior therapy and cognitive behavior therapy in the treatment of generalized anxiety disorder. *Journal of Consulting and Clinical Psychology, 59*, 167–175.

Chambless, D. L., Baker, M. J., Baucom, D. H., Beutler, L. E., Calhoun, K. S., Crits-Christoph, P., et al. (1998). Update on empirically validated therapies, II. *Clinical Psychologist, 51*, 3–15.

Clark, D. M., Salkovskis, P. M., Hackmann, A., Middleton, H., Anastasiades, P., & Gelder, M. (1994). A comparison of cognitive therapy, applied relaxation and imipramine in the treatment of panic disorder. *British Journal of Psychiatry, 164*, 759–769.

Craske, M. G., & Rowe, M. K. (1998). A comparison of behavioral and cognitive treatments of phobias. In G. C. L. Davey (Ed.), *Phobias* (pp. 247–280). Toronto: Wiley.

Dugas, M. J. (2002, November). *Cognitive–behavioral therapy for generalized anxiety disorder: Learning to tolerate uncertainty and emotional arousal.* Workshop presented at the annual convention of the Association for Advancement of Behavior Therapy, Reno, NV.

Dugas, M. J., Gagnon, F., Ladouceur, R., & Freeston, M. H. (1998). Generalized anxiety disorder: A preliminary test of a conceptual model. *Behaviour Research and Therapy, 36*, 215–226.

Dugas, M. J., Ladouceur, R., Léger, E., Freeston, M. H., Langlois, F., Provencher, M. D., & Boisvert, J.-M. (2003). Group cognitive–behavioral therapy for generalized anxiety disorder: Treatment outcome and long-term follow-up. *Journal of Consulting and Clinical Psychology, 71*, 821–825.

Durham, R. C., Fisher, P. L., Treliving, L. R., Hau, C. M., Richard, K., & Stewart, J. B. (1999). One year follow-up of cognitive therapy, analytic psychotherapy and anxiety management training for generalized anxiety disorder: Symptom change, medication usage and attitudes to treatment. *Behavioural and Cognitive Psychotherapy, 27*, 19–35.

Fava, G. A., Zielezny, M., Savron, G., & Grandi, S. (1995). Long-term effects of behavioural treatment for panic disorder with agoraphobia. *British Journal of Psychiatry, 166*, 87–92.

Feske, U., & Chambless, D. L. (1995). Cognitive behavioral versus exposure only treatment for social phobia: A meta-analysis. *Behavior Therapy, 26,* 695–720.

Frost, R. O., & Hartl, T. L. (1996). A cognitive–behavioral model of compulsive hoarding. *Behavior Research and Therapy, 34,* 341–350.

Greenberg, P. E., Sisitsky, T., Kessler, R. C., Finkelstein, S. N., Berndt, E. R., Davidson, J. R. T., et al. (1999). The economic burden of anxiety disorders in the 1990s. *Journal of Clinical Psychiatry, 60,* 427–435.

Heimberg, R. G., Dodge, C. S., Hope, D. A., Kennedy, C. R., Zollo, L. J., & Becker, R. E. (1990). Cognitive behavioral group treatment for social phobia: Comparison with a credible placebo control. *Cognitive Therapy and Research, 14,* 1–23.

Heimberg, R. G., Liebowitz, M. R., Hope, D. A., Schneier, F. R., Holt, C. S., Welkowitz, L. A., et al. (1998). Cognitive–behavioral group therapy vs. phenelzine therapy for social phobia. *Archives of General Psychiatry, 55,* 1133–1141.

Hiss, H., Foa, E. B., & Kozak, M. J. (1994). Relapse prevention program for treatment of obsessive–compulsive disorder. *Journal of Consulting and Clinical Psychology, 62,* 801–808.

Keane, T. M., Fairbank, J. A., Caddell, J. M., & Zimmering, R. T. (1989). Implosive (flooding) therapy reduces symptoms of PTSD in Vietnam combat veterans. *Behavior Therapy, 20,* 245–260.

Kessler, R. C., McGonagle, K. A., Zhao, S., Nelson, C. B., Hughes, M., Eshleman, S., et al. (1994). Lifetime and 12-month prevalence of DSM-III-R psychiatric disorders in the United States. *Archives of General Psychiatry, 51,* 8–19.

Ladouceur, R., Dugas, M. J., Freeston, M. H., Léger, E., Gagnon, F., & Thibodeau, N. (2000). Efficacy of a cognitive–behavioral treatment for generalized anxiety disorder: Evaluation in a controlled clinical trial. *Journal of Consulting and Clinical Psychology, 68,* 957–964.

Ley, R. (1985). Agoraphobia, the panic attack and the hyperventilation syndrome. *Behavior Research and Therapy, 23,* 79–81.

Liebowitz, M. R., Heimberg, R. G., Schneier, F. R., Hope, D. A., Davies, S., Holt, C. S., et al. (1999). Cognitive–behavioral group therapy versus phenelzine in social phobia: Long term outcome. *Depression and Anxiety, 10,* 89–98.

Marks, I., Lovell, K., Noshirvani, H., Livanou, M., & Thrasher, S. (1998). Treatment of PTSD by exposure and/or cognitive restructuring: A controlled study. *Archives of General Psychiatry, 55,* 317–325.

McLean, P. D., Whittal, M. L., Thordarson, D. S., Taylor, S., Söchting, I., Koch, W. J., et al. (2001). Cognitive versus behavior therapy in the group treatment of obsessive–compulsive disorder. *Journal of Consulting and Clinical Psychology, 69,* 205–214.

Meyer, V. (1966). The modification of expectations in cases with obsessional rituals. *Behavior Research and Therapy, 4,* 273–280.

Öst, L.-G. (1996). Long-term effects of behavior therapy for specific phobia. In M. R. Mavissakalian & R. F. Prien (Eds.), *Long-term treatments of anxiety disorders.* Washington, DC: American Psychiatric Press.

Öst, L.-G., Alm, T., Brandberg, M., & Breitholtz, E. (2001). One vs. five sessions of exposure and five sessions of cognitive therapy in the treatment of claustrophobia. *Behavior Research and Therapy, 39*, 167–183.

Öst, L.-G., Salkovskis, P. M., & Hellström, K. (1991). One-session therapist-directed exposure vs. self-exposure in the treatment of spider phobia. *Behavior Therapy, 22*, 407–422.

Öst, L-G., Westling, B. E., & Hellstrom, K. (1993). Applied relaxation, exposure in vivo and cognitive methods in the treatment of panic disorder with agoraphobia. *Behavior Research and Therapy, 31*, 383–394.

Paul, G. L. (1967). Insight versus desensitization in psychotherapy: Two years after termination. *Journal of Consulting Psychology, 31*, 333–348.

Power, K. G., Simpson, R. J., Swanson, V., & Wallace, L. A. (1990). A controlled comparison of cognitive–behaviour therapy, diazepam, and placebo, alone and in combination, for the treatment of generalised anxiety disorder. *Journal of Anxiety Disorders, 4*, 267–292.

Price, R. P., Bader, B. C., & Ketterer, R. F. (1980). Prevention in community mental health. In R. H. Price (Ed.), *Prevention in mental health: Research, policy, and practice.* Beverly Hills, CA: Sage.

Rachman, S. (1998). A cognitive theory of obsessions: Elaborations. *Behavior Research and Therapy, 36*, 385–401.

Rachman, S., & Hodgson, R. (1980). *Obsessions and compulsions.* Englewood Cliffs, NJ: Prentice-Hall.

Radomsky, A. S., & Otto, M. W. (2001). Cognitive–behavioral therapy for social anxiety disorder. *Psychiatric Clinics of North America, 24*, 805–815.

Radomsky, A. S., Rachman, S., Thordarson, D. S., Teachman, B. A., & McIsaac, H. (2001). The Claustrophobia Questionnaire. *Journal of Anxiety Disorders, 15*, 287–297.

Rapee, R. M., & Heimberg, R. G. (1997). A cognitive–behavioral model of anxiety in social phobia. *Behavior Research and Therapy, 35*, 741–756.

Resick, P. A., & Schnicke, M. K. (1992). Cognitive processing therapy for sexual assault victims. *Journal of Consulting and Clinical Psychology, 60*, 748–756.

Richards, D. A., Lovell, K., & Marks, I. (1994). Post-traumatic stress disorder: Evaluation of a behavioral treatment program. *Journal of Traumatic Stress, 60*, 669–680.

Salkovskis, P. M. (1985). Obsessional–compulsive problems: A cognitive–behavioral analysis. *Behavior Research and Therapy, 23*, 571–583.

van Oppen, P., de Haan, E., van Balkom, A. J. L. M., Spinhoven, P., Hoogduin, K., & van Dyck, R. (1995). Cognitive therapy and exposure in vivo in the treatment of obsessive compulsive disorder. *Behavior Research and Therapy, 33*, 379–390.

Westen, D., & Morrison, K. (2001). A multidimensional meta-analysis of treatments for depression, panic, and generalized anxiety disorder: An empirical examination of the status of empirically supported therapies. *Journal of Consulting and Clinical Psychology, 69*, 875–899.

Wilson, S. A., Becker, L. E., & Tinker, R. H. (1995). Eye movement desensitization and reprocessing (EMDR) treatment for psychologically traumatized individuals. *Journal of Consulting and Clinical Psychology, 63*, 928–937.

Wolpe, J. (1958). *Psychotherapy by reciprocal inhibition*. Stanford, CA: Stanford University Press.

8

PRIMARY PREVENTION
OF DEPRESSION

CECILIA A. ESSAU

Depression is one of the most common disorders in adolescents, with an estimated lifetime prevalence ranging from 15% to 20% (see Essau & Dobson, 1999). Depression also co-occurs frequently with other psychiatric disorders. After reviewing six community studies, Angold and Costello (1993) concluded that the presence of depression in adolescents increased the probability of the presence of another disorder by at least 20 times. The most common comorbid disorder with depression is anxiety, with anxiety problems typically preceding the onset of a depressive disorder (Essau, 2002). Disruptive behavior (e.g., attention-deficit/hyperactivity disorder, conduct disorder, oppositional defiant disorder) and substance use disorders also frequently co-occur with depression.

Depression is a recurrent disorder and is accompanied by impairment in various life areas, not only during the worst depressive episode but also when the criteria for depression are no longer even met. Despite this impairment, a large proportion of depressed adolescents in the community do not receive

185

professional help (Essau, Conradt, & Petermann, 2000; McGee, Feehan, & Williams, 1995). One study, for example, found that only 2% of adolescents who met the diagnostic criteria for major depression sought professional help (mainly from general practitioners) for their disorder (Essau, 2002). Among those who seek professional assistance, depression is often misdiagnosed or undetected. Consequently, depressed adolescents often do not receive appropriate treatment for their disorder and may undergo several unnecessary medical examinations. This underdetection may lead to an inappropriately high cost for the health system and, more important, may contribute to the chronicity of depression. Studies have also shown that individuals with an early onset of depression generally do not respond well to treatment (Essau, 2002; Lewinsohn, Rohde, & Seeley, 1998). Lewinsohn et al. (1998) found that adolescents who received treatment were as likely to have another depressive episode during young adulthood as those who did not receive treatment. In the Bremen Adolescent Study (Essau, 2002), 40% of the adolescents who received treatment for depression remained depressed at follow-up investigation.

The finding that only a small portion of depressed youths actually seek professional help is an important issue. Children do not usually refer themselves to treatment for behavioral problems; rather, this decision is typically made by adults (usually a parent or teacher). Mash and Krahn (1995) argued that the likelihood that parents will seek help for their children may be influenced by (a) the extent to which the child's behavior is noticeable and bothersome, (b) the parent's own mental health status and treatment history, and (c) the perceived benefits of treatment. The child's clinical features are also important determinants of treatment utilization. Among these features are a history of attempted suicide, the existence of comorbid disorders, the severity of the depression, the number of past depressive episodes, academic problems, a disruptive family structure, and being female (Essau, 2002; Lewinsohn et al., 1998). Other factors that determine whether professional help is sought are the availability of mental health services and the cost and mechanism of financing (Essau et al., 2000).

All these findings stress the importance of developing, evaluating, and implementing evidence-based prevention programs that target adolescent depression. Primary prevention in youth—the main focus of this chapter—has several advantages (Andrews, Szabo, & Burns, 2002). First, because this level of prevention involves targeting whole populations (e.g., a particular school cohort), it avoids the problems associated with labeling and stigmatization that result from certain selection procedures (e.g., when adolescents are singled out from their peers to participate in prevention programs; Durlak & Wells, 1997). In recent years, numerous school-based primary approaches have been developed and implemented routinely as part of the school curriculum. These programs offer a possible solution to the problems of recruitment and potential stigmatization (e.g., Shochet et al.,

2001). Second, primary prevention programs may help individuals develop and enhance various cognitive, emotional, and social skills that reduce the likelihood of the onset of depression. Third, primary prevention allows intervention to reach a large number of people. Because this level of prevention also provides intervention to a large number of "false positives" (i.e., individuals who would not likely become depressed anyway), primary prevention may not be as efficient or cost effective as secondary or tertiary prevention. Still, primary prevention may optimally decrease the number of individuals who ultimately experience depression. In this chapter, I present some major primary prevention programs for depression in children and adolescents and briefly discuss some general programs that promote both the physical and the psychological health of these young people. Before doing so, I review some risk and protective factors for the development of depression.

RISK AND PROTECTIVE FACTORS IN CHILD AND ADOLESCENT DEPRESSION

Knowledge about risk factors is critical for psychologists to identify those individuals who are at elevated risk so that they can be targeted for preventing the onset of depression. A summary of the main risk factors for depression is presented in Table 8.1. Most of the information in the table is reviewed elsewhere (see Essau, 2002; Essau & Dobson, 1999; Lewinsohn & Essau, 2002). The most commonly identified broad risk factors for depression include family factors, life events, and cognitive factors.

Family Factors

Children of depressed parents have up to six times higher rates of depression than do children of nondepressed mothers; they also have an earlier age of onset of the disorder (for a review, see Essau & Merikangas, 1999; Gotlib & Sommerfeld, 1999). A high proportion of depressed adolescents report the presence of other disorders in their parents, including alcohol, drug, and anxiety disorders. The mechanisms responsible for the transmission of depression from parents to children are unclear. However, dysfunctional parent–child interactions, marital conflict, emotional unavailability of the parents, and genetic factors have been proposed (Essau & Merikangas, 1999; Gotlib & Sommerfeld, 1999). For example, maternal depression may lead to marital discord or to divorce, increasing the probability that children will be exposed to interparental conflict (Fendrich, Warner, & Weissman, 1990). Parental depression may also affect children through depression-related parental behaviors, such as emotional unavailability and cognitive dysfunction. Communication within the family of depressed patients is also frequently impaired (Essau, 2002).

TABLE 8.1
Major Risk Factors for Depression and Their Implication for Prevention

Factors	Main findings	Prevention strategies
Cognitive factors	Low self-esteem Negative body image Pessimistic explanatory styles Depressogenic attributional style Negative expectation Hopelessness Low perceived competence	Cognitive behavioral skills programs Cognitive restructuring Problem-solving and decision-making skill training Self-control therapy
Family factors	Parental Dysfunctional parent–child interactions Marital conflict Emotional unavailability of parents	Early identification of children and families at risk through socioeconomic adversity and psychopathology Parent training Family and marital support programs Training parents to model effective cognitive and behavioral coping Parent training to foster positive parenting and secure attachment
Life events	Negative life events prior to depression Negative coping styles	Support for family and youth problems, breakdown, and homelessness Training positive coping Interpersonal problem-solving skills
Individual factors	Poor social skills Comorbid disorders Academic difficulties Difficult temperament Interpersonal difficulties Alienation Physical disease and disease-related functional impairment	Social skills training Relaxation training Assertive skills training Problem-solving and decision-making skills training Interpersonal skills Skills to increase self-control and self-esteem Mental health services use Academic assistance–cooperative learning Improve school environment and teaching practice Provide recreational–physical activities

Life Events

Numerous studies have linked negative life events and chronic stressors with concurrent depression (e.g., Essau, 2002; Lewinsohn, Clarke, Seeley, & Rohde, 1994). In the Commonwealth Fund 1997 Adolescent Health Survey (Schraedley, Gotlib, & Hayward, 1999), the presence of many stressful life events tripled the likelihood of reporting high levels of depressive symptoms. Specific life events that significantly predicted depression included the death of a parent before age 15 years, pregnancy, and health problems that interfered with daily functioning, especially in females (Reinherz et al., 1993). Monroe, Rohde, Seeley, and Lewinsohn (1999) found that the breakup of a relationship was an important event for the first depressive episode, but not for its recurrence. In the Bremen Adolescent Study (Essau, 2002), negative life events, such as the end of a romantic relationship, were associated with the onset of depression, whereas chronic life conditions (e.g., daily hassles) were related to the recurrence of depression.

Because of the cross-sectional nature of most studies, however, the direction of the relationship between life events and depression is uncertain. There is also evidence that depression may contribute to the occurrence of stressors themselves. Hammen, Rudolph, Weisz, Rao, and Burge (1999), for example, proposed that depression develops as a result of the interaction between personal vulnerability (i.e., a cognitive propensity toward depression-inducing interpretations or appraisals of events) and external stress and that exposure to the latter may activate this underlying cognitive predisposition. Goodyer, Cooper, Vize, and Ashby (1993) suggested that some families may be "life event prone" as a consequence of lifetime episodes of parental psychopathology.

The mechanisms that increase an individual's vulnerability to depression are unclear, as not all adolescents who have been exposed to negative life events become depressed. Individual differences in how adolescents cope with such events may be important. Given the same level of stress, people who use more effective coping strategies will presumably experience less disruption of their behavior and, consequently, less distress. Consistent with this hypothesis, depressed adolescents have been found to use less effective coping styles (e.g., becoming intoxicated, isolating themselves, or running away from home), whereas nondepressed adolescents tend to use more effective strategies (e.g., minimizing the importance of the events, engaging in problem-solving behavior), to deal with negative life events (Essau, 2002). Moreover, depression is consistently and positively correlated with emotion-focused strategies and cognitive avoidance and is negatively associated with problem-focused coping (see Lewinsohn & Essau, 2002).

Cognitive Factors

In line with cognitive theories of depression, negative or maladaptive belief systems play an important role in the onset and maintenance of the disorder. For example, depressed adolescents—especially girls—frequently exhibit low self-esteem and negative body image, and depressed adolescents of both sexes show low perceived control and competence, and excessive pessimism. These individuals also display evidence of depressotypic attributional styles (e.g., they blame themselves for failures and attribute positive experiences to external sources; Essau, 2002; King, Naylor, Segal, Evans, &

Shain, 1993; Lewinsohn et al., 1994; Renouf & Harter, 1990). In a series of longitudinal studies by Cole and colleagues (e.g., Hoffman, Cole, Martin, Tram, & Seroczynski, 2000), depressed symptoms at six-month follow-up were predicted by low perceived competence in various life domains.

One should note that the preceding factors do not seem to represent specific risks for depression. For example, Kendler, Neale, Kessler, Heath, and Eaves (1992) found that parental loss before the age of 17 years was significantly related to the presence of five different psychiatric disorders. Other complexities in understanding risk factors of depression include their co-occurrence and interaction with each other, as well as their multiplicative effects (Essau, 2002; Essau & Petermann, 1997).

For children at risk for depressive disorders, protective factors reduce the possibility of maladaptation. Protective factors are "conditions that buffer young people from the negative consequences of exposure to risk by either reducing the impact of the risk or changing the way a person responds to the risk" (Hawkins, 1995, p. 14). Factors that may protect individuals against the effects of risk factors and that may confer resilience on those in high-risk environments include (a) high intelligence or problem-solving skills (Herrenkohl, Herrenkohl, & Egolf, 1994); (b) strong interests outside the family or the presence of a confiding adult outside the family (Jenkins & Smith, 1990); (c) a warm, nurturant, or supportive relationship with at least one parent (Bradley et al., 1994; Herrenkohl et al., 1994); (d) having parents in good mental health, who have effective parenting skills and harmonious marital relations (Cicchetti & Toth, 1995); (e) a secure attachment history (Pearson, Cohn, Cowan, & Cowan, 1994); (f) having a supportive family (McFarlane, Bellissimo, Norman, & Lange, 1994); and (g) competence in academic domains (Kellam, Rebok, Mayer, Ialongo, & Kalodner, 1994). Despite our increased knowledge of the protective factors for depression, we know little about the processes through which these factors modify the impact of risk factors.

PREVENTION PROGRAMS
FOR DEPRESSION

Most prevention programs for depression revolve around the tenets of cognitive–behavioral therapy (CBT). The primary goal of cognitive therapy is to confront, challenge, and modify maladaptive cognitive processes, whereas the main focus of behavioral therapy in this context is to increase pleasurable experiences and specific response repertoires (e.g., social skills). Parallel to the problems seen in depressed adolescents, the techniques used in the CBT-oriented prevention programs generally target cognitive, behavioral, and affect or mood regulation deficits. Some examples of these techniques, discussed next, are cognitive restructuring, self-control therapy, pleasant event scheduling, social skills training, relaxation training, and problem-solving training (Weisz, Valeri, McCarty, & Moore, 1999). In practice, cognitive and behavioral strategies are integrated into a single package.

The *cognitive restructuring* aspect of the CBT enables children to learn to identify, challenge, and change their maladaptive thoughts. In most programs, this technique usually begins with learning to recognize the differences between thoughts (cognition) and emotions (affects), and to correctly identify specific emotions (e.g., sad, happy).

Self-control therapy is based on Rehm's (1977) model, which posits that depression is associated with deficiencies in self-monitoring, self-evaluation, and self-reinforcement. An important part of self-control therapy involves training youth to evaluate and reinforce their own efforts at improvement and the steps that they take toward the accomplishment of specific goals. Self-monitoring involves systematically observing oneself by maintaining a daily record of experiences and their associated moods.

Pleasant event scheduling involves teaching youth to increase their frequency of experiencing pleasant activities, on the premise that high rates of socially reinforcing events may reduce depression. Children perform a systematic monitoring of their current activities and seek to increase their rates of engaging in pleasant activities. Attempts are made to track events that are associated with elevated mood and to increase the occurrence of these events through the deliberate planning of the child's daily schedule. This exercise helps youth to recognize what makes them feel good and to focus their attention on more positive experiences.

Social skills training involves teaching children assertiveness, communication, ways of accepting and giving feedback, social problem solving, and conflict resolution skills to increase the frequency of their positive social interactions (Fine, Forth, Gilbert, & Haley, 1991). Direct instruction, modeling, and rehearsal with corrective feedback are three methods that are used in social skills training.

Since depression is related to deficits in interpersonal problem-solving skills, CBT frequently involves teaching youths *problem solving* steps, such as identifying problems, generating alternative responses or solutions, evaluating the potential consequences of each alternative, and selecting the most promising alternative. These techniques help children identify events that contribute to depressed feelings and also help them deal with stressors (Nezu, Nezu, & Perri, 1989).

Finally, given a high comorbidity between anxiety and depression (see Nottelmann & Jensen, 1999), *relaxation training* is another important component of CBT. Children are taught to tense and relax various muscle groups to achieve a relaxed state. Guided imagery is often paired with relaxation training, and the children are taught to imagine pleasant scenarios that evoke positive feelings in them.

PREVENTION PROGRAMS FOR DEPRESSION
AND THEIR EFFICACY

Numerous prevention programs for depression have been developed in which the different components of the CBT are integrated into a single package. Despite their similarities, these programs differ in many ways (e.g., number of sessions offered, duration of the sessions, age range, and parental involvement). Two programs established by Australian research groups are the Resourceful Adolescent Program—Adolescents (RAP–A; Shochet, Holland, & Whitefield, 1997) and the Problem Solving for Life Program (Spence, Sheffield, Donovan, & Price, 1997). These programs have been used as primary prevention interventions in schools. Three other programs—the Adolescent Coping with Depression Course (Lewinsohn, Clarke, Rohde, Hops, & Seeley, 1996), the Penn Prevention Program (Jaycox, Reivich, Gillham, & Seligman, 1994), and the Primary and Secondary Control Enhancement Training program (Weisz, Thurber, Sweeney, Proffitt, & LeGagnoux, 1997)— also focus on school-age children, but are secondary prevention efforts in that they target individuals who exhibit certain levels of depressive symptoms.

The Resourceful Adolescent Program

The Resourceful Adolescent Program—Adolescents (RAP–A) is a highly structured training program that comprises 11 group sessions conducted weekly for 40 to 50 minutes during school class time (Shochet et al., 1997). The first seven sessions follow CBT approaches and include such activities as promoting self-management and self-calming skills in the face of stress, cognitive restructuring, and problem solving. Sessions 8 to 10 address interpersonal risk and protective factors relevant to adolescent development. Specific topics covered during these sessions include role transitions during adolescence (e.g., moving toward greater independence while maintaining positive relations with parents) and the use of skills to promote harmony, avoid escalation of conflicts, resolve conflicts, and enhance perspectives. The last session reviews and discusses the main topics presented in the previous sessions.

The RAP also has a component that comprises three group sessions with parents. These sessions are conducted at 3-week intervals over the 11-week duration of the adolescent program. The main aims of the parent sessions are to help parents identify their strengths, to manage stress, to enhance calm and effective parenting, to provide information on (and address misconceptions about) normal adolescent development, to impart strategies for promoting adolescent self-esteem, and to teach techniques that promote family harmony and enhance conflict management.

The efficacy of the RAP in preventing depression has been examined, within the constraints of the school environment, in two separate studies.

In the first study (Shochet et al., 2001), 260 adolescents (M age = 13.5 years) were assigned to one of three groups: (a) Resourceful Adolescent Program—Adolescents (RAP–A), as part of the school curriculum; (b) Resourceful Adolescent Program—Family (RAP–F), which was essentially the same as the RAP–A, but also included a three-session parent-participation program; and (c) Adolescent Watch (AW), a comparison group in which adolescents simply completed the measures. The adolescents in all groups were assessed pre- and post-intervention, as well as at a 12-month follow-up period. Adolescents in either RAP program reported significantly lower levels of both depressive symptomatology and hopelessness post-intervention and at follow-up than did those individuals in the comparison group. No significant differences were found between the RAP–A and the RAP–F groups. Subclinical adolescents with moderately elevated depressive and hopelessness symptoms at pretest showed the greatest benefit from the program. Adolescents in the RAP groups in particular were more likely to fall within a healthy range, and less likely to fall into the clinical range, than were those individuals in the comparison group. Of the subclinical adolescents, 71.4% in the RAP group moved into the healthy category post-intervention and 75% did at follow-up. Among subclinical children in the AW group, only 31.6% and 41% moved into the healthy category post-intervention and at follow-up, respectively. None of the subclinical adolescents in the RAP program moved into the clinical range post-intervention or at 10-month follow-up. Among the AW subclinical adolescents, 10.5% and 17.6% fell into the clinical range post-intervention and at follow-up, respectively.

The effectiveness of the RAP programs, when implemented by teachers and local mental health professionals, was evaluated in a second study (Shochet, Montague, & Dadds, in press). Participants were 1,003 secondary school students drawn from three pairs of matched Grade-9 cohorts. The students were assigned to either the RAP or a comparison condition. Both boys and girls reported positive overall benefits from the RAP intervention. Program effects on depressive symptoms in favor of the RAP intervention were found for the girls both post-intervention and at six-month follow-up. Teachers did not differ from health professionals in terms of their effects on reducing depressive symptoms, perceived program benefits, and their likeability. The authors concluded that teachers could be effective resources for implementing such CBT prevention programs.

The Problem Solving for Life Program

The aim of the Problem Solving for Life Program (Spence et al., 1997) is to enhance youths' coping skills, optimistic thinking styles, and life problem-solving skills. This program involves eight group sessions and focuses on two major content areas. The first area emphasizes cognitive styles and highlights the association between cognition, affect, and behavior. The second area focuses on teaching the skills necessary for effective problem solving. In particular, four main steps used in problem solving are taught: Stop (i.e., learn to stop, consider the situation, and find a solution to the problem); State (i.e., learn to set goals in a specific, realistic, and achievable way); Search (i.e., practice generating possible solutions to specific problems and predicting and evaluating the consequences of each solution); and Solve (i.e., attempt to develop and implement a plan).

The Problem Solving for Life Program is currently being tested in almost 3,000 eighth-grade children from various schools in and around the city of Brisbane, Australia (Spence & Sheffield, 2000). The evaluation of this program is based on a randomized-control-trial design, in which children who participated in the program are compared with those who did not participate. Preliminary data based on 600 children who completed the program and on 600 control participants showed positive short-term effects of the program. That is, adolescents in the prevention group displayed a significant reduction in depressive symptoms and greater improvements in problem-solving skills at the end of the program, compared with children in the control group. The efficacy of the program was particularly strong among children who presented as a high risk for depression and who were identified as having elevated (but not at the clinical level) depressive symptoms prior to the program.

Prevention of Depression Through Other Mental Health Prevention Programs

In addition to programs that are specifically designed to prevent depression, programs developed to prevent other psychiatric disorders may be useful in that regard. As mentioned earlier, there are high comorbidity rates between depression and other disorders. Among those with comorbid disorders, there seems to be a specific sequence of onset. For example, among adolescents with anxiety and depression, depression is generally preceded by problems with anxiety (Essau, 2002). Thus, it seems important to prevent the development of a disorder that may put the child at risk for other disorders. Prevention should also disrupt the transition from one disorder to the next.

Furthermore, depression and a range of psychiatric disorders (e.g., anxiety) in adolescents seem to share a number of risk factors (see Essau, 2002, for a review). It has been argued that some of the developmental pathways to depression may exist through other internalizing disorders as well as through externalizing disorders. Greenberg, Domitrovich, and Bumbarger (1999) similarly argued that diverse developmental pathways may interweave and influence alternative developmental trajectories. On this theoretical basis, and on the basis of empirical findings showing the comorbidity and temporal sequence of depression with other disorders, interventions aimed at reducing those other disorders may also reduce the prevalence of depression. Indeed, prevention programs that have been developed to address such problems as internalizing disorders (e.g., anxiety), coping with bereavement, managing stress, and externalizing conditions may have beneficial effects on depression outcomes as well (see Greenberg et al., 1999).

FURTHER STRATEGIES TO PREVENT DEPRESSION

Numerous strategies that include the promotion of physical health, positive coping, day care and after-school care, and positive parenting may also be useful in mental health promotion and primary prevention. In this section, I present the possible contribution of each of these programs to the prevention of depression. Prevention in relation to societal risk factors such as poverty and unemployment is not discussed. The relief of these adverse features is surely a desirable goal; however, their connections with causal mechanisms seem to be rather indirect.

Promotion of Physical Health

The usefulness of promoting physical health in the prevention of depression stems from at least two lines of research. First, the presence of physical disease and disease-related functional impairment appear to be a strong predictor of depression. Lewinsohn and his colleagues (1996), for instance, found that 8.4% of the adolescents who reported no reduced activity due to physical disease met the diagnosis of depression, compared with 15.1% of those with reduced activity. Second, behaviors that promote overall health and a sense of physical well-being tend to protect children from becoming depressed (Lewinsohn et al., 1994) and make them less likely to be vulnerable to depression. Third, physical exercise has been found to counteract the vegetative aspects of depression (e.g., Raymer, 1992).

Previous studies have also shown that, compared with non-physically fit children, physically fit children are more resistant to fatigue and stress (Krogam, 1980), have improved academic performance (Bailey, 1975), and exhibit healthier self-concepts. Other researchers have argued that participating in sports or other outdoor adventures may enhance self-esteem, develop skills, and foster important relationships between youth and adults (Jeffs & Smith, 1990). By setting goals, meeting challenges, and performing at an optimum level, youths may develop skills, self-discipline, a sense of responsibility and leadership, and decision-making abilities. The development of these competencies may, in turn, help youth in other life domains.

A major challenge involves motivating youth to participate in physical activity. Although a high number of adolescents (especially girls) have positive attitudes toward physical activity, citing its relation to health, few are actually involved in such activity, because of "conflicting" interests (Hendry

& Singer, 1981). Thus, efforts must be made to help youth to focus on the sociability, enjoyment, and competence-related benefits of physical activity. Physically active role models, such as parents, peers, and athletes and actors presented in the mass media, may also positively influence youth participation in regular physical activity.

Positive Parenting

Accumulative studies have shown that cognitive styles are associated with depression in children and adolescents (e.g., Gotlib & Sommerfeld, 1999). Studies indicate that similar to adults, depressed youths generally exhibit dysfunctional cognition. Despite the strong evidence of the relationship between cognitive dysfunction and depression, little is known about the origins of cognitive styles. Acknowledging that negative cognitive styles (e.g., pessimistic thinking) likely result from childhood experiences, Seligman (1995) proposed four possible causes of childhood pessimism: (a) genetics, (b) criticism from parents, teachers, or coaches that is pessimistic, (c) experiences that hinder mastery and foster helplessness, and (d) pessimism in parents. Indeed, children of depressed mothers exhibit significantly lower perceived self-worth and more depressive attributional styles compared with children of nondepressed mothers (Garber & Robinson, 1997; Goodman, Adamson, Riniti, & Cole, 1994).

According to Bowlby (1980), cognitive styles emerge out of a person's internal representations of his or her relationship with attachment figures. The insecure child–caregiver attachment is often associated with the internal representation of oneself as a failure or as unlovable and is associated with the expectation of negative events, hostility, or rejection by others. Such cognitive representations (working models) may increase adolescents' vulnerability to depression. Consistent with Bowlby's (1980) model, numerous studies have shown a significant association among insecure attachment in childhood, depressogenic cognition, and depressive symptomatology (e.g., Hammen & Goodman-Brown, 1990; Renouf & Harter, 1990).

Parents can prevent depression in their offspring by establishing a strong parent–child relationship with them. Therefore, programs that teach parents how to communicate effectively with their children, develop problem-solving skills, and provide appropriate reinforcement are important. One example of such a family-based program is the Seattle Social Development Project (Hawkins, Catalano, Kosterman, Abbott, & Hill, 1999). This six-year intervention includes teacher–classroom, parent, and child components. The teacher–classroom component is intended to enhance attachment and commitment to school through active classroom management, interactive teaching strategies, and cooperative learning. The parent component is designed to reward children's prosocial involvement in both school and family settings. Parents are also taught to support their children's progress at school by creating a positive learning environment in the home, positively reinforcing desired behavior, and providing consistent negative consequences for inappropriate behavior. The final component is intended to help the child develop skills related to problem solving, communication, decision making, negotiation, and conflict resolution. The project has been tested for its efficacy with students in grades 4 to 6. Results were positive for students in the experimental group in terms of reduced antisocial behavior, improved academic skills, increased commitment to school, reduced levels of alienation, and reduced school misbehavior. The positive effects of this prevention project were maintained six years after the end of the intervention (Hawkins et al., 1999). These findings support the importance of starting prevention early and of using the main systems involved in the child's life (i.e., involving the whole school and parents).

Day Care and After-School Care

In most industrialized countries, there has been an increasingly high proportion of mothers working outside the home, and more and more infants are receiving alternative forms of care. Such changes have led to the establishment of day care and after-school care programs. These programs, however, differ in terms of quality, ranging from "social addresses," where children gather largely unsupervised, to "well-run programs," with trained staff and curricula for various age-appropriate activities (e.g., sports, computer activities).

The benefits of day care and after-school care programs have been the subject of several investigations. According to numerous studies, high-quality alternative care can have social and intellectual benefits and may buffer children against the risks associated with forming insecure attachments due to insensitive or unresponsive parenting (National Institute of Child Health and Human Development Early Child Care Research Network, 1997; Ramey & Ramey, 1998). A study by Posner and Vandell (1994) also showed that children from high-risk neighborhoods who attended a supervised after-school-care program were more academically competent, better adjusted, and less likely to be involved in antisocial activities than were children who were not supervised by an adult after school. Given the importance of having high quality programs to influence social, emotional, and intellectual outcomes in a positive manner (Broberg, Wessels, Lamb, & Hwang, 1997), it is important to find ways to optimize developmental outcomes and to prevent children of working mothers from being alone after school. From a political point of view, governments need to subsidize high-quality day care (i.e., staffed programs with trained child-care professionals) that is widely available to all citizens from all social backgrounds at a modest fee.

Another important issue is related to maternity leave. To assist working parents in establishing and maintaining more secure ties with their children, and to otherwise optimize the children's development, the regulation of maternity and paternity leave needs to be revised. One such effort would be to have longer paid leaves, given findings that the length of maternal leave is associated with positive child development. Clark, Hyde, Essex, and Klein (1997), for instance, found that mothers who took four-month maternity leaves displayed less negative affect when interacting with their babies than did mothers whose leaves lasted for only two months. Longer leaves tended to be even more beneficial to mothers with symptoms of depression and to those who had babies with difficult temperaments. In these cases, longer leaves enable the mothers to be more confident with their role as caregivers while, at the same time, affording them the opportunity to establish a "good fit" between their parenting styles and the infants' temperamental characters.

Schoolwide Programs and Positive Coping

Given that a large proportion of the waking lives of school-age children is spent in schools, schools can be regarded as both social organizations and educational institutions. As such, schools can have a strong effect on children's behavior and attainment (Rutter, Giller, & Hagell, 1998). Age-appropriate activities that promote competence in athletic skills, academic skills, behavioral self-control, and social skills and that provide opportunities to compare and compete with same-age peers and to interact with caregivers will advance self-esteem and counteract depressive symptomatology. Kellam, Rebok, Mayer, Ialongo, and Kalodner (1994) reported that symptoms of depression tended to decrease over the course of the first grade in those children who participated in an intervention program that addressed poor reading achievement. These findings imply that improving schools in ways that enhance social competence and positive coping should in turn prevent depression.

Numerous programs geared to the prevention of several problems (e.g., substance use disorders and aggression) have been included in the curriculum of many schools. Children may also benefit from participating in programs such as Botvin's Life Skills Training (Botvin, 1990), which could be used to enhance social competence and social problem solving, and the Yale–New Haven program (Weissberg, Jackson, & Shriver, 1993), which focuses on how to cope with stressful life events.

The area of positive coping is of importance, given the strong association between life events and depression. It has also been argued that because all youth will be exposed to some degree of stress (Compas, 1995), the ability to evoke positive coping skills is important in preventing the development of depression. Positive coping skills have been defined as the ability to tolerate negative emotions that are associated with stressors and to respond in ways that will lead to positive growth and development

(McCauley, Kendall, & Pavlidis, 1995). In line with this definition, Compas (1995) suggested that coping programs should focus on the following:

> development of attitudes and behaviors that foster positive feelings toward the self, mutually adaptive relations with others, and skills to solve life problems and stressors. These include, but are not limited to a sense of self-efficacy; the ability to control one's emotions under stress, the ability to act assertively in changing one's environment in response to a problem, the ability to consider alternative solutions to a problem; the capacity to pursue goal-directed behavior; the capacity to resist pressure from others and concomitantly; to experience a sense of autonomy and personal control over one's behavior; and the capacity to evaluate the effectiveness of one's actions and pursue alternative solutions if necessary. (p. 262)

Acquiring such skills should help children and adolescents develop a positive sense of self and enhance their subjective well-being. The same skills may also enable individuals to maintain these positive attributes in the presence of stress.

CONCLUSION

Despite numerous advantages of primary prevention of depression, there are several difficulties and challenges in its implementation and evaluation. The first issue pertains to what strategies are needed to prevent depression. Given that numerous risk factors of depression have been identified, it is difficult to pinpoint what specifically should be targeted for preventative intervention. A related problem is that risk factors tend to come in "packages" or "chains," with the occurrence of one risk factor leading to the occurrence of another.

A second issue relates to the practicalities surrounding the implementation of prevention programs. Although most programs have been conducted in schools, schools are often overburdened with academic curriculum demands. Adding a separate multisession curriculum to prevent depression, in addition to other programs that prevent, for example, substance abuse, would overwhelm schools. This problem could be addressed by having depression prevention goals subsumed within a multicomponent general mental health preventive program. Such a program would be able to address multiple problem areas in a cohesive, but not too burdensome, package. This type of prevention program seems justifiable because many adverse outcomes in children and adolescents (e.g., substance abuse, suicide, depression) share several common risk factors.

Finally, little is known about the cost of prevention programs for depression. Therefore, an important area of future research would involve conducting cost–benefit analyses. Specifically, the cost of providing primary prevention should be compared with the reduction in the cost of treatment for depression. Also included in this analysis should be the costs that are associated with subclinical and clinical depression in terms of long-term treatment, time off from work, hospitalization, and the impact on both the family and the individual with depression.

REFERENCES

Andrews, G., Szabo, M., & Burns, J. (2002). Preventing major depression in young people. *British Journal of Psychiatry, 181,* 460–462.

Angold, A., & Costello, E. J. (1993). Depressive comorbidity in children and adolescents: Empirical, theoretical, and methodological issues. *American Journal of Psychiatry, 150,* 1779–1791.

Bailey, D. A. (1975). The growing child and the need for physical activity. In M. S. Smart & R. C. Smart (Eds.), *School-age children: Development and relationship* (pp. 50–61). New York: Macmillan.

Botvin, G. J. (1990). Substance abuse prevention: Theory, practice and effectiveness. In M. Tonry & J. Q. Wilson (Eds.), *Communities and crime* (pp. 101–162). Chicago: University of Chicago Press.

Bowlby, J. (1980). *Loss: Sadness and depression.* New York: Basic Books.

Bradley, R. H., Whiteside, L., Mundfrom, D. J., Casey, P. H., Kelleher, K. J., & Pope, S. K. (1994). Early indicators of resilience and their relation to experiences in the home environments of low birthweight, premature children living in poverty. *Child Development, 65,* 346–360.

Broberg, A. G., Wessels, H., Lamb, M. E., & Hwang, C. P. (1997). Effects of day care on the cognitive development of 8-year-olds: A longitudinal study. *Developmental Psychology, 33,* 62–69.

Cicchetti, D., & Toth, S. (1995). Developmental psychopathology and disorders of affect. In D. Cicchetti & D. J. Cohen (Eds.), *Developmental psychopathology, Vol. 2: Risk, disorder, and adaptation* (pp. 369–420). New York: Wiley.

Clark, R., Hyde, J. S., Essex, M. J., & Klein, M. H. (1997). Length of maternity leave and quality of mother–infant interactions. *Child Development, 68,* 364–383.

Compas, B. E. (1995). Promoting successful coping during adolescence. In M. Rutter (Ed.), *Psychosocial disturbances in young people: Challenges for prevention* (pp. 247–273). Cambridge, England: Cambridge University Press.

Durlak, J. A., & Wells, A. M. (1997). Primary prevention mental health programs for children and adolescents: A meta-analytic review. *American Journal of Community Psychology, 25,* 115–152.

Essau, C. A. (2002). *Lehrbuch: Depression bei Kindern und Jugendlichen* [Textbook: Depression in children and adolescents]. Munich, Germany: Ernst Reinhardt Verlag.

Essau, C. A., Conradt, J., & Petermann, F. (2000). Frequency, comorbidity, and psychosocial impairment of depressive disorders in adolescents. *Journal of Adolescent Research, 15*, 470–481.

Essau, C. A., & Dobson, K. S. (1999). Epidemiology of depressive disorders. In C. A. Essau & F. Petermann (Eds.), *Depressive disorders in children and adolescents: Epidemiology, risk factors, and treatment* (pp. 69–103). Northvale, NJ: Jason Aronson.

Essau, C. A., & Merikangas, K. R. (1999). Familial and genetic factors. In C. A. Essau & F. Petermann (Eds.), *Depressive disorders in children and adolescents: Epidemiology, risk factors, and treatment* (pp. 261–285). Northvale, NJ: Jason Aronson.

Essau, C. A., & Petermann, F. (1997). Introduction and general issues. In C. A. Essau & F. Petermann (Eds.), *Developmental psychopathology: Epidemiology, diagnostics, and treatment* (pp. 1–18). London: Harwood Academic.

Fendrich, M., Warner, V., & Weissman, M. M. (1990). Family risk factors, parental depression, and psychopathology in offspring. *Developmental Psychology, 26*, 40–50.

Fine, S., Forth, A., Gilbert, M., & Haley, G. (1991). Group therapy for adolescent depressive disorder: A comparison of social skills and therapeutic support. *Journal of the American Academy of Child and Adolescent Psychiatry, 30*, 79–85.

Garber, J. S., & Robinson, N. S. (1997). Cognitive vulnerability in children at risk for depression. *Cognitions and Emotions, 11*, 619–635.

Goodman, S. H., Adamson, L. B., Riniti, J., & Cole, S. (1994). Mothers' expressed attitudes: Associations with maternal depression and children's self-esteem and psychopathology. *Journal of the American Academy of Child and Adolescent Psychology, 33*, 1265–1274.

Goodyer, I., Cooper, P. J., Vize, C. M., & Ashby, L. (1993). Depression in 11–16-year-old girls: The role of past parental psychopathology and exposure to recent life events. *Journal of Child Psychology and Psychiatry, 34*, 1103–1115.

Gotlib, I. H., & Sommerfeld, B. K. (1999). Cognitive functioning in depressed children and adolescents: A developmental perspective. In C. A. Essau & F. Petermann (Eds.), *Depressive disorders in children and adolescents: Epidemiology, risk factors, and treatment* (pp. 195–236). Northvale, NJ: Jason Aronson.

Greenberg, M. T., Domitrovich, C., & Bumbarger, B. (1999). Preventing mental disorders in school age children: A review of the effectiveness of prevention programmes. CITY: Pennsylvania State University.

Hammen, C., & Goodman-Brown, T. (1990). Self-schemas and vulnerability to specific life stress in children at risk for depression. *Cognitive Therapy and Research, 14*, 215–227.

Hammen, C., Rudolph, K., Weisz, J., Rao, U., & Burge, D. (1999). The context of depression in clinic-referred youth: Neglected areas in treatment. *Journal of the American Academy of Child and Adolescent Psychiatry, 38*, 64–71.

Hawkins, J. D. (1995). Controlling crime before it happens: Risk-focused prevention. *National Institute of Justice, 229*, 10–18.

Hawkins, J. D., Catalano, R. F., Kosterman, R., Abbott, R., & Hill, K. G. (1999). Preventing adolescent health-risk behaviors by strengthening protection during childhood. *Archives of Pediatrics and Adolescent Medicine, 153*, 226–234.

Hendry, L., & Singer, F. (1981). Sport and the adolescent girl: A case study of one comprehensive school. *Scottish Journal of Physical Education, 9*, 19–29.

Herrenkohl, E. C., Herrenkohl, R. C., & Egolf, B. (1994). Resilient early school-age children from maltreating homes: Outcomes in late adolescence. *American Journal of Orthopsychiatry, 64*, 301–309.

Hoffman, K. B., Cole, D. A., Martin, J. M., Tram, J., & Seroczynski, A. D. (2000). Are the discrepancies between self and others appraisals of competence predictive or reflective of depressive symptoms in children and adolescents: A longitudinal study, Part II. *Journal of Abnormal Psychology, 109*, 651–662.

Jaycox, L. H., Reivich, K. J., Gillham, J., & Seligman, M. E. P. (1994). Prevention of depressive symptoms in school children. *Behaviour Research and Therapy, 32*, 801–816.

Jeffs, T., & Smith, M. (1990). *Young people, inequality and youth work.* London: Macmillan.

Jenkins, J. N., & Smith, M. A. (1990). Factors protecting children living in disharmonious homes: Maternal reports. *Journal of the Academy of Child and Adolescent Psychiatry, 29*, 60–69.

Kellam, S. G., Rebok, G. W., Mayer, L. S., Ialongo, N., & Kalodner, C. R. (1994). Depressive symptoms over first grade and their response to a developmental epidemiologically based preventive trial aimed at improving achievement. *Development and Psychopathology, 6*, 463–481.

Kendler, K. S., Neale, M. C., Kessler, R. C., Heath, A. C., & Eaves, L. J. (1992). Childhood parental loss and adult psychopathology in women. *Archives of General Psychiatry, 49*, 109–116.

King, C. A., Naylor, M. W., Segal, H. G., Evans, T., & Shain, B. N. (1993). Global self-worth, specific self-perceptions of competence, and depression in adolescents. *Journal of the American Academy of Child and Adolescent Psychiatry, 32*, 745–752.

Krogam, W. M. (1980). *Child growth.* Ann Arbor: University of Michigan Press.

Lewinsohn, P. M., Clarke, G., Rohde, P., Hops, H., & Seeley, J. (1996). A course in coping: A cognitive–behavioral approach to the treatment of adolescent depression. In E. D. Hibbs & P. S. Jensen (Eds.), *Psychosocial treatments for child and adolescent disorders: Empirically based strategies for clinical practice* (pp. 109–135). Washington, DC: American Psychological Association.

Lewinsohn, P. M., Clarke, G. N., Seeley, J. R., & Rohde, P. (1994). Major depression in community adolescents: Age at onset, episode duration, and time to recurrence. *Journal of the American Academy of Child and Adolescent Psychiatry, 33*, 714–722.

Lewinsohn, P. M., & Essau, C. A. (2002). Depression in adolescents. In I. Gotlib & C. Hammen (Eds.), *Handbook of depression* (pp. 541–559). New York: Guilford.

Lewinsohn, P. M., Rohde, P., & Seeley, J. R. (1998). Treatment of adolescent depression: Frequency of services and impact on functioning in young adulthood. *Depression and Anxiety, 7,* 47–52.

Mash, E. J., & Krahn, G. L. (1995). Research strategies in child psychopathology. In M. Hersen & R. T. Hammerman (Eds.), *Advanced abnormal child psychology* (pp. 105–133). Hillsdale, NJ: Erlbaum.

McCauley, E., Kendall, K., & Pavlidis, K. (1995). The development of emotional regulation and emotional response. In I. M. Goodyer (Ed.), *The depressed child and adolescent: Developmental and clinical perspectives* (pp. 53–80). Cambridge, England: Cambridge University Press.

McFarlane, A. H., Bellissimo, A., Norman, G. R., & Lange, P. (1994). Adolescent depression in a school-based community sample: Preliminary findings on contributing social factors. *Journal of Youth and Adolescence, 23,* 601–620.

McGee, R., Feehan, M., & Williams, S. (1995). Long-term follow-up of a birth cohort. In F. C. Verhulst & H. M. Koot (Eds.), *The epidemiology of child and adolescent psychopathology* (pp. 366–384). Oxford, England: Oxford University Press.

Monroe, S. M., Rohde, P., Seeley, J. R., & Lewinsohn, P. M. (1999). Life events and depression in adolescence: Relationship loss as a prospective risk factor for first onset of major depressive disorder. *Journal of Abnormal Psychology, 108,* 606–614.

National Institute of Child Health and Human Development Early Child Care Research Network. (1997). The effects of infant child care on mother–infant attachment security: Results of the NICHD study of early child care. *Child Development, 68,* 860–879.

Nezu, A. M., Nezu, C. M., & Perri, M. G. (1989). *Problem-solving therapy for depression: Theory, research, and clinical guidelines.* New York: Wiley.

Nottelmann, E. D., & Jensen, P. S. (1999). Comorbidity of depressive disorders in children and adolescents: Rates, temporal sequencing, course and outcome. In C. A. Essau & F. Petermann (Eds.), *Depressive disorders in children and adolescents: Epidemiology, risk factors, and treatment* (pp. 137–191). Northvale, NJ: Jason Aronson.

Pearson, J. L., Cohn, D. A., Cowan, P. A., & Cowan, C. P. (1994). Earned-and-continuous security in adult attachment: Relation to depressive symptomatology and parenting style. *Development and Psychopathology, 6,* 359–373.

Posner, J. K., & Vandell, D. L. (1994). Low-income children's after-school care: Are there beneficial effects of after-school programs? *Child Development, 65,* 440–456.

Ramey, C. T., & Ramey, S. L. (1998). Early intervention and early experience. *American Psychologist, 53,* 109–120.

Raymer, K. A. (1992). Inpatient treatment of depression. In M. Shafii & S. L. Shafii (Eds.), *Clinical guide to depression in children and adolescents* (pp. 233–248). Washington, DC: American Psychiatric Press.

Rehm, L. P. (1977). A self-control model of depression. *Behavior Therapy, 8,* 787–804.

Reinherz, H. Z., Giaconia, R. M., Pakiz, B., Silverman, A. B., Frost, A. K. & Lefkowitz, E. S. (1993). Psychosocial risks for major depression in late adolescence: A longitudinal community study. *Journal of the American Academy of Child and Adolescent Psychiatry, 32*, 1155–1163.

Renouf, A. G., & Harter, S. (1990). Low self-worth and anger as components of the depressive experience in young adolescents. *Development and Psychopathology, 2*, 293–310.

Rutter, M., Giller, H., & Hagell, A. (1998). *Antisocial behavior by young people*. Cambridge, England: Cambridge University Press.

Schraedley, P. K., Gotlib, I. H., & Hayward, C. (1999). Gender differences in correlates of depressive symptoms in adolescents. *Journal of Adolescent Health, 25*, 98–108.

Seligman, M. E. P. (1995). *The optimistic child*. New York: Houghton Mifflin.

Shochet, I. M., Dadds, M. R., Holland, D., Whitefield, K., Harnett, P. H., & Osgarby, S. M. (2001). The efficacy of a school-based program to prevent adolescent depression. *Journal of Clinical Child Psychology, 30*, 303–315.

Shochet, I., Holland, D., & Whitefield, K. (1997). *The Griffith Early Intervention Depression Project: Group leader's manual*. Brisbane, Australia: Griffith Early Intervention Project.

Shochet, I. M., Montague, R., & Dadds, M. (in press). Preventing adolescent depression with sustainable resources: Evaluation of a school-based universal effectiveness trial.

Spence, S. H., & Sheffield, J. (2000). Problem solving for life program: Preventing depression in Australian youth. *Reaching Today's Youth, 4*, 67–72.

Spence, S. H., Sheffield, J., Donovan, C., & Price, C. (1997). *Problem solving for life manual*. Brisbane, Australia: University of Queensland.

Weissberg, R. P., Jackson, A. S., & Shriver, S. (1993). Promoting positive social development and health practices in young urban adolescents. In M. J. Elias (Ed.), *Social decision making and life skills development: Guidelines for middle school educators* (pp. 45–77). Gaithersburg, MD: Aspen.

Weisz, J. R., Thurber, C. A., Sweeney, L., Proffitt, V. D., & LeGagnoux, G. L. (1997). Brief treatment of mild to moderate child depression using primary and secondary control enhancement training. *Journal of Consulting and Clinical Psychology, 65*, 703–707.

Weisz, J. R., Valeri, S. M., McCarty, C. A., & Moore, P. S. (1999). Interventions for child and adolescent depression: Features, effects, and future directions. In C. A. Essau & F. Petermann (Eds.), *Depressive disorders in children and adolescents: Epidemiology, risk factors, and treatment* (pp. 383–435). Northvale, NJ: Jason Aronson.

9

SECONDARY PREVENTION OF DEPRESSION: RISK, VULNERABILITY, AND INTERVENTION

RICK E. INGRAM, MICA ODOM,
AND TISH MITCHUSSON

As Dozois and Westra made clear in chapter 2 (this volume), depression constitutes a significant public health concern. The National Comorbidity Survey (Kessler et al., 1994) found overall lifetime rates of depression of 17.1%; the National Institute of Mental Health Epidemiologic Catchment Area study (Weissman, Bruce, Leaf, Florio, & Holzer, 1991) estimated a lifetime prevalence rate of 5.8%. Even the more conservative of these estimates suggests that depression is one of the most common mental disorders found in the population, affecting millions of people worldwide, and is also the most common condition for which individuals receive inpatient psychiatric treatment (Gotlib & Hammen, 1992). As alarming as these rates are, some data suggest that the incidence of depression is yet increasing—so much so, that some researchers have argued that the public faces an epidemic of the disorder (Seligman, 1990).

Aside from the emotional misery associated with depression, the condition is linked to a variety of other problems, including social withdrawal, occupational disability, and interpersonal turmoil. Moreover, left untreated, depressive disorders typically last as long as 6 months to a year (Keller, Shapiro, Lavori, & Wolfe, 1982), and in some cases individuals can experience significant symptoms for up to 2 years (see Goodwin & Jamison, 1990). Depression can also be a chronic condition; relapse and recurrence rates are quite high (Hammen, 1991; Ingram, Miranda, & Segal, 1998), and individuals who experience recurrent depression are also at significant risk for developing dysthymia as well as other psychiatric conditions. Suicide and attempted suicide are not uncommon during depressive episodes, and prevalence rates suggest that women are at least twice as likely to be diagnosed with a major depressive disorder. Thus, it is no wonder that interest in the prevention of depression may be at an all-time high.

As noted in more detail throughout this volume, primary prevention is typically viewed as those activities aimed either at precluding the occurrence of depression in large samples or at reducing the overall incidence of depression in the population. From a public health perspective, few would disagree that primary prevention is always preferable to other forms of prevention or to initiating treatment after the occurrence of an onset. Yet, primary prevention is also notoriously difficult to implement successfully (Clarke, 1999); hence, when primary prevention is unsuccessful or not feasible, secondary prevention serves an increasingly important function. In this chapter, we examine a number of facets of secondary prevention, ranging from conceptual issues to its implementation in several informative studies. Because it is not feasible to examine all of these issues and studies in a single chapter, we focus on several of the most important conceptual issues, along with examining those studies which not only provide informative data on the efficacy of secondary prevention, but also may afford models and insights for future efforts in the secondary prevention of depression in particular.

Before discussing the secondary prevention of depression, however, it is important to recognize that depression is not a homogenous disorder. Indeed, many forms, and some subtypes, of depressive disorders have been recognized. All are, arguably, worthy of prevention efforts. For instance, both theory and empirical data not only recognize unipolar depression, but also distinguish it from bipolar disorder. Although bipolar disorder is a debilitating psychiatric condition, because unipolar depression is much more common and has more often been the target of prevention attempts, our focus in this chapter is on unipolar major depressive disorder as defined by sources such as the fourth edition of the *Diagnostic and Statistical Manual of Mental Disorders* (*DSM–IV–TR*; American Psychiatric Association, 2000).[1] In addition,

---

[1]Unless otherwise specified, throughout this chapter we will use the term *depression* to refer to unipolar major depressive disorder of the type described in *DSM–IV*.

although depressive symptoms can be a legitimate focus of prevention efforts (Gillham, Shatte, & Freres, 2000), our focus is on the prevention of depressive *disorders*. We thus begin our exploration of the secondary prevention of depression with a discussion of what constitutes secondary prevention and then examine the idea of risk and differentiate it from ideas about vulnerability. We next note various risk factors for depression and examine studies that have documented efforts toward the secondary prevention of the disorder. We conclude by offering some thoughts on future issues in the secondary prevention of depression.

DEFINITIONS OF SECONDARY PREVENTION

Prevention can have numerous definitions (Cowen, 1997), and although the term is sometimes defined in a way that explicitly differentiates it from treatment, at least in the case of secondary prevention this is a false dichotomy. Indeed, secondary prevention almost always involves the provision of some kind of treatment (Muñoz & Ying, 1993; Muñoz, Le, Clarke, & Jaycox, 2002). As we shall subsequently see—and in detail—secondary prevention involves the identification of high-risk individuals and then the provision of some form of intervention, either individually or through groups, to prevent the full onset of the disorder (Heller, Wyman, & Allen, 2000). For our purposes, secondary prevention and its associated treatment can be thought of in one of two ways. The first focuses on the early identification of cases of depression as targets of treatment before the disorder becomes fully realized. We discuss this tack only briefly, because most efforts at preventing depression emphasize a second approach, one that focuses on the identification of risk factors even when no symptoms are present and then, ideally at least, intervening before the occurrence of the disorder. In both cases, the goal is to avert the onset of depression (again, ideally) or to decrease its severity and duration (Heller et al., 2000).

Whereas *secondary* prevention aims to prevent or diminish the onset of symptoms in high-risk individuals, *tertiary* prevention focuses on preventing relapses and recurrences of depression (see chap. 4, this volume). However, in many cases, the differentiation between secondary and tertiary prevention may be more implied than real. As we note later in this chapter, prior depression is a clear risk factor for later depression, and if it can be safely assumed that a person is in full remission from a previous episode of depression, then secondary prevention can legitimately focus on individuals who have experienced such a previous episode. Although it is unclear exactly where to draw the line between relapse (i.e., the recurrence of an existing or "old" episode) and the occurrence of a new and different episode (Hollon, DeRubeis, & Evans, 1996), efforts to prevent a future onset can properly be considered secondary prevention at least in cases of full recovery.

Early Case Identification

As a general rule, prevention efforts focusing on early case identification seek to identify the prodromal or early signs of an emergent disorder and then attempt to prevent the development of the fully developed disorder. In the case of depression, prodromal functioning can be conceptualized in different ways. In the official classification scheme of the American Psychiatric Association, *bereavement* does not constitute a depressive disorder; thus, in the most technical sense, treatment efforts aimed at preventing the development of a major depressive disorder in bereaved individuals could be considered secondary prevention. Indeed—and with mixed success—some research has been aimed at preventing the onset of depression as the result of bereavement. For example, Marmar, Horowitz, Weiss, and Wilner (1988) reported success using brief therapy and self-help when they specifically targeted bereaved persons who were experiencing prolonged grief.

Despite the fact that strategies for treating grief are important, they may not be particularly relevant to the true secondary prevention of depression. That is, if we concentrate on symptomatology without reference to precipitating events, a reasonable case can be made that depression as the result of bereavement is already a fully developed depressive disorder (see Beckham, Leber, & Youll, 1995) and thus treatment efforts could not legitimately be considered to be preventive, at least from the standpoint of secondary prevention.

A more clear-cut case of early symptomatology represents a subclinical or subthreshold depressive disorder; such cases are widely recognized as a risk factor for major depressive disorder (Horwath, Johnson, Klerman, & Weissman, 1992; Judd, 1997). However, defining subclinical depression can be tricky. For example, the *DSM–IV–TR* lists minor depressive disorder as a condition involving "fewer symptoms and less impairment" (p. 775) than is seen in a diagnosis of major depressive episode. Specifically, only two to four symptoms, rather than a minimum of five, need to be present for making this diagnosis. Minor depressive disorder currently represents a state designated for further study and is thus not officially recognized as a diagnostic category. The *DSM* also lists "adjustment disorder with depressed mood" as an official diagnostic category, although the criteria for this disorder are vague. In this regard, the *DSM–IV–TR* notes that this adjustment disorder is characterized by symptoms that are clinically significant and that may be linked to "marked distress" or by "significant impairment" (p. 679). However, few criteria for clinical significance, marked distress, or significant impairment are specified.

The construct of mild or subclinical depression is perhaps the most difficult to pin down operationally. Such states are frequently the focus of research, but rather than denoting a specific focus on a subclinically depressed state, the term tends to be used by studies that simply did not include a diagnostic assessment; thus, no conclusions can be inferred about the diagnostic status of research participants (Ingram & Hamilton, 1999). Most studies using this methodology probably recruit groups that are composed of some clinically depressed individuals, some individuals who have a depressive syndrome that does not reach clinical significance, and some individuals who have simply had a rough couple of weeks (Ingram & Siegle, 2002). Despite these methodological issues, subclinical depression, defined as symptoms that are of insufficient intensity or number to necessitate a diagnosis of major depression, can be considered an important focus of secondary prevention programs.

Issues in the Definition of Risk

Although early signs and symptoms of depression provide one key for directing secondary prevention attempts, the more general construct of risk is an important focus of theory and research on preventing depression and is in fact the central concept in most of the research that has explored secondary prevention interventions. Data on the risk factors for depression are abundant (Kaelber, Moul, & Farmer, 1995), and we subsequently discuss some of the more virulent risk factors and how they have been used in prevention research. Before doing so, however, it is important to note distinctions between two related, but different, constructs: risk and vulnerability.

The Relationship Between Risk and Vulnerability

Differentiating between risk and vulnerability factors has important implications for the secondary prevention of depression. Although *risk* and *vulnerability* are terms that are often used interchangeably, they are not in fact synonymous. *Risk* refers to any and all factors associated with increased odds of experiencing the onset of depression or of experiencing more severe and chronic depressive states (Heller et al., 2000). Such factors, however, can be seen as *correlates* of depression and are not necessarily informative about the *causes* of the disorder (Ingram et al., 1998).

To illustrate this distinction, consider gender differences in depression; female gender is recognized as a risk factor for the condition (Ingram et al., 1998; Kaelber et al., 1995). Yet, that alone does not tell us anything about the actual processes or mechanisms which bring about depression in women. Indeed, numerous and different possibilities as to why women are at heightened risk for depression, ranging from biological to psychological to social reasons, have been proposed (Nolen-Hoeksema, 2002).

Moreover, and consistent with a lack of information about causal factors, the identification of a presumed risk variable does not rule out the possibility that the variable may be a *consequence* of depression, rather than a cause. For instance, being unmarried is a risk factor for depression, but given the interpersonal turmoil that is associated with a depressive disorder, the dissolution of a marriage may be the result, rather than a precipitant, of the depression. In either case, people who are unmarried are statistically more likely to experience depression. To the extent that a variable is related to an increased likelihood of experiencing depression, the variable can be considered a risk factor, but this alone is informative only about probability, not about causality.

The number of risk factors for depression that have been empirically identified is impressive. In examining the myriad of potential risk factors, Kaelber et al. (1995) classified factors as either highly plausible, plausible, or possible. It is important to note that, although differing in probability, these factors are not necessarily independent. For instance, divorce is a highly plausible risk factor, and being unmarried is a plausible risk factor. Of course, becoming unmarried is the result of divorce; hence, the difference between these variables is temporal, and the person who has survived divorce without experiencing a depressive episode may still be at risk for depression at a later time. In general, knowledge of these kinds of factors is important in efforts to prevent depression, but as we shall see shortly, such knowledge alone is not sufficient for effective prevention efforts.

In contrast to risk factors, *vulnerability* factors are defined as reflecting presumed causal mechanisms of depression (Luthar & Zigler, 1991). Hence, if the occurrence of depression is rooted in the disruption of a certain neurotransmitter, then this disruption constitutes a vulnerability factor because it represents a presumed causal mechanism that underlies the emergence of depression. Of course, different theoretical perspectives suggest different vulnerability factors; for example, cognitive perspectives argue that depression is the result of the activation of negative self-schemas, and it is thus the presence of such schemas that constitutes vulnerability. No matter what the theoretical perspective, however, vulnerability is defined as information about causality (e.g., Ingram et al., 1998).

Given these definitions of risk and vulnerability, vulnerability factors must also logically constitute risk factors. That is, because risk is defined as *any* variable that is associated with an increased probability of depression, vulnerability factors also qualify as risk factors; by definition, they are linked to an increased likelihood of the disorder. Because vulnerability processes represent a subset of risk variables, risk thus comprises a much broader conceptual network than does vulnerability.

Although conceptually separate, risk and vulnerability are nonetheless related. In noting a similar distinction, Luthar and Zigler (1991) suggested that risk and vulnerability interact to produce the onset of psychopathology. For example, people who are at increased risk because they live in a stressful environment will see this risk eventuate in depression if they *also* possess a vulnerability mechanism. As one example of a diathesis–stress model, consider individuals who live in impoverished circumstances; living in poverty may produce the stress that triggers the dysregulation processes that lead to the onset of depression. In sum, then, although they reflect no causal significance per se, risk factors are important predictive variables that may act in concert with vulnerability factors to bring about the onset of depression.

Given that much of the enterprise of secondary prevention focuses on identifying individuals who are at risk, but who are not (yet) depressed, the need to differentiate between risk and vulnerability becomes apparent. In particular, the identification of individuals who are at risk allows clinicians or researchers to identify groups of individuals toward whom secondary prevention efforts *should be targeted*. However, using risk factors in such a manner is far from straightforward: Even variables that are highly plausible may be too broadly defined to be of much utility from a secondary prevention perspective. Consider gender; it would make little sense to target secondary prevention efforts at individuals simply because they are women (although primary prevention may more appropriately focus solely on women). To be useful for secondary prevention, such risk factors would need to be combined with other risk factors to narrow the target groups. Hence, targeting prevention efforts at women who are living in stressful circumstances would be far more likely to pay off in effective secondary prevention than would focusing on women alone. Alternatively, some high-risk groups (e.g., individuals who have previously experienced an episode of depression) may be narrowly enough defined that little additional information is needed to target these groups for secondary prevention.

Distinguishing Risk and Vulnerability in Prevention

Effective secondary prevention requires knowledge of both the risk and vulnerability factors. The identification of risk factors provides data on *which* groups or individuals should be targeted for secondary prevention efforts. A wealth of data, for example, indicates that children whose mothers are depressed are at risk for depression (discussed later) and are thus appropriate targets for prevention trials. The same could be true for virtually any presumed risk group, such as individuals living in poverty, divorcing couples, and so on. The point of identifying risk then is to identify individuals who could benefit from secondary prevention programs.

Although the identification of risk is a necessary first step, in many cases it will not be sufficient for successful secondary prevention. Specifically, the identification of presumed vulnerability factors may also be critical for prevention efforts, because such identification focuses on the processes or mechanisms (rather than individuals) to be targeted in the prevention process. Thus, to the extent that cognitive perspectives are correct in suggesting that the presence of negative self-schemas reflects a vulnerability mechanism, prevention efforts might profitably focus on identifying individuals at risk and then modifying such schemas before they can initiate a depressive episode when stress occurs.

Of course, some prevention treatment options may be less theoretically developed and, therefore, need to rely less on the identification of mechanisms. In this regard, although selective serotonin reuptake inhibitors have been found to be effective in the treatment of depression (Thase, 2000), there is little consensus on whether they affect the mechanisms that bring about depression. That is, a treatment which successfully targets a given process cannot, in and of itself, verify that it was that process which initially caused the disorder. Regardless of whether causal mechanisms are affected by psychopharmacological (or psychological) treatments, there is likely to be little disagreement that if the precise causal mechanisms could be determined in high-risk individuals, prevention efforts would likely take a quantum leap forward. The discovery of vulnerability mechanisms is thus important in maximizing the prospects for effective secondary prevention.

WHO IS AT RISK?

In the previous section, we noted risk factors that have been described by various investigators. The list of potential risk factors is quite large, but in this section we discuss several that are both narrowly enough defined and sufficiently empirically documented that they merit consideration as primary targets of secondary prevention efforts.

Negative Cognition

Cognitive factors must be included in any discussion of risk for depression. Not only is the vast majority of contemporary psychosocial research on depression cognitive in nature, but cognitive factors have long been featured in models of vulnerability to depression. Although the conceptual details of various cognitive models differ to some degree, they typically converge on several important concepts (Ingram et al., 1998). Several cognitive models suggest that dysfunctional cognitive self-structures, or *schemas*, constitute central elements in the onset and maintenance of depression, thus making them ideal risk candidates (see Beck, 1967, 1987). In addition, cognitive models of depression are typically of the diathesis–stress variety in nature. Schemas determine personal meaning and self-concept in various situations, thus setting the stage for depression when stressful life circumstances are encountered. More specifically, diathesis–stress perspectives argue that schemas are dormant or inactive until they become energized by stressful events (e.g., Beck, 1967; Ingram et al., 1998; Ingram, 1984; Teasdale, 1983). Segal and Shaw (1986) have described these cognitive structures as "latent but reactive" and argue that, once they are triggered, a pattern of negative self-referenced information processing is initiated that leads to depression.

Support for cognitive diathesis–stress models has grown substantially. As Segal and Ingram (1994) and Ingram et al. (1998) have noted, several converging lines of research suggest that vulnerable individuals process information dysfunctionally when they encounter situations that stimulate depressive cognitive structures (e.g., Miranda & Persons, 1988). Moreover, the processes articulated in diathesis–stress models have been shown to predict a relapse into depression in previously treated patients (Segal, Gemar, & Williams, 1999) and to function in the offspring (as young as 8 years) of depressed mothers (Taylor & Ingram, 1999).

Models emphasizing schemas as the core of depressive risk processes are one of the two major conceptual themes in this arena. A related, but different, approach emphasizes attributional style, as originally articulated by Abramson, Seligman, and Teasdale (1978). More recently, Abramson, Metalsky, & Alloy (1989) presented a revised version of the attributional model, with a specific focus on hopelessness as a major causal factor for at least some kinds of depression (see also Abramson, Alloy, & Hogan, 1997). To the extent that individuals are inclined to believe that desired outcomes are unlikely to occur or, conversely, that aversive outcomes are likely and that no response can alter this likelihood, Abramson et al. (1989) argue that people are at increased risk for depression.

Support for this model, as well as for schema models of depression, has been reported by the Temple–Wisconsin Cognitive Vulnerability to Depression Project (Alloy & Abramson, 1999), which assessed a group of individuals who, upon entry into college, were identified as possessing negative inferential styles (and negative self-schemas). These at-risk individuals were compared with individuals not showing evidence of the same cognitive characteristics with regard to the likelihood that they would experience depression in the future. Data reported from this project thus far have suggested a number of cognitive factors that may be linked to vulnerability. Most critically, those identified as being a high cognitive risk do appear more likely to experience depression at some point in the future (Alloy & Abramson, 1999).

A variation on cognitive models that is important to note in an examination of risk are two personality types that have been suggested to constitute specific vulnerabilities for depression. Beck (1987) and Blatt and Zuroff (1992) have described these types as reflecting either sociotropy or autonomy. Sociotropic individuals are thought to value interpersonal relationships, intimacy, and acceptance by others as a way of maintaining their own self-esteem, and correspondingly, they are considered to be vulnerable to depression when they experience a loss or rejection in social relationships. Autonomous individuals, in contrast, are invested in maintaining their independence and achieving goals and standards; they are at risk if they experience failure in an achievement or individual accomplishment domain (e.g., a demotion at work). Although these specific personality types may be at risk, longitudinal studies have shown only somewhat mixed success in predicting self-reported distress or depression in sociotropic and autonomic individuals (Coyne & Whiffen, 1995). Nevertheless, it seems clear that negative cognitive patterns can constitute a risk factor for depression and, because this category of risk also encompasses vulnerability, may also be informative about the processes to target in prevention programs.

Children of Depressed Parents

It has traditionally been assumed that the children of individuals with psychological disorders are at heightened risk for the development of similar disorders (e.g., Rosenthal et al., 1968). In the case of depression, most research has focused specifically on depressed mothers. Data tend to show that the children of depressed mothers are at increased risk for a range of problems (Beardslee, Bemporad, Keller, & Klerman, 1983; Hammen et al., 1987) that include deficits in academic performance, in school behavior, and in social competence (Weintraub, Winters, & Neale, 1986). A wealth of data also show that the children of depressed mothers are vulnerable to depression (Beardslee, Versage, Gladstone, & Tracy, 1998; Cummings & Davis, 1999; Goodman & Gotlib, 1999; Hammen, 1991; Garber & Flynn, 2001a, 2001b), with some investigators suggesting that more than half of the offspring of depressed mothers will experience depressive disorders and that adolescents with a depressed mother are up to 6 times more likely to experience depression than those with nondepressed mothers (Downey & Coyne, 1990).[2]

As we noted in our discussion of risk versus vulnerability factors, the fact that a child of a depressed mother is at increased risk for depression is not informative per se about the mechanisms underlying that risk (Hammen, 1991). We next review several possibilities in this regard because they suggest promise in providing guidance on how secondary prevention interventions might be structured.

Genetic Variables

Certainly, genetic factors can and do play a role in the acquisition of vulnerability to depression in the offspring of depressed mothers. This idea is based on evidence showing that higher levels of depression are found in the relatives of depressed patients than are found in the general population (Winokur, Coryell, Keller, Endicott, & Leon, 1995) and that higher levels

---

[2]Having a depressed father may also represent a risk factor, but we focus on mothers because the overwhelming majority of research has focused on maternal risk (Phares, 1996; Phares & Compas, 1992).

of depressive concordance are found in monozygotic twins than in dizygotic twins (McGuffin, Katz, Watkins, & Rutherford, 1996). Davidson's (1994; see also Davidson, Pizzagalli, & Nitschke, 2002) findings that depressed patients exhibit left frontal lobe hypoactivation, coupled with some research showing similar hypoactivation in the offspring of depressed mothers (Jones, Field, Fox, Lundy, & Davalos, 1997) also suggest a genetic link.

Cognitive Variables

It is clear that depressed mothers' emotional difficulties have a profound effect, not only on the way their children feel about themselves, but also on the way their children perceive and cope with stressful events. In this regard, Garber and Flynn (2001b) found that a history of maternal depression was associated with negative cognitions in their offspring; specifically, these children evidenced deficits in self-worth, higher levels of hopelessness, and an attributional style that tended to match the negative attributional style of their mothers. Similarly, in a longitudinal study, Garber, Keiley, and Martin (2002) found that attributions and stress interacted to predict the onset of depressive symptoms in the children of depressed mothers. Goodman, Adamson, Riniti, and Cole (1994) found that, compared with low-risk children, children who were at high risk because their mothers were depressed had lower levels of self-worth, and Garber and Robinson (1997) reported that high-risk children reported more self-criticism and lower levels of perceived academic competence, behavioral competence, and self-worth than did low-risk children. In addition, children whose mothers were more chronically depressed had a more depressotypic attributional style than did high-risk children whose mothers were less chronically depressed.

Employing a somewhat different approach to the assessment of cognitive factors in the offspring of depressed mothers, Jaenicke et al. (1987) found that the children of unipolar depressed mothers had a significantly less positive self-concept, a more negative attributional style (i.e., more internal, stable, and global attributions for negative events), and less positive information processing than did the offspring of nonpsychiatric control groups. Dysfunctional information processing in the offspring of depressed mothers was also reported by Taylor and Ingram (1999), who showed that, when in a sad mood, high-risk children display negative cognition of the sort that has been linked to depression. In sum, both information-processing research and work on attributional styles suggest that dysfunctional cognition in the children of depressed mothers would make an appropriate prevention target.

Interpersonal Disruptions: Marital Discord

Data suggest that there are any number of disruptions in interpersonal functioning that might be linked to increased risk for depression (Gotlib

& Hammen, 1992; Joiner & Coyne, 1999). Within this domain, we focus on marital disruptions. There is a large body of research showing a link between depression and problematic marriages. For example, in a review of over two dozen studies, Whisman (2001) reported a meta-analytic effect size of .66 between depression and marital adjustment. It is, however, important to clarify the nature of this link, because it may be that it is depression that leads to marital problems rather than the other way round (Fincham, Beach, Harold, & Osborne, 1997). In fact, data clearly support the idea that depression can precede the development of marital difficulties. In general, interactional approaches to depression (see Joiner & Coyne, 1999) provide models that suggest a good fit for this relationship. Interactional frameworks argue that depression is an aversive state not only for the affected individual, but for people who interact with depressed people (Coyne 1999; Hammen, 1999)—a particularly problematic situation for individuals who are in a close relationship (Anderson, Beach, & Kaslow, 1999).

The fact that depression can lead to marital difficulties, however, does not obviate the possibility that marital difficulties can also predispose a person to depression. For example, data from the landmark National Institute of Mental Health Epidemiologic Catchment Area Study (see Robins & Regier, 1991) suggest a twenty-five-fold rise in depression risk for individuals in discontented marriages, with 6-month prevalence rates of over 45% among women in troubled marriages (Weissman, 1987). A tenfold risk among newlyweds also has been reported (O'Leary, Christian, & Mendell, 1994). While our focus is on *marital* discord (because the overwhelming majority of research focuses on married couples), it is worth noting that similar increases in risk may accrue for individuals who are not married, but who are in significant relationships that may be discordant. Clearly, disruptions in marriage (and in close relationships) appear to be a risk factor for the development of depression.

A number of processes in troubled marriages may result in depression. One concept that has inspired research in several areas of psychopathology, including depression, is the idea of *expressed emotion* (Vaughn & Leff, 1976; Wearden, Tarrier, Barrowclough, Zastowny, & Rahill, 2000), which has been found to play a role in relapse in schizophrenia and depression. Some researchers have suggested that it may serve as a risk factor for depression in marriage. Although expressed emotion encompasses a number of constructs, central to this concept is the idea of criticism. Adapting the concept of expressed emotion to risk, some researchers suggest that spousal criticism plays a significant role in the development of depression in troubled marriages. Indeed, Gottman (1999) has metaphorically referred to criticism in the context of marriage as one of the "Four Horsemen of the Apocalypse" (p. 41). Certainly, other processes may contribute to the risk that emanates from problematic marital relationships, but spousal criticism may be a particularly important factor.

Previous Depression and Subclinical Depression

We address the issues of previous depression and subclinical depression only briefly because (a) most research employing previous depression as an organizational concept reflects tertiary rather than secondary prevention and (b) even though subclinical depression may be a precursor of clinical depression, few secondary prevention trials have been reported in this area.

There is little doubt that a previous depressive episode is a significant risk factor for future depression (Angst, 1997; Angst, Sellaro, & Merikangas, 2000; Judd, 1997). Although a substantial number of individuals may experience only one depressive episode, depression is generally recognized as a recurrent psychiatric problem (Boland & Keller, 2002). Also, relapse rates for depression are quite high even after successful treatment (Keller, Lavori, Lewis, & Klerman, 1983).

Earlier, we discussed issues revolving around the idea of subclinical depression as a significant risk factor for major depressive disorders. In this regard, it is worth noting parenthetically that subclinical depression is not the only psychological state that may precede depression; anxiety states may also constitute significant risk factors (chap. 2, this volume; Kendall & Ingram, 1989). A reasonably large body of data shows that anxiety often precedes depression; hence, clinicians who are interested in preventing the onset of depression might profitably view anxiety as a precursor to depression in many individuals (Dobson, 1985).

SECONDARY PREVENTION TRIALS

Prevention trials employ a variety of models and thus defy easy classification. To organize our discussion, we group prevention studies into one of three broad categories: *risk-based models, intervention based models*, and *broad-spectrum models*.[3] The primary aim of a risk-based trial is to focus on the identification of a specific risk sample and then employ an intervention, which need not be specific to the particular group at risk. For example, studies identifying risk on the basis of being the offspring of a depressed parent may use a variety of prevention approaches. In contrast, an intervention-based model attempts to match risk identification and prevention more closely, as illustrated by studies that identify risk on the basis of negative cognitions and then employ methods to alter those cognitions. Finally, some studies do not focus on risk identification at all, or only in the broadest sense; such broad-spectrum approaches implement prevention programs with a large number of participants, some whom may or may not be at risk.

---

[3]Some researchers have used the term "targeted prevention" to denote a focus on a high-risk sample (Clarke, 1999). Both the risk-based model and the intervention-based model fall into this category.

Risk-Based Approaches

Two broad categories of studies fall into the category of risk-based approaches. The first tends to focus on the children of depressed parents. Most of the basic research in this area examines risk as a function of maternal depression, but prevention research tends to be more inclusive, focusing on the children of depressed parents, regardless of the parents' genders. The second category tends to focus on the identification of early or mild symptoms, with the goal of preventing the onset of a clinically significant depressive disorder.

Children of Depressed Parents

Several secondary prevention trials have been conducted with the children of depressed parents. For instance, Beardslee et al. (1993) identified problematic family functioning as a key mediating process in the risk for depression and thus designed an intervention to modify the problematic behaviors. In particular, they employed a family-based intervention focused on enhancing parenting behaviors, increasing communication within the family, and providing information about treatments for depression. They also designed their approach to be useful to clinicians with a wide variety of theoretical backgrounds and orientations and to be used by general practitioners who may be called upon to implement intervention approaches. Diagnoses of depression were unaffected by this intervention, although positive effects were found for family functioning, particularly when the intervention was delivered by a clinician rather than in a lecture format. These family effects were sustained over time (Beardslee, 2000; Beardslee & Gladstone, 2001).

Another secondary prevention trial, aimed at reducing depression in the adolescent (age 13–18 years) offspring of depressed parents, was reported by Clarke et al. (2001). In particular, they compared a cognitive-based intervention with a usual-care condition (e.g., youths were permitted to initiate or continue seeking health services). Reflecting an assumption that cognitive factors might create the link between depression in parents and offspring (Garber & Flynn, 2001a, 2001b), Clarke and colleagues' treatment approach focused on teaching, in group settings, cognitive restructuring methods such as identifying and challenging irrational or negative thoughts. Results indicated that the group receiving the cognitive intervention reported fewer depressive symptoms and better overall global functioning and, during a median 15-month follow-up, had significantly fewer depressive onsets than the control group reported. In fact, adolescents in the usual-care condition were found to be 5 times more likely to experience the onset of a depressive disorder than were those who received cognitive treatment. Despite these initial gains, the groups showed evidence of converging on many of the measures after 2 years, suggesting the need for booster sessions to maintain gains.

Early Symptoms

Although some secondary prevention interventions aimed at individuals with mild depression levels as a risk indicator have not been successful (Clarke, Hawkins, Murphy, & Sheeber, 1993), positive results have also been reported. For instance, at a 6-month and a 12-month follow-up, Clarke et al. (1995) found that a cognitive group prevention treatment for mildly depressed adolescents resulted in fewer depressive symptoms and diagnosable cases than did a "usual-care" control condition. In another study using similar cognitive methods, Jaycox, Reivich, Gillham, and Seligman (1994) reported an intervention program for children aged 10 to 13 years. Their focus was on modifying cognitions in children who were experiencing some depressive symptoms that were of insufficient magnitude to warrant a positive diagnosis. Although the risk factor identified in this sample was early depressive symptoms, the presumed risk mechanism was dysfunctional cognitive patterns. In particular, Jaycox et al. (1994) structured treatment around distinctions between *cognitive distortions* (inaccurate processing of information) and *cognitive deficiencies* (an impulsive lack of cognitive processing). Jaycox et al. (1994) thus taught social problem solving to help facilitate efficient cognitive processing and employed procedures to help correct cognitive distortions. Results indicated an immediate decrease in depressive symptoms and reductions in acting-out behaviors, but more important from a prevention perspective, also fewer depressive symptoms 6 months later. The results were maintained at a 2-year follow-up (Gillham, Reivich, Jaycox, & Seligman, 1995) and further suggested that modifications in explanatory style may have played a mediative role.

Although prevention trials frequently focus on the application of psychosocial approaches (and, most commonly, cognitive approaches), some research has suggested the efficacy of psychopharmacological interventions for mild depressive symptoms. Rapaport and Judd (1998), for instance, treated adults with subsyndromal depressive symptomatology with fluvoxamine (a selective serotonin reuptake inhibitor) for an 8-week period and found decreases in their depressive symptoms. This result suggests that psychopharmacological treatments may interrupt the transition from mild depression to major depression. Similar psychopharmacological approaches have been used in the treatment of depressed adolescents (Kutcher, 1999), but studies evaluating this approach for prevention in adolescents are sparse.

Intervention-Based Approaches

Recall that intervention-based approaches focus on the selection of individuals whose risk mechanisms appear to match the particular intervention approach. Although several different groups could theoretically fall under this category, the extant research focuses on negative cognition.

Negative Cognition

A number of studies dealing specifically with the secondary prevention of depression have used risk assumptions and findings from cognitive perspectives on depression (e.g., Alloy & Abramson, 1999) both to select the sample and to guide the intervention. As is common among prevention studies, this research has focused on children and adolescents. In line with the theoretical perspective that guides such research is the idea that cognitive principles found to be successful in the treatment of depression and that presumably affect mechanisms linked to the emergence of the disorder can be applied to the prevention of depression in young people.

Seligman, Schulman, DeRubeis, and Hollon (1999) examined the prevention of depression in college students who had no diagnosable disorder, but who were found to consistently evince a pessimistic explanatory style. Participants were first-year students who were initially randomized into a prevention workshop group or a control group. The workshop group met once a week for 2 hours over the course of 8 weeks, in addition to holding occasional individual meetings between a workshop participant and a workshop trainer. Consistent with a focus on cognitive mechanisms of risk, workshops emphasized the development of cognitive coping skills based on the principles developed by Beck (e.g., Beck, Rush, Shaw, & Emery, 1979). After a follow-up period of 3 years, results indicated that the workshop group had significantly fewer episodes of generalized anxiety disorder (GAD), a trend toward fewer self-reported depressive symptoms, fewer dysfunctional thoughts and less hopelessness, and a more positive explanatory style than did the control group.

Although Seligman and colleagues' (1999) study did not find significant differences in depressive episodes, their results are noteworthy for two reasons. First, the intervention was fairly brief: Workshop participants received less than 1 day's worth (i.e., less than 24 hours) of prevention training. Though the participants were young (e.g., 18–19 years), they've spent their whole lifetime developing a negative explanatory style, and the amount of intervention provided was thus exceptionally minimal. Yet, there was some evidence 3 years later that fewer depressive symptoms were seen, and there were fewer cases of GAD, another potentially debilitating condition. Second, as the results for GAD suggest, the prevention interventions may not have been specific to depression (as was the case also in Gillham et al., 1995, and Jaycox et al., 1994). In psychopathology research, a finding of nonspecificity can be a fatal blow to a theory (Ingram, 1990), but in prevention research such nonspecificity can clearly be seen as a positive feature. Given the high rate of comorbidity between depression and anxiety (see chap. 2, this volume; Kendall & Ingram, 1989) and a number of similar cognitive features that have been known for some time in both depression and anxiety (Ingram, Kendall, Smith, Donnell, & Ronan, 1987), it is perhaps not surprising that the likelihood of developing GAD was also affected.

BROAD-SPECTRUM APPROACHES

Although most prevention efforts focus on the identification of risk factors for depression, Shochet et al. (2001) reported a different approach examining the prevention of depression in an entire grade level of children.[4] Even though such large-scale efforts are expensive, Shochet and colleagues argued that programs directed toward at-risk children may stigmatize those children. Thus, all ninth-year students in a secondary school in Australia were recruited to participate in the program, with an 88% initial recruitment rate and an approximately 6% attrition rate. Two prevention approaches were implemented, one with adolescents and one with parents. The adolescent intervention focused on coping and problem-solving skills, cognitive restructuring, and teaching interpersonal skills. The parent approach was the same, but included three sessions on stress management training and information on adolescent development. Compared with a control group (a cohort from a different school year), both prevention groups showed fewer depressive symptoms at a 10-month follow-up, although there were no significant differences between the groups. These data suggest that such school-based approaches may be both feasible and effective.

SUMMARY

In sum, results from the various secondary prevention trials point to several findings. Although not all trials demonstrated that depression was prevented, on the whole the data clearly suggest the effectiveness of secondary prevention for depression. Moreover, in some cases data suggest that prevention, even though aimed at depression, was also helpful for other types of emotional (e.g., GAD) and behavior (e.g., acting-out) problems.

In general, three themes from this research tend to stand out. First, of the psychosocial approaches that were tested, those employing a cognitive framework and methods are the most prevalent. To be sure, other methods (e.g., coping, social skills training) were combined with the cognitive approach. Nevertheless, given the latter's demonstrated effectiveness in

---

[4]The nature of this trial comes close to primary prevention. However, we describe it under secondary prevention because the rationale for the study was to deal with the stigmatization that may come from being classified as being at risk and it thus represents a way to resolve this problem through secondary prevention efforts.

the treatment of depression, it is not unexpected that such methods were commonly incorporated into prevention intervention packages. Second, data from the prevention research tend to suggest that these approaches can in fact be effective in preventing, or at least diminishing the incidence and symptoms of, depression. Third, many of the trials incorporating cognitive approaches examine prevention in children or adolescents and suggest that depression can be prevented or diminished in these groups, perhaps more effectively than can be accomplished in adults. Given that children and adolescents are still in the formative stages of biological, emotional, and social development, it is perhaps not surprising that they can be taught skills that are effective in reducing the development of depression.

CONCLUSIONS AND FUTURE DIRECTIONS

Although not in its infancy, the secondary prevention of depression is still a young field. Research has focused extensively on risk factors for depression for some time now (Ingram et al., 1998), but the development and implementation of prevention efforts that could capitalize on the results obtained has lagged behind. There are few reports of secondary prevention efforts that occurred before the 1990s. By all indications, however, prevention research is beginning to catch up to more basic risk research and is showing some progress in establishing efficacy. In this chapter, we have sought to examine some of the conceptual, methodological, and research issues that are relevant to the idea of secondary prevention. For instance, we examined definitions of secondary prevention and risk, differentiated between risk and vulnerability, reviewed research on risk groups, and then examined some noteworthy trials aimed at eliminating or reducing the risk for depression.

As we noted, various secondary prevention trials have proven somewhat successful in reducing the incidence of depression. The natural question, then, is where does the field go from here? Although there is probably no limit to answers to this question, we note several major themes that may be important for future research on secondary prevention.

First, secondary prevention is difficult to accomplish, a situation that will probably always be the case. Yet, we think there is much promise in the model of prevention. Most interventions are extremely limited in comparison to the time that individuals have had to acquire risk. Even children in prevention trials, either through social and parental influences or through genetic factors, have had years to acquire vulnerability. Most prevention efforts, by contrast, accumulate to less than a day's worth (24 hours) of intervention. There is no guarantee, of course, that more extensive prevention efforts will pay off in reducing depression, but it does not seem yet that prevention trials have reached a point of diminishing returns vis-à-vis the length and intensity of treatment. Until individuals have passed the most critical ages for the onset of depression (e.g., late adolescence to young adulthood), it may be helpful for prevention interventions to make use of occasional booster sessions similar to those which many researchers and clinicians include in their research on treatment efficacy and effectiveness.

Another reason that prevention is difficult is that precise markers of risk and vulnerability have not been established. Clearly, the field has some sound ideas and data on what constitutes risk, but they are far from precise. For example, being the child of a depressed mother is indisputably a risk factor for depression, but not all children of depressed mothers eventually become depressed, and not all individuals who become depressed had a depressed mother. Obviously, there is significant room for improvement in our understanding of risk, vulnerability, and effective intervention. Precision, however, is not a prerequisite for effective intervention. Indeed, if it were, then psychotherapy would never be effective, because the discipline's understanding of change processes is far from complete (Heller et al., 2000). Yet, there is little doubt that improved treatment methods, along with a clearer understanding of the factors that constitute risk and vulnerability, will yield more effective prevention.

The data tend to show that those who are most helped by prevention programs are children and adolescents. It would be premature to give up on adults who are at risk, but the biggest payoffs in prevention may come if children and adolescents are considered the primary targets. That is, because interventions can target cognitive and affective processes and structures before they become relatively static, a special emphasis on prevention in children seems reasonable. Moreover, prevention efforts in children can also pay off because successful prevention may have a proportionally larger impact on their lives. For example, the 15-year-old who can be taught ways to ward off depression will probably not only be better able to accommodate this procedural and semantic knowledge than the 35-year-old will, but will have the advantage of 20 more years without the experience of significant and debilitating depression. Moreover, given data showing that depression is related to earlier mortality (Irwin, 2002; Saz & Dewey, 2001), prevention efforts in children and adolescents not only might improve their quality of life, but also might lead to longer life. Children and adolescents will thus likely be the biggest beneficiaries of prevention research and trials.

Most prevention research has focused on the application of psychosocial treatment methods, with an emphasis on modifying cognitive factors. Research shows the promise of these methods and offers individuals the possibility of learning how to modify their cognitive and behavioral functioning with potentially lasting effects. At the same time, however, it would be ill advised to suggest that psychosocial methods are necessarily the best or only route to prevention: Although psychopharmacological approaches have been the focus of considerably less prevention research than psychological methods, such approaches may be helpful in preventing depression in some individuals in some situations. For instance, not only is the early or prodromal appearance of symptoms a possible reason to use psychopharmacological treatment (e.g., it may interrupt a developing depressive episode), but also the empirical data suggest efficacy in this regard (e.g., Rapaport & Judd, 1998). To be sure, there is little in the way of data on the use of these methods to prevent depression in children and adolescents, but some data suggest their efficacy in already depressed children and adolescents, giving reason to believe that psychopharmacological methods could be effective in preventing the full-blown development of depression in those age groups. Certainly, this is a worthy area of research.

The core element of any prevention program must be not only the outcome at the end of the intervention, but long-term follow-up. Prevention trials virtually always report follow-ups, usually up to 2 years after completion of the intervention. Because prevention research is still a young area, longer follow-ups may be forthcoming. Ultimately, however, the field needs data on the life course of individuals who have received prevention interventions. Of course, it will be some time, if ever, before we are able to see data on the incidence of depression and quality of life in 50-year-olds who were the focus of a prevention intervention at age 15, but such issues should be a legitimate goal of prevention research and of agencies that fund such research.

Finally, we note that, although the prevention of unipolar depression is an extremely worthwhile goal, the prevention of other disorders is also worthy. As was observed in some of the research reviewed in this chapter, there may in fact be collateral prevention for disorders other than depression (e.g., GAD). These data are important, but a specific focus on the prevention of other kinds of mood disorders (e.g., bipolar disorder), as well as other disorders, will also be important. For example, because Axis II personality disorders frequently (if not always) underlie Axis I disorders (Benjamin, 1993), a focus on the prevention of these disorders might yield an impressive payoff in improving personality functioning and in reducing the incidence of associated Axis I disorders. Certainly, numerous complex issues would need to be considered in such research, but there is little argument that, if successfully developed, preventing other disorders would constitute an important advancement in prevention science.

Some researchers have argued that a focus on treatment after the development of a disorder, rather than preventing the development of the disorder, is anything but optimal (Albee, 2000). Although there is much to recommend in this view, treating depression after it has reached clinical significance will always be an approach that is used, if not embraced, by mental health professionals. Yet, prevention does offer enormous promise, and there is little argument that the secondary prevention of depression may provide much greater benefits to society and to individuals than will the treatment of one depressed individual at a time.

REFERENCES

Abramson, L. Y., Alloy, L. B., & Hogan, M. E. (1997). Cognitive/personality subtypes of depression: Theories in search of disorders. *Cognitive Therapy and Research, 21,* 247–265.

Abramson, L. Y., Metalsky, G. I., & Alloy, L. B. (1989). Hopelessness depression: A theory-based subtype of depression. *Psychological Review, 96,* 358–372.

Abramson, L. Y., Seligman, M. E. P., & Teasdale, J. (1978). Learned helplessness in humans: Critique and reformulation. *Journal of Abnormal Psychology, 87,* 49–74.

Albee, G. (2000). Critique of psychotherapy in American society. In C. R. Snyder & R. E. Ingram (Eds.), *Handbook of psychological change: Psychotherapy processes and practices for the 21st century* (pp. 689–705). New York: Wiley.

Alloy, L. B., & Abramson, L. Y. (1999). The Temple–Wisconsin Cognitive Vulnerability to Depression Project: Conceptual background, design, and methods. *Journal of Cognitive Psychotherapy, 13,* 227–262.

American Psychiatric Association. (2000). *Diagnostic and statistical manual of mental disorder* (4th ed., text rev.). Washington, DC: Author.

Anderson, P., Beach, S., & Kaslow, N. (1999). Marital discord and depression: The potential of attachment theory to guide integrative clinical intervention. In T. E. Joiner & J. C. Coyne (Eds.), *The interactional nature of depression* (pp. 271–298). Washington, DC: American Psychological Association.

Angst, J. (1997). Epidemiology of depression. In A. Honig & H. M. van Praag (Eds), *Depression: Neurobiological, psychopathological and therapeutic advances* (pp. 17–29). New York: Wiley.

Angst, J., Sellaro, R., & Merikangas, K. R. (2000). Depressive spectrum diagnoses. *Comparative Psychiatry, 4,* 39–47.

Beardslee, W. R. (2000). Prevention of mental disorders and the study of developmental psychopathology: A natural alliance. In J. L. Rapoport (Ed.), *Childhood onset of "adult" psychopathology: Clinical and research advances.* American Psychopathological Association series (pp. 333–355). Washington, DC: American Psychiatric Press.

Beardslee, W. R., Bemporad, J., Keller, M. B., & Klerman, G. L. (1983). Children of parents with major affective disorder: A review. *American Journal of Psychiatry, 140,* 825–832.

Beardslee, W. R., & Gladstone, T. R. G. (2001). Prevention of childhood depression: Recent findings and future prospects. *Biological Psychiatry, 49,* 1101–1110.

Beardslee, W. R., Salt, P., Porterfield, K., Rothberg, P. C., Swatling, S., Hoke, L., et al. (1993). Comparison of preventive interventions for families with parental affective disorder. *Journal of the American Academy of Child and Adolescent Psychiatry, 32,* 254–263.

Beardslee, W. R., Versage, E. M., Gladstone, T. R. G., & Tracy, R. G. (1998). Children of affectively ill parents: A review of the past 10 years. *Journal of the American Academy of Child and Adolescent Psychiatry, 37,* 1134–1141.

Beck, A. T. (1967). *Depression: Causes and treatment*. Philadelphia, PA: University of Pennsylvania Press.

Beck, A. T. (1987). Cognitive models of depression. *Journal of Cognitive Psychotherapy, 1*, 5–37.

Beck, A. T., Rush, A. J., Shaw, B. F., & Emery, G. (1979). *Cognitive therapy of depression*. New York: Guilford.

Beckham, E. E., Leber, W. R., & Youll, L. K. (1995). The diagnostic classification of depression. In E. E. Beckham & W. R. Leber (Eds.), *Handbook of depression* (2nd ed., pp. 36–60). New York: Guilford.

Benjamin, L. S. (1993). *Interpersonal diagnosis and treatment of personality disorders*. New York: Guilford.

Blatt, S. J., & Zuroff, D. C. (1992). Interpersonal relatedness and self-definition: Two prototypes for depression. *Clinical Psychology Review, 12*, 527–562.

Boland, R. J., & Keller, M. B. (2002). Course and outcome of depression. In I. H. Gotlib & C. L. Hammen (Eds.), *Handbook of depression* (pp. 43–60). New York: Guilford.

Clarke, G. N. (1999). Prevention of depression in at risk samples of adolescents. In C. A. Essau & F. Petermann (Eds.), *Depressive disorders in children and adolescents* (pp. 341–360). Northvale, NJ: Jason Aronson.

Clarke, G. N., Hawkins, W., Murphy, M., & Sheeber, L. (1993). School-based primary prevention of depressive symptomatology in adolescents: Findings from two studies. *Journal of Adolescent Research, 8*, 183–204.

Clarke, G. N., Hawkins, W., Murphy, M., Sheeber, L., Lewinsohn, P. M., & Seeley, J. R. (1995). Targeted prevention of unipolar depressive disorder in an at-risk sample of high school adolescents: A randomized trial of group cognitive intervention. *Journal of the American Academy of Child and Adolescent Psychiatry, 34*, 312–321.

Clarke, G. N., Hornbrook, M., Lynch, F., Polen, M., Gale, J., Beardslee, W., et al. (2001). A randomized trial of a group cognitive intervention for preventing depression in adolescent offspring of depressed parents. *Archives of General Psychiatry, 58*, 1127–1134.

Cowen, E. L. (1997). On the semantics and operations of primary prevention (or will the real primary prevention please stand up). *American Journal of Community Psychology, 25*, 245–255.

Coyne, J. C. (1999). Thinking interactionally about depression: A radical restatement. In T. E. Joiner & J. C. Coyne (Eds.), *The interactional nature of depression* (pp. 365–391). Washington, DC: American Psychological Association.

Coyne, J. C., & Whiffen, V. E. (1995). Issues in personality as diathesis for depression: The case of sociotropy dependency and autonomy self criticism. *Psychological Bulletin, 118*, 358–378.

Cummings, E. M., & Davis, P. T. (1999). Depressed parents and family functioning: Interpersonal effects and children's functioning and development. In T. E. Joiner & J. C. Coyne (Eds.), *The interactional nature of depression* (pp. 299–327). Washington, DC: American Psychological Association.

Davidson, R. J. (1994). Asymmetric brain function, affective style, and psychopathology: The role of early experience and plasticity. *Development and Psychopathology, 6,* 741–758.

Davidson, R. J., Pizzagalli, D., & Nitschke, J. (2002). The representation and regulation of emotion in depression. In I. H. Gotlib & C. L. Hammen (Eds.), *Handbook of depression* (pp. 219–244). New York. Guilford.

Dobson, K. S. (1985). The relationship between anxiety and depression. *Clinical Psychology Review, 5,* 307–324.

Downey, G., & Coyne, J. C. (1990). Children of depressed parents: An integrative review. *Psychological Bulletin, 108,* 50–75.

Fincham, F. D., Beach, S. R. H., Harold, G. T., & Osborne, L. N. (1997). Marital satisfaction and depression: Different causal relationships for men and women? *Psychological Science, 8,* 351–357.

Garber, J., & Flynn, C. (2001a). Vulnerability to depression in children and adolescents. In R. E. Ingram & J. M. Price (Eds.), *Handbook of vulnerability to psychopathology: Risk across the lifespan* (pp. 175–225). New York: Guilford Press.

Garber, J., & Flynn, C. (2001b). Predictors of depressive cognitions in young adolescents. *Cognitive Therapy and Research, 4,* 353–376.

Garber, J., Keiley, M. K., & Martin, N. C. (2002). Developmental trajectories of adolescents' depressive symptoms: Predictors of change. *Journal of Consulting and Clinical Psychology, 70,* 79–95.

Garber, J., & Robinson, N. S. (1997). Cognitive vulnerability in children at risk for depression. *Cognition and Emotion, 11,* 619–635.

Gillham, J. E., Reivich, K. J., Jaycox, L. H, & Seligman, M. E. P. (1995). Prevention of depressive symptoms in schoolchildren: Two-year follow-up. *Psychological Science, 6,* 343–351.

Gillham, J. E., Shatte, A. J., & Freres, D. R. (2000). Preventing depression: A review of cognitive–behavioral and family interventions. *Applied and Preventive Psychology, 9,* 63–88.

Goodman, S. H., Adamson, L. B., Riniti, J., & Cole, S. (1994). Mothers' expressed attitudes: Associations with maternal depression and children's self-esteem and psychopathology. *Journal of the American Academy of Child and Adolescent Psychiatry, 33,* 1265–1274.

Goodman, S. H., & Gotlib, I. H. (1999). Risk for psychopathology in the children of depressed mothers: A developmental model for understanding mechanisms of transmission. *Psychological Review, 106,* 458–490.

Goodwin, F. K., & Jamison, K. R. (1990). *Manic–depressive illness.* New York: Oxford University.

Gotlib, I. H., & Hammen, C. L. (1992). *Psychological aspects of depression: Toward a cognitive–interpersonal integration.* Chichester, England: Wiley.

Gottman, J. M. (1999). *The marriage clinic: A scientifically based marital therapy.* New York, Norton.

Hammen, C. (1991). *Depression runs in families: The social context of risk and resilience in children of depressed mothers.* New York: Springer-Verlag.

Hammen, C. (1999). The emergence of an interpersonal approach to depression. In T. E. Joiner & J. C. Coyne (Eds.), *The interactional nature of depression* (pp. 21–36). Washington, DC: American Psychological Association.

Hammen, C., Gordon, G., Burge, D., Adrian, C., Jaenicke, C., & Hiroto, G. (1987). Maternal affective disorders, illness, and stress: Risk for children's psychopathology. *American Journal of Psychiatry, 144,* 736–741.

Heller, K., Wyman, M. F., & Allen, S. M. (2000). Future direction for prevention science: From research to adoption. In C. R. Snyder & R. E. Ingram (Eds.), *Handbook of psychological change: Psychotherapy processes and practices for the 21st century* (pp. 660–680). New York: Wiley.

Hollon, S. D., DeRubeis, R. J., & Evans, M. D. (1996). Cognitive therapy in the treatment and prevention of depression. In P. M. Salkovskis (Ed.), *Frontiers of cognitive therapy* (pp. 293–317). New York: Guilford.

Horwath, E., Johnson, J., Klerman, G. L., & Weissman, M. M. (1992). Depressive symptoms as relative and attributable risk factors for first-onset major depression. *Archives of General Psychiatry, 49,* 817–823.

Ingram, R. E. (1990). Depressive cognition: Models, mechanisms, and methods. In R. E. Ingram (Ed.), *Contemporary psychological approaches to depression* (pp. 169–195). New York: Plenum.

Ingram, R. E. (1984). Toward an information processing analysis of depression. *Cognitive Therapy and Research, 8,* 443–478.

Ingram, R. E., & Hamilton, N. A. (1999). Evaluating precision in the social psychological assessment of depression: Methodological considerations, issues, and recommendations. *Journal of Social and Clinical Psychology, 18,* 160–180.

Ingram, R. E., Kendall, P. C., Smith, T. W., Donnell, C., & Ronan, K. (1987). Cognitive specificity in emotional distress. *Journal of Personality and Social Psychology, 53,* 734–742.

Ingram, R. E., Miranda, J., & Segal, Z. (1998). *Cognitive vulnerability to depression.* New York: Guilford.

Ingram, R. E., & Siegle, G. J. (2002). Methodological issues in depression research: Not your father's Oldsmobile. In I. Gotlib & C. Hammen (Eds.), *Handbook of depression* (pp. 86–114). New York: Guilford.

Irwin, M. (2002). Psychoneuroimmunology of depression: Clinical implications. *Brain, Behavior, and Immunity, 16,* 1–16.

Jaenicke, C., Hammen, C. L., Zupan, B., Hiroto, D., Gordon, D., Adrian, C., & Burge, D. (1987). Cognitive vulnerability in children at risk for depression. *Journal of Abnormal Child Psychology, 15,* 559–572.

Jaycox, L. H., Reivich, K. J., Gillham, J., & Seligman, M. E. P. (1994). Prevention of depressive symptoms in school children. *Behaviour Research and Therapy, 32,* 801–816.

Joiner, T. E., & Coyne, J. C. (Eds.). (1999). *The interactional nature of depression.* Washington, DC: American Psychological Association.

Jones, N., Field, T., Fox, N. A., Lundy, B., & Davalos, M. (1997). EEG activation in 1-month-old infants of depressed mothers. *Development and Psychopathology, 9,* 491–505.

Judd, L. L. (1997). The clinical course of unipolar major depressive disorders. *Archives of General Psychiatry, 54*, 989–991.

Kaelber, C. T., Moul, D. E., & Farmer, M. E. (1995). Epidemiology of depression. In E. E. Beckham & W. R. Leber (Eds.), *Handbook of depression* (2nd ed., pp. 3–35). New York: Guilford.

Keller, M. B., Lavori, P. W., Lewis, C. E., & Klerman, G. L. (1983). Predictors of relapse in major depressive disorder. *Journal of the American Medical Association, 250*, 3299–3304.

Keller, M. B., Shapiro, R. W., Lavori, P. W., & Wolfe, N. (1982). Relapse in RDC major depressive disorders: Analysis with the life table. *Archives of General Psychiatry, 39*, 911–915.

Kendall, P. C., & Ingram, R. E. (1989). Cognitive–behavioral perspectives: Theory and research on negative affective states. In P. C. Kendall & D. Watson (Eds.), *Anxiety and depression: Distinctive and overlapping features* (pp. 27–53). San Diego: Academic Press.

Kessler, R. C., McGonagle, K. A., Zhao, S., Nelson, C. B., Hughes, M., Eshleman, S., et al. (1994). Lifetime and 12-month prevalence of results from the National Comorbidity Survey. *Archives of General Psychiatry, 51*, 8–19.

Kutcher, S. P. (1999). Pharmacotherapy of depression: A review of current evidence and practical clinical directions. In C. A. Essau, & F. Petermann (Eds.), *Depressive disorders in children and adolescents: Epidemiology, risk factors, and treatment* (pp. 437–458). Northvale, NJ: Jason Aronson.

Luthar, S. S., & Zigler, E. (1991). Vulnerability and competence: A review of research on resilience in childhood. *American Journal of Orthopsychiatry, 61*, 6–22.

Marmar, C. R., Horowitz, M. J., Weiss, D. S., & Wilner, N. R. (1988). A controlled trial of brief psychotherapy and mutual-help group treatment of conjugal bereavement. *American Journal of Psychiatry, 145*, 203–209.

McGuffin, P., Katz, R., Watkins, S., & Rutherford, J. (1996). A hospital-based twin registry study of the hereditability of DSM-IV unipolar depression. *Archives of General Psychiatry, 53*, 129–136.

Miranda, J., & Persons, J. B. (1988). Dysfunctional attitudes are mood-state dependent. *Journal of Abnormal Psychology, 97*, 76–79.

Muñoz, R. F., Le, H., Clarke, G., & Jaycox, L. (2002). Preventing the onset of major depression. In I. Gotlib & C. Hammen (Eds.), *Handbook of depression* (pp. 343–359). New York: Guilford.

Muñoz, R. F., & Ying, Y. (1993). *The prevention of depression: Research and practice.* Baltimore: Johns Hopkins.

Nolen-Hoeksema, S. (2002). Gender differences in depression. In I. Gotlib & C. Hammen (Eds.), *Handbook of depression* (pp. 492–509). New York: Guilford.

O'Leary, K. D., Christian, J. L., & Mendell, N. R. (1994). A closer look at the link between marital discord and depressive symptomatology. *Journal of Social and Clinical Psychology, 4*, 33–41.

Phares, V. (1996). *Fathers and developmental psychopathology*. New York: Wiley.

Phares, V., & Compas, B. E. (1992). The role of fathers in child and adolescent psychopathology: Make room for daddy. *Psychological Bulletin, 111*, 387–412.

Rapaport, M., & Judd, L. L. (1998). Minor depressive disorder and subsyndromal depressive symptoms: Functional impairment and response to treatment. *Journal of Affective Disorders, 48*, 227–232.

Robins, L. N., & Regier, D. A. (1991). *Psychiatric disorders in America: The epidemiologic catchment area study*. New York: The Free Press.

Rosenthal, D., Wender, P. H., Kety, S. S., Schulsinger, F., Welner, J., & Ostergaard, L. (1968). Schizophrenics' offspring reared in adoptive homes. In D. Rosenthal & S. S. Kety (Eds.), *Transmission of schizophrenia* (pp. 97–113). Oxford: Pergamon.

Saz, P., & Dewey, M. (2001). Depression, depressive symptoms and mortality in persons aged 65 and over living in the community: A systematic review of the literature. *International Journal of Geriatric Psychiatry, 16*, 622–630.

Segal, Z. V., Gemar, M., & Williams, S. (1999). Differential cognitive response to a mood challenge following successful cognitive therapy or pharmacotherapy for unipolar depression. *Journal of Abnormal Psychology, 108*, 3–10.

Segal, Z. V., & Ingram, R. E. (1994). Mood priming and construct activation in tests of cognitive vulnerability to unipolar depression. *Clinical Psychology Review, 14*, 663–695.

Segal, Z. V., & Shaw, B. F. (1986). Cognition in depression: A reappraisal of Coyne & Gotlib's critique. *Cognitive Therapy and Research, 10*, 671–694.

Seligman, M. E. P. (1990). Why is there so much depression today? The waxing of the individual and the waning of the commons. In R. E. Ingram (Ed.), *Contemporary psychological approaches to depression: Theory, research and treatment*. (pp. 1–10). New York: Plenum.

Seligman, M. E. P., Schulman, B. S., DeRubeis, R. J., & Hollon, S. D. (1999). The prevention of depression and anxiety. *Prevention & Treatment, 2*, 1–22.

Shochet, I. M., Dadds, M. R., Holland, D., Whitefield, K., Harnett, P. H., & Osgarby, S. M. (2001). The efficacy of a universal school-based program to prevent adolescent depression. *Journal of Clinical Child Psychology, 30*, 303–315.

Taylor, L., & Ingram, R. E. (1999). Cognitive reactivity and depressotypic information processing in the children of depressed mothers. *Journal of Abnormal Psychology, 108*, 202–210.

Teasdale, J. D. (1983). Negative thinking in depression: Cause, effect, or reciprocal relationship? *Advances in Behaviour Therapy and Research, 5*, 3–25.

Thase, M. E. (2000). Psychopharmacology in conjunction with psychotherapy. In C. R. Snyder & R. E. Ingram (Eds.), *Handbook of psychological change: Psychotherapy processes and practices for the 21st century* (pp. 474–498). New York: Wiley.

Vaughn, C. E., & Leff, J. P. (1976). The influence of family and social factors on the course of psychiatric illness: A comparison of schizophrenic and depressed neurotic patients. *British Journal of Psychiatry, 129*, 125–137.

Wearden, A. J., Tarrier, N., Barrowclough, C., Zastowny, T. R., & Rahill, A. A. (2000). A review of expressed emotion research in health care. *Clinical Psychology Review, 20,* 633–666.

Weintraub, S., Winters, K. C., & Neale, J. M. (1986). Competence and vulnerability in children with an affectively disordered parent. In M. Rutter, C. E. Izard, & P. B. Read (Eds.), *Depression in young people* (pp. 236–258). New York: Guilford.

Weissman, M. M. (1987). Advances in psychiatric epidemiology: Rates and risks for major depression. *American Journal of Public Health, 77,* 445–451.

Weissman, M. M., Bruce, M. L., Leaf, P., Florio, L. P., & Holzer, C. (1991). Affective disorders. In L. N. Robins & D. Regier (Eds.), *Psychiatric disorders in America: The epidemiologic catchment area study* (pp. 53–80). New York: Free Press.

Whisman, M. A. (2001). The association between depression and marital dissatisfaction. In S. R. H. Beach (Ed.), *Marital and family processes in depression: A scientific foundation for clinical practice* (pp. 3–24). Washington, DC: American Psychological Association.

Winokur, G., Coryell, W., Keller, M., Endicott, J., & Leon, A. (1995). A family study of manic–depressive (bipolar I) disease: Is it a distinct illness separable from primary unipolar depression. *Archive of General Psychiatry, 55,* 367–373.

10

TERTIARY INTERVENTION FOR DEPRESSION AND PREVENTION OF RELAPSE

KEITH S. DOBSON AND NICOLE D. OTTENBREIT

Clinical depression is widely acknowledged to be a significant public health concern. It is one of the most common problems seen in clinical practice (Eaton et al., 1989), and there is evidence that rates of depression are increasing with time (Ormel et al., 1994). Research has consistently shown that women are at twice the risk of experiencing depression compared with men (American Psychiatric Association, 2000). On the basis of the prevalence and incidence of depression, as well as associated costs in health care, lost productivity, and even mortality, the World Health Organization has predicted that depression will have the highest total burden of care of any disorder worldwide by the year 2020 (Murray & Lopez, 1997).

Depression is increasingly recognized as a recurrent disorder. Although estimates of the risk of relapse vary, it is generally believed that 40% to 60% of individuals who recover from an episode of depression can be expected to have at least one additional such episode at some later point in their lifetime

(Belsher & Costello, 1988; Keller, Lavori, Rice, Coryell, & Hirschfeld, 1986). Research also indicates that a person who experiences a single episode of depression can expect to experience an estimated total of 4.3 major depressive episodes in his or her lifetime (Perris, 1992) and that each additional episode further increases the future probability of relapse (American Psychiatric Association, 2000).

A focus on preventing relapse in depression is important for a number of reasons. First, it serves to highlight the psychosocial aspects of this typically chronic and recurrent disorder. Recurrent depression causes significant impairment in individuals' intimate and social relationships and occupational functioning (Ormel et al., 1994) and is associated with worse general health and greater disability for individuals (Murray & Lopez, 1997; Sartorius, Ustun, Lecrubier, & Wittchen, 1996). Second, the risk of suicide increases in the absence of effective treatment for depression, because rates of suicide are significantly higher in depressed individuals relative to the general population (Angst, Angst, & Stassen, 1999; Chen & Dilsaver, 1996). Thus, a more complete understanding of relapse processes may also advance our knowledge of suicide and its prevention. Third, a focus on relapse will help to address conceptual issues related to partial versus complete recovery and to the differential risk of relapse associated with various levels of clinical outcome in depression (Judd et al., 1998; Judd et al., 2000). Fourth, a focus on minimizing relapse into depression will also naturally encourage the study of, and intervention into, common comorbid conditions such as anxiety disorders and substance abuse or dependence (Rohde, Lewinsohn, & Seeley, 1991; Sartorius et al., 1996). Finally, if effective strategies for preventing relapse in depression can be identified and developed, it could be expected that there would be a commensurate increase in the focus on health care costs associated with preventive strategies. Such a dual emphasis on clinical outcome and cost-effectiveness will be important for the integration of prevention strategies into the health care system.

Understanding relapse in clinical depression is of fundamental importance to the promotion of public health. The rates and recurrent nature of depression dictate that the cost of the disorder, both in terms of health care utilization and human suffering, is enormous (Keller et al., 1986). The National Advisory Mental Health Council Workgroup on Mental Disorders Prevention Research, of the National Institute of Mental Health (NIMH), recently recognized the importance and utility of preventing relapse in the group's major review of prevention strategies: "prevention strategies are critically needed to prevent relapse and comorbid conditions as part of comprehensive treatment approaches" (National Advisory Mental Health Council Workgroup on Mental Disorders Prevention Research, 2001).

There are also methodological advantages for researchers who study relapse in the context of depression (Belsher & Costello, 1988; Wilson, 1992a). First, because individuals who experience clinical depression often present to primary health care settings, it is relatively easy to identify those who are vulnerable to relapse. Second, because the percentage of people who experience relapse after an episode of depression is higher than it is for the population at large, smaller sample sizes are required to obtain sufficient statistical power in prediction studies. Finally, relapse lends itself to examination using prospective and longitudinal research designs, which are generally viewed as optimal for the study of causal models of psychopathology.

Given the evidence regarding the high rates of relapse in depression, it is not surprising that theorists and clinicians have placed great emphasis in recent years on trying to understand the relapse process and on devising strategies to minimize the likelihood of relapse. In this chapter, some primary conceptual issues that arise in the literature are discussed. The major risk variables that have been examined for relapse and that should be addressed in relapse prevention programs are reviewed. Evidence pertaining to relapse associated with various treatment approaches to depression is then examined and discussed. The chapter concludes with recommendations for future theory and research, as well as for clinical practice.

REFINING THE PREVENTION OF RELAPSE IN PREVENTION TERMS

One of the critical issues in the prevention of relapse is the manner in which recovery from depression is defined. If different investigators employ different definitions of when a given person has recovered from an episode of depression, their definitions of relapse will also differ. Although a strong logical argument can be made to define recovery as a change in symptoms such that a formerly depressed person can no longer be diagnosed with major depression (American Psychiatric Association, 2000), other approaches to the issue of definition also exist. For example, as opposed to "recovery" from depression, as defined by the condition's no longer being diagnosable in the individual, "response" to psychopharmacological treatment has been identified as a reduction of symptoms by at least 50% (Stahl, 1999). Also, in some trials, significant changes in depression severity scores are treated as indicating improvement, regardless of diagnostic status.

The most comprehensive set of criteria yet devised to frame the discussion around the outcome of treatment consists of the consensus criteria proposed by Frank, Prien, et al. (1991). These criteria distinguish between "remission" and "recovery." "Remission" refers to the condition's no longer being diagnosable, whereas "recovery" represents a more stringent standard, composed of both fewer than two symptoms of depression reported for at least 2 weeks, using a structured interview, and low scores on a standardized depression inventory. Frank, Prien, et al. further specify that the term "relapse" should be employed only when a previously depressed person has entered remission, but not yet met the full-recovery criteria. As regards yet another situation, Frank, Prien, and colleagues argue that if a person has recovered from depression, but then develops a subsequent depressive episode, the appropriate term is "recurrence."

A primary advantage of the Frank, Prien, et al. (1991) criteria is that these criteria maintain the nosological distinction of major depression by discriminating individuals above and below the *DSM* diagnostic threshold. The criteria also reflect changes in overall severity of symptoms and the fact that a formerly depressed patient may have gone into remission from a previous higher level of depression, but still experience what are sometimes referred to as "residual symptoms" (Paykel, 2001; Paykel et al., 1999). Frank, Prien, et al. criteria also help to encourage research on the degree of change in depression (remission vs. recovery) a person might experience, as well as the associated likelihood of future depression (Judd et al., 1998; Judd et al., 2000).

Depending on the theoretical underpinnings of the investigator, different strategies for investigating and preventing relapse are recommended in the literature. If a clinical "response" is the focus of the intervention, then the ongoing management of "residual symptoms" will be the focus of prevention efforts. This approach is perhaps most prominent in the psychopharmacology literature. If one conceptualizes clinical outcome as the "remission" of an episode of major depression, then a concern about continuing treatment or providing booster sessions as a means of staving off "relapse" is logically warranted. This approach to the prevention of recurrent depression is seen in both the psychopharmacology and psychosocial treatment literature (Jarrett et al., 1998). Finally, if the focus of treatment in the first instance is full "recovery," then the optimization of mental health and the prevention of "recurrence" become the foci of treatment. True relapse prevention treatments are scarce in the depression literature, but the primary efforts to date are found in the psychosocial treatment literature.

Each of the foregoing approaches to considering outcome and preventing relapse in depression contains its own strengths and weaknesses. For example, complete recovery may be difficult to achieve or may require a considerable deployment of resources, making it an impracticable goal in many cases of depression. Certainly, one would expect remission and clinical response to be more achievable clinical outcomes. However, if complete recovery is associated with lower rates of relapse, it may be more cost effective in the long term to retain this treatment goal.

The next section briefly summarizes the literature on risk factors for relapse in depression, as these factors constitute potential targets for strategies to prevent relapse. Following the literature review, the existing models of relapse prevention based upon the preceding three approaches to treatment and relapse in depression are examined.

PREDICTORS OF RELAPSE:
IDENTIFYING POTENTIAL TARGETS
FOR PREVENTING RELAPSE

The list of possible risk factors for relapse into depression is both extensive and likely highly redundant with the risk factors for the onset of depression (see chaps. 2 & 9, this volume). While a comprehensive model of the factors associated with relapse is still awaited, there are some emerging trends in this area. The sections that follow will review some of the major areas of inquiry pertaining to the risk for relapse. The majority of this research has been conducted in the context of particular treatment studies, with only a few studies focusing primarily on the prevention of relapse into depression. Most of the research also has employed fairly indeterminate or liberal definitions of "relapse" more in line with what would be termed "recurrence" on the basis of the Frank, Prien, et al. (1991) criteria.

Residual Symptoms and Chronicity

One of the characteristics that has been shown to distinguish depressed persons in remission who will subsequently experience a relapse from those who will not is the individual's very experience of depression. On the basis of accumulating evidence, it appears that the existence of residual symptoms in depressed patients who are in remission is associated with an elevated risk of relapse (Judd et al., 1998, 2000). Further, a greater number of previous episodes is associated with a greater likelihood of relapse (Gonzales, Lewinsohn, & Clarke, 1985). These findings suggest that relapse prevention strategies should focus on first episodes of depression and the complete recovery from symptoms, as opposed to a reduction of symptoms or simple remission. This idea is further elaborated in a subsequent section.

Life Events

A considerable body of literature has examined the role of life events as a risk factor for depression. Generally, these studies indicate that both major negative life events and minor "hassles" are associated with increased risk of depression (Paykel & Cooper, 1992) and that events which specifically require a major life adjustment predict the onset of a depressive episode (Brown & Harris, 1978; Brown & Prudo, 1981). Further, both the clinical literature and the research literature support the conclusion that events which involve either loss or personal diminishment convey a particular risk for depression (Clark, Beck, & Alford, 1999).

Despite the fact that a significant relationship exists between life events and depression, several issues complicate the conclusions that can be drawn from this research. First, the observed relationships between life events and depression are typically modest to moderate (Andrews, 1978), leaving room for alternative explanatory variables. Second, the direction of causality cannot be determined from the existence of a correlational relationship. It is possible that individuals who are prone to depression engage in their environment in a manner which serves to increase the probability of negative life events (Hammen, 1991) or that even the early symptoms of depression themselves make it difficult for those affected to gain positive interactions in their social world (Paykel, 1994; Paykel & Hollyman, 1984). Most models that examine life events in the context of depression thus postulate a diathesis–stress model, in which life events interact with some individual risk factors or vulnerabilities to predict depression (Kessler, 1997; Paykel, 1994). Finally, most models of life events in depression fail to consider the potentially divergent role of those events in first episodes of depression and in subsequent relapse. If there are erosive processes that occur with the recurrence of depression, as has been suggested (Dobson, 2000; Ingram, Miranda, & Segal, 1998; Joiner, 2000), it may be the case that first episodes of depression require a more potent negative life event to activate them than do subsequent episodes.

Cognitive Factors

An enormous literature has accrued which has established that depressed individuals can be distinguished from nondepressed individuals on the basis of the following cognitive variables: selective attention, information-processing speed, tendency to ruminate, attribution errors, memory, organization of information, and thought content (see Clark et al., 1999; Ingram et al., 1998). The identified patterns are in line with what one might expect, given that negative cognition is reflected in the potential diagnostic features of depression (American Psychiatric Association, 2000). However, the literature has moved beyond the investigation of correlational associations between cognition and depression to examine potentially causal links.

One avenue of research in the search for a causal role of cognition in depression has been to look for cognitive correlates of depression that persist following patients' recovery from depression. Although this literature has generally been disappointing, a few studies have revealed residual phenomena that could be markers of depression (Clark et al., 1999; Haaga, Dyck, & Ernst, 1991). In a major review of the literature, including 29 studies of "recovered" depressed samples, Clark et al. (1999) observed, "An inescapable conclusion from the majority of these studies is that depressive cognition is largely state dependent. Little evidence was found for the existence of an enduring proximal predisposition that does not change with treatment" (p. 157).

A major concern regarding using recovered depressed individuals (i.e., someone who was previously diagnosed with depression, but does not currently meet the criteria for diagnosis) to study cognitive vulnerability to depression is that the cognitive model itself suggests that, in the absence of some precipitant, the important causal cognitive variables should be silent or latent (Beck, Rush, Shaw, & Emery, 1979). Thus, activation of schemas and the cognitive phenomena associated with such a process should be seen only when specific cognitive systems are themselves activated or primed (Segal, 1988). A number of studies have now examined the effects of either mood induction or cognitive primes on activating these cognitive systems (for a review, see Clark et al., 1999). In general, there is some support for similarity in the thinking styles of currently depressed individuals and recovered individuals who have undergone priming or induction procedures, suggesting the persistence of cognitive phenomena following recovery from depression.

Even if residual cognitive effects are found to exist in depression, either with or without priming, the research methodology employed in the majority of these studies precludes the formulation of any causal conclusions. Prospective or longitudinal research designs must be utilized in order to evaluate the causal role of research variables. Research employing such designs has been conducted to examine the role of cognitive variables in relapse into depression. It has been found that depressed patients who endorse more negative attitudes tend to show longer times to achieve remission from a depressive episode (Dent & Teasdale, 1988). Of even greater importance has been the finding that future relapse can be predicted by using a priming task at the time of recovery (Segal, Gemar, & Williams, 1998). These results seem to provide some support for the predictive role of cognition in depression.

Two well-documented data sets commend themselves as the best evidence to date for a causal role of cognition in depression. The first of these data sets was collected from an earlier prospective study led by Lewinsohn and conducted in the 1980s in Eugene, Oregon (Lewinsohn, Steinmetz, Larson, & Franklin, 1981); the other is the Temple–Wisconsin Vulnerability to Depression Project (Alloy & Abramson, 1999). Both studies employed a wide battery of psychosocial measures, including cognitive and other dispositional measures, historical descriptors, and life event measures, to examine relationships between these psychosocial variables and both changes in depression severity scores and the development of new cases of depression. Although data from the more recent study are still emerging, the general findings to this point in time suggest that cognitive variables alone do not possess significant predictive power, but, in interaction with matching life events, contribute significantly to the prediction of new cases of depression (cf. Lewinsohn et al., 1981).

These findings are in line with Beck's diathesis–stress model of depression, featuring the vulnerability characteristics of sociotropy and autonomy (Beck et al., 1979; Clark et al., 1999). In principle, sociotropic individuals (those who are sensitive to actual or perceived social loss) should be most at risk for depression when they are confronted with interpersonal life events that threaten loss in relation to their connection to, or acceptance from, others. In contrast, autonomous individuals (those who value independence and self-control) should be at risk for depression only when confronted with a loss or limitation of independence, control, or achievement. The *congruency hypothesis*, which estimates depressive risk for individuals by matching cognitive vulnerabilities and life events, has now been evaluated in a number of studies (for a review, see Nietzel & Harris, 1990). In general, the evidence is supportive of this model (Coyne & Whiffen, 1995) and, in particular, of the match between a sociotropic style and negative interpersonal events in the prediction of depression. Thus, further inquiry in the area appears promising and indicated (Coyne & Whiffen, 1995; Segal, Shaw, Vella, & Katz, 1992).

Social Support

Social support has been examined as a vulnerability factor for depression in a large number of studies over the years. Both the "direct effects" model, in which social support is hypothesized to be a direct risk factor for depression, and the "buffering hypothesis" (Alloway & Bebbington, 1987), in which social support is viewed as a buffer or moderator of negative life events, have been evaluated (Cohen & Wills, 1985; Thoits, 1982). A large number of cross-sectional studies, in which clinically depressed participants are compared with control groups, have validated the idea that social support is diminished in depression (for a review, see Paykel & Cooper, 1992). Evidence has been found for both a direct effect of social support on depression (e.g., Andrews, 1978; Parry & Shapiro, 1986) and the buffering hypothesis (e.g., Brown & Harris, 1978; Brown & Prudo, 1981; Flannery & Wieman, 1989).

A few longitudinal studies to date have examined the role of social support specifically in the onset of depression. The existing evidence suggests that social support has predictive power regarding the onset of depression, particularly as a buffer of negative life events (Brown, Andrews, Harris, Adler, & Bridge, 1986; Brugha et al., 1990). Unfortunately, a number of these studies failed to contrast the direct and buffering models of social support, rendering the nature of the contribution of social support to both duration of an indexical episode and subsequent recovery or relapse unclear. Further investigation of the role of social support in depressive relapse in particular is a critical area of investigation required for developing relapse and relapse prevention models in the area of depression.

Coping Models

The concept of psychological coping involves the attempts or strategies that one uses to overcome, reduce the effects of, or tolerate a stressful situation or experience (Endler & Parker, 1990). As such, the concept inherently encompasses an interaction between negative life events and the various coping strategies that might be employed. Different conceptual frameworks for coping have been developed, including (a) problem- or task-focused coping, which reflects the orientation of trying to confront and overcome stressful events directly, (b) emotion-focused coping, which involves a self-directed orientation of attempting to deal with or overcome the negative emotional and other consequences of confronting negative life experiences, and (c) avoidance strategies, which include attempts to cope by using distraction or behavioral avoidance to limit one's exposure to stressful events (Folkman & Lazarus, 1986).

The results of a large number of studies have established that coping strategies are significantly associated with the onset, course, and severity of depression. In particular, depressed individuals are more likely to use emotion-oriented coping strategies and less likely to employ problem-focused coping strategies, compared with nondepressed individuals (Billings, Cronkite, & Moos, 1983; Endler & Parker, 1990; Kuyken & Brewin, 1994). The somewhat more limited data on the use of avoidance-oriented coping responses again implicates this strategy as being more typical for depressed, as opposed to nondepressed, individuals (Billings et al., 1983; Billings & Moos, 1982; Kuyken & Brewin, 1994).

As has been noted for other risk factors in depression, there is relatively little evidence that supports a causal role for coping strategies in the prediction of cases of clinical depression (Holahan & Moos, 1991; Swindle, Cronkite, & Moos, 1989). There is some evidence that relapse can be predicted on the basis of the lack of problem-focused coping (Swindle et al., 1989). However, the role of coping strategies, both alone and in interaction with other variables such as life events, in the prediction of relapse in depression has not received sufficient research attention to offer definitive conclusions about the contribution of coping to relapse into depression (Kuyken & Brewin, 1994).

Integrating Risk Factors

Risk factors for relapse in depression are often studied in isolation from one another or, at best, in simplistic two-factor models. Although these approaches have identified factors associated with the differential risk of relapse, a more comprehensive and integrated model of relapse is needed. In particular, the potential utility of a more conceptual approach to studying risk for relapse in depression warrants consideration. A recent model proposed by Joiner (2000) examines risk factors from the perspective of whether they serve to propagate depression (i.e., whether they are risk factors in the sense typically considered), are erosive factors (i.e., are markers and possible risk factors that erode over time or with repeated occurrences of depression), or are self-propagatory processes (i.e., things that depressed individuals do themselves that actually increase their risk for depression). In an extension of this model, Dobson (2000) has argued that some of the factors identified by Joiner might also be combinations of erosive and self-propagatory processes contributing to relapse. It may be that examining risk factors within a conceptual framework is a direction for future theory to take that will have advantages in attempting to understand and prevent the risk of relapse in depression.

EFFORTS TOWARD PREVENTING RELAPSE

As previously stated, there are three different areas of investigation in the treatment literature that address the issues of recurrence and relapse in depression: (a) the utilization of optimal treatment during the acute phase of depression in order to maximize recovery and reduce the risk of relapse, (b) the continued treatment of residual symptoms as a means of reducing the likelihood of relapse, and (c) the development and evaluation of targeted relapse prevention strategies. The rest of this section presents a number of empirical findings and conclusions in each of these areas of investigation.

Optimizing Acute-Phase Treatment

One strategy that has been shown to reduce the risk of relapse in depression is the optimization of acute-phase treatment. Because patients with residual symptoms at the termination of treatment have been found to show an elevated risk of relapse into depression (Judd et al., 1998, 2000), a logical expectation is that more complete recovery from symptoms should be associated with reducing such risk. In general, while various treatments for the acute phase of depression have not shown markedly different outcomes, considerable evidence now exists regarding the differential risk of relapse associated with those treatments.

On the basis of trials of tricyclic medication, Belsher and Costello (1988) estimated that, following remission or recovery from depression, approximately 50% of patients would experience a relapse within a year after the termination of treatment. This estimate has held up well with newer data, which also indicate that about 50% of patients relapse following the discontinuation of selective serotonin reuptake inhibitors (Paykel et al., 1999; Rafanelli, Park, & Fava, 1999). On the basis of the newer studies, some psychiatrists recommend that the focus of psychopharmacological treatment in depression change from acute-phase treatment to long-term use of medication for maintenance (Donoghue & Hyla, 2001; Keller & Boland, 1998). In contrast to the recommendation of maintenance medication, an alternative strategy that has been employed is to have patients strategically cross over from one medication to another if the first medication is unsuccessful. Koran et al. (2001), for example, found that more aggressive combinations of medication can result in a better clinical outcome and, presumably, a better long-term prognosis than can be obtained from any single medication.

Although most investigators offer the opinion that active treatments for depression have relatively similar short-term outcomes (Clark et al., 1999; Hollon & Najavits, 1988), it appears that different types of treatment for depression are associated with a differential risk of relapse (Clark et al., 1999; Dobson, Backs-Dermott, & Dozois, 2000). In an update of a previous study by Dobson (1989), Gloaguen, Cottraux, Cucherat, & Blackburn (1998) conducted a meta-analysis of the effects of cognitive therapy for depression. They reported that cognitive therapy showed significantly—albeit not remarkably—better outcomes than were obtained from medication and other therapies, with the exception of behavior therapy, in the acute phase of depression. Most notably, the average risk of relapse after cognitive therapy was reported to be 25%, as opposed to 60% following pharmacotherapy, at follow-up periods of 1 to 2 years.

The evidence in favor of long-term reduced risk of relapse following cognitive therapy is sizable and accumulating (Overholser, 1998). In the most recent of the trials in this area, Hollon and DeRubeis (Barclay, 2002) compared the results obtained with cognitive therapy with those yielded by selective serotonin reuptake inhibitors. Although both treatments resulted in equal outcomes of 57% remission in the acute phase of treatment, the risk of relapse after cognitive therapy over a 1-year follow-up period was 25%, compared with 40% in the group that received continued medication. Notably, the cognitive therapy group not only exhibited better long-term clinical results, but also required lower overall costs than did continued medication.

If cognitive therapy is associated with a lower risk of relapse than that afforded by medication, the reasons for this differential outcome must be explored. It does not appear that the reasons are related to a better short-term outcome (i.e., fewer residual symptoms) for cognitive therapy, as the differences in this regard are likely insufficient to account for the more substantial differences in relapse rates (Dobson, 1989; Glogcuen et al., 1998). Moreover, because cognitive therapy has higher rates of completion than other treatments have, it is also unlikely that those people who recover from depression following cognitive therapy are a more select and resilient group.

Further study of the mechanisms of change in cognitive therapy is clearly warranted (Whisman, 1993). For example, the issue of sudden change in cognitive therapy needs to be examined. This phenomenon, in which a rapid reduction in depressive symptoms is observed with cognitive therapy treatment (Tang & DeRubeis, 1999), has been associated with better long-term outcome. Although the response does not occur in all cognitive therapy patients and may not be specific to cognitive therapy (Tang, Luborsky, & Andrusyna, 2002), it seems that an important shift takes place in some patients that requires further investigation. It also appears that recovered patients who have negative cognitions that can be activated show an elevated risk for relapse into depression (Segal et al., 1998). Thus, it seems likely that the greatest reduction in risk of relapse will be seen in those patients who achieve lasting cognitive changes as a result of cognitive therapy. It may also be that cognitive therapy teaches skills that aid in coping with new adversities in life and that these skills are enhanced in cognitive therapy relative to other treatments. Although the mechanisms of cognitive therapy themselves continue to require investigation (cf. Jacobson et al., 1996), examining why this treatment is associated with significantly lower rates of relapse relative to the relapse rates of other treatments is clearly a promising avenue of study.

Overall, the literature suggests that the risk of relapse in depression can be minimized through the provision of optimal acute-phase treatment, including cognitive therapy (Overholser, 1998) and the strategic use of alternative medication if only partial success is obtained with a first drug (Montgomery, 1999). As research designs in this area improve (Storosum, van Zwieten, Vermeulen, Wohlfarth, & van den Brink, 2001), and the mechanisms of change associated with reduced risk of relapse are elucidated, it may be possible to develop more targeted forms of treatment that would result in improved long-term outcomes.

Treating Residual Symptoms and Maintenance Treatment

Other methods of minimizing the risk of relapse in depression include ensuring that treatment effects are prolonged and that residual symptoms that might remain after remission continue to be a focus of treatment. As has already been noted, because of the relatively high rates of relapse in the medical treatment of depression, the strategy of continuation medication has been recommended (Fava & Kaji, 1994; Nierenberg, 2001). On the basis of a review of 91 articles that examined continuation or maintenance pharmacotherapy for depression, Forshall and Nutt (1999) recommended that antidepressant medication be continued at the same dosage as during the acute phase of treatment for depression for 4 to 6 months following remission of symptoms. Further, in patients with more chronic patterns of depression, these authors recommend long-term medication.

The strategy of continuation medication for depression has now been evaluated in a number of studies, and the results generally support a reduced risk of relapse. For example, in an open trial of the continued use of citalopram in recovered patients with recurrent depression, 32 of the 36 participants were able to use the medication for a 24-month period, and only 34% of the group experienced a relapse (Franchini, Spagnolo, Rampoldi, Zanardi, & Smeraldi, 2001; Franchini, Zanardi, Gasperini, & Smeraldi, 1999). In a similarly designed study using mirtazapine as the continuation medication and a 40-week follow-up period, Thase, Nierenberg, Keller, and Papagides (2001) reported a 19.7% relapse rate with continued medication, versus a rate of 43.9% with placebo. Similar reductions in rates of relapse with continuation medication have been reported for other medications (Feiger et al., 1999; Montgomery, 1999), leading some to recommend ongoing or continuation medication treatment as a standard part of clinical care, particularly in recurrent depression (Dunner, 2001; Nierenberg, 2001; Paykel, 2001).

Although there appears to be good reason to expect that an effective treatment for depression, such as some kind of medication, will produce benefits with continued use, caution is warranted for several reasons. First, it appears that some medications lose their effectiveness with continued use (Byrne & Rothschild, 1998), suggesting the need to transfer patients from one medication to another (Brown & Harrison, 1995). Second, there often are notable side effects with prolonged use of medication. Prominent among these side effects are sexual problems (Rothschild, 2000), apathy and mental dulling (Stahl, 2000), and weight gain (Sussman & Ginsberg, 1998). These side effects, as well as the ongoing costs associated with continued medication, reduce the acceptability of the long-term use of antidepressants.

An alternative to using continuation medication is employing other psychosocial treatments for residual symptoms. In particular, the two most effective treatments for the acute-phase treatment of depression—cognitive–behavioral therapy and interpersonal therapy—have been evaluated. The available evidence suggests that interpersonal therapy does not confer any particular benefit in the prevention of relapse. For example, Frank and colleagues (1990; Frank, Kupfer, et al., 1991) conducted a trial in which interpersonal therapy was compared with treatment with imipramine both in the acute phase and as a follow-up or continuation treatment for depression. Patients who were recovered at the end of the acute phase of treatment were randomly assigned to continuation medication or psychotherapy, with appropriate placebo comparisons. Three years after completion of the test, the proportion of patients remaining in the analysis who had relapsed were 90% in the placebo condition, 32% in the medication condition, 67% in the interpersonal therapy condition, and 29% in the combined interpersonal therapy and medication condition. Thus, although interpersonal therapy had a preventive effect relative to no treatment, it was significantly less effective than continued medication and conferred no benefit above and beyond medication in the combined condition in terms of preventing relapse into depression. Clearly, further research is needed to elucidate the relative effect of interpersonal therapy in preventing relapse.

Fava and colleagues have reported on the long-term results of a cognitive–behavioral treatment (CBT) for patients who went into remission after being treated with antidepressant medications, but who continued to show residual symptoms. In the trial, 40 patients were randomly assigned to a brief 10-session course of CBT or standard clinical management and were followed for 6 years posttreatment (Fava, Grandi, Zielezny, Canestrari, & Morphy, 1994; Fava, Grandi, Zielezny, Rafanelli, & Canestrari, 1996; Fava,

Rafanelli, Grandi, Canestrari, & Morphy, 1998). Relapse rates following CBT were 15% at 2 years, compared with 35% in the clinical management condition. For the group that was assessed at 4 years posttreatment, relapse rates were 35% for CBT versus 70% for clinical management. Both of these results were statistically significant and suggested a relapse prevention effect for CBT. By 6 years, however, the differential relapse rates of 50% for CBT and 75% for clinical management no longer achieved statistical significance. However, the numbers of new episodes of depression in the two groups during the 6-year follow-up period were significantly different, with CBT associated with a lower number of new episodes of depression than standard care (Fava, Rafanelli, Grandi, Canestrari, & Morphy, 1998). In a recent replication of this study (Fava, Rafanelli, Grandi, Conti, & Belluardo, 1998), the results were even stronger in favor of CBT having a relapse prevention effect for patients with residual symptoms, with the 2-year relapse rate for CBT being 25%, as opposed to 80% in the clinical management condition. Long-term results from this latter trial will help to determine the long-term benefit of a brief CBT intervention in preventing relapse into depression.

Paykel et al. (1999) have also reported on the relapse prevention potential of CBT in residual depression. In their study, 158 patients who were in remission from major depression, but who still had residual symptoms, were randomized to clinical management or clinical management plus 16 sessions of CBT (and 2 booster sessions at a later point) and then were followed after treatment. As reported by the authors, "Cognitive therapy significantly reduced the relapse over 17 months on clinical management from a high level of 47%, which occurred despite continued treatment with antidepressants. The reduction to a 29% rate of relapse by the addition of CT was definitely worthwhile" (Paykel et al., 1999, p. 832). These results mirror others (Blackburn & Moore, 1997) which have shown that the use of CBT in depressed patients in remission is associated with lower rates of relapse than continuation medication alone or than continuation medication following successful CBT.

One other study warrants review at this point. In what was described as an optional "aftercare" program for discharged depressed patients, Kuehner, Angermeyer, and Veiel (1996) reported on the benefits of a group format intervention based on Lewinsohn's Coping with Depression course (CWD; Lewinsohn, Antonuccio, Steinmetz, & Teri, 1984). Over a 6-month follow-up period, the relapse rates were 14.3% for the individuals who participated in the program, as opposed to 42.9% in a matched control group. The relapse rates for the treatment group were particularly favorable in the subset of patients who were in full remission at discharge. Further, the authors anecdotally report that the course "was especially attractive to those patients who still displayed extensive depressive residual symptoms after discharge and those who had experienced an early relapse during the 6-month period preceding the CWD intervention" (p. 405). These results, while again encouraging for the preventive effects of cognitive–behavioral treatments, need to be replicated in a randomized controlled trial.

In sum, it appears that continued treatment for patients who show residual symptoms can be an effective strategy to reduce the risk of relapse into depression. Both continuation medication and CBT provided to patients with residual symptoms are associated with reduced rates of relapse. The evidence to date indicates that this preventive effect is stronger for CBT than for medication, with CBT relapse rates being consistently lower than those associated with continued medication. There are both theoretical and practical issues to consider in interpreting these results. At a conceptual level, it must be inquired whether it in fact is CBT that is actually lowering the risk of depression in these studies, and if so, what mechanism or mechanisms are responsible for the effect (DeRubeis et al., 1990; Shaw & Segal, 1999; Teasdale, 1999). Teasdale and colleagues (2001) have suggested, for example, that successful CBT may change the manner in which previously depressed persons respond to negative thoughts. If mechanisms associated with reducing the risk of relapse into depression can be identified, it may be possible to select patients who are most likely to be subject to these mechanisms and perhaps even to administer CBT or medication to them selectively, in accordance with what is appropriate for a given patient. Further, the ongoing costs of medication and their side effects suggest that the issue of acceptability of treatment will be important in the choice of continuation treatments. However, the differential availability of CBT, on the one hand, and various medications, on the other, suggests that even if CBT has significantly better relapse prevention effects than continuation medication does, its relative lack of availability may limit its use in clinical care.

Targeted Relapse Prevention Programs

A third strategy for reducing the incidence of relapse in depression is to design and implement programs for those formerly depressed patients who have fully recovered. These programs would constitute "true" relapse prevention programs, in that they would involve strategies to undermine or negate processes that otherwise might be associated with a risk of relapse. In this final subsection, we review the limited evidence in this area.

From a biological perspective, the neurotransmitters associated with depression are well established. Although, as we have seen, continuing medication treatment for previously depressed patients with residual symptoms or a recurrent course of depression has been recommended, and although there have been philosophical discussions of the value of medicating entire groups of society to prevent them from lapsing into depression (Kingwell, 1999), no individual, to our knowledge, has suggested using psychotropic medication with fully recovered patients. Thus, the review of "true" relapse prevention efforts in the area of depression is confined to psychological approaches.

Four psychological approaches to preventing relapse have appeared to date in the literature. In the earliest of these, Berlin (1985) developed a targeted relapse prevention program focused on self-criticism. Twenty-two recovered self-critical women were randomly assigned to either a standard CBT program or a focused intervention. Six months later, the effects between the groups in terms of targeted outcome variables were not significantly different. While the small sample size used in this study precludes any firm conclusions, the idea of targeting processes associated with risk of depressive relapse warrants merit and continues to be an idea that is explored in the research.

In another study, Wilson and his colleagues evaluated the benefits of booster sessions in preventing relapse in recovered depressed patients. Baker and Wilson (1985), for example, randomly assigned patients to receive CBT booster sessions, nonspecific booster sessions, or no booster sessions, but failed to find any differences in the rates of relapse across the groups. The study's negative results were qualified by (a) the researchers' failure to distinguish between recovered patients and those with residual symptoms at the beginning of the program and (b) the nonindividualized format of the CBT intervention. In a subsequent study designed to overcome these problems, Kavanagh and Wilson (1987) failed to find a significant benefit associated with targeted CBT booster sessions in terms of reducing the risk of relapse. Wilson (1992b) has speculated that the timing or spacing of the booster sessions may not have been optimal, but these limitations have not yet been addressed empirically. Thus, although, in principle, the idea of booster sessions makes eminent sense (Eifert, Beach, & Wilson, 1995), and although the likely effective components of such a program could be identified, this approach requires further examination. One idea might be to integrate these interventions into primary-care settings (Ludman et al., 2000) in much the same manner as ongoing dental checkups have become standard care in dentistry.

The third relapse prevention approach to appear in the literature has yet to be subjected to adequate empirical evaluation. This approach, which has been labeled Well-Being Therapy, consists of self-monitoring of symptoms, together with six other components: environmental mastery, personal growth, purpose in life, autonomy, self-acceptance, and developing positive relationships (Ryff & Singer, 1996). Well-Being Therapy has been developed by Fava and colleagues (Fava, Rafanelli, Cazzaro, Conti, & Grandi, 1998) as a program to emphasize positive aspects of functioning and to optimize well-being in recovered depressed persons. The preliminary evaluation of Well-Being Therapy in a small sample of recovered depressed patients showed it to be as effective as CBT in preventing relapse (Fava, Rafanelli, Cazzaro, et al., 1998). Further evaluation of the therapy in larger controlled trials is needed.

The most innovative and successful effort to date to design and test a true relapse prevention program for recovered depressed patients has been reported by Teasdale and colleagues (Teasdale et al., 2000). Their intervention, named Mindfulness Based Cognitive Therapy (MBCT), is based upon the idea that changing a person's emotional processing can reduce the individual's risk of relapse (Teasdale, 1999; Teasdale, Segal, & Williams, 1995). In Teasdale and colleagues' trial, 145 recovered depressed patients were randomly assigned to either continued treatment as usual or treatment as usual plus MBCT. The MBCT included exercises to help the patient disengage from the potential depressive effects of both depression-related thoughts and feelings and exercises to allow patients to experience these thoughts and feelings fully, but without feeling the need to respond to them or sense them as catastrophic (see also Segal, Williams, & Teasdale, 2002). This "decentering" and experiential MBCT process was associated with significantly less relapse (40%, versus 66% in treatment as usual at 60-week follow-up). It was also observed that, although the risk of relapse increased as a function of the number of previous episodes of depression in the treatment-as-usual condition, no such effect was observed in MBCT, as the relapse rates were independent of the effects of chronic depression for this group. These results have since been replicated in a second trial that has yet to be published (J. D. Teasdale, personal communication, May 22, 2002), suggesting that MBCT may indeed show preventive effects in recovered depressed persons.

Despite the recent intriguing relapse prevention results of Teasdale et al. (2000) and the innovative, but unsuccessful, early work of Wilson and colleagues, true relapse prevention in depression has been insufficiently studied. This is in some respects quite surprising, given that the risk of relapse is well documented and the target population relatively easy to identify. Logically, a program, such as MBCT or the even more generic CBT, that combines ongoing assessment of symptoms, family education and awareness, monitoring of life events or other risk factors for relapse, and training of effective techniques for reducing the risk of relapse should have significant potential to reduce the risk of relapse in depression (Kuehner et al., 1996; Ludman et al., 2000). Although engaging recovered depressed patients in ongoing treatment may be difficult, the evaluation of such strategies appears to be the next step in advancing relapse prevention efforts.

ISSUES FOR FUTURE DEVELOPMENT AND RESEARCH

As the preceding review has documented, a number of promising avenues for the prevention of relapse in depression are beginning to be identified and evaluated. These strategies include optimizing treatment during the acute phase of the disorder, applying continuing treatment in patients who are in remission, but who are not fully recovered, and developing specific relapse prevention programs. In general, CBT appears to be associated with the lowest risk of relapse, based on acute-phase treatment. Both pharmacological therapies and CBT recommend themselves as maintenance therapies. In terms of psychological approaches to preventing relapse, to date only MBCT has been adequately evaluated and found to have a specific relapse prevention effect in recovered depressed patients. Thus, despite the cautious optimism that the current literature allows, there remain a large number of theoretical and practical issues that need to be addressed. In the remainder of this chapter, we identify the primary issues requiring consideration in research on the tertiary prevention of depression.

Standardizing Terminology and Methodology in Studying Relapse

Although the criteria proposed by Frank, Prien, et al. (1991) for defining remission, recovery, recurrence, and relapse in depression have decreased the confusion in the literature, it is apparent that variability still exists in the conceptualization of outcomes in this area. For example, some investigators have used "modified" Frank et al. criteria. Such inconsistency presents difficulties in determining whether the results of a given study are comparable to those seen in other studies. In addition, the extensive collection of severity measures in the area of depression (see chap. 3, this volume) provides for a number of options in assessing outcomes in depression research, further complicating the comparability and integration of research in the area. To maximize the future ease of interpreting and integrating research outcomes, we encourage investigators to utilize the Frank, Prien, et al. (1991) criteria in depression research. If a variation of these criteria is desired, we propose that that variation be used in addition to the standard criteria, with a clear description of the variation employed. We also recommend that all studies in depression use either or both the Beck Depression Inventory or the Hamilton Rating Scale for Depression. Although these measures may be supplemented with other ones, they are so commonly employed in depression research that, in effect, they have become the benchmarks against which other outcomes can be compared.

Relapse Vulnerability Research

As the preceding sections have documented, a considerable body of literature addresses risk factors for relapse into depression (Joiner, 2000). The established risk factors for depression include a history of depression, life events, cognitive factors, social support, and coping style. Further, our review has determined that there is a differential risk of relapse associated with various types of treatment. To date, most of the research on relapse prevention has focused on either variables in isolation from each other or, in some cases, two interacting variables. Models of prediction need to move beyond more simplistic formulations to those which involve several simultaneous predictors. As almost all of these relapse prevention models include the role of negative life events, issues pertaining to the conceptualization and measurement of life events must be clarified in future depression research. Finally, models in the area of relapse prevention in depression need to examine not only the presence of negative risk factors in relapse, but also positive and potentially protective factors. For example, Brown and colleagues (1986) have found that "fresh-start events" (i.e., events that permit a new chance for success or the development of positive relationships) may be associated with recovery from depression and lower risk of relapse. Other positive variables, such as the development of hope, increased social support, and enhanced coping, all deserve future attention in research on well-being (Ryff & Singer, 1996) and relapse into depression.

Major Depression and Related Disorders

As other chapters in this volume note, there is a very high rate of comorbidity between anxiety and depression. Hence, investigators who are working in one of these areas need to be cognizant about developments in the other, as variables and intervention strategies in one domain may have direct implications for the other. Similarly, as new relapse prevention research is conducted on related mood disorders, depression investigators should consider the implications for their area. For example, Lam et al. (2003) recently formulated a series of strategies to identify and address prodromes associated with the risk of relapse in bipolar disorder. This type of purposeful, innovative work can likely serve as a model after which studies can be designed and adapted in the area of depression.

Treatment Development and Randomized Trials

This review has brought to light the clear need for the development and evaluation of innovative relapse prevention programs. As previously indicated, only two true relapse prevention strategies have been developed to date. Of these, Mindfulness Based Cognitive Therapy (Segal et al., 2002; Teasdale et al., 2000) has been shown in a randomized controlled trial to have relapse prevention potential for recovered depressed patients. Well-being Therapy (Fava, Rafanelli, Cazzaro, et al., 1998), although showing promise in a preliminary trial, has yet to be evaluated with the use of stringent empirical standards. There is thus considerable room for the design and evaluation of other strategies.

In developing relapse prevention-focused programs in the area of depression, three options are evident (Cardemil & Barber, 2001). First, established treatments such as medications, CBT, and interpersonal therapy could be adapted for use with either all recovered patients or those individuals for whom there are indications of potential relapse into depression. Such a purposeful adaptation and evaluation of existing therapies would be fairly easy to implement and would likely be a productive area for future research. A second strategy is to build on our current knowledge of risk factors associated with relapse (Dobson, 2000; Joiner, 2000; Wilson, 1992b) and design a customized prevention program to address these factors. Indeed, such a development could be "modularized" such that if the overall program is demonstrated to have relapse prevention benefit, it could be dismantled and evaluated to determine the effects of different program components. A third strategy, one that is to date perhaps best exemplified by the Well-Being Therapy model (Fava, Rafanelli, Cazzaro, et al., 1998), is to shift the focus of intervention for recovered depressed patients from the prevention of relapse to the maintenance of health. Whereas many recovered depressed individuals may find prevention-of-relapse strategies acceptable (cf. Kuehner et al., 1996; Ludman et al., 2000), it is quite possible that these individuals would be even more receptive to a program that emphasizes maintenance of mental health.

One particularly innovative idea that holds evident promise is the design and evaluation of "First Episode Clinics" in depression. Given the high relapse rates in the disorder and the negative, erosive consequences that might be associated with recurrent depression (Joiner, 2000), it seems that intervention in first episodes of depression has great potential to maximize clinical outcomes and reduce long-term health care costs. Such clinics could provide (a) early identification, perhaps in association with primary-care settings, (b) the delivery of treatment to those persons experiencing their first episode of depression, with the goal of effecting recovery, as opposed to remission, (c) maintenance treatment, (d) continued monitoring following recovery, and (e) targeted interventions for those exhibiting relapse or recurrence. If developed, such clinics should be evaluated on the basis of not only efficacy criteria, but also effectiveness criteria, including the acceptability of the program to depressed individuals and the program's long-term cost-effectiveness compared with standard treatment.

SUMMARY

The purposes of this chapter have been to discuss the established variables associated with risk of relapse in clinical depression, to review the evidence regarding prevention of relapse, and to suggest areas of development for the future. Based on the evidence to date, it appears that, although considerable data exist regarding the risk factors for relapse into depression, these data have not consistently or strategically been used in the design and evaluation of relapse prevention programs. Optimization of the acute-phase treatment of depression, the employment of continuation treatments to maximize recovery from depression, and the design of targeted relapse prevention programs are three major strategies with a demonstrated potential to reduce the proportion of formerly depressed persons who will experience relapse. Given that one of the strongest predictors of future depression is past depression and that depression often follows a chronic course, we have argued, in particular, that the identification and treatment of first episodes of depression should be a priority. Thus, although much is already known about the process of relapse in depression, much remains to be accomplished to reduce the human suffering and health care costs associated with the disorder and to maximize the mental health of recovered depressed persons.

REFERENCES

Alloway, R., & Bebbington, P. (1987). The buffer theory of social support: A review of the literature. *Psychological Medicine, 17,* 91–108.

Alloy, L. B., & Abramson, L. Y. (1999). The Temple–Wisconsin Cognitive Vulnerability to Depression (CVD) Project: Conceptual background, design and methods. *Journal of Cognitive Psychotherapy: An International Quarterly, 13,* 227–262.

American Psychiatric Association. (2000). *Diagnostic and statistical manual of mental disorders* (4th ed., text revision). Washington, DC: American Psychiatric Association.

Andrews, J. G. (1978). Life event stress and psychiatric illness. *Psychological Medicine, 8,* 545–549.

Angst, J., Angst, F., & Stassen, H. H. (1999). Suicide risk in patients with major depressive disorder. *Journal of Clinical Psychiatry, 60*(Suppl. 2), 57–62.

Baker, A. L., & Wilson, P. H. (1985). Cognitive–behavior therapy for depression: The effects of booster sessions on relapse. *Behavior Therapy, 16,* 335–344.

Barclay, L. (2002). *Cognitive therapy for depression sustains improvement longer than drugs.* Posted by Medscape.Com, May 24, 2002. Retrieved August 15, 2002 from http://www.medscape.com/viewarticle/434073

Beck, A. T., Rush, A. J., Shaw, B. F., & Emery, G. (1979). *Cognitive therapy of depression.* New York: Guilford.

Belsher, G., & Costello, C. G. (1988). Relapse after recovery from unipolar depression: A critical review. *Psychological Bulletin, 104,* 84–96.

Berlin, S. (1985). Maintaining reduced level of self-criticism through relapse-prevention treatment. *Social Work Research and Abstracts, 21,* 21–33.

Billings, A. G., Cronkite, R. C., & Moos, R. H. (1983). Social-environmental factors in unipolar depression: Comparisons of depressed patients and nondepressed controls. *Journal of Abnormal Psychology, 92,* 119–133.

Billings, A. G., & Moos, R. H. (1982). Psychosocial theory and research on depression: An integrative framework and review. *Clinical Psychology Review, 2,* 213–237.

Blackburn, I. M., & Moore, R. G. (1997). Controlled acute and follow-up trial of cognitive therapy and pharmacotherapy in outpatients with recurrent depression. *British Journal of Psychiatry, 171*, 328–334.

Brown, G. W., Andrews, B., Harris, T., Adler, Z., & Bridge, L. (1986). Social support, self-esteem and depression. *Psychological Medicine, 16*, 813–831.

Brown, G. W., & Harris, T. (Eds.). (1978). *The social origins of depression*. New York: Free Press.

Brown, G. W., & Prudo, R. (1981). Psychiatric disorder in a rural and an urban population: I. Aetiology of depression. *Psychological Medicine, 11*, 581–599.

Brown, W. A., & Harrison, W. (1995). Are patients who are intolerant to one selective serotonin reuptake inhibitor intolerant to another? *Journal of Clinical Psychiatry, 56*, 30–34.

Brugha, T. S., Bebbington, P. E., McCarthy, B., Sturt, E., Wykes, T., & Potter, J. (1990). Gender, social support and recovery from depressive disorders: A prospective clinical study. *Psychological Medicine, 20*, 147–156.

Byrne, S., & Rothschild, A. J. (1998). Loss of antidepressant efficacy during maintenance therapy: Possible mechanisms and treatments. *Journal of Clinical Psychiatry, 59*, 279–288.

Cardemil, E. V., & Barber, J. P. (2001). Building a model for prevention practice: Depression as an example. *Professional Psychology: Research and Practice, 32*, 392–401.

Chen, Y.-W., & Dilsaver, S. C. (1996). Lifetime rates of suicide attempts among subjects with bipolar and unipolar disorders relative to subjects with other Axis I disorders. *Biological Psychiatry, 39*, 896–899.

Clark, D. A., Beck, A. T., & Alford, B. (1999). *Scientific foundations of the cognitive theory and therapy of depression*. New York: Wiley.

Cohen, S., & Wills, T. A. (1985). Stress, social support, and the buffering hypothesis. *Psychological Bulletin, 98*, 310–357.

Coyne, J. C., & Whiffen, V. E. (1995). Issues in personality as diathesis for depression: The case of sociotropy-dependency and autonomy–self-criticism. *Psychological Bulletin, 118*, 358–378.

Dent, J., & Teasdale, J. D. (1988). Negative cognition and the persistence of depression. *Journal of Abnormal Psychology, 97*, 29–34.

DeRubeis, R. J., Evans, M., Hollon, S. D., Garvey, M. J., Grove, W. M., & Tucson, V. B. (1990). How does cognitive therapy work? Cognitive change and symptom change in cognitive therapy and pharmacotherapy for depression. *Journal of Consulting and Clinical Psychology, 58*, 862–869.

Dobson, K. S. (1989). A meta-analysis of the efficacy of cognitive therapy for depression. *Journal of Consulting and Clinical Psychology, 57*, 414–419.

Dobson, K. S. (2000). Chronic process in depression: Differentiating self and other influences in onset, maintenance, and relapse/recurrence. *Clinical Psychology: Science and Practice, 7*, 236–239.

Dobson, K. S., Backs-Dermott, B., & Dozois, D. J. A. (2000). Cognitive and cognitive–behavioral therapies. In R. Ingram & C. R. Snyder (Eds.), *Handbook of psychological change: Psychotherapy processes and practices for the 21st century* (pp. 409–428). New York: Wiley.

Donoghue, J., & Hyla, T. R. (2001). Antidepressant use in clinical practice: Efficacy vs. effectiveness. *British Journal of Psychiatry, 179*(Suppl. 42), S9–S17.

Dunner, D. L. (2001). Acute and maintenance treatment of chronic depression. *Journal of Clinical Psychiatry, 62*(Suppl. 6), 10–16.

Eaton, W. W., Kramer, M., Anthony, J. C., Dryman, A., Shapiro, S., & Locke, B. Z. (1989). The incidence of specific DIS/DSM-III mental disorders: Data from the NIMH Epidemiologic Catchment Area program. *Acta Psychiatrica Scandinavica, 79*, 163–178.

Eifert, G. H., Beach, B. K., & Wilson, P. H. (1995). Depression: Behavioral principles and implications for treatment and relapse prevention. In J. J. Plaud & G. H. Eifert (Eds.), *From behavior theory to behavior therapy* (pp. 68–97). Needham Heights, MA: Allyn and Bacon.

Endler, N. S., & Parker, J. D. (1990). The multidimensional assessment of coping: A critical evaluation. *Journal of Personality and Social Psychology, 58*, 844–854.

Fava, G. A., Grandi, S., Zielezny, M., Canestrari, R., & Morphy, M. A. (1994). Cognitive behavioral treatment of residual symptoms in primary major depressive disorder. *American Journal of Psychiatry, 151*, 1295–1299.

Fava, G. A., Grandi, S., Zielezny, M., Rafanelli, C., & Canestrari, R. (1996). Four-year outcome for cognitive behavioral treatment of residual symptoms in major depression. *American Journal of Psychiatry, 153*, 945–947.

Fava, G. A., Rafanelli, C., Cazzaro, M., Conti, S., & Grandi, S. (1998). Well-being therapy. *Psychological Medicine, 28*, 475–480.

Fava, G. A., Rafanelli, C., Grandi, S., Canestrari, R., & Morphy, M. A. (1998). Six year outcome for cognitive behavioral treatment of residual symptoms in major depression. *American Journal of Psychiatry, 155*, 1443–1445.

Fava, G. A., Rafanelli, C., Grandi, S., Conti, S., & Belluardo, P. (1998). Prevention of recurrent depression with cognitive behavioral therapy. *Archives of General Psychiatry, 55*, 816–820.

Fava, M., & Kaji, J. (1994). Continuation and maintenance treatments of major depressive disorder. *Psychiatric Annals, 24*, 281–290.

Feiger, A. D., Bielski, R. J., Bremner, J., Heiser, J. F., Trivedi, M., Wilcox, C. S., et al. (1999). Double-blind, placebo-substitution study of nefazodone in the prevention of relapse during continuation treatment of outpatients with major depression. *International Clinical Psychopharmacology, 14*, 19–28.

Flannery, R. B., & Wieman, D. (1989). Social support, life stress, and psychological distress: An empirical assessment. *Journal of Clinical Psychology, 45*, 867–872.

Folkman, S., & Lazarus, R. S. (1986). Stress processes and depressive symptomatology. *Journal of Abnormal Psychology, 95*, 107–113.

Forshall, S., & Nutt, D. J. (1999). Maintenance pharmacotherapy of unipolar depression. *Psychiatric Bulletin, 23*, 370–373.

Franchini, L., Spagnolo, C., Rampoldi, R., Zanardi, R., & Smeraldi, E. (2001). Long-term treatment with citalopram in patients with highly recurrent forms of unipolar depression. *Psychiatry Research, 105*, 129–133.

Franchini, L., Zanardi, R., Gasperini, M., & Smeraldi, E. (1999). Two-year maintenance treatment with citalopram, 20 mg, in unipolar subjects with high recurrence rate. *Journal of Clinical Psychiatry, 60,* 861–865.

Frank, E., Kupfer, D. J., Perel, J. M., Cornes, C., Jarret, D. B., Mallinger, A. G., et al. (1990). Three year outcomes for maintenance therapies in recurrent depression. *Archives of General Psychiatry, 47,* 1093–1099.

Frank, E., Kupfer, D. J., Wagner, E. F., McEacheran, A. M., & Cornes, C. (1991). Efficacy of interpersonal psychotherapy as a maintenance treatment of recurrent depression: Contributing factors. *Archives of General Psychiatry, 48,* 1053–1059.

Frank, E., Prien, R. F., Jarrett, R., Keller, M. B., Kupfer, D. J., Lavori, P. W., et al. (1991). Conceptualization and rationale for consensus definitions of terms in major depressive disorder: Remission, recovery, relapse, and recurrence. *Archives of General Psychiatry, 48,* 851–855.

Gloaguen, V., Cottraux, J., Cucherat, M., & Blackburn, I. (1998). A meta-analysis of the effects of cognitive therapy in depression. *Journal of Affective Disorders, 49,* 59–72.

Gonzales, C. R., Lewinsohn, P. M., & Clarke, G. N. (1985). Longitudinal followup of unipolar depressives: An investigation of predictors of relapse. *Journal of Abnormal Psychology, 94,* 461–469.

Haaga, D., Dyck, M. J., & Ernst, D. (1991). Empirical status of cognitive theory of depression. *Psychological Bulletin, 110,* 215–236.

Hammen, C. L. (1991). Generation of stress in the course of unipolar depression. *Journal of Abnormal Psychology, 100,* 555–561.

Holahan, C. J., & Moos, R. H. (1991). Life stressors, personal and social resources, and depression: A 4-year structural model. *Journal of Abnormal Psychology, 100,* 31–38.

Hollon, S. D., & Najavits, L. (1988). Review of empirical studies on cognitive therapy. In A. J. Frances & R. E. Sales (Eds.), *American Psychiatric Press Review of Psychiatry* (Vol. 7, pp. 643–666). Washington, DC: American Psychiatric Press.

Ingram, R. E., Miranda, J., & Segal, Z. V. (1998). *Cognitive vulnerability to depression.* New York: Guilford.

Jacobson, N., Dobson, K. S., Truax, P. A., Addis, M. E., Koerner, K., Gollan, J., et al. (1996). A component analysis of cognitive–behavioral treatment for depression. *Journal of Consulting and Clinical Psychology, 64,* 295–304.

Jarrett, R. B., Basco, M. R., Risser, R., Ramanan, J., Marwill, M., Kraft, D., et al. (1998). Is there a role for continuation phase cognitive therapy for depressed outpatients? *Journal of Consulting and Clinical Psychology, 66,* 1036–1040.

Joiner, T. E. (2000). Depression's vicious scree: Self-propagating and erosive processes in depression chronicity. *Clinical Psychology: Science and Practice, 7,* 203–218.

Judd, L. L., Akiskal, H. S., Maser, J. D., Zeller, P. J., Endicott, J., Coryell, W., et al. (1998). Major depressive disorder: A prospective study of residual subthreshold depressive symptoms as predictors of rapid relapse. *Journal of Affective Disorders, 50*, 97–108.

Judd, L. L., Paulus, M. J., Schettler, P. J., Akiskal, H. S., Endicott, J., Leon, A. C., et al. (2000). Does incomplete recovery from first lifetime major depressive episode herald a chronic course of illness? *American Journal of Psychiatry, 157*, 1501–1504.

Kavanagh, D. J., & Wilson, P. H. (1987). Prediction of outcome with group cognitive therapy for depression. *Behavior Research and Therapy, 27*, 333–343.

Keller, M. B., & Boland, R. J. (1998). Implications of failing to achieve successful long-term maintenance treatment of recurrent unipolar major depression. *Biological Psychiatry, 44*, 348–360.

Keller, M. B., Lavori, P. W., Rice, J., Coryell, W., & Hirschfeld, R. M. A. (1986). The persistent risk of chronicity in recurrent episodes of nonbipolar major depressive disorder: A prospective follow-up. *American Journal of Psychiatry, 143*, 24–28.

Kessler, R. C. (1997). The effects of stressful life events on depression. *Annual Review of Psychology, 48*, 191–214.

Kingwell, M. (1999). *Better living in the pursuit of happiness: From Plato to Prozac.* Toronto: Penguin.

Koran, L. M., Gelenberg, A. J., Kornstein, S. G., Howland, R. H., Friedman, R. A., DeBattista, C., et al. (2001). Sertraline versus imipramine to prevent relapse in chronic depression. *Journal of Affective Disorders, 65*, 27–36.

Kuehner, C., Angermeyer, M. C., & Veiel, H. O. G. (1996). Cognitive–behavioral group intervention as a means of tertiary prevention in depressed patients: Acceptance and short-term efficacy. *Cognitive Therapy and Research, 20*, 391–409.

Kuyken, W., & Brewin, C. R. (1994). Stress and coping in depressed women. *Cognitive Therapy and Research, 18*, 403–412.

Lam, D. H., Watkins, E. R., Hayward, P., Bright, J., Wright, K., Kerr, N., et al. (2003). A randomized controlled study of cognitive therapy for relapse prevention for bipolar affective disorder: Outcome of the first year. *Archives of General Psychiatry, 60*, 145–152.

Lewinsohn, P. M., Antonuccio, D. O., Steinmetz, J. L., & Teri, L. (1984). *The Coping with Depression course: A psychoeducational intervention for unipolar depression.* Eugene, OR: Castalia.

Lewinsohn, P. M., Steinmetz, J. L., Larson, D. W., & Franklin, J. (1981). Depression-related cognitions: Antecedents or consequences? *Journal of Abnormal Psychology, 90*, 213–219.

Ludman, E., Von Korff, M., Katon, W., Lin, E., Simon, G., Walker, E., et al. (2000). The design, implementation, and acceptance of a primary care-based intervention to prevent depression relapse. *International Journal of Psychiatry in Medicine, 30*, 229–245.

Montgomery, S. A. (1999). Managing the severely ill and long-term depressed. *International Journal of Psychiatry in Clinical Practice, 3*(Suppl. 1), S13–S17.

Murray, C. J. L., & Lopez, A. D. (1997). Alternative projections of mortality and disability by cause 1900–2020: Global Burden of Disease Study. *Lancet, 349*, 1498–1504.

National Advisory Mental Health Council Workgroup on Mental Disorders Prevention Research. (2001, June 26). Priorities for Prevention Research at NIMH. *Prevention and Treatment, 4*, Article 17. Retrieved November 1, 2001, from http://journals.apa.org/prevention/volume 4/pre0040017namhc.html

Nierenberg, A. A. (2001). Long-term management of chronic depression. *Journal of Clinical Psychiatry, 62*, 17–21.

Nietzel, M. T., & Harris, M. J. (1990). Relationship of dependency and achievement/autonomy to depression. *Clinical Psychology Review, 10*, 279–297.

Ormel, J., Von Korff, M., Ustun, B., Pini, S., Jorten, A., & Oldehinkel, T. (1994). Common mental disorders and disability across cultures: Results from the WHO Collaborative Study on Psychological Problems in General Health Care. *Journal of the American Medical Association, 272*, 1741–1748.

Overholser, J. C. (1998). Cognitive–behavioral treatment of depression: X. Reducing the risk of relapse. *Journal of Contemporary Psychotherapy, 28*, 381–396.

Parry, G., & Shapiro, D. A. (1986). Social support and life events in working class women. *Archives of General Psychiatry, 43*, 315–323.

Paykel, E. S. (1994). Life events, social support and depression. *Acta Psychiatrica Scandinavica, Suppl. 377*, 50–58.

Paykel, E. S. (2001). Continuation and maintenance therapy in depression. *British Medical Journal, 57*, 145–159.

Paykel, E. S., & Cooper, Z. (1992). Life events and social stress. In E. S. Paykel (Ed.), *Handbook of affective disorders* (2nd ed., pp. 147–170). New York: Guilford.

Paykel, E. S., & Hollyman, J. A. (1984). Life events and depression: A psychiatric view. *Trends in Neuroscience, 7*, 478–481.

Paykel, E. S., Scott, J., Teasdale, J. D., Johnson, A. L., Garland, A., Moore, R., et al. (1999). Prevention of relapse in residual depression by cognitive therapy: A controlled trial. *Archives of General Psychiatry, 56*, 829–835.

Perris, C. (1992). Bipolar–unipolar distinction. In E. S. Paykel (Ed.), *Handbook of affective disorders* (2nd ed., pp. 57–75). New York: Guilford.

Rafanelli, C., Park, S. K., & Fava, G. A. (1999). New psychotherapeutic approaches to residual symptoms and relapse prevention in unipolar depression. *Clinical Psychology and Psychotherapy, 6*, 194–201.

Rohde, P., Lewinsohn, P. M., & Seeley, J. R. (1991). Comorbidity of unipolar depression: II: Comorbidity with other mental disorders in adolescents and adults. *Journal of Abnormal Psychology, 100*, 214–222.

Rothschild, A. J. (2000). Sexual side effects of antidepressants. *Journal of Clinical Psychiatry, 61*(Suppl. 11), 28–36.

Ryff, C. D., & Singer, B. (1996). Psychological well-being: Meaning, measurement, and implications for psychotherapy research. *Psychotherapy and Psychosomatics, 65*, 14–23.

Sartorius, N., Ustun, T. B., Lecrubier, Y., & Wittchen, H. (1996). Depression comorbid with anxiety: Results from the WHO study on psychological disorders in primary health care. *British Journal of Psychiatry, 168*(Suppl. 30), 38–43.

Segal, Z. V. (1988). Appraisal of the self-schema construct in cognitive models of depression. *Psychological Bulletin, 103*, 147–162.

Segal, Z. V., Gemar, M., & Williams, S. (1998). Differential cognitive response to a mood challenge following successful cognitive therapy or pharmacotherapy for unipolar depression. *Journal of Abnormal Psychology, 108*, 3–10.

Segal, Z. V., Shaw, B. F., Vella, D. D., & Katz, R. (1992). Cognitive and life stress predictors of relapse in remitted unipolar depressed patients: Test of the congruency hypothesis. *Journal of Abnormal Psychology, 101*, 26–36.

Segal, Z. V., Williams, J. M. G., & Teasdale, J. D. (2002). *Mindfulness-based cognitive therapy for depression: A new approach to preventing relapse*. New York: Guilford.

Shaw, B. F., & Segal, Z. V. (1999). Efficacy, indications, and mechanisms of action of cognitive therapy of depression. In D. S. Janowsky (Ed.), *Psychotherapy indications and outcomes* (pp. 173–195). Washington, DC: American Psychiatric Press.

Stahl, S. M. (1999). Why settle for silver, when you can go for gold? Response vs. recovery as the goal of antidepressant therapy. *Journal of Clinical Psychiatry, 60*, 213–214.

Stahl, S. M. (2000). *Essential psychopharmacology* (2nd ed.). Boston: Cambridge University Press.

Storosum, J. G, van Zwieten, B. J., Vermeulen, H. D. B, Wohlfarth, T., & van den Brink, S. (2001). Relapse and recurrence prevention in major depression: A critical review of placebo-controlled efficacy studies with special emphasis on methodological issues. *European Psychiatry, 16*, 327–335.

Sussman, N., & Ginsberg, D. (1998). Weight gain associated with SSRIs. *Primary Psychiatry*, 28–37. Retrieved July 4, 2003 from http://www.mvelectric.com/ssri

Swindle, R. W., Cronkite, R. C., & Moos, R. H. (1989). Life stressors, social resources, coping, and the 4-year course of unipolar depression. *Journal of Abnormal Psychology, 98*, 468–477.

Tang, T. Z., & DeRubeis, R. J. (1999). Sudden gains and critical sessions in cognitive–behavioral therapy for depression. *Journal of Consulting and Clinical Psychology, 67*, 894–904.

Tang, T. Z., Luborsky, L., & Andrusyna, T. (2002). Sudden gains in recovering from depression: Are they also found in psychotherapies other than cognitive–behavioral therapy? *Journal of Consulting and Clinical Psychology, 70*, 444–447.

Teasdale, J. D. (1999). Emotional processing, three modes of mind and the prevention of relapse in depression. *Behaviour Research and Therapy, 37*(Suppl. 1), 53–77.

Teasdale, J. D., Scott, J., Moore, R. G., Hayhurst, H., Pope, M., & Paykel, E. S. (2001). How does cognitive therapy prevent relapse in residual depression? Evidence from a controlled trial. *Journal of Consulting and Clinical Psychology, 69*, 347–357.

Teasdale, J. D., Segal, Z. V., & Williams, J. M. G. (1995). How does cognitive therapy prevent depressive relapse and why should attentional control (mindfulness) training help? *Behaviour Research and Therapy, 33,* 25–39.

Teasdale, J. D., Segal, Z. V., Williams, J. M. G., Ridgeway, V. A., Soulsby, J. M., & Lau, M. A. (2000). Prevention of relapse/recurrence in major depression by mindfulness-based cognitive therapy. *Journal of Consulting and Clinical Psychology, 68,* 615–623.

Thase, M. E., Nierenberg, A. A., Keller, M. B., & Papagides, J. (2001). Efficacy of mirtazapine for prevention of depressive relapse: A placebo-controlled double-blind trial of recently remitted high-risk patients. *Journal of Clinical Psychiatry, 62,* 782–788.

Thoits, P. (1982). Conceptual, methodological, and theoretical problems in studying social support as a buffer against life stress. *Journal of Health and Social Behavior, 23,* 145–159.

Whisman, M. A. (1993). Mediators and moderators of change in cognitive therapy of depression. *Psychological Bulletin, 114,* 248–265.

Wilson, P. H. (1992a). Relapse prevention: Conceptual and methodological issues. In P. H. Wilson (Ed.), *Principles and practice of relapse prevention* (pp. 1–22). New York: Guilford.

Wilson, P. H. (1992b). Depression. In P. H. Wilson (Ed.), *Principles and practice of relapse prevention* (pp. 128–156). New York: Guilford.

11

THE COMORBIDITY OF ANXIETY AND DEPRESSION, AND THE IMPLICATIONS OF COMORBIDITY FOR PREVENTION

DAVID J. A. DOZOIS, KEITH S. DOBSON, AND HENNY A. WESTRA

Although most of the chapters of this volume and other chapters that deal specifically with anxiety or depression treat these disorders as discrete, it is widely acknowledged that anxiety and depression are in fact highly co-occurring conditions (Mineka, Watson, & Clark, 1998). This co-occurrence manifests itself in the high correlation that has been observed among anxiety and depression measures, as well as in the comorbidity of anxiety-related and depressive diagnoses (see chap. 2, this volume). In this chapter, we review some of the common features of anxiety and depression as well as identify factors that may be specific to either of these disorders. We illustrate that some of the more distal factors (e.g., constitutional variables such as genetics, early childhood experiences) share considerable variance with anxiety and depression. In contrast, some of the more proximal variables are where greater specificity may be found.

Just as anxiety and depression are often presented as discrete phenomena, even though it is recognized that this is often not the case, we also recognize that, although we discuss the variables in this chapter independently, as if they operate in isolation, in truth these variables rarely operate in isolation in the real world. Rather, most of these mechanisms and risk factors relate to, and interact with, one another in complex, dynamic, and reciprocal ways. Thus, a richer understanding of anxiety and depression, and of the prevention of these disorders, necessitates the adoption of a developmental, life span perspective and the use of more complex longitudinal research designs (Ingram & Price, 2001; Mash & Dozois, 2003; National Advisory Mental Health Council [NAMHC] Workgroup on Child and Adolescent Mental Health Intervention Development and Deployment, 2001; NAMHC Workgroup on Mental Disorders Prevention Research, 1998).

In the review that follows, we examine four broad classes of vulnerability factors: parental psychopathology and parenting, biological vulnerability factors, cognitive vulnerability, and stressful life events. Each area is reviewed in turn, with an emphasis on both the shared and the unique risk implications for anxiety and depression. In a final section of the chapter, we also examine the implications of these issues for prevention models in this area.

PARENTAL PSYCHOPATHOLOGY AND PARENTING

In this section, we review the growing literature on the role of parents and parenting as risk factors for anxiety and depression. Several issues emerge in this context: the manner in which parent and child reports concur, the increased risk of anxiety and depression in children of parents with those disorders, and studies of parental behavior. Each of these areas is discussed in turn.

Concordance of Parent and Child Mood and Anxiety Disorders

A number of studies have examined the degree of concordance between parents' and children's expressions of emotional disturbance, often of both depression and anxiety concurrently. In these studies, researchers have used two types of methodology: top down (i.e., investigating rates of dysfunction in children of depressed or anxious parents) and bottom up (i.e., examining dysfunction in parents of depressed or anxious children). Both types of studies have consistently reflected strong concordance rates between parents and children with regard to emotional distress, highlighting parental psychopathology as a significant risk factor for emotional difficulty in children. In fact, parental psychopathology has emerged as one of the strongest risk factors for later emotional disturbance in children (Goodman & Gotlib, 1999; Hammen, 2000; Wickramaratne & Weissman, 1998). Although disorder-specific transmission appears to exist, particularly for anxiety, these data are inconsistent, and the bulk of the evidence is consistent with the transmission of a generalized vulnerability for emotional disorders in children of parents with anxiety or depression.

Children of Depressed or Anxious Parents

Most of the research on concordance rates between parent and child psychopathology has used a top-down methodology. These studies consistently demonstrate that parental emotional disturbance confers a heightened risk of psychopathology in offspring. Using structured diagnostic interviews of parents and children, Beidel and Turner (1997) demonstrated that only 10% of children with normal parents had a psychiatric diagnosis, compared with 36% to 45% of children with an anxious or depressed parent. Significantly higher rates of childhood anxiety also have been found in samples of parents with anxiety, depression, and mixed anxiety/depression, compared with nonpsychiatric control participants (e.g., Biederman et al., 2001; Lieb et al., 2000; Unnewehr, Schneider, Floring, & Margraf, 1998; Warner, Mufson, & Weissman, 1995). In comparison to control participants, significantly higher rates of mood disorders have also been observed in children of depressed parents (Hammen, Burge, & Stansbury, 1990; Hammen, 2000; Dierker, Merikangas, & Szatmari, 1998; Lewinsohn, Rohde, Seeley, Klein, & Gotlib, 2000). In addition, higher rates of other types of disorders, such as behavioral problems and medical dysfunction, have been identified in children of depressed parents, compared with control participants (Beidel & Turner, 1997; Hammen, 1991; Weissman, Warner, Wickramaratne, Moreau, & Olfson, 1997). In general, the psychopathology of children of anxious parents tends to be anxiety related, whereas children of depressed parents exhibit a wider range of psychopathology, including mood, anxiety, and other behavioral problems.

Another consistent finding that emerges from the literature is the increased risk conferred on children by comorbidity in parents. For example, Beidel and Turner (1997) found the highest rates of disturbance in the offspring of parents with comorbid anxiety–depression, with 45% of these children having a psychiatric diagnosis. Using odds ratio calculations and comparisons with children of normal parents, these investigators noted that children of parents with either anxiety or depression were five times more likely to have a psychiatric diagnosis, whereas children of parents with comorbid anxiety–depression were almost seven times more likely to carry a psychiatric diagnosis. The latter group of children was also more likely to have been referred for treatment than were children of parents with either anxiety or depression alone.

Such findings are consistent with the results of studies showing a significant increase in the risk for emotional disturbance in children, *both* of whose parents had an emotional disorder, compared with children for whom only a single parent experienced anxiety or depression. For example, Merikangas, Avenevoli, Dierker, and Grillon (1999) reported a threefold increased risk of social phobia in children with both parents with an anxiety disorder, compared with youths with only one parent with an anxiety disorder (see also Dierker et al., 1998). Similarly, in a sample of parents with depression, Nomura, Warner, and Wickramaratne (2001) estimated the risk of depression to be nearly seven times higher, and the risk of anxiety over eight times higher, in children when both parents had depression, compared with the risk to children when neither parent had major depressive disorder (MDD). Lewinsohn et al. (2000) also identified an increased proportion of family members with MDD as a significant risk factor in the prediction of recurrence of depression in adulthood in those with adolescent-onset depression.

Parents of Anxious or Depressed Children

Elevated rates of parental emotional disturbance have been identified in studies examining children with anxiety or depression. Anxious children are significantly more likely to have one or more parents who meet the diagnostic criteria for an anxiety disorder, compared with the parents of control children without psychopathology (Cooper & Eke, 1999; Last, Hersen, Kazdin, Orvaschel, and Perrin, 1991; Martin, Cabrol, Bouvard, Lepine, & Mouren-Simeoni, 1999). For example, Last et al. (1991) found that 40% of parents of anxious children had an anxiety disorder, compared with 18% of parents of normal children in the control group. Depression is also significantly more common among parents of depressed children. Ferro, Verdeli, Pierre, and Weissman (2000), for instance, found that 31% of mothers who brought children in for outpatient treatment of depression screened positive for a current psychiatric disorder, including 14% with major depression (59% subthreshold for major depression) and 17% with an anxiety disorder. Hammen (2000) has reported that in a sample of depressed children and adolescents referred for treatment, fully 70% of their mothers had a lifetime history of MDD or dysthymic disorder, and 30% were currently depressed.

Studies using longitudinal methodologies have also found a high concordance between parents and children in rates of psychopathology. In a 10-year longitudinal study, Wickramaratne and Weissman (1998) reported that, compared with the condition in normal control participants, parental MDD was associated with an eightfold increase in childhood-onset MDD and a fivefold increase in early adult onset of the condition, with a threefold increase in anxiety. The highest risk was observed in young children of parents with a mood disorder onset before the age of 30, who exhibited a thirteenfold increase in the risk of childhood-onset depression. These findings are consistent with those of another study showing that young children with depressed parents are at a substantially increased risk of developing depression by age 21, compared with those without depressed parents in childhood (Reinherz, Giaconia, Hauf, Wasserman, & Paradis, 2000). Moreover, of those individuals who went on to develop depression, 33% were found to have at least one parent with a history of depression, compared with 17% of children who did not develop psychiatric problems.

Overall, the results of these investigations consistently reveal that parental psychopathology is a substantive risk factor in children—particularly, young children—for the development of anxiety and mood disorders. This risk is greatest among parents with comorbid psychiatric emotional disorders and in situations where both parents are affected by mood or anxiety disorders. In all likelihood, a combination of genetic, biological, and psychosocial factors operate to explain the high concordance rates of parent and child psychopathology.

Parental Behavior

A number of studies have investigated the hypothesized influence of parental behavior on children's risk for psychopathology through direct observation of interactions between parents and children. Nolen-Hoeksema, Wolfson, Mumme, and Guskin (1995), for example, compared a group of young children with depressed mothers with a comparable group of children with nondepressed mothers, on a jointly completed puzzle task. They found that low degrees of maternal responsiveness and encouragement, and not the presence of depression per se, accounted for differences in helplessness in children during the task. Reiss et al. (1995) reported findings from a large community sample of families in which low warmth and low support, as well as a high degree of monitoring or control, were predictive of adolescent depressive symptoms. In general, depressed mothers' interactions with their children are characterized by more inconsistency, greater criticism, more negativity, and less involvement than matched control participants (for reviews, see Downey & Coyne, 1990; Goodman & Gotlib, 1999).

Anxious mothers' interactions with their children have been observed to be less warm and positive, more critical and catastrophic, and less granting of autonomy, compared with nonanxious mothers' interactions. Dumas, LaFreniere, and Serketich (1995), for instance, observed that mothers of anxious children were significantly more controlling and likely to exercise control through negative behaviors (being coercive or nonresponsive) and negative affect (e.g., criticism or sarcasm) during the completion of a board game task than were mothers of either aggressive or socially competent preschool children. Anxious children have also been found to adopt more anxious interpretations of ambiguous scenarios following discussion with their parents, compared with nonpsychiatric controls (Barrett, Rapee, & Dadds, 1993; Chorpita, Albano, & Barlow, 1996), suggesting that parental behavior may play a significant role in cognitive responding in anxious children.

Self-report methods, albeit weaker methodologically than the observational studies just cited, also consistently support this relationship between parenting behavior and anxiety or depression. Stark, Humphrey, Crook, and Lewis (1990) had 51 children diagnosed with either an anxiety or a mood disorder report on their family interactions. Compared with nonpsychiatric control participants, these children rated their parents as less supportive and less willing to involve them in family decisions. Muris, Meesters, Merckelbach, and Hülsenbeck (2000) also observed that increased worry in primary school children was associated with child-reported parental behaviors of rejection and parental anxiety. Compared with nonsocially anxious peers, socially anxious adolescents report that their parents are more socially avoidant and overly concerned with others' opinions (Caster, Inderbitzen, & Hope, 1999). In general, such studies consistently report that anxious children depict their parents as exerting excessive control, being less supportive, and failing to promote independence. Retrospective self-reports of adult patients with anxiety and mood disorders relate perceptions of less parental affection and greater parental overprotection and control in childhood in anxious and depressed adult samples, compared with control participants (Gerlsma, Emmelkamp, & Arrindell, 1990; Silove, Parker, Hadzi-Pavlovic, Manicavasagar, & Blaszcynski, 1991).

Although parenting behavior may be one mechanism through which parental psychopathology contributes to the risk of emotional disturbance in children, the pathways from parental disturbance to emotional problems in children, adolescents, and adults are complex and varied. Goodman and Gotlib (1999) outline a developmental model that attempts to account for the transmission of depression between parents and children. Factors identified as contributory include heritability, innate dysfunctional neuroregulatory mechanisms, exposure to negative maternal cognitions and behaviors, and the stressful context surrounding children's lives (e.g., high levels of parental marital conflict). Goodman and Gotlib also outline a number of hypothesized protective factors, including child characteristics (e.g., higher intelligence) and the presence of other supportive adults. Barlow (2002) has proposed a comprehensive model that includes a role for early life experience with uncontrollability as pivotal to increased vulnerability for later anxiety or depression. In particular, parental control and experiences with uncontrollability are hypothesized to interfere with children's development of autonomy and self-efficacy and their acquisition of effective problem-solving skills that, in turn, render them more vulnerable to dealing unsuccessfully with stress and to later depression and anxiety.

BIOLOGICAL VULNERABILITY FACTORS

As we have seen, a number of studies of children and adults suggest that anxiety and depression often cluster in families. These studies are useful inasmuch as they indicate whether different disorders have discrete patterns of familial transmission. As Garber and Flynn (2001) aptly point out, however, they do not help to ascertain whether familial aggregation is due to shared genes or shared psychosocial influences, such as maladaptive parenting or the modeling of maladaptive cognitive styles. Fortunately, more methodologically satisfying bivariate twin analyses have been conducted.

On the basis of these more sophisticated twin studies, it appears that, at least for some of the anxiety disorders, there may be a common genetic link with major depression (cf. Eley & Stevenson, 1999; Roy, Neale, Pedersen, Mathé, & Kendler, 1995; Thapar & McGuffin, 1997). For example, Thapar and McGuffin reported that most of the covariation in anxious and depressive symptoms in a study of 172 pairs of twins (ages 8–16 years) could be explained by a common set of genetic factors. Two large-scale twin studies have also revealed that genetic factors were entirely shared between generalized anxiety disorder (GAD) and MDD. The likelihood that an individual would ultimately develop depression or generalized anxiety was, however, also due to environmental circumstances (Kendler, Neale, Kessler, Heath, & Eaves, 1992; Roy et al., 1995).

Genes may predispose an individual to general distress that is later manifested as either anxiety or depression, depending on the environmental circumstances faced by the individual. Eley and Stevenson (1999), for instance, assessed 395 pairs of same-sex twins aged 8 to 16 years. Using self-report measures, the two researchers found that genetic factors seemed to account for the majority of the variance in the correlation between anxiety and depression, but that specificity to either disorder was more related to environmental influences. An important qualification of this conclusion, however, is due to the fact that most twin studies have focused on GAD to the relative exclusion of other anxiety disorders. More specific research on these other anxiety disorders is needed to assess the conclusion more fully.

In sum, much of the covariation and comorbidity between anxiety and depression may be explained by common genetic influences (Thapar & McGuffin, 1997). However, at least in the case of the relationship between GAD and MDD (Kendler et al., 1992; Roy et al., 1995), genes seem to predispose an individual to general distress (being "high strung" or nervous), rather than contributing differentially to the development of anxiety or depression (Barlow, 2002). It is also possible that depression represents a more severe variant of initial anxiety, perhaps arising out of general negative affect. At least three sets of findings are congruent with this idea. First, data indicate that the offspring of individuals with comorbid anxiety and depression tend to show patterns of psychopathology similar to those of children of depressed parents (cf. Thapar & McGuffin, 1997). Second, in the temporal relationship between anxiety and depression, anxiety often precedes depression. Third, related literature suggests that the transition from anxiety to depression may follow the cognitive shift from helplessness to hopelessness (see *Helplessness and Hopelessness* section, later in this chapter; see also Beck et al., 2001). As a final note, it is important to emphasize that, although the data demonstrating a genetic link between anxiety and depression are strong, some studies have also shown that a more modest relationship may exist between the two disorders (see Mineka et al., 1998).

COGNITIVE VULNERABILITY

A number of approaches have been developed in which the cognitive content or information processing between anxiety and depression have been compared. In this section, four such approaches are reviewed, with a focus on both the common and the unique elements of these disorders.

Content Specificity and Information Processing

A. T. Beck proposed that anxiety and depression are governed by similar cognitive processes, but that they vary in content (Beck & Clark, 1988; Clark, Beck, & Alford, 1999). Anxiety, held Beck, is related to a future orientation with a focus on cognitions of harm or danger, whereas the emphasis in depression is more on the past, with the content of cognition relating to loss, deprivation, worthlessness, and hopelessness. Research in experimental psychopathology has generally supported this content-specificity hypothesis (e.g., Beck & Perkins, 2001; Clark et al., 1999; Westra & Kuiper, 1997). Westra and Kuiper (1997, Experiment 1), for instance, conducted a study in which undergraduates made self-descriptive ratings on several adjectives sampled from the depression, anxiety, bulimia, and the Type A personality literature. Partial correlations revealed that dysphoria was uniquely related to adjectives pertaining to loss, failure, and hopelessness, whereas the themes in anxiety centered on threat and stigmatization. Using a visual probe detection task (Experiment 2), these researchers also found content-specificity effects for selective attention in dysphoria, anxiety, and bulimia. On an incidental recognition measure, enhanced memory performance was found for domain-specific adjectives, but only in the dysphoric and bulimic groups. Greenberg and Alloy (1989) performed a more stringent analysis of the content-specificity hypothesis by comparing depressed individuals, anxious individuals, and control participants on depression-relevant, anxiety-relevant, and control adjectives. Depressed participants were unique in their balanced endorsements and processing of positive and negative content. Anxious participants showed an effect unique to anxiety-relevant words. Although the content-specificity hypothesis has received support, the findings are not unequivocal and are typically more robust in clinical than in nonclinical samples (Clark, Steer, Beck, & Snow, 1996).

The idea that anxiety and depression are related to similar information-processing mechanisms has also been reported in the literature, although not consistently. Although anxiety and depression both involve attentional and other cognitive processes, anxiety seems to relate more to automatic processing and attentional biases, whereas depression is associated more with strategic and elaborative processing and memory biases (Clark et al., 1999; Mineka & Nugent, 1995). In other words, individuals with anxiety are said to be in an *orienting* mode, whereas those with depression operate more in an *oriented* mode (Mineka et al., 1998).

Negative Affect and Cognition

Different models have attempted to elaborate the linkage between cognition and negative affect. In this section, we review the tripartite model, as it is a major paradigm that has attempted to account for the relationship between anxiety and depression. According to the tripartite model, there are both shared and unique affective features of anxiety and depression. The two disorders are similar to one another in terms of being characterized by high *negative affect,* a construct that is related to behavioral inhibition, neuroticism, and anxious apprehension (Barlow, 2002). Negative affect is characterized by distress, anger, disgust, fear, and worry. *Positive affect* in contrast, appears to be specific to depression and is described by mood descriptors such as "excited," "delighted," "interested," "enthusiastic," and "proud" (see Mineka, Pury, & Luten, 1995). Depressed individuals differ from anxious persons by exhibiting low positive affect. The third branch of the model is *hyperphysiological arousal,* which is hypothetically specific to anxiety.

The tripartite model has been well supported empirically (Beck et al., 2001; Brown, Chorpita, & Barlow, 1998; Dozois & Dobson, 2001; Eley & Stevenson, 1999; but see also Wetherell, Gatz, & Pedersen, 2001). To date, the most comprehensive analysis of this model is by Brown and colleagues (1998), who investigated various competing models as well, using confirmatory factor analysis in a sample of 350 outpatients. The results indicated that the most parsimonious model was one in which there were two higher order factors consisting of negative affect and positive affect. Negative affect was nonspecifically related to both mood and anxiety disorders. Compared with anxiety, depression was characterized by low positive affect. Hyperphysiological arousal has recently been reconceptualized in terms of its specificity to anxiety. Formerly hypothesized to be associated with all anxiety disorders, the construct now is held to be related primarily to panic disorder (see Barlow, 2002).

Worry and Rumination, and Self-Focused Attention

Another commonality between anxiety and depression is negative repetitive thinking. A number of researchers have found that depression is related to rumination and self-focused attention. Rumination has been associated with longer and more severe episodes of depression or dysphoria (Nolen-Hoeksema, 2000), biased and negative interpretations of hypothetical scenarios, less optimism regarding future positive events (Lyubomirsky & Nolen-Hoeksema, 1995), excessive seeking of support (Nolen-Hoeksema, 2000) and impaired problem-solving ability (Lyubomirsky & Nolen-Hoeksema, 1995). Nolen-Hoeksema (2000) argued that rumination is conceptually distinct from self-focused attention by its emphasis on depressive symptoms rather than on negative experiences per se. However, self-focused attention also makes the significance of adverse events more pronounced and interacts reciprocally with dysphoria (e.g., Pyszczynski, Holt, & Greenberg, 1987).

If rumination and self-focused attention are categorized under the rubric of negative repetitive thought, then anxiety and depression appear to share that phenomenon. For example, Nitschke, Heller, Imig, McDonald, and Miller (2001) found that "anxious apprehension involves worry and is characterized by verbal rumination, typically about possible negative outcomes of future events" (p. 3). Thus, although anxiety and depression may be differentiated by the specific content of the repetitive thinking, the underlying processes may be similar (Beck et al., 2001; Segerstrom, Tsao, Alden, & Craske, 2000). This postulation of similarity is also consistent with findings that the most common comorbid diagnosis in GAD is MDD (Barlow, 2002). Consistent with the notion that negative repetitive thinking is represented cognitively in both disorders are approaches to prevent relapse in depression (Segal, Williams, & Teasdale, 2002) and anxiety (Papageorgiou & Wells, 2000), which specifically involve attention control training and which attempt to interfere with negative ruminative processes.

Helplessness and Hopelessness

Another common mechanism in anxiety and depression appears to be a diminished sense of control (Barlow, 2002; Mineka et al., 1998). Mineka and Nugent (1995), for example, discussed a biphasic response to stressful events, in which anxiety and agitation occur first, followed by depression and despair. Increased helplessness appears to be related to anxiety, and when helplessness becomes prolonged, a person may eventually give up, lose hope, and become depressed. Beck et al. (2001) found that hopelessness showed specificity as a cognitive correlate of depression, whereas worry was nonspecifically related to both anxiety and depression. These findings are congruent with the tripartite model, as the researchers also found that worry was a relatively nonspecific cognitive component of high negative affect. Hopelessness, by contrast, was related to low positive affect and differentiated significantly between depression and anxiety. As Barlow (2002) noted, depression may be an extreme psychological manifestation of high unpredictability and high uncontrollability.

STRESSFUL LIFE EVENTS

The majority of people who experience a major depressive episode report the prior occurrence of a severe stressful life event (Brown & Harris, 1989; Hammen, 1988; van Os & Jones, 1999). Environmental stress has been associated with the onset and occurrence of anxiety symptoms in children and adolescents (cf. Nolen-Hoeksema, Girgus, & Seligman, 1992). Specific stressful life events are also clearly factors in the development of some phobias (Öst, 1987; Thyer, Neese, Cameron, & Curtis, 1985) and posttraumatic stress disorder (Barlow, 2002).

The researcher needs to take into account the context of the individual's life events in considering the impact of stressful events in the etiology of emotional disturbance. Rarely, though, is this a simple direct effect, and most theorists have stressed the importance of the person–environment interaction, in which individual factors (e.g., cognitive style, personality variables) mediate the impact of stress. Moreover, the reciprocal nature of psychopathology and stress has also been highlighted by investigators. For example, both children (Kashani & Orvaschel, 1990) and adults (Hammen et al., 1987) with anxiety or depression report experiencing more stressful life events compared with what control participants report experiencing.

There is evidence that individuals with repeated and chronic emotional disturbance become more sensitive to the negative effects of stressful life events. For example, sensitivity to stress increases with the number of depressive episodes (Kessler & Magee, 1994) and a history of mental disorder has been found to modify individual response to stress such that fewer stressful life events are needed to trigger future mood episodes (Post, 1992; van Os & Jones, 1999). Hammen, Henry, Daley, and Burge (1999) have also observed that depressed women with exposure to early adversity (violence, parental death, divorce) were less likely to experience a severe stressor prior to the onset of depression and had lower levels of stress compared with depressed women who did not experience such adversity. On the basis of these findings, the authors argued that early acquisition of vulnerability is essential to later expression of psychopathology.

Among the numerous stressful life experiences that have been linked to increased expression of emotional distress, anxiety, and depression in children are change of school (Braden & Hightower, 1998), low socioeconomic status (Beidel & Turner, 1997; Fergusson, Horwood, & Lawton, 1990), parental death (Finkelstein, 1988), larger family size (Reinherz et al., 1993), divorce and parental separation (Hetherington, Bridges, & Insabella, 1998), violence (Briggs-Gowan, McCue Horwitz, Schwab-Stone, Leventhal, & Leaf, 2000), strained peer relationships and bullying (Bond, Carlin, Thomas, Rubin, & Patton, 2001), family conflict (Rueter, Scaramella, Wallace, & Conger, 1999), and financial stress (Briggs-Gowan et al., 2000). In adulthood, particular stressors related to increased risk of emotional disturbance include unemployment (Caplan, Vinokur, & Price, 1997; Comino, Silove, Manicavasagar, Harris, & Harris, 2000), financial strain (Kessler, Turner, & House, 1987), marital instability and divorce (Bruce & Kim, 1992; Gotlib & Beach, 1995; Kessler, Walters, & Forthofer, 1998), and single parenthood (Briggs-Gowan et al., 2000).

Although numerous stressors have been implicated in the expression of anxiety and depression, interpersonal stressors have been highlighted as particularly important in this regard (Joiner & Coyne, 1999). For example, interpersonal variables are among the best predictors of depressive relapse and chronicity (Joiner, 2000). In their longitudinal study, Reinherz et al. (2000) reported that 41% of unpopular 9-year-old children had developed depression by age 21, compared with only 17% of their more popular peers. Moreover, there is evidence that, at least in depression, being depressed introduces a variety of interpersonal changes (e.g., increased self-focus, conversational negativity). These interaction styles have been found to play a role in perpetuating dysphoria through eliciting feelings of depression, anxiety, and hostility in others (Joiner, 2000).

Family disruption has repeatedly been linked to increased risk of, and perpetuation of, emotional disturbance in children. Parental divorce is one of the most common and serious negative life events confronting children and adolescents (Hetherington et al., 1998) and is associated with many deleterious effects in children, including depression and anxiety. Marital discord is, in fact, more strongly related to child psychopathology than is maternal depression (Goodman & Gotlib, 1999), and children have been found to be sensitive to mere exposure to marital conflict, independently of any effects that such conflicts might have on parenting (Cummings & Davies, 1994). In their longitudinal study of families, Rueter et al. (1999) found that among adolescents, level of disagreements with parents and changes in such levels were strongly related to the presence of internalizing symptoms and the onset of disorder by age 20. Similarly, Lewinsohn et al. (2000) identified conflict with parents as a significant risk factor in the prediction of recurrence of major depression in adulthood in females with adolescent-onset depression.

Investigators have postulated that various protective factors may mediate the deleterious impact of the preceding stressors on the individual. Among the factors cited are the presence of a supportive parent (Goodman & Gotlib, 1999), level of social support (White, Bruce, Farrell, & Kliewer, 1998), and, in children, characteristics of cognitive ability (Crow, Done,

& Sacker, 1995; van Os, Lewis, Jones, & Murray, 1997) and coping skills (Donovan & Spence, 2000).

THE IMPLICATIONS OF COMORBIDITY FOR PREVENTION

The purpose of this chapter has been to review some of the major factors that exhibit either commonality or distinctiveness between anxiety and depression. As we have demonstrated, a number of factors do show commonality. Some represent common features of the topography of these conditions (e.g., high negative affect), but many also imply common risk factors. The general pattern appears to be that, whereas some factors confer risk for both anxiety and depression, extra factors need to be present for depression to ensue. Also, as has been noted in other chapters, anxiety itself is often a precursor to depression and hence, in and of itself, confers risk.

These common and specific factors lead to several implications as regards prevention. First, it seems apparent that focusing on common factors in prevention can reap a larger benefit than can intervening with risk factors that are specific to only one or the other condition. For example, intervening with young children of parents with anxiety or depression, particularly if both parents are affected, may hold promise in reducing rates of future dysfunction in that group. This argument assumes, of course, that common factors can be identified early enough for intervention to be effective. It may be, however, that once anxiety or depression symptoms emerge and prevention efforts shift to secondary, or indicated, modes of intervention, a focus on common elements will not be as effective.

Second—and although this inference is somewhat more speculative than the first—it seems that, to the extent that prevention efforts have to be focused on either anxiety or depression alone, it might be more efficacious to target those related to anxiety. Inasmuch as anxiety often precedes depression (see Mineka et al., 1998), targeting anxiety and its related symptoms may have preventive implications for depression, whereas the reverse is less likely. Incorporating recent advancements in the management of worry (e.g., Ladouceur et al., 2000), for instance, may have particular promise for preventing *both* anxiety and depression, whereas coping with loss might be effective only for the prevention of depression.

A third direction for future work is to examine the specific factors that are either common to both anxiety and depression, or specific to each, and to systematically vary which factors are targeted in prevention efforts. Such research could help to establish the most effective combination of intervention practices or targets that will minimize the likelihood of dysfunction.

A fourth implication of the comorbidity between anxiety and depression is that programs which target one or the other disorder should look for indirect effects in the other domain. For example, treating a given anxiety disorder produces a decline in other anxiety and mood disorders that are not specifically addressed in treatment (Brown, Antony, & Barlow, 1995). The hypothetical causal direction from anxiety to depression can be evaluated effectively only if data about such indirect effects are gathered. Clinicians and researchers working in these areas are encouraged to assess outcomes comprehensively. Finally, in addition to investigating prevention programs in the presence of specific positive risk factors, further efforts might be directed toward identifying and enhancing common or unique protective factors that may limit the probability of developing anxiety or depression or that may buffer the severity of these disorders.

As the literature and theory related to common and distinct elements of anxiety and depression grows, and in particular as longitudinal research related to risk and resilience factors is expanded, we may expect to be able to develop more comprehensive and focused intervention strategies. It is possible that our knowledge related to specific risk factors will lead to highly effective, but circumscribed, prevention efforts. An interesting question for future examination will be whether the efficacy of prevention will be traded off against the specificity of those efforts—that as prevention efforts become broader in their focus (i.e., addressing both risk factors for anxiety and risk factors for depression), the efficacy of those efforts decreases. Such results might call for an integrated approach, which targets both common and distinct factors, to be maximally efficient *and* effective. Clearly, considerable work needs to be conducted in order for researchers to be more authoritative about such matters.

REFERENCES

Barlow, D. H. (2002). *Anxiety and its disorders* (2nd ed.). New York: Guilford.

Barrett, P. M., Rapee, R. M., & Dadds, M. R. (1993, November). *Cognitive and family processes in childhood anxiety*. Paper presented at the 27th annual convention of the Association for Advancement of Behavior Therapy, Atlanta, GA.

Beck, A. T., & Clark, D. A. (1988). Anxiety and depression: An information processing perspective. *Anxiety Research, 1*, 23–36.

Beck, R., & Perkins, T. S. (2001). Cognitive content-specificity for anxiety and depression: A meta-analysis. *Cognitive Therapy and Research, 25*, 651–663.

Beck, R., Perkins, T. S., Holder, R., Robbins, M., Gray, M., & Allison, S. H. (2001). The cognitive and emotional phenomenology of depression and anxiety: Are worry and hopelessness the cognitive correlates of NA and PA? *Cognitive Therapy and Research, 25*, 829–838.

Beidel, D. C., & Turner, S. M. (1997). At risk for anxiety: Psychopathology in the offspring of anxious parents. *Journal of the American Academy of Child and Adolescent Psychiatry, 36*, 918–924.

Biederman, J., Faraone, S. V., Hirshfeld-Becker, D. R., Friedman, D., Robin, J. A., & Rosenbaum, J. F. (2001). Patterns of psychopathology and dysfunction in high-risk children of parents with panic disorder and major depression. *American Journal of Psychiatry, 158,* 49–57.

Bond, L., Carlin, J. B., Thomas, L., Rubin, K., & Patton, G. (2001). Does bullying cause emotional problems? A prospective study of young teenagers. *British Medical Journal, 323,* 480–484.

Braden, J. P., & Hightower, A. D. (1998). Prevention. In R. J. Morris & T. R. Kratochwill (Eds.), *The practice of child therapy* (3rd ed., pp. 510–539). Needham Heights, MA: Allyn & Bacon.

Briggs-Gowan, M. J., McCue Horwitz, S., Schwab-Stone, M. E., Leventhal, J. M., & Leaf, P. J. (2000). Mental health in pediatric settings: Distribution of disorders and factors related to service use. *Journal of the American Academy of Child and Adolescent Psychiatry, 39,* 841–849.

Brown, G. W., & Harris, T. O. (1989). Depression. In G. Brown and T. Harris (Eds.), *Life events and illness* (pp. 49–93). New York: Guilford.

Brown, T. A., Antony, M. M., & Barlow, D. H. (1995). Diagnostic comorbidity in panic disorder: Effect on treatment outcome and course of comorbid diagnosis following treatment. *Journal of Consulting and Clinical Psychology, 63,* 408–418.

Brown, T. A., Chorpita, B. F., & Barlow, D. H. (1998). Structural relationships among dimensions of the DSM–IV anxiety and mood disorders and dimensions of negative affect, positive affect, and autonomic arousal. *Journal of Abnormal Psychology, 107,* 179–192.

Bruce, M. L., & Kim, K. M. (1992). Differences in the effects of divorce on major depression in men and women. *American Journal of Psychiatry, 149,* 914–917.

Caplan, R. D., Vinokur, A. D., & Price, R. H. (1997). From job loss to reemployment: Field experiments in prevention-focused coping. In G. W. Albee & T. P. Gullotta (Eds.), *Primary prevention works* (pp. 341–379). Thousand Oaks, CA: Sage.

Caster, J., Inderbitzen, H., & Hope, D. (1999). Relationship between youth and parent perceptions of family environment and social anxiety. *Journal of Anxiety Disorders, 13,* 237–251.

Chorpita, B. F., Albano, A. M., & Barlow, D. H. (1996). Cognitive processing in children: Relation to anxiety and family influences. *Journal of Clinical Child Psychology, 25,* 170–176.

Clark, D. A., Beck, A. T., & Alford, B. A. (1999). *Scientific foundations of cognitive theory and therapy of depression.* Philadelphia: Wiley.

Clark, D. A., Steer, R. A., Beck, A. T., & Snow, D. (1996). Is the relationship between anxious and depressive cognitions and symptoms linear or curvilinear? *Cognitive Therapy and Research, 20,* 135–154.

Comino, E. J., Silove, D., Manicavasagar, V., Harris, E., & Harris, M. F. (2000). Agreement in symptoms of anxiety and depression between patients and GPs: The influence of ethnicity. *Family Practice, 18,* 71–77.

Cooper, P., & Eke, M. (1999). Childhood shyness and maternal social phobia: A community study. *British Journal of Psychiatry, 174,* 439–443.

Crow, T. J., Done, D. J., & Sacker, A. (1995). Birth cohort study of the antecedents of psychosis: Ontogeny as witness to phylogenetic origins. In H. Hafner and W. F. Gattaz (Eds.), *Search for the causes of schizophrenia III* (pp. 3–21). Berlin, Germany: Springer.

Cummings, E. M., & Davies, P. T. (1994). Maternal depression and child development. *Journal of Child Psychology and Psychiatry, 35,* 73–112.

Dierker, L. C., Merikangas, K. R., & Szatmari, P. (1998). Influence of parental concordance for psychiatric disorders on psychopathology in offspring. *Journal of the American Academy of Child and Adolescent Psychiatry, 38,* 280–288.

Donovan, C. L., & Spence, S. H. (2000). Prevention of childhood anxiety disorders. *Clinical Psychology Review, 20,* 509–531.

Downey, G., & Coyne, J. C. (1990). Children of depressed parents: An integrative review. *Psychological Bulletin, 108,* 50–76.

Dozois, D. J. A., & Dobson, K. S. (2001). Information processing and cognitive organization in unipolar depression: Specificity and comorbidity issues. *Journal of Abnormal Psychology, 110,* 236–246.

Dumas, J. E., LaFreniere, P. J., & Serketich, W. J. (1995). "Balance of power": A transactional analysis of control in mother–child dyads involving socially competent, aggressive, and anxious children. *Journal of Abnormal Psychology, 104,* 104–113.

Eley, T. C., & Stevenson, J. (1999). Using genetic analyses to clarify the distinction between depressive and anxious symptoms in children. *Journal of Abnormal Child Psychology, 27,* 105–114.

Fergusson, D. M., Horwood, L. J., & Lawton, J. M. (1990). Vulnerability to childhood problems and family social background. *Journal of Child Psychology and Psychiatry, 31,* 1145–1160.

Ferro, T., Verdeli, H., Pierre, F., & Weissman, M. M. (2000). Screening for depression in mothers bringing their offspring for evaluation or treatment of depression. *American Journal of Psychiatry, 157,* 375–379.

Finkelstein, H. (1988). The long-term effects of early parent death: A review. *Journal of Clinical Psychology, 44,* 3–9.

Garber, J., & Flynn, C. (2001). Vulnerability to depression in childhood and adolescence. In R. E. Ingram & J. M. Price (Eds.), *Vulnerability to psychopathology: Risk across the lifespan* (pp. 175–225). New York: Guilford.

Gerlsma, C., Emmelkamp, P. M. G., and Arrindell, W. A. (1990). Anxiety, depression, and perception of early parenting: A meta-analysis. *Clinical Psychology Review, 10,* 251–277.

Goodman, S. H., & Gotlib, I. H. (1999). Risk for psychopathology in the children of depressed mothers: A developmental model for understanding mechanisms of transmission. *Psychological Review, 106,* 458–490.

Gotlib, I. H., & Beach, S. R. H. (1995). A marital/family discord model of depression: Implications for therapeutic intervention. In N. S. Jacobson & A. S. Gurman (Eds.), *Clinical handbook of couple therapy* (pp. 411–436). New York: Guilford.

Greenberg, M. S., & Alloy, L. B. (1989). Depression versus anxiety: Processing of self- and other-referent information. *Cognition and Emotion, 3,* 207–223.

Hammen, C. (1988). Self cognitions, stressful events, and the prediction of depression in children of depressed mothers. *Journal of Abnormal Child Psychology, 16,* 347–360.

Hammen, C. (1991). *Depression runs in families: The social context of risk and resilience in children of depressed mothers.* New York: Springer-Verlag.

Hammen, C. (2000). Interpersonal factors in an emerging developmental model of depression. In S. L. Johnson, A. Hayes, T. M. Field, N. Schneiderman, and P. McCobe (Eds.), *Stress, coping, and depression* (pp. 71–88). London: Lawrence Erlbaum.

Hammen, C., Burge, D., & Stansbury, K. (1990). Relationship of mother and child variables to child outcomes in a high risk sample: A causal modelling analysis. *Developmental Psychology, 26,* 24–30.

Hammen, C., Gorson, D., Burge, D., Adrian, C., Jaenicke, C., & Hiroto, D. (1987). Maternal affective disorders, illness, and stress: Risk for children's psychopathology. *American Journal of Psychiatry, 144,* 736–741.

Hammen, C., Henry, R., Daley, S., & Burge, D. (1999). *Sensitization to stressful life events as a function of early adversity.* Manuscript under review.

Hetherington, E. M., Bridges, M., & Insabella, G. M. (1998). What matters? What does not? Five perspectives on the association between marital transitions and children's adjustment. *American Psychologist, 53,* 167–184.

Ingram, R. E., & Price, J. M. (Eds.). (2001). *Vulnerability to psychopathology: Risk across the lifespan.* New York: Guilford.

Joiner, T. E., Jr. (2000). Depression's vicious scree: Self-propagating and erosive processes in depression chronicity. *Clinical Psychology: Science & Practice, 7,* 203–218.

Joiner, T., & Coyne, J. C. (Eds.). (1999). *The interactional nature of depression.* Washington, DC: American Psychological Association.

Kashani, J. H., & Orvaschel, H. (1990). A community study of anxiety in children and adolescents. *American Journal of Psychiatry, 147,* 313–318.

Kendler, K. S., Neale, M. C., Kessler, R. C., Heath, A. C., & Eaves, L. J. (1992). Major depression and generalized anxiety disorder: Same genes, (partly) different environments? *Archives of General Psychiatry, 49,* 716–722.

Kessler, R. C., & Magee, W. J. (1994). The disaggregation of vulnerability to depression as a function of determinants of onset and recurrence. In W. R. Avison & I. H. Gotlib (Eds.), *Stress and mental health: Contemporary issues and prospects for the future* (pp. 239–258). New York: Plenum.

Kessler, R. C., Turner, J. B., & House, J. (1987). Intervening processes in the relationship between unemployment and health. *Psychology and Medicine, 17,* 949–961.

Kessler, R. C., Walters, E. E., & Forthofer, M. S. (1998). The social consequences of psychiatric disorders, III: Probability of marital stability. *American Journal of Psychiatry, 155,* 1092–1095.

Ladouceur, R., Dugas, M. J., Freeston, M. H., Liger, E., Gagnon, F., & Thibodeau, N. (2000). Efficacy of a cognitive–behavioural treatment for generalized anxiety disorder: Evaluation in a controlled clinical trial. *Journal of Consulting and Clinical Psychology, 68,* 957–964.

Last, C. G., Hersen, M., Kazdin, A., Orvaschel, H., and Perrin, S. (1991). Anxiety disorders in children and their families. *Archives of General Psychiatry, 48,* 928–934.

Lewinsohn, P. M., Rohde, P., Seeley, J. R., Klein, D. N., & Gotlib, I. H. (2000). Natural course of adolescent major depressive disorder in a community sample: Predictors of recurrence in young adults. *American Journal of Psychiatry, 157,* 1584–1591.

Lieb, R., Wittchen, H., Hoefler, M., Fuetsch, M., Stein, M. B., & Merikangas, K. R. (2000). Parental psychopathology, parenting styles, and the risk of social phobia in offspring: A prospective-longitudinal community study. *Archives of General Psychiatry, 57,* 859–866.

Lyubomirsky, S., & Nolen-Hoeksema, S. (1995). Effects of self-focused rumination on negative thinking and interpersonal problem solving. *Journal of Personality and Social Psychology, 69,* 176–190.

Martin, C., Cabrol, S., Bouvard, M. P., Lepine, J. P., & Mouren-Simeoni, M. (1999). Anxiety and depressive disorders in fathers and mothers of anxious school-refusing children. *Journal of the American Academy of Child and Adolescent Psychiatry, 38,* 916–922.

Mash, E. J., & Dozois, D. J. A. (2003). Child psychopathology: A developmental-systems perspective. In E. J. Mash & R. A. Barkley (Eds.), *Child psychopathology* (2nd ed., pp. 3–71). New York: Guilford.

Merikangas, K., Avenevoli, S., Dierker, L., & Grillon, C. (1999). Vulnerability factors among children at risk for anxiety disorders. *Biological Psychiatry, 29,* 611–619.

Mineka, S., & Nugent, K. (1995). Mood-congruent memory biases in anxiety and depression. In D. L. Schacter (Ed.), *Memory distortions: How minds, brains, and societies reconstruct the past* (pp. 173–193). Cambridge, MA: Harvard University Press.

Mineka, S., Pury, C. L., & Luten, A. G. (1995). Explanatory style in anxiety and depression. In G. M. Buchana & M. E. P. Seligman (Eds.), *Explanatory style* (pp. 135–158). Hillsdale, NJ: Erlbaum.

Mineka, S., Watson, D., & Clark, L. A. (1998). Comorbidity of anxiety and unipolar mood disorders. *Annual Review of Psychology, 49,* 377–412.

Muris, P., Meesters, C., Merckelbach, H., & Hülsenbeck, P. (2000). Worry in children is related to perceived parental rearing and attachment. *Behaviour Research & Therapy, 38,* 487–497.

National Advisory Mental Health Council Workgroup on Child and Adolescent Mental Health Intervention Development and Deployment. (2001). *Blueprint for change: Research on child and adolescent mental health.* Washington, DC: National Institute of Mental Health.

National Advisory Mental Health Council Workgroup on Mental Disorders Prevention Research. (1998). *Priorities for prevention research at NIMH.* Bethesda,

MD: National Institutes of Health/National Institute of Mental Health. NIH Publication No: 98-4321.

Nitschke, J. B., Heller, W., Imig, J. C., McDonald, R. P., & Miller, G. A. (2001). Distinguishing dimensions of anxiety and depression. *Cognitive Therapy and Research, 25,* 1–22.

Nolen-Hoeksema, S. (2000). The role of rumination in depressive disorders and mixed anxiety/depressive symptoms. *Journal of Abnormal Psychology, 109,* 504–511.

Nolen-Hoeksema, S., Girgus, J. S., & Seligman, M. E. P. (1992). Predictors and consequences of childhood depressive symptoms. A 3-year longitudinal study. *Journal of Abnormal Psychology, 101,* 405–422.

Nolen-Hoeksema, S., Wolfson, A., Mumme, D., and Guskin, K. (1995). Helplessness in children of depressed and nondepressed mothers. *Developmental Psychology, 31,* 377–387.

Nomura, Y., Warner, V., and Wickramaratne, P. (2001). Parents concordant for major depressive disorder and the effect of psychopathology in offspring. *Psychological Medicine, 31,* 1211–1222.

Öst, L. G. (1987). Age of onset of different phobias. *Journal of Abnormal Psychology, 96,* 223–229.

Papageorgiou, C., & Wells, A. (2000). Treatment of recurrent major depression with attention training. *Cognitive and Behavioral Practice, 7,* 407–413.

Post, R. M. (1992). Transduction of psychosocial stress into the neurobiology of recurrent affective disorder. *American Journal of Psychiatry, 149,* 999–1010.

Pyszczynski, T., Holt, K., & Greenberg, J. (1987). Depression, self-focused attention, and expectancies for positive and negative future life events for self and others. *Journal of Personality and Social Psychology, 52,* 994–1001.

Reinherz, H. Z., Giaconia, R. M., Hauf, A. C., Wasserman, M. S., & Paradis, A. D. (2000). General and specific childhood risk factors for depression and drug disorders by early adulthood. *Journal of the American Academy of Child and Adolescent Psychiatry, 39,* 223–231.

Reinherz, H. Z., Giaconia, R. M., Pakiz, B., Silverman, A. B., Frost, A. K., & Lefkowitz, E. S. (1993). Psychosocial risks for major depression in late adolescence: A longitudinal community study. *Journal of the American Academy of Child and Adolescent Psychiatry, 32,* 1155–1163.

Reiss, D., Hetherington, E. M., Plomin, R., Howe, G. W., Simmens, S. J., Henderson, S. H., et al. (1995). Genetic questions for environmental studies: Differential parenting and psychopathology in adolescence. *Archives of General Psychiatry, 52,* 925–936.

Roy, M. A., Neale, M. C., Pedersen, N. L., Mathé, A. A., & Kendler, K. S. (1995). A twin study of generalized anxiety disorder and major depression. *Psychological Medicine, 25,* 1037–1049.

Rueter, M. A., Scaramella, L., Wallace, L. E., & Conger, R. D. (1999). First onset of depressive or anxiety disorders predicted by the longitudinal course of internalizing symptoms and parent–adolescent disagreements. *Archives of General Psychiatry, 56,* 726–732.

Segal, Z. V., Williams, J. M., & Teasdale, J. D. (2002). *Mindfulness Based Cognitive Therapy for Depression*. New York: Guilford.

Segerstrom, S. C., Tsao, J. C. I., Alden, L. E., & Craske, M. G. (2000). Worry and rumination: Repetitive thought as a concomitant and predictor of negative mood. *Cognitive Therapy and Research, 24*, 671–688.

Silove, D., Parker, G., Hadzi-Pavlovic, D., Manicavasagar, V., & Blaszcynski, A. (1991). Parental respresentations of patients with panic disorder and generalized anxiety disorder. *British Journal of Psychiatry, 159*, 835–841.

Stark, K. D., Humphrey, L. L., Crook, K., & Lewis, K. (1990). Perceived family environments of depressed and anxious children: Child's and maternal figure's perspective. *Journal of Abnormal Child Psychology, 18*, 527–547.

Thapar, A., & McGuffin, P. (1997). Anxiety and depressive symptoms in childhood: A genetic study of comorbidity. *Journal of Child Psychology and Psychiatry and Allied Disciplines, 38*, 651–656.

Thyer, B. A., Neese, R. M., Cameron, O. G., & Curtis, G. C. (1985). Agoraphobia: A test of the separation anxiety hypothesis. *Behavior Research and Therapy, 23*, 75–78.

Unnewehr, S., Schneider, S., Floring, I., & Margraf, J. (1998). Psychopathology in children of patients with panic disorder or animal phobia. *Psychopathology, 31*, 69–84.

van Os, J., & Jones, P. B. (1999). Early risk factors and adult person–environment relationships in affective disorder. *Psychological Medicine, 29*, 1055–1067.

van Os, J., Lewis, G., Jones, P., & Murray, R. M. (1997). Developmental precursors of affective illness in a general population birth cohort. *Archives of General Psychiatry, 54*, 625–632.

Warner, V., Mufson, L., & Weissman, M. M. (1995). Offspring at high and low risk for depression and anxiety: Mechanisms of psychiatric disorder. *Journal of the American Academy of Child and Adolescent Psychiatry, 34*, 786–797.

Weissman, M. M., Warner, V., Wickramaratne, P., Moreau, D., & Olfson, M. (1997). Offspring of depressed parents: Ten years later. *Archives of General Psychiatry, 54*, 932–940.

Westra, H. A., & Kuiper, N. A. (1997). Cognitive content specificity in selective attention across four domains of maladjustment. *Behavior Research and Therapy, 35*, 349–365.

Wetherell, J. L., Gatz, M., & Pedersen, N. L. (2001). A longitudinal analysis of anxiety and depressive symptoms. *Psychology and Aging, 16*, 187–195.

White, K. S., Bruce, S. E., Farrell, A. D., & Kliewer, W. (1998). Impact of exposure to community violence on anxiety: A longitudinal study of family social support as a protective factor for urban children. *Journal of Child and Family Studies, 7*, 187–203.

Wickramaratne, P. J., & Weissman, M. M. (1998). Onset of psychopathology in offspring by development phase and parental depression. *Journal of the American Academy of Child and Adolescent Psychiatry, 37*, 933–942.

III

CONCLUSIONS

12

THE PREVENTION OF ANXIETY AND DEPRESSION: PROMISES AND PROSPECTS

KEITH S. DOBSON AND DAVID J. A. DOZOIS

The logic of prevention is ineluctable. If it is possible to know the risk factors for a given disorder and to intervene with these factors, then surely it is more humane to prevent that disorder than to have members of society suffer needlessly. Presumably, because the cost of repairing lives that are damaged by mental health problems is also more expensive than it is to prevent the onset of a given condition, prevention strategies also make economic sense. Two conditions are necessary to make the foregoing logic succeed, though. First, it is important to have a clear conceptual model that enables scientists and practitioners to understand and measure the risk factors for a given disorder. Second, there must be effective means to intervene with those risk factors. The development of a knowledge base on risk factors for any disorder takes decades to evolve, and the notion of any "final" model for either anxiety or depression is certainly some time away.

In this final chapter, we summarize the principal themes that emerge in the area of prevention of anxiety and depression. Overall, we have been impressed by the large number of theoretical, methodological, and empirical developments that have already occurred in the field. We also note, however, the enormous number of challenges that face the field's future development. We have been in the privileged position to read the contributions of the chapter authors in this volume. On the basis of our understanding of those chapters, as well as our further readings, we have identified no fewer than 21 different areas that warrant attention. We present these areas next in several conceptual clusters, related to (a) theoretical issues, (b) population issues, (c) measurement issues, and (d) treatment issues.

THEORETICAL ISSUES

One of the fundamental questions for the field of prevention, broadly speaking, is how to conceptualize different levels or forms of prevention (see chaps. 4 & 9, this volume). We note two related, but somewhat divergent, frameworks for thinking about prevention in the field. The earlier and perhaps better known framework divides prevention into primary, secondary, and tertiary levels. From this framework, primary prevention aims at population-level interventions to try to prevent the very occurrence of signs or symptoms of a given problem. By definition, such intervention efforts are provided to "healthy" individuals, with a view to keeping those individuals healthy. Secondary prevention is focused on individuals in a given group who are already beginning to manifest signs or symptoms; such prevention efforts rest on the need for early identification of individuals requiring intervention and for effective strategies to conduct those treatments. Finally, tertiary prevention involves both early identification and treatment of individuals who have developed a full index case of the problem that is being focused on and the minimization of negative long-term consequences (Heller, Wyman, & Allen, 2000).

A relatively recent alternative to the framework just set forth proposes the use of *universal, selective,* and *indicated* categories of prevention (Mrazek & Haggerty, 1994; National Advisory Mental Health Council Workgroup on Child and Adolescent Mental Health Intervention Development and Deployment [NAMHC Workgroup], 2001). Universal prevention is largely analogous to the concept of primary prevention, targeting an entire population. Like primary prevention, universal prevention requires knowledge of the risk factors for a given disorder and the development of effective, wide-reaching methods of intervention, such as the media or school systems. Selective and indicated types of prevention are both subsumed under secondary prevention. In selective prevention, groups at risk of developing a disorder are selectively chosen for prevention. For example, children of depressed parents are known to have higher risk of depression than children from families without depressed parents (Garber & Flynn, 2001); they therefore could be selectively targeted for prevention efforts. Indicated prevention, in contrast, is used when an individual begins to demonstrate signs or symptoms of a disorder. As such, indicated prevention is most similar to the first framework's notion of secondary prevention. According to the newer model, once an individual experiences a disorder, the concept of prevention is not appropriate. Thus, early identification, assessment, and treatment become the focus of research and practice.

In developing this book, we naturally had to consider which of the foregoing two frameworks was more appropriate to the areas of anxiety and depression. We opted for the earlier distinction between primary, secondary, and tertiary prevention because we believe that this set of prevention levels better fits what is known about risk, resilience, onset, maintenance, and recurrence or relapse in these disorders. We also note that, because secondary prevention incorporates each of the concepts of selective and indicated prevention, it is a more comprehensive framework for prevention. Neither framework, however, captures the treatment phenomena of recurrence and relapse well. What seems to be absent in prevention frameworks is the idea of *reindicated* prevention, denoting individuals who have suffered a previous episode of a given disorder and who are currently asymptomatic, but who are at risk of a subsequent index episode. Thus, although we have adopted the primary, secondary, and tertiary formulation for examining anxiety and depression in this volume, we have expanded the concept of tertiary prevention somewhat to include the prevention of recurrence and relapse.

When prevention is considered, it is usually with regard to the signs or symptoms of a given disorder. Such a perspective is appropriate, but only insofar as the sole interest is in the disorder itself. As is reflected in the chapters in this volume, however, in the area of mental health, it may be necessary to expand our set of considerations to other phenomena. For example, there is now good evidence that early shyness may be a warning sign for later social anxiety disorder or agoraphobia (see chap. 6, this volume). Although shyness is not a particular sign of the more fully developed anxiety disorders, it might still be a useful and legitimate focus of prevention of anxiety disorders. As another example, the field is increasingly aware of the often chronic nature of depression. In some cases, an argument could be advanced that, although prevention of the disorder should be a continuing concern, other outcomes, such as optimizing the individual's quality of life or continuing to integrate the person into mainstream society (i.e., avoiding hospitalization) should have equal weight in the development of prevention strategies. The general point is that outcomes in the area of prevention, especially in mental health, need to be expanded beyond the targeted focus on symptoms of disorder.

One of the critical issues in the prevention of anxiety and depression is the knowledge of risk factors. Risk factors require organization into models of etiology, which can then form the basis of prevention efforts. Fortunately, because anxiety disorders and depression are ubiquitous conditions, much is known about them. Indeed, there are several competing models describing these conditions, as noted in the contributions to this volume. Which model, in the final analysis, will prove to be the "best" is indeterminate at present, but at least there are established models.

One of the benefits of having sets of risk factors is that they can be targeted for further research and intervention efforts. There are risks, however, to being too determinate. Such overemphasis on known factors might lead to less work on new or less examined factors. Also, it is quite possible that risk factors vary, depending on characteristics of individuals or stages of the disorder itself. For example, the risk factors for anxiety may be different in children than in adults. The risk factors for depression may be different in groups with a low socioeconomic status, versus those with a high socioeconomic status. The risk factors for first onset might be different from those for relapse in both anxiety and depression. Thus, investigators and theorists need to be purposeful in the evaluation of risk factors and clear in their reports about the conceptual model being investigated.

As the chapters of this book make plain, there appears to be a major divergence in the approaches taken to prevention, based on either psychosocial or biological models. In general, psychosocial models of risk and resilience emphasize factors that can be assessed and modified, such as negative cognitions, social skills, or reduced activity. These models also emphasize primary or secondary prevention and generally have the goal of stopping the onset of anxiety or depression. In contrast, biological models of prevention emphasize primarily the management or reduction of symptoms once they have emerged. Hence, these models are used mainly as tertiary prevention strategies—that is, for the prevention of relapse or recurrence through maintenance medication regimens.

Are there optimal strategies that combine the use of psychosocial and biological interventions in the areas of anxiety and depression? Probably, but to date, the field is not clear about what these strategies might be. For example, the literature on preventing relapse into depression is currently equivocal about the value of combination treatments, relative to either alone. Again, this appears to be a domain that is rich with research possibilities.

Models of the acute treatment of both anxiety disorders and depression tend to focus on the individual with the mental health problem. Even those treatments which do exist (e.g., interpersonal therapy) focus on helping the individual attain insight and on teaching the individual how better to negotiate his or her social environment. Yet, much is known about the social context of anxiety and depression. We know that such factors as socioeconomic status, family relations, peer status and relationships, psychosocial trauma, and interpersonal coping styles all correlate with anxiety and depression. Similarly, such variables as social support and social networks have been identified as protective factors. Even more, in some areas it has been demonstrated that these other variables predate, or potentially exert, a causal role.

Knowledge about the social context of anxiety and depression can be used in at least two important ways. First, to the extent that these variables predict a problem, but are "fixed" (e.g., socioeconomic status), they can be used to identify high-risk groups for selective prevention efforts. Second, for those socially oriented variables that can be modified, interventions can be constructed either to minimize the effects of negative predictors or to enhance the positive effects of protective factors. Such strategies as teaching adolescents how to assert themselves in various situations or how to build their circle of social support are fairly straightforward examples of how this knowledge can be built into prevention.

Social variables have a particular etiological role in the onset of psychopathology: Not only do they form the distal background to risk or resilience, but they also can serve in the role of proximal or even activating events. Many models of mental health problems now invoke a vulnerability/diathesis-stress formulation, in which a vulnerable person requires an eliciting psychosocial stressor to bring on the onset of a given disorder. Such models exist in the areas of both anxiety and depression. If these models are valid, it becomes clear that prevention efforts must also be directed toward understanding the nature of the activating events, learning how to predict them, and teaching at-risk persons how to respond with the least possible distress, should those events materialize. A number of related research questions emerge in this context: How do we best conceptualize and measure stressors? How can we identify vulnerability in the absence of activating events? Can we develop challenge tasks, in the form of hypothetical events, questionnaires, or mood induction procedures, to help predict who is at risk? (cf. Segal, 1997). Are there effective ways to mitigate the negative effects of stressors before their actual occurrence? These and other questions can serve as a fruitful basis for considerable research into the nature and identification of vulnerability.

Studies of the natural development of anxiety and depression indicate that there may be a developmental progression in the symptoms and syndromes of psychopathology (see chap. 2, this volume). Accordingly, the field should resist the urge to develop a prevention model or strategy in one age group and then assume that it will apply across the developmental spectrum. Historically, the tendency has been for primary prevention to be oriented toward children and secondary and tertiary prevention toward adolescents or adults. Instead, we suggest that there should be more cross-fertilization of models and strategies across the age span. Certainly, the age appropriateness of prevention models and strategies must be a consideration when treatments are developed and applied and risk factors are assessed.

Even beyond the effects of social variables within a given culture, it is becoming increasingly clear that both anxiety and depression exhibit significant cultural variation. This variation occurs in the incidence and prevalence of the disorders, the manner in which they are experienced, common wisdoms about their causal factors, and acceptable treatments. It is possible that there exist intercultural differences in risk factors for the two disorders. Our point here is that the success (or failure) of a given prevention strategy in one culture should not be assumed to apply universally. Cross-cultural replication and fertilization of research are needed to maximize the development of prevention efforts for both of these common disorders.

POPULATION ISSUES

One of the well-known features of anxiety and depression is that they correlate highly when considered from a quantitative perspective and are highly comorbid when considered qualitatively as diagnoses (Barlow, 2002; Brown, Chorpita, & Barlow, 1998). Further, the evidence for covariance between anxiety and depression tends to support the idea that anxiety more frequently precedes the onset of depression than vice versa (e.g., Cole, Peeke, Martin, Truglio, & Seroczynski, 1998) and that either anxiety is a risk factor for depression or there is some risk factor common to the two disorders that expresses itself differently over time. This high degree of covariation raises a number of conceptual and methodological issues for prevention research. For example, should efforts at prevention be addressed to anxiety and depression separately, or should they be aimed at a more unified phenomenon? If prevention efforts have an effect, should we expect specific results related to either anxiety or depression, or is it perhaps more realistic to expect the same result in both dimensions? Should we target childhood anxiety, with a view toward reaping benefits with respect to depression at a later point in time? At present, the answers to these questions are not at all clear. Further research on conceptual models of anxiety and depression, their relationship over time, and prevention efforts will be needed to evaluate these issues more fully.

In addition to having diagnosable anxiety and depressive disorders, many individuals experience subsyndromal levels of anxiety and depression symptoms. In some cases, these individuals go on to develop mental health disorders, but in other cases they do not. It remains important, therefore, to be aware of issues having to do with the range of symptoms that individuals might experience and to develop prevention efforts with an eye on the symptoms, severity, and clinical disorders related to anxiety and depression. It is also worth recalling that significant debates continue about the optimal way to view anxiety and depression-related experience—as either continuous or dichotomous phenomena. It appears prudent for researchers to use symptom-level, severity-related, and diagnostic outcomes in evaluating the efficacy of prevention, as the various perspectives on both anxiety and depression may yield somewhat divergent conclusions about the efficacy and utility of prevention efforts.

MEASUREMENT ISSUES

Any research domain can answer the questions it asks only to within the fidelity of the measurement tools it uses. It logically follows that the field of prevention of anxiety and depression requires reliable and valid measurement tools. Fortunately for investigators in this area, a large amount of development has already taken place, particularly as regards the measurement of the constructs of anxiety and depression themselves. Both the diagnostic framework for these constructs and the models that conceptualize them as dimensional variables are well articulated, and reliable and valid measures from each of these perspectives have been published and made widely available (chap. 3, this volume). What is more, measures of anxiety and depression have been developed for specific age groups and even in the context of other disorders or conditions. Although construct measures related to mechanisms need further development, there is already a sizable number of such instruments available to investigators (Antony, Orsillo, & Roemer, 2001; Nezu, Ronan, Meadows, & McClure, 2000).

One of the conundrums facing the field of prevention is whether we need to have a common set of outcome measures. Although certain instruments seem to be more or less favored in the literature, investigators are still free to elect whatever validated measurement tools they wish to answer a given question. This freedom, while advantageous from the perspective of assessing the generalizability of results across different instruments, poses a challenge to those who read the literature to know exactly how one set of results relates to another. When such difficulties are further complicated by different studies examining different levels of prevention or developmental stages, making sense of the overall pattern becomes extremely difficult.

Just as the measurement tools adopted in a given study affect the generalizability of that study, so, too, do decisions about the sample that is investigated. One of the dilemmas pertaining to the design of a study is how homogeneous or heterogeneous the sample should be (Kazdin, 1992). Homogeneous samples have the virtue of clearer results; from a statistical perspective, they are associated with a reduced error variance and a consequent increase in statistical power and in the opportunity to obtain significant results. Heterogeneous samples, in contrast, have higher levels of error variance and reduced statistical power. There is, consequently, a need for larger sample sizes, in order to obtain significant results. Yet another important factor is that studies with homogeneous samples are not easily generalizable, whereas studies with heterogeneous samples afford the investigator considerable scope in generalizing their results.

The level of prevention that is being studied complicates the extent to which generalizability is a problem in prevention research. For primary prevention, almost by definition, large heterogeneous samples are required to examine population-based interventions. For secondary prevention studies, particularly of the indicated variety, the criteria whereby participants are selected will inevitably reduce the heterogeneity of the sample, increasing its precision and predictive power, but at the expense of generalizability of the study's results. In tertiary prevention, it is necessary to have well-defined samples with known inclusion and exclusion criteria, because, at that level of prevention, investigators are studying known disorders.

Our point here is not that there is one best or optimal strategy with regard to the sample that is being studied. Rather, the stage of intervention and other specific dimensions of the hypotheses being examined will drive the particular characteristics of the sample. It will remain critical for investigators to articulate clearly the extent to which they have employed any selection criteria, as such choices will inevitably affect the generalizability of their results and the decisions that subsequent investigators make when designing research in order to refer to those results.

One of the unique features of prevention research is that, by definition, it is longitudinal in nature. Hence, it is imperative that measurement tools have not only concurrent validity, but also predictive validity. Measurement needs to be particularly stable in this area, so that the relationships among variables over time can be assessed. Further, the tools that are used as predictors of subsequent functioning need to be assessed for their predictive utility. These unique demands of instrumentation in the field of prevention require studies of questionnaires and other measures that are at times significantly beyond the demands imposed in other research areas. Investigators of prevention are accordingly encouraged to collect and report the evidence regarding the predictive validity of the measures they employ and to examine multiple tools simultaneously in their studies, so that the relative predictive utility of various measures can be determined.

At present, it is difficult to say with much confidence how potent various prevention strategies are in the fields of anxiety and depression. The effect sizes associated with various prevention strategies have yet to be determined. Even so, those conducting prevention research should already take effect sizes into account. For example, as previously alluded to, primary prevention likely has the lowest power, because it is typically aimed at the most heterogeneous samples. Still, some individuals in the population do not have vulnerability for later symptomatology and tend therefore to "wash out" any possible intervention effects. Consequently, the effect sizes in such studies will necessarily be reduced, and there will be a need for larger samples to obtain true effects. We recommend that, in addition to reporting statistical significance of various prevention strategies, investigators also report power where possible, to enable subsequent investigators to plan their studies with adequate power. Describing the clinical significance of findings with the reliable change index (Jacobson & Truax, 1991) or by employing normative comparisons (Kendall, Marrs-Garcia, Nath, & Sheldrick, 1999) is also important for effective research and clinical utility.

TREATMENT ISSUES

As previously noted, prevention strategies require knowledge about risk and resilience factors, as well as the ability to target these factors for intervention. As documented in the chapters of this volume, there is now a considerable body of research that has identified risk and resilience factors in both anxiety and depression. The extent to which these factors are amenable to prevention, however, likely varies. Some factors are more distal to the onset of symptoms or syndromes and are probably less easy to identify and prove to be preventive factors than are those which are more proximal to the onset of problems (see Ingram & Price, 2001). Some factors, by contrast, may be specific to particular symptoms or syndromes related to anxiety or depression, and it thus might be relatively easy to document their potential in prevention research, relative to those factors which are nonspecific or general for a wider range of symptoms or diagnoses. Similarly, some factors may be necessary, but not sufficient, for effective prevention, whereas others may be necessary and sufficient.

Identifying the relationships among different risk and resilience factors, as well as the relationships among these factors and the symptoms and syndromes related to anxiety and depression, will require a sustained effort over many years. It will require investigators to examine a range of factors and how they relate to a variety of outcomes, using multivariate methods within a given study. It may be that studies will have to be dismantled systematically; that is, different studies might have to be employed to examine the relative use of intervening with different factors. Thus, while the literature has already developed to a considerable extent, further systematic efforts are required.

In general, relatively little has been written in the field of psychotherapy about how innovative treatments are initially developed. Although various theoretical frameworks drive many treatments, it is clear that many treatments employ inventions and techniques that are simply known to have positive outcomes. For example, it is now well established that, at some stage of treatment for most anxiety disorders, the patient needs to be exposed to the stimulus or situation that he or she is fearful of (Barlow, 2002).

How, then, do we develop prevention programs? Should we edit or modify existing treatment technologies—perhaps even those developed primarily for the treatment of acute disorders? If so, the chapters in this volume suggest that the field should look chiefly to cognitive–behavioral interventions for effective places to start. However, such an approach almost inevitably minimizes the significant efforts made to document other risk and resilience factors. An alternative model to prevention, therefore, is to begin with a comprehensive analysis of the established risk and resilience factors and then design an intervention (or perhaps a set of interventions) that specifically targets these factors for intervention. To date, it appears that most of the prevention work either has been significantly affected by the theoretical perspective of the individuals doing the research or has focused on a relatively small set of potential targets of intervention. Although the logic of comprehensive prevention strategies is strong, there are obvious limitations on the ability of any one person or group to review and design such large-scale intervention studies.

Building on the point just made, our overall conclusion from the many excellent chapters in this volume is that the "ultimate prevention program" will need to be multidimensional, drawing on a number of divergent and developmentally sensitive theoretical models and focusing on both risk and resilience factors. Within the domains of anxiety and depression, there likely will be general vulnerability factors that can be applied across the spectrum of those disorders (Mineka, Watson, & Clark, 1998), but there may well also be the need for specific preventive strategies for particular symptoms or diagnostic categories. To develop such a multifaceted framework for prevention, investigators from various disciplines and theoretical perspectives, as well as researchers who study different disorders and age groups, will need to work together, share their results, and collaborate on the development and evaluation of innovative intervention protocols.

In designing and evaluating prevention programs, the primary question must be related to the efficacy of those programs. Obviously, even if a program has high theoretical value and makes conceptual sense, if it cannot affect the subsequent likelihood of anxiety or depression symptoms, it has little prevention value. In addition to carrying out studies of the efficacy of intervention, we argue that investigators must assess the fidelity of the interventions they are using and studying. *Fidelity* refers to the assessment of the extent to which the ingredients of the program are adhered to (and the extent to which techniques or methods from other approaches do not appear in these studies) and the skill or competence with which programs are administered (Waltz, Addis, Koerner, & Jacobson, 1993). Effective prevention strategies that are poorly delivered are not likely to yield significant benefits in terms of prevention. Accordingly, we recommend that investigators in this field develop and apply measures of treatment fidelity when prevention studies are conducted.

Although the initial emphasis in the development of any prevention strategies must be on their efficacy, if these strategies are to be translated into general practice, it will also be necessary to evaluate the effectiveness of prevention. In this regard, *effectiveness* refers to such aspects as the ease of teaching effective prevention strategies, the acceptability of successful strategies, and the cost-effectiveness of prevention programs. Certainly, for the acceptance and integration of prevention programs into general public health policy, data on both the efficacy and the effectiveness of prevention will be required (Miller & Magruder, 1999). Again, we encourage those who are interested in the development and evaluation of prevention to gather both types of evidence in their various research efforts.

The chapters in this volume, together with our summary comments presented here, generally agree on the need for more increasingly complex models for the prevention of anxiety and depression. With increasing conceptual and methodological complexity comes the need for increasingly sophisticated and multivariate statistical analysis strategies. Investigators in the domain of prevention will thus need to be schooled in the methods of not just multiple regression, but also logistic regression, trend analysis, latent growth curve analysis, nonlinear dynamics, and other advanced statistical techniques. We also believe that increasingly complex statistics will need to be developed to fully explore and explain the patterns of results seen in various data sets. In this regard, our statistical tools will increasingly need to go beyond the examination of linear effects to determine other trends and patterns in data as well.

Finally, although the predominant perspective in the field of prevention is to achieve the minimal occurrence of signs, symptoms, or syndromes, we need to recall that anxiety and depression have adaptive roles, too, and contribute to variety in life. For example, anxiety can serve a valuable signaling function informing us that something is wrong in our environment or the way we are interacting with our environment and so can provide the impetus for creative and adaptive change. Similarly, in the face of significant and irreversible loss, depression may well be the most appropriate and adaptive responsive. Accordingly, our belief is that we do not want to prevent all anxiety and depression. We need to respect the diversity of feelings and emotional expressivity seen in others and intervene only to the extent that it is appropriate and welcomed. From a slightly different way of thinking about this issue, we need to know when to promote change and reduction in symptomatology, as opposed to accepting—or even encouraging—the expression of such phenomena as anxiety and depression.

CONCLUDING COMMENTS

Despite the significant developments that have been made to date, as reflected in the chapters in this volume, there remain a large number of theoretical, methodological, and even ethical directions that need to be considered for the optimal development of the field of prevention of anxiety and depression. Although considerable rhetoric has been given over to the value of prevention (Holden & Black, 1999; Mrazek & Haggerty, 1994; NAMHC Workgroup, 2001), it remains the case that considerably more attention to, and funding of, research and treatment are provided for disorders that have already developed. Those individuals who are responsible for the funding of health research may need to consider the allocation of specific monies for prevention-oriented research and development. Similarly, and notwithstanding the enormous pressures caused by extant illnesses on health care systems, those responsible for health care need the continuing support of experts in prevention to allocate funds for preventive efforts.

How can the field best advise the health research agenda and health policymakers? We believe that, in addition to paying attention to the existing frameworks for research and development, a fruitful strategy would be to convene an international panel of experts in anxiety and depression to come to some conceptual and methodological conclusions and to provide a template for future investigation. Issues such as the standardization of outcomes and assessment, the identification of the most promising theoretical models of risk and resilience, the development of the most effective strategies for modifying factors associated with these theoretical models, and the establishment of a coordinated set of intervention trials could all emerge from such a review process. We believe that our knowledge base is sufficient for such a panel to be effective, and although we recognize the inherent difficulties associated with such an organizational task, we end this book with the recommendation that this process take place.

REFERENCES

Antony, M. M., Orsillo, S. M., & Roemer, L. (2001). *Practitioner's guide to empirically based measures of anxiety*. New York: Kluwer/Plenum.

Barlow, D. H. (2002). *Anxiety and its disorders: The nature and treatment of anxiety and panic* (2nd ed.). New York: Guilford.

Brown, T. A., Chorpita, B. F., & Barlow, D. H. (1998). Structural relationships among dimensions of the *DSM–IV* anxiety and mood disorders and dimensions of negative affect, positive affect, and autonomic arousal. *Journal of Abnormal Psychology, 107,* 179–192.

Cole, D. A., Peeke, L. G., Martin, J. M., Truglio, R., & Seroczynski, A. D. (1998). A longitudinal look at the relation between depression and anxiety in children and adolescents. *Journal of Consulting and Clinical Psychology, 66,* 451–460.

Garber, J., & Flynn, C. (2001). Vulnerability to depression in childhood and adolescence. In R. E. Ingram & J. M. Price (Eds.), *Vulnerability to psychopathology: Risk across the lifespan* (pp. 175–225). New York: Guilford.

Heller, K., Wyman, M. F., & Allen, S. M. (2000). Future directions for prevention science: From research to adoption. In C. R. Snyder & R. E. Ingram (Eds.), *Handbook of psychological change: Psychotherapy processes and practices for the 21st Century* (pp. 660–680). New York: Wiley.

Holden, E. W., & Black, M. M. (1999). Theory and concepts of prevention science as applied to clinical psychology. *Clinical Psychology Review, 19,* 391–401.

Ingram, R. E., & Price, J. M. (2001). (Eds.), *Vulnerability to psychopathology: Risk across the lifespan*. New York: Guilford.

Jacobson, N. S., & Truax, P. (1991). Clinical significance: A statistical approach to defining meaningful change in psychotherapy research. *Journal of Consulting and Clinical Psychology, 59*, 12–19.

Kazdin, A. E. (1992). *Research design in clinical psychology* (2nd ed.). Boston: Allyn & Bacon.

Kendall, P. C., Marrs-Garcia, A., Nath, S. R., & Sheldrick, R. C. (1999). Normative comparisons for the evaluation of clinical significance. *Journal of Consulting and Clinical Psychology, 67*, 285–299.

Miller, N. E., & Magruder, K. M. (1999). (Eds.). *Cost-effectiveness of psychotherapy: A guide for practitioners, researchers, and policymakers.* London: Oxford University Press.

Mineka, S., Watson, D., & Clark, L. A. (1998). Comorbidity of anxiety and unipolar mood disorders. *Annual Review of Psychology, 49*, 377–412.

Mrazek, P. J., & Haggerty, R. J. (Eds.). (1994). Committee on Prevention of Mental Disorders, Institute of Medicine. *Reducing risks for mental disorders: Frontiers for preventive intervention research.* Washington, DC: National Academy Press.

National Advisory Mental Health Council Workgroup on Child and Adolescent Mental Health Intervention Development and Deployment. (2001). *Blueprint for change: Research on child and adolescent mental health.* Washington, DC: National Institute of Mental Health.

Nezu, A. M., Ronan, G. F., Meadows, E. A., & McClure, K. S. (2000). *Practitioner's guide to empirically-based measures of depression. Clinical assessment series, Volume 1.* New York: Kluwer/Plenum.

Segal, Z. V. (1997). Implications of priming for measures of change following psychological and pharmacological treatments. In H. H. Strupp, L. M. Horowitz, & M. J. Lambert (Eds.), *Measuring patient changes in mood, anxiety, and personality disorders: Toward a core battery* (pp. 81–99). Washington, DC: American Psychological Association.

Waltz, J., Addis, M. E., Koerner, K., & Jacobson, N. (1993). Testing the integrity of a psychotherapy protocol: Assessment of adherence and competence. *Journal of Consulting & Clinical Psychology, 61*, 620–630.

AUTHOR INDEX

Numbers in italics refer to listings in the reference sections.

Dobson, K. S., 17, 23, 24, 25, 26, 28, *33,
*41, 68, 90, 95, 96, 115, *123,* 185,
187, *201,* 217, *227,* 238, 242, 243,
252, *254, 256,* 269, *276*
Dodge, C. S., *182*
Dodge, K. A., 105, *126*
Dollinger, S. J., 106, *123,* 139, *155*
Domitrovich, C., 101, *124,* 194, *201*
Donahoe, C. P., 107, *122*
Done, D. J., 272, *276*
Donnell, C., 220, *228*
Donoghue, J., 242, *255*
Donovan, C. L., 101, 104, 108, 118, *123,*
133, 136, 137, *155,* 192, *204,* 273,
276
Downey, G., 214, *227,* 265, *276*
Dozois, D. J. A., 17, 23, 24, 25, 28, 29, *33,*
37, 51, 67, 243, *254,* 262, 269,
276, 278
Druss, B., 28, *38*
Dryman, A., *34, 255*
Dubois, D. L., *124*
Dubow, E. F., 112, *123*
Dudek, D., 24, *33*
Dugas, M. J., 149, *155,* 177, 178, 180, *181,*
182, 278
Duggan, C. F., 22, 23, *34*
Dumas, J. E., 265, *276*
Duncan, E. M., 22, *37*
Dunner, D. L., 245, *255*
Durham, R. C., 15, *34,* 176, 179, *181*
Durlak, J. A., 75, 76, 96, 110, *123,* 186,
200
Dusenbury, L., 111, *122*
Dweck, C. S., 16, *34*
Dyck, M. J., 238, *256*

Eaton, W. W., 20, 21, *34,* 133, 146, 151,
155, 160, 233, *255*
Eaves, L. J., 105, *126,* 133, *157,* 190, *202,*
267, *277*
Ediger, J. M., 98
Edwards, S., 112, *123*
Egeland, B., 104, *124, 128, 129*
Egolf, B., 190, *202*
Ehlers, A., 141, 145, 146, 149, *155, 156,*
157
Eifert, G. H., 248, *255*
Eisen, A. R., 12, *34*
Eisen, J., 16, *37*
Eke, M., 264, *275*

Eley, T. C., 26, *34,* 85, 96, 267, 269, *276*
Elias, M. J., 114, 115, *122, 124*
Elliott, C. H., 140, 141, *156*
Emery, G., 220, 226, 239, *253*
Emmelkamp, P. M. G., 134, *159,* 266, *276*
Endicott, J., 214, *231, 256, 257*
Endler, N. S., 240, 241, *255*
Enns, M. W., 55, 80, 95
Epstein, N., 58, 66
Epstein, R. S., 147, *155*
Erickson, M. F., 104, *124*
Erkanli, A., 12, 30, *34*
Ernst, D., 238, *256*
Eshleman, S., 36, 96, *126, 157, 182,* 229
Essau, C. A., 185, 186, 187, 188, 189, 190,
194, *200, 201, 202*
Essex, M. J., 198, *200*
Evans, M. D., *155,* 207, *228, 254*
Evans, T., 189, *202*
Eyeson-Annan, M. L., 24, *31*
Eysenck, H., 133, 134, *155*
Eysenck, M. W., 134, *160*
Ezpeleta, L., 12, 16, *34*

Fairbank, J. A., 172, *182*
Faraone, S. V., *31, 122, 125, 128, 153,*
156, 275
Farmer, M. E., 20, 36, 209, *229*
Farrell, A. D., 107, *129,* 272, *280*
Fava, G. A., 170, *181,* 242, 245, 246, 248,
251, 252, *255, 258*
Fava, M., 26, *34,* 244, *255*
Feehan, M., 186, *203*
Feeny, N. C., 149, *155*
Feiger, A. D., 245, *255*
Feiring, C., 104, *126*
Felner, R. D., 115, *124*
Fendrich, M., 187, *201*
Fennell, M., 175, *181*
Ferdinand, R. F., 109, *129*
Fergusson, D. M., 24, *34,* 109, *124,* 271,
276
Ferro, T., 264, *276*
Feske, U., 166, *182*
Field, T., 215, *228*
Figgit, D. P., 15, *34*
Fincham, F. D., 216, *227*
Fine, S., 191, *201*
Finkelstein, H., 272, *276*
Finkelstein, S. N., 22, *35, 124, 156, 182*
First, M. B., 62, 63, 67

Gorham, D. R., 61, 69
Gorman, J. M., 70
Gorson, D., 277
Gorsuch, R. L., 57, 70
Gotlib, I. H., 1, 6, 17, 22, 24, 25, *34, 35,*
    80, 85, *95, 96,* 187, 188, 196,
    201, 204, 205, 214, 215, *227,*
    263, 265, 266, *272,* 276, *278*
Gottman, J. M., 216, 227
Gracely, E. J., 57, 67
Grandi, S., 170, *181,* 245, 246, 248, *255*
Gray, M., *31, 274*
Greenberg, J., 270, 279
Greenberg, M. S., 268, 277
Greenberg, M. T., 101, 108, 110, 111,
    124, 194, 195, *201*
Greenberg, P. E., 16, 22, 25, 35, 102, *124,*
    131, *156, 162, 182*
Greenwald, S., *40*
Greenwood, K., 108, *125*
Greist, J. H., 16, *36*
Griens, A. M. G. F., 22, *35*
Griffin, K. W., 64, 69
Grillon, C., 264, *278*
Grisham, J. R., 25, *32,* 82, *95*
Gross, A. M., 106, *127*
Grove, W. M., *254*
Grubb, H. J., 104, *126*
Gruen, R. J., 108, *124*
Guardino, M., *32*
Guilleminault, C., 20, *38*
Gursky, D. M., 57, 69, 145, *158*
Guskin, K., 265, *279*
Gusman, F. D., 66

Haaga, D., 238, *256*
Hackmann, A., *181*
Hadzi-Pavlovic, D., 266, *280*
Haffmans, P. M. J., 22, *35*
Hagell, A., 198, *204*
Haggerty, R. J., 30, *38,* 73, 74, 75, 76,
    78, 79, 80, 84, 89, 90, 91, 92, *97,*
    132, *158,* 284, *293, 295*
Hahn, S. R., 70
Hajak, G., *121*
Haley, G., 191, *201*
Hamilton, M., 56, 58, 68
Hamilton, N. A., 209, *228*
Hammen, C. L., 1, 6, 17, 19, 21, 22, 23,
    24, 25, 26, 29, *34, 35,* 86, *96,*
    189, 196, *201,* 205, 206, 214,

216, *227, 228,* 238, *256, 263, 264,*
    271, *277*
Hampson, J., 114, *122*
Harkness, K. L., 86, 96
Harnett, P. H., *204, 230*
Harnett-Sheehan, K., *70*
Harold, G. T., 216, *227*
Harris, E., 272, *275*
Harris, J. R., 106, *125*
Harris, M., *154*
Harris, M. F., 272, *275*
Harris, M. J., 240, *258*
Harris, T. O., 86, *95,* 237, 240, *254,* 271,
    275
Harrison, W., 245, *254*
Harrison, W. M., *39*
Harter, S., 190, 196, *204*
Hartl, T. L., 169, *182*
Hartlage, S., 80, *94*
Hartup, W. W., 102, 105, 106, *125*
Harvey, A. G., 148, *156*
Hau, C. M., *181*
Hauf, A. C., 265, *279*
Hautzinger, M., 22, *37*
Hawes, R., 140, *157*
Hawkins, J. D., *123,* 190, 196, 197, *201,*
    202
Hawkins, W., 78, *95,* 219, *226*
Hayhurst, H., *38, 259*
Hayward, C., 132, *156,* 188, *204*
Hayward, P., *257*
Hazlett, R. L., 27, *35*
Hearst-Ideka, D., 49, *68*
Heath, A. C., 105, *126, 133, 157,* 190,
    202, 267, 277
Heckelman, L. R., 16, *39*
Heim, C., 135, *156*
Heimberg, R. G., 14, *36,* 120, *123, 125,*
    142, *154, 164,* 165, *182, 183*
Heiser, J. F., *255*
Heller, K., 76, *96,* 207, 209, 223, 228, 284,
    294
Heller, W., 270, *279*
Hellström, K., 163, 170, *183*
Henderson, A. S., 105, *121, 125*
Henderson, S. H., *279*
Hendry, L., 195, *202*
Henin, A., *126*
Heninger, G. R., *68*
Henry, R., 271, *277*
Herbert, J. D., 134, *156*
Herbst, J. H., 46, *71*

McPhee, A. E., *155*

McQuaid, J. R., 23, 24, 25, *37*

Meadows, E. A., 53, 69, 149, *155*, 289, *295*

Mechanic, D., 25, *37*

Meesters, C., 103, *127*, 266, *278*

Melamed, B. G., 140, *157*

Melançon, G., 115, *127*

Mellsop, G. W., 24, *31*

Melton, B., 133, *155*

Meltzer-Brody, S. E., 28, *33*

Melville, L. F., 105, *127*

Mendell, N. R., 216, *229*

Mendlowicz, M. V., 16, *37*

Merckelbach, H., 12, *38*, 105, *127*, 143, 150, *158*, 266, *278*

Merikangas, K. R., 104, *123*, *129*, 187, *201*, *217*, *225*, 263, 264, 276, *278*

Merk, F. L., 112, *123*

Messenger, C., 145, *157*

Messer, S. C., 106, *127*

Metalsky, G. I., 69, 81, 94, 213, *225*

Metz, C., 109, *121*

Metzger, R. L., 59, 69

Meyer, A. L., 78, 97

Meyer, D. A., 56, *71*

Meyer, T. J., 59, 69

Meyer, V., 167, *182*

Miceli, R. J., *39*

Mickelson, K., *32*

Middleton, H., *181*

Miller, G. A., 270, *279*

Miller, I., 22, *39*

Miller, M. L., 59, 69

Miller, N. E., 292, *295*

Miller, P. P., 14, *33*

Mills, R. S., 108, *128*

Mills, R. S. L., 106, *128*

Mineka, S., 25, 26, 30, *37*, 85, 86, 97, 139, *154*, 261, 269, 270, 273, *278*, 292, *295*

Miranda, J., 56, 68, 80, 96, 206, 213, *228*, *229*, 238, *256*

Mitchell, D., 143, *158*

Mitchell, J. T., 148, *157*

Mojtabai, R., 25, 28, *37*

Monk, C., 135, *158*

Monroe, S. A., 80, 81, *95*

Monroe, S. M., 80, 87, 88, 89, *97*, 189, *203*

Monson, R. R., 20, *38*

Montague, R., 193, *204*

Montgomery, S. A., 244, 245, *257*

Moodie, E., *40*

Moore, P. S., 191, *204*

Moore, R., *258*

Moore, R. G., 246, *254*, *259*

Moos, R. H., 241, *253*, *256*, *259*

Moreau, D., 14, *37*, 263, *280*

Moreno, F. A., 14, *37*

Morphy, M. A., 245, 246, *255*

Morris, T. L., 60, 66, 106, *127*

Morris-Yates, A., 105, *121*

Morrison, K., 15, *40*, 162, *183*

Morselli, P. L., *32*

Moscicki, E. K., 76, 96

Moul, D. E., 20, *36*, 209, *229*

Mouren-Simeoni, M., 264, *278*

Mrazek, P. J., 30, *38*, 73, 74, 75, 76, 78, 79, 80, 84, 89, 90, 91, 92, 97, 132, *158*, 284, *293*, *295*

Mueller, T. I., *33*, *40*

Mufson, L., 263, *280*

Mulhall, P. F., *124*

Muller, N., *40*

Mullins, M., *154*

Mumme, D., 265, *279*

Mundfrom, D. J., 200

Muñoz, R. F., 75, 76, 97, 207, *229*

Muris, P., 12, *38*, 103, 105, *127*, 142, 143, 150, *153*, *158*, 266, *278*

Murphy, J. M., 20, *38*

Murphy, M., 78, *95*, 219, *226*

Murray, C. J. L., 233, 234, *258*

Murray, R. M., 273, *280*

Myers, J. K., *39*

Mylle, J., 106, *126*

Mystkowski, J. L., 151, *160*

Nagy, L. M., 66

Najavits, L., 243, *256*

Narrow, W. E., *39*

Nath, S. R., 290, *295*

Nathan, P. E., 15, *38*

National Institute of Child Health and Human Development Early Child Care Research Network, 197, *203*

National Institute of Mental Health, 2, 6, 23, 30, *38*, 45, 62, 69, 74, 75, 76, 77, 78, 79, 82, 89, 90, 92, 93, *97*, 101, *127*, 234, *258*, 262, *278*, 284, *293*, *295*

Naylor, M. W., 189, *202*

Neale, J. M., 214, *231*
Neale, M. C., 26, *39*, 105, *126*, 133, *157*,
    190, *202*, 267, *277*, *279*
Neese, R. M., 271, *280*
Nelson, C., *157*
Nelson, C. B., 36, 96, *126*, *182*, *229*
Nemeroff, C. B., 135, *156*
Nezu, A. M., 53, 54, *69*, 191, *203*, 289,
    295
Nezu, C. M., 191, *203*
Nierenberg, A. A., *34*, 244, 245, *258*, *260*
Nietzel, M. T., 240, *258*
Nitschke, J., 215, *227*
Nitschke, J. B., 270, *279*
Nolen-Hoeksema, S., 21, *38*, 209, *229*,
    265, 270, 271, *278*, *279*
Nomura, Y., 264, *279*
Norman, G. R., 190, *203*
Norton, R., 133, 145, *158*
Noshirvani, H., 172, *182*
Nottelmann, E. D., 191, *203*
Noyes, R., 14, *38*, 133, *158*
Nugent, K., 269, 270, *278*
Nurrish, J., *160*
Nutt, D., 26, *38*
Nutt, D. J., 244, *255*

Oberklaid, F., 141, *158*
O'Donnell, J. P., 106, *123*, 139, *155*
Oei, T. P. S., 90, *97*
Offord, D., 89, *96*
Ohayon, M. M., 20, 25, 27, *38*
Okkes, I., 28, *36*
Oldehinkel, T., *258*
O'Leary, K. D., 216, *229*
Olfson, M., 25, 27, 28, *32*, 36, 37, *38*, 263,
    280
Oliveau, D. C., 14, *30*
Ollendick, T. H., 2, 5, 15, 22, *32*, 57, *69*,
    102, *126*
Oosterlaan, J., 135, *158*
Opila, J., *33*
Orbach, I., 111, *127*
Ormel, J., 233, 234, *258*
Orsillo, S. M., 53, 66, 289, *294*
Orvaschel, H., 13, 36, 132, *156*, 264, *278*
O'Ryan, D., *160*
Osborne, L. N., 216, *227*
Osgarby, S. M., 204, *230*
Öst, L. G., 141, *158*, 163, 170, *182*, *183*,
    271, *279*

Ostergaard, L., *230*
Otto, M. W., *32*, 164, 165, 166, 180,
    183
Ovaschel, H., 271, *277*
Overall, J. E., 61, *69*
Overholser, J. C., 243, 244, *258*

Padgett, M. B., *155*
Pakiz, B., 204, *279*
Panichelli-Mindel, S., *126*
Panzarino, P. J., 25, *38*
Papageorgiou, C., 270, *279*
Papagides, J., 244, *260*
Paradis, A. D., 265, *279*
Park, S. K., 242, *258*
Parker, G., 266, *280*
Parker, J. D., 240, 241, *255*
Parker, J. D. A., 80, *95*
Parkerson, G. R., Jr., 63, *69*
Parry, G., 240, *258*
Partridge, F., *37*
Patten, S. B., 20, *38*
Patton, G., 272, *275*
Paul, G. L., 164, 179, *183*
Paulus, M. J., *35*, *257*
Pava, J., *34*
Pavlidis, K., 198, *203*
Paykel, E. S., 28, *38*, 236, 237, 238,
    240, 242, 245, 246, *258*, *259*
Pearson, J. L., 190, *203*
Pedersen, N. L., 26, *39*, 40, 267, 269,
    279, *280*
Pedro-Carroll, J. L., 107, *123*
Peeke, L. G., 25, 26, *32*, 102, *123*, 288,
    294
Penava, S. J., *32*
Peppe, J., *155*
Pepper, C. M., 19, *33*
Perel, J. M., *256*
Peri, T., 147, *159*
Perkins, T. S., *31*, 86, *95*, 268, *274*
Perri, M. G., 191, *203*
Perrin, S., 14, *37*, 264, *278*
Perris, C., 234, *258*
Perry, K. J., 49, 57, 67, *68*
Persons, J. B., 213, *229*
Petermann, F., 186, 190, *201*
Peterson, B. S., 144, *158*
Peterson, C., 54, *69*
Peterson, L., 140, *158*
Peterson, R., 145, *158*

Storosum, J. G., 244, *259*
Strachowski, D., *156*
Strauss, C. C., 102, 106, *129*
Sturt, E., *254*
Summerfeldt, L. A., 63, 66
Summerfeldt, L. J., 47, 61, 62, 65, 70
Sussman, N., 245, *259*
Swanson, V., *40*, 175, *183*
Swartz, A. L., *155*
Swartz, M. S., 20, *31*
Swatling, S., *225*
Swedo, S. E., *153*
Sweeney, L., 192, *204*
Swindle, R. W., 241, *259*
Swinson, R., 146, *159*
Swinson, R. P., 5, *5*, 49, 55, 63, 66, *70*
Szabo, M., 186, *200*
Szatmari, P., 263, *276*
Szollos, A., 103, 106, *127*
Szymaczek, M., *33*

Tallis, F., 143, *159*
Tang, T. Z., 90, *95*, 243, *259*
Tanielian, T., 28, *38*
Tarrier, N., 216, *230*
Tashman, N. A., *30*
Taylor, C. B., 132, *156*
Taylor, K. L., 57, 68
Taylor, L., 213, 215, *230*
Taylor, S., *182*
Teachman, B., 143, *158*
Teachman, B. A., 164, *183*
Teasdale, J., 213, *225*
Teasdale, J. D., 23, *39, 40*, 212, *230*, 239, 247, 249, 251, *254, 258, 259, 260*, 270, *279*
Tellegen, A., 86, 98
Teri, L., 246, *257*
Terr, L. C., 106, *129*
Thapar, A., 267, 268, *280*
Thase, M. E., 22, *39*, 212, *230*, 244, *260*
Thibodeau, N., 143, *155, 182, 278*
Thoits, P., 240, *260*
Thomas, J., *155*
Thomas, L., 272, *275*
Thomsen, P. H., 144, *159*
Thordarson, D. S., 143, *159*, 164, *182, 183*
Thrasher, S., 172, *182*
Thurber, C. A., 192, *204*
Thyer, B. A., 271, *280*
Tiet, Q. Q., 107, *129*

Timmerman, I. G., 134, 151, *159*
Tinker, R. H., 173, *184*
Torgersen, S., 105, *129*
Tortu, S., 111, *122*
Toth, C. S., 113, *124*
Toth, S., 190, *200*
Tracy, R. G., 214, *225*
Tram, J., 190, *202*
Trant, J., 143, *158*
Treadwell, K. R., 138, *157*
Treliving, L. R., *181*
Trivedi, M., *255*
Truax, P. A., 68, 256, 290, *295*
Trufan, S. J., *154*
Truglio, R., 25, 26, *32*, 102, *123*, 288, *294*
Tsao, J. C. I., 151, *160*, 270, *280*
Tse, C., 24, *32*
Tse, C. K. J., 63, 69
Tucson, V., *254*
Tuma, J., 27, *40*
Tupler, L. A., 67
Tupper, C., 15, *35*
Turner, C., 115, 116, *122*, 142, *153*
Turner, J. B., 272, *277*
Turner, S. M., 57, 60, 66, *71*, 104, *129*, 263, 271, *274*
Turovsky, J., 13, *31*
Twaite, J., 107, *125*
Tylee, A., 26, *40*
Tyrer, P., 105, *129*

U.S. Department of Health and Human Services, 101, *129*
Ubriaco, M., *124*
Udwin, O., *160*
United States Preventative Services Task Force, 46, 48, 49, *71*
Unnewehr, S., 263, *280*
Ursano, R. J., 115, *128*, 147, *155*
Ustun, B., *39, 258*
Ustun, T. B., 234, *259*

Vagg, P. R., 57, *70*
Valentine, J., 134, *160*
Valentine, J. D., 147, *154*
Valeri, S. M., 191, *204*
Valla, J. P., 12, *32*
van Balkom, A. J. L. M., *183*
van den Brink, S., 244, *259*
van der Ende, J., 109, *129*

van Dyck, R., 122, 183
van Oosten, A., 142, 153
van Oppen, P., 167, 183
van Os, J., 27, 40, 271, 273, 280
van Tilburg, W., 122
van Zwieten, B. J., 244, 259
Vandell, D. L., 197, 203
Vaughn, C. E., 216, 230
Veiel, H. O. G., 246, 257
Vella, D. D., 240, 259
Verdeli, H., 264, 276
Verhulst, F. C., 109, 129
Verma, S. K., 16, 32
Vermeulen, H. D. B., 244, 259
Versage, E. M., 214, 225
Vinokur, A. D., 272, 275
Vize, C. M., 189, 201
von Baeyer, C., 69
Von Korff, M., 257, 258
Vredenburg, K., 80, 96, 98

Wagner, E. F., 256
Wagner, G., 64, 69
Wakefield, J. C., 20, 40
Walker, E., 257
Walker, J. R., 80, 98
Walker, L. M., 86, 98
Wallace, L. A., 175, 183
Wallace, L. E., 28, 39, 272, 279
Walsh, B. T., 41
Walsh, J. M., 134, 160
Walters, E. E., 16, 36, 39, 272, 277
Waltz, J., 47, 71, 292, 295
Wang, P. S., 27, 40
Ware, J. E., 64, 71
Warman, M., 126
Warman, M. J., 108, 129
Warner, V., 187, 201, 263, 264, 279, 280
Warren, M., 102, 122
Warren, S. L., 104, 129
Warshaw, M. G., 36
Wasserman, M. S., 265, 279
Watkins, E., 143, 159
Watkins, E. R., 257
Watkins, S., 215, 229
Watson, D., 25, 37, 80, 82, 85, 86, 95, 97, 98, 261, 278, 292, 295
Watt, M. C., 145, 159
Watt, N. F., 123
Wearden, A. J., 216, 230

Weathers, F. W., 66
Wegner, D. M., 143, 160
Weinstein, P., 140, 160
Weintraub, S., 214, 231
Weiss, D. S., 208, 229
Weissberg, R. P., 198, 204
Weissman, A. N., 55, 71
Weissman, M. M., 5, 6, 12, 16, 19, 20, 21, 35, 37, 40, 46, 68, 81, 96, 104, 129, 187, 201, 205, 208, 216, 228, 231, 263, 264, 276, 280
Weisz, J., 189, 201
Weisz, J. R., 191, 192, 204
Welkowitz, L. A., 182
Wells, A., 150, 154, 160, 270, 279
Wells, A. M., 75, 76, 96, 110, 123, 186, 200
Wells, K. B., 25, 41
Welner, J., 230
Wender, P. H., 230
Wesler, R. H., 67
Wessels, H., 197, 200
West, S. G., 123
Westen, D., 15, 40, 162, 183
Westling, B. E., 170, 183
Westra, H. A., 15, 29, 40, 268, 280
Wetherell, J. L., 26, 40, 269, 280
Whatley, S. L., 108, 129
Whiffen, V. E., 80, 81, 88, 95, 214, 226, 240, 254
Whisman, M. A., 216, 231, 243, 260
Whitaker, A., 13, 41, 153, 155
White, K. S., 107, 129, 272, 280
White, T. L., 143, 160
Whitefield, K., 192, 204, 230
Whitehouse, W. G., 30, 65
Whiteside, L., 200
Whittal, M., 26, 41
Whittal, M. L., 182
Wickramaratne, P., 263, 264, 279, 280
Wickramaratne, P. J., 263, 264, 280
Wieman, D., 240, 255
Wiener, M. R., 113, 124
Wignall, A., 102, 127
Wilcox, C. S., 255
Wilding, J., 134, 160
Williams, C., 57, 67
Williams, J. B. W., 62, 67, 70
Williams, J. M., 23, 39, 40, 270, 279
Williams, J. M. G., 249, 259, 260

Williams, N. L., 58, 70
Williams, R., 106, 130
Williams, S., 37, 56, 70, 109, 121, 186, 203, 213, 230, 239, 259
Wills, T. A., 240, 254
Wilner, N. R., 208, 229
Wilson, K. G., 80, 98
Wilson, L., 15, 35
Wilson, P. H., 234, 248, 252, 253, 255, 257, 260
Wilson, S. A., 173, 184
Wilson, W., 67
Winett, R. A., 118, 129
Winokur, G., 33, 214, 231
Winters, K. C., 214, 231
Wittchen, H., 234, 259, 278
Wittchen, H. U., 39, 40, 151, 160
Wohlfarth, T., 244, 259
Wolfe, N., 206, 229
Wolfson, A., 265, 279
Wollman, D., 148, 149, 160
Wolpe, J., 163, 169, 184
Woodman, C. L., 158
Woods, S. W., 70
Woodward, L. J., 24, 34
Woody, S., 104, 129
Worden, T., 107, 128
World Health Organization, 62, 71
Worthington, J. J., III, 32
Wright, E. C., 34
Wright, K., 257

Wykes, T., 254
Wyman, M. F., 207, 228, 284, 294

Ying, Y., 207, 229
Yonkers, K. A., 36
Youll, L. K., 208, 226
Young, A. S., 25, 41
Young, R. C., 56, 71
Yule, W., 106, 130, 147, 160
Yurcheson, R., 140, 157

Zanardi, R., 244, 255, 256
Zastowny, T. R., 216, 230
Zeidner, M., 108, 130
Zeller, P. J., 35, 256
Zhao, S., 36, 96, 126, 151, 157, 160, 182, 229
Zheng, D., 24, 41
Zieba, A., 33
Ziegler, V. E., 56, 71
Zielezny, M., 170, 181, 245, 255
Zigler, E., 210, 229
Zimmering, R. T., 172, 182
Zlotnick, C., 147, 148, 160
Zoellner, L. A., 149, 155
Zollo, L. J., 182
Zonderman, A. B., 46, 71
Zucker, B. G., 133, 143, 144, 151, 154, 160
Zupan, B., 228
Zuroff, D. C., 213, 226

SUBJECT INDEX

quality of life, 63–64
recovery from depression, 235–236, 250
social context, 287
subsyndromal pathology, 12, 28
See also Measurement
Attachment style
anxiety and, 104
depression and, 196
Attention deficit hyperactivity disorder, 144
Attentional processes, 269
Attributional style, depression risk and, 213, 215
Attributional Style Questionnaire, 54
Avoidance behavior
in anxiety, 9–10
parental reinforcement of, 105

Beck Anxiety Inventory, 58
Beck Depression Inventory, 54
Behavior therapy
anxiety disorder, 179–180
generalized anxiety disorder, 175–176
obsessive–compulsive disorder, 167, 168–170
one-session exposure therapy, 163–164
panic disorder, 170
phobic disorder, 163
social phobia, 164, 166–167
Bereavement, 208
Biological models
neurobiology of anxiety, 135
physiologic correlates of behavioral inhibition, 139–140
risk and resilience in, 286
See also Genetic risk
Biopsychosocial research, 286
Bipolar disorder, 206
Body image, depression and, 189
Brief Psychiatric Rating Scale, 61

Children and adolescents
anxiety assessment instruments, 59, 60
anxiety disorder course, 14, 27, 132
anxiety disorder diagnosis, 10
anxiety disorder epidemiology, 13, 132
anxiety prevention, 27, 110, 111–113, 114–118, 137–139, 152
anxiety risk factors, 103, 104, 105–106, 134–137

attachment style, 104
concordance of parent–child mood and anxiety disorders, 262–263, 264–265
of depressed or anxious parents, 263–264
depression prevalence, 21, 185
depression prevention programs, 186–187, 192–195, 218, 223
depression prevention strategies, 190–191, 195–199
depression risk factors, 187–190, 272
depression treatment, 185–186
depressive disorder manifestations, 19
help-seeking behavior, 27, 185–186
parent–child interactions, 265–266, 272
peer relations as anxiety risk factor, 105–106
phobic disorder prevention, 140–141
phobic disorder risk, 139–140
physical health, 195–196
primary prevention evaluation, 48
rationale for early assessment and diagnosis, 27
social phobia/social anxiety disorder, 141–142
stress management training, 112–113
substance abuse prevention, 111–112
Children's Depression Inventory, 55
Citalopram, 244–245
Classic model of prevention, 2, 3, 44–45, 284
alternative model and, 284, 285
developmental context, 287
Clinician-Administered PTSD Scale, 58
Cognitive functioning
anxiety disorder relapse predictors, 180
anxiety disorder risk factors, 86–87, 268–271
attributional style, 86
catastrophic misinterpretation, 143
congruency hypothesis, 240
content specificity, 268–269
coping with depression, 21, 23–24
covariance of anxiety and depression risk, 268–271
depression manifestations, 238
depression prevention goals, 191
depression prevention programs, 219, 220–221
depression relapse risk and, 238–240

depression risk and, 86–87, 189–190, 196, 212–214, 215, 219

depression vulnerability assessment, 56–57

hopelessness, 270–271

information processing, 269

mechanism of change in PTSD treatment, 174–175

mechanism of change in social phobia treatment, 166–167

negative affect and, 269

negative self-referent cognition, 24–25, 86–87, 106

in obsessive–compulsive disorders, 143

rumination, 270

threat perception, 9–10, 103–104

worry, 150, 270–271

Cognitive therapy, 90

depression prevention, 218, 219, 220–221, 221–222

depression relapse prevention, 243–244, 246

generalized anxiety disorder, 176–177

mechanisms of change, 243–244

panic disorder, 170–171, 172

posttraumatic stress disorder, 173–174

Cognitive–behavioral therapies, 2

anxiety disorder, 15, 178–180

depression prevention, 190–193, 192

depression relapse prevention, 245–246, 247, 248–250

generalized anxiety disorder prevention, 150–151

generalized anxiety disorder treatment, 175–176, 177–178

obsessive–compulsive disorder, 167–168, 169–170

phobic disorder prevention, 140–141

relapse prevention, 29

social phobia treatment, 164–167

for specific phobic, 163–164

Comorbidity

anxiety, 25–26, 29, 81–82, 251

depression, 25–26, 29, 81–82, 185, 194–195, 251

implications for prevention, 82, 194–195, 288

intergenerational transmission of psychopathology, 263

successive, 14, 26, 82, 194, 288

symptom severity and, 26

See also Covariance of anxiety and depression

Congruency hypothesis, 240

Coping style

anxiety risk and, 107–108

definition, 108

depression risk and, 189, 198–199, 240–241

emotion-oriented, 241

problem-focused, 241

Coping with Depression course, 246–247

Corticotropin-releasing factor, 135

Costs of anxiety and depression, 16–17, 24–25, 102, 131, 233, 234

prevention costs and, 199–200, 234

Course of disease, 287

anxiety disorders, 13–15, 132

depression, 21–24

Covariance of anxiety and depression

cognitive vulnerability, 268–271

comorbidity, 25–26, 29, 81–82, 185, 251

continuum model, 80–81

distal factors, 261–262

genetic linkages, 267–268

implications for prevention, 81, 194, 251, 273–274, 288

interaction among variables, 262

parental factors, 262–266

proximal variables, 261–262

psychopathology in both parents, 264

research needs, 29, 251

stressful life experiences and, 271–273

temporal relationship, 14, 26, 82, 288

tripartite model, 269, 270–271

Critical incident stress debriefing, 148–149

Cultural context

anxiety and depression in, 287–288

of prevention intervention research, 90

Day care programs for depression prevention, 197

Debriefing procedures, 148–149

Delivery systems research, 45, 77

secondary prevention evaluation, 49–50

Dental phobias, 140

Depression Anxiety and Stress Scale, 55

Depression/depressive disorders

access to care, 185–186

acute-phase treatment, 242–244

adaptive function, 293
anxiety and. *See* Covariance of anxiety
 and depression
assessment instruments, 52–53, 54–57
bereavement and, 208
case identification challenges in
 prevention research, 80–81,
 93–94, 208–209
classification, 17, 206–207
clinical conceptualization, 3–4
clinical features, 17–20
comorbid disorders, 29, 81–82, 185,
 194–195, 251
conceptualization of clinical outcomes,
 235–236, 250
costs of disease and prevention, 24–25,
 199–200, 233
course, 21–24, 206
current treatment approaches, 1–2
diathesis–stress model, 87, 212–213,
 238, 239–240
epidemiology, 20–21, 82–83, 185, 205,
 233
first episode response, 252
help-seeking behavior, 22, 185–186
heritability, 214–215
as internalizing disorder, 194–195
interpersonal relationships and, 189,
 213–214, 215–216
models of prevention, 2–3, 284–285
mood-cognition activation paradigm,
 56–57
need for prevention research, 2, 4
parental, 263–264
pharmacotherapy, 219, 223–224,
 242–243, 244–247
prevention rationale, 205–206, 224, 234
prevention strategies, 27–30
primary prevention
 interventions, 78, 190–191
 program efficacy, 192–195
 rationale, 186–187
 strategies, 190–191, 195–199, 199
protective factors, 190
relapse
 research, 234–235
 risk, 22–23, 233–234, 237–242
research needs, 23, 222–224, 249–252
risk factor research, 84, 85–89, 93–94
risk factors, 187–190, 196, 212–217
risk identification, 208–212, 217,
 218–219, 223

secondary prevention, 49, 84, 217–224
stigmatization, 186–187, 221
subclinical, 19–20, 25, 28, 208–209, 217
suicide risk, 24
tertiary prevention, 85
 rationale, 233–234
 strategies, 242–249
vulnerability after initial episode, 86,
 233–234
Desensitization procedures
 phobic disorder treatment, 163
 social phobia treatment, 164
Developmental context, 287
 anxiety disorders, 10, 14–15
 anxiety prevention interventions,
 114–115, 152
 anxiety risk, 137
 depression course, 21–22
 depression etiology, 194
 See also Children and adolescents
*Diagnostic and Statistical Manual of Mental
 Disorders*, 10, 17, 52, 80, 81
Diagnostic Interview Schedule for
 Children, 62
Diathesis–stress model, 211, 287
 complex interactions in, 88–89
 conceptual basis, 87
 depression risk, 212–213, 238, 239–240
 diathesis qualities, 88
 research challenges, 87–88
 stress identification, 88
Divorce, 136–137, 272
Dose of treatment, 90–91
 depression prevention, 222–223, 248
Duke Health Profile, 63
Dysfunctional Attitude Scales, 55

Efficacy and effectiveness studies
 adolescent depression prevention
 programs, 192–195
 conceptual challenges in, 45, 91–92
 phobic disorder treatment, 163
 research in low base rate disorders,
 82–83
 research needs, 292–293
 secondary prevention of depression,
 221–222
Epidemiology
 anxiety disorders, 12–13, 82–83, 109,
 131, 132, 133
 comorbidity, 81–82

Iatrogenic effects of prevention
    interventions, 118–120
Illness Intrusiveness Rating Scale, 63
Imipramine, 171, 245
Implosive therapy, 172
Improving Social Awareness–Social
    Problem Solving, 114–115
Indicated interventions
    classic model of prevention and, 284,
        285
    definition, 2–3, 79, 284–285
    measurement issues, 48–51
Inhibited temperament, 103, 134–135,
    139–140, 141
Interdisciplinary treatment, 292
Interpersonal relationships
    depression risk factors in, 189, 213–214,
        215–216, 239–240, 272
    parent–child interactions, 265–266
    peer relations as anxiety risk factor,
        105–106
    social reservedness, 106
    social support as protective factor, 107
    See also Social phobia
Interpersonal therapy, depression relapse
    prevention, 245

Latent inhibition, 136, 139, 152
Learning theory, 135–136
Life Skills Training, 111–112
Longitudinal research, 91–92, 290
Looming Maladaptive Style
    Questionnaire-Revised, 58–59

Major depressive disorder, 19–20, 25–26
    genetic risk, 267
    parent–child concordance, 264–265
Maternity leave, 197–198
Measurement, 4, 5
    anxiety and depression knowledge base,
        289
    anxiety assessment instruments, 57–61
    depression assessment instruments,
        54–57
    effect size, 290
    of functioning, 52
    interviewer-rated scales, 53, 61–63
    population samples, 47, 90, 289–290
    in primary prevention, 46–48
    relevant instruments, 52–53

requirements for prevention research,
    43–44, 45–46, 64–65, 290
    in secondary prevention, 48–51
    self-report scales, 53
    statistical analyses, 293
    subclinical symptoms, 46
    in tertiary prevention, 51–52
    treatment adherence, 46–47
    validity requirements, 290
    See also Outcome measures
Medical health assessment, 63
Mindfulness Based Cognitive Therapy,
    248–249, 251
Mini International Neuropsychiatric
    Interview, 62
Mirtazapine, 244–245
Modeling, phobic disorder treatment,
    163
Models of anxiety and depression, 3–4,
    10–12, 285–286
Models of prevention, 2–3, 284–285, 286
    developmental considerations, 287
Mood-cognition activation paradigm,
    56–57
Multidimensional Anxiety Scale for
    Children, 59

Negative affect, 149, 198, 265, 267, 269,
    271, 273
Negative life events, 85, 86
    anxiety risk, 106–107, 136–137
    covariance of anxiety and depression
        risk, 271–273
    depression risk, 212–213
        among adolescents, 188–189
        relapse, 237–238
    diathesis–stress model, 238, 239–240
Neuroticism, anxiety risk and, 134
Normative data, 51

Obsessive–compulsive disorder
    assessment instruments, 60–61
    epidemiology, 13
    prevention, 144
    risk factors, 142–144
    subclinical symptoms, 144
    tertiary prevention, 167–170
    treatment challenges, 167
Outcome measures, 65
    anxiety disorder treatment, 15

covariance of anxiety and depression, 288

depression recovery, 235–236, 250

efficacy and effectiveness studies, 91–92, 285, 288, 292–293

follow-up period, 91–92, 162

generalizability of anxiety and depression research, 289

for low base rate disorders, 82–83

primary prevention evaluation, 46, 47

secondary prevention evaluation, 49

tertiary prevention evaluation, 51

Panic attacks, 10

anxiety sensitivity and, 145

epidemiology, 145–146

panic disorder and, 145–146

risk factors, 145

Panic disorder, 10

age of onset, 14

assessment instruments, 57–58, 59

clinical features, 145

course, 14

depression and, 26

hyperphysiological arousal and, 269

prevention, 146–147

risk factors, 145–146

tertiary prevention, 170–172

therapeutic change models, 171–172

Panic Disorder Severity Scale, 59

Parents/parenting

adolescent depression prevention programs, 192–193, 196–197

anxiety risk and, 104–105, 135–136

children of depressed or anxious parents, 263–264

concordance of disorders in families, 262–263, 264–265

covariance of anxiety and depression, 262–266

depression prevention strategies, 218

depression transmission, 187, 190, 214–215

generalized anxiety disorder in children and, 150

maternity leave, 197–198

parent–child interactions, 265–266

parents of depressed or anxious children, 264–265

phobic disorder risk in children, 139

psychopathology in both parents, 264

social anxiety in children and, 142

Penn State Worry Questionnaire, 59

Personality factors

anxiety risk, 102, 134–135

depression risk, 213–214

Pharmacotherapy

anxiety disorder treatment, 15, 179

depression prevention and treatment, 219, 223–224, 242–243, 244–247

follow-up data, 162

generalized anxiety disorder treatment, 175

panic disorder, 171

phobic disorder prevention, 140–141

prolonged use, 245

social phobia treatment, 165–166

treatment efficacy, 1–2

Phenelzine, 165

Phobic disorders

age of onset, 14, 26

course, 14

dental, 140

epidemiology, 13

latent inhibition in formation of, 136, 139

prevention, 140–141

risk factors, 139–140

tertiary prevention, 163–164

See also specific disorder

Physical exercise, 152–153, 195–196

Pleasant event scheduling, 191

Population, 288

research samples, 47, 90, 289–290

targets of prevention models, 2–3, 45

Positive affect, 86, 269, 271

Posttraumatic stress disorder, 178

assessment, 58

epidemiology, 147

mechanism of change, 174–175

prevention interventions, 115, 148–149

protective factors, 107

risk factors, 147–148

tertiary prevention, 172–175

Pregnancy, 135

Preintervention prevention research, 45, 77

Prevention research, 93–94

biopsychosocial, 286

classification of interventions, 78–79

covariance of anxiety and depression, 29, 273–274, 288

cultural considerations, 287–288

measurement issues in intervention
evaluation, 51–52
in models of prevention, 2–3, 285
predictors of, 28
preventive psychotherapy, 28–29
tertiary prevention goals, 79, 161–162
See also Tertiary prevention
Relaxation exercises, 111, 113
depression prevention among
adolescents, 191
generalized anxiety disorder treatment,
175–176
panic disorder treatment, 170–171
posttraumatic stress disorder treatment,
174
Remission, 235–236
Resilience. *See* Protective factors
Resourceful Adolescent Program, 192–193
Reynolds Adolescent Depression Scale, 56
Risk assessment, depression, 208–209, 223
Risk factors
activating triggers, 87–88
anxiety/anxiety disorders, 102–107,
133–137, 149–150, 152
anxiety sensitivity, 57–58, 145
causality and, 209–211
challenges in prevention research,
83–89
clinical models of anxiety and
depression, 285–286
conceptual models of prevention, 2–3,
284–285, 286
covariance of anxiety and depression,
29, 262–273, 288
definition, 75
depression, 187–190, 209–217
depression relapse, 237–242, 252
etiological classification, 86
genetic, 214–215, 267–268
individual characteristics, 103–104,
134–137
interactions among, 88–89, 262
knowledge base needs for prevention,
44, 283
major depressive disorder, 19–20
negative life events, 85, 86, 106–107,
136–137
obsessive–compulsive disorder, 142–144
panic disorder, 145–146
parental characteristics, 104–105,
135–137, 262–266
phobias, 139–140

posttraumatic stress disorder, 147–148
relapse, 28–29
research needs, 241–242, 287, 291–292
risk reduction model, 84
secondary prevention research, 50,
84–85
sensitivity of screening tests, 50–51
social, 287
social phobia, 141–142
specificity of, 85–87
specificity of screening tests, 50–51
subclinical symptomatology and, 49
vulnerability and, 75, 209–211
Risk reduction model, 84

Schema(s), depression risk model,
212–213
School intervention for depression
prevention, 198, 221
School Transitional Environment Project,
115
Screen for Child Anxiety Related
Emotional Disorders, 60
Seattle Social Development Project,
196–197
Secondary prevention, 4–5
advantages of, as model for anxiety and
depression, 285
alternative model of prevention and,
284, 285
anxiety disorders, 152–153
definition, 2, 45, 48–49, 207, 284
depression, 206, 217–224
developmental context, 287
generalized anxiety disorder, 150–152
goals, 78, 207
knowledge base needs, 284
measurement issues in performance
evaluation, 48–51
obsessive–compulsive disorder, 144
panic disorder, 146–147
phobic disorders, 140–141
posttraumatic stress disorder, 148–149
research methodology, 289–290
risk and vulnerability identification in,
211–212
risk factor research in, 50, 84–85
social anxiety/phobia, 142
targets of intervention, 78, 84–85
tertiary prevention and, 79, 207
treatment and, 207

Selected interventions
  classic model of prevention and, 284
  definition, 2, 78, 284
Self concept
  depression prevention strategies, 195
  depression risk, 189–190, 212–213, 215
  negative self-referent cognition, 24–25,
    86–87, 106
  self-descriptions correlated with mood
    and anxiety, 268–269
Self-control therapy, 191
Sensitivity of screening tests, 50–51
Separation anxiety, 14
Serotonin reuptake inhibitors, 243
SF-36 Health Survey, 64
Sheehan Disability Scale, 64
Shyness, 134–135, 141, 285
Social and Occupational Functioning
    Assessment Scale, 52
Social anxiety/social phobia
  age of onset, 14, 26
  assessment instruments, 60
  familial risk factors, 105
  parent–child interactions and, 266
  prevention, 142
  risk factors, 141–142
  tertiary prevention, 164–167
Social context
  anxiety disorder burden, 16
  clinical conceptualization of anxiety
    and depression, 286–287
  costs of anxiety and depression, 16–17,
    24–25, 102
  depression risk, 240
  etiological significance, 287
  prevention intervention research, 90
  prevention strategies, 287
  See also Interpersonal relationships
Social Phobia and Anxiety Inventory for
    Children, 60
Social Phobia Inventory, 60
Social skills training for depression
    prevention among adolescents,
    191
Sociotropy, 213–214, 239–240
Somatic arousal in anxiety, 9–10, 269
Specificity
  of prevention intervention, 220
  of risk factors, 85–87
  of screening tests, 50–51
Spence Anxiety Scale for Children, 60
Stress prevention, 112–114

Structured Clinical Interview for *DSM–IV*
    Axis I Disorders, 62–63
Subclinical symptomatology, 288
  anxiety disorder conceptualization,
    11–12
  case identification challenges in
    prevention research, 80–81,
    208–209
  depressive, 19–20, 208–209, 217
  implications for prevention, 28
  measurement, 46
  obsessive–compulsive disorder, 144
  risk factors and, 49
  secondary prevention goals, 48–49, 78
Substance abuse
  anxiety prevention intervention,
    111–112
  depression and, 185
Successive comorbidity, 14, 26, 82, 194,
    288
Suicide, 24, 206, 234
Symptoms of disease
  anxiety disorders, 9–12
  cause and effect identification, 86
  conceptualization of anxiety and
    depression, 3–4, 80–81, 288
  conceptualization of prevention
    outcomes, 285
  cultural context, 287–288
  depressive disorders, 17–20
  severity of, in comorbidity, 26
  subclinical, 11–12, 46, 80–81, 288
  tertiary prevention evaluation, 51–52

Temporal orientation, 268
Tertiary prevention
  anxiety disorders, 178–180
  case identification challenges in
    prevention research, 81
  definition, 2, 161–162
  depression, 234–235, 242–253
  developmental context, 287
  generalized anxiety disorder, 175–178
  goals, 51, 79, 284
  measurement issues in performance
    evaluation, 51–52
  obsessive–compulsive disorder, 167–170
  by optimizing acute-phase treatment,
    242–244
  panic disorder, 170–172
  phobic disorder treatment, 163–164

posttraumatic stress disorder, 172–175
research methodology, 289–290
risk factor research, 85
secondary prevention and, 79, 207
social anxiety/social phobia, 164–167
Threat cognition in anxiety, 9–10,
103–104

Universal interventions
classic model of prevention and, 284
definition, 2, 78
knowledge base needs, 284
measurement issues, 46–48
negative effects, 119–121

Validity of measures, 290
Vulnerability, 287
after initial episode of depression, 86,
233–234
causality and, 210–211

definition, 75
depression, 223
depression relapse, 224–235, 250–251
diathesis–stress model, 87
looming model of anxiety, 59
normative data, 51
predictive value of screening tests,
50–51
risk and, 209–211
secondary prevention research, 84–85
See also Risk factors

Well-Being Therapy, 248
Workplace interventions, 113–114
maternity leave, 197–198
Worry, 150, 270–271

Yale-Brown Obsessive Compulsive Scale,
60–61
Young Mania Rating Scale, 56–57

ABOUT THE EDITORS

David J. A. Dozois, PhD, is an assistant professor in the Departments of Psychology and Psychiatry at the University of Western Ontario in London, Ontario, Canada. He completed his doctoral work in clinical psychology at the University of Calgary in 1999. Dr. Dozois's research focuses on the role of cognition in depression and anxiety. Additional research interests include cognitive–behavioral theories and therapy, the assessment of psychopathology, and professional issues in psychology. Dr. Dozois has published more than 30 scientific articles and book chapters and has presented nearly 100 research posters and papers at national and international conferences. Dr. Dozois was honored recently with an early career award from the Canadian Psychological Association (CPA) and a Brain Star award from the Canadian Institutes of Health Research: Institute of Neurosciences, Mental Health and Addiction; he is also a recipient of a New Investigator Fellowship from the Ontario Mental Health Foundation. Dr. Dozois has been quite involved with various professional organizations. He currently serves as chair-elect for the CPA Section on Clinical Psychology.

Keith S. Dobson, PhD, is a professor of clinical psychology at the University of Calgary, Alberta, Canada. His research is in the area of cognitive aspects of depression and cognitive–behavioral therapy. He has been the author or editor of seven books, including the *Handbook of Cognitive–Behavioral Therapies* (1988; 2001), and *Empirically Supported Therapies: Best Practice in Professional Psychology* (1998). He has also published over 140 research articles and chapters and participated widely in conferences related to his research. Dr. Dobson has also provided training both in Canada and abroad, including the United States, Mexico, New Zealand, Australia, Europe, and Eastern Europe. In addition to his research area, Dr. Dobson has been active in professional domains. He has served as president of the licensing board for psychologists in British Columbia, as a member or chair for a large number of committees of national and international organizations, and as a term as president of the CPA. Related to his professional interests, he has authored or coauthored a number of articles in the area of professional psychology, and coedited *Professional Psychology in Canada* (1993). In addition, he has been a committee chair for the Association for Advancement of Behavior Therapy and is on the board of directors of both the Academy of Cognitive Therapy and the International Association of Cognitive Psychotherapy. He won the 2001 Canadian Psychological Association award for contributions to the profession of psychology. Dr. Dobson is a licensed psychologist and practices cognitive therapy in Calgary, Alberta, Canada.